Bath and Beyond

This book re-examines spa and assembly culture as key venues for sociability in the eighteenth century.

Focused chiefly on the eighteenth century, this book looks forward into the nineteenth and early twentieth centuries. While many of the chapters concern aspects of the city of Bath, the book stretches beyond Bath's confines, taking in comparative British towns such as Tunbridge Wells, European spa towns, such as Nice, and the impact Bath had on spa towns in America. The chapters not only reconsider familiar themes such as the marriage market but also offer new insights into the architectural development of the city and the role of Masters of Ceremonies: the officials who oversaw Assembly Rooms' rules and culture. There are also insights into the musical culture of spa towns and the varied backgrounds of the artists and performers. As places that attracted the wealthy and powerful, the book rounds off with consideration of Bath and other spa towns' importance as centres of culture and diplomacy and of their place in the tourist industry.

This accessibly written book appeals to a broad readership, including undergraduate and postgraduate students as well as academics and informed non-specialists interested in social and cultural history, British history, and modern history.

Dr Hillary Burlock is a British Academy Postdoctoral Fellow at the University of Liverpool, working on a project on British assembly rooms, and a historian of eighteenth-century dance and sociability, with interests in politics, embodiment, and performance. She previously worked on the Eighteenth-Century Political Participation and Electoral Culture project and publications include 'Party Politics: Dancing in London's West End, 1780–9' (2021).

Dr Robin Eagles is the Editor of the House of Lords 1660–1832 section at the History of Parliament, whose research interests include the history of Parliament from the late seventeenth to the close of the eighteenth century; the old Palace of Westminster; Frederick, Prince of Wales and the development of opposition politics at Leicester House; John Wilkes. Publications include *Champion of English Freedom: the life of John Wilkes, MP and Lord Mayor of London, 1725–1797* (2024).

Tatjana LeBoff is the Project Curator at the Bath Assembly Rooms for the National Trust and is working on a new visitor experience at the Bath Assembly Rooms which will bring to life the Georgian heyday of the Rooms. Research interests include eighteenth- and nineteenth-century social history, as well as considering how curatorial practice can weave together heritage, social history, and contemporary arts and programming.

Routledge Studies in Eighteenth-Century Cultures and Societies

Series Editors: Elaine Chalus and Deborah Simonton

The long eighteenth century sits as a pivotal point between the early-modern and modern worlds. By actively encouraging an international focus for the series overall, both in terms of wide-ranging geographical topics and authorial locations, the series aims to feature cutting-edge research from established and recent scholars, and capitalize on the breadth of themes and topics that new approaches to research in the period reveal. This series provides a forum for recent and established historians to present new research and explore fresh approaches to culture and society in the long eighteenth century. As a crucial period of transition, the period saw developments that shaped perceptions of the place of the individual and the collective in the construction of the modern world. Eighteenth-Century Cultures and Societies is a series that is globally ambitious in scope and broad in its desire to publish cutting-edge research that takes an innovative, multi-vocal and increasingly holistic approach to the period. The series will be particularly sensitive to questions of gender and class, but aims to embrace and explore a variety of fresh approaches and methodologies.

Letters and the Body, 1700–1830
Writing and Embodiment
Edited by Sarah Goldsmith, Sheryllynne Haggerty and Karen Harvey

Gender, Space and Illicit Economies in Eighteenth-Century Europe
Uncontrolled Crossings
Anne Montenach

Bath and Beyond
The Social and Cultural World of the Georgian Assembly Room
Edited by Hillary Burlock, Robin Eagles, and Tatjana LeBoff

For more information about this series, please visit: www.routledge.com/Routledge-Studies-in-Eighteenth-Century-Cultures-and-Societies/book-series/RSECCS

Bath and Beyond
The Social and Cultural World of the Georgian Assembly Room

Edited by Hillary Burlock,
Robin Eagles, and Tatjana LeBoff

NEW YORK AND LONDON

Designed cover image: Thomas Rowlandson, Comforts of Bath. Plate 10, 1798, hand-coloured etching and aquatint, 19.6 x 21cm, Metropolitan Museum of Art, The Elisha Whittelsey Collection, The Elisha Whittelsey Fund, 1959.

First published 2025
by Routledge
605 Third Avenue, New York, NY 10158

and by Routledge
4 Park Square, Milton Park, Abingdon, Oxon, OX14 4RN

© 2025 selection and editorial matter, Hillary Burlock, Robin Eagles, and Tatjana LeBoff; individual chapters, the contributors

The right of Hillary Burlock, Robin Eagles, and Tatjana LeBoff to be identified as the authors of the editorial material, and of the authors for their individual chapters, has been asserted in accordance with sections 77 and 78 of the Copyright, Designs and Patents Act 1988.

All rights reserved. No part of this book may be reprinted or reproduced or utilised in any form or by any electronic, mechanical, or other means, now known or hereafter invented, including photocopying and recording, or in any information storage or retrieval system, without permission in writing from the publishers.

Trademark notice: Product or corporate names may be trademarks or registered trademarks, and are used only for identification and explanation without intent to infringe.

ISBN: 978-1-032-49447-0 (hbk)
ISBN: 978-1-032-49446-3 (pbk)
ISBN: 978-1-003-39385-6 (ebk)

DOI: 10.4324/9781003393856

Typeset in Sabon
by Apex CoVantage, LLC

Contents

List of Figures	*vii*
List of Contributors	*x*
Foreword	*xiii*
Acknowledgements	*xvi*
List of Abbreviations	*xviii*

1 Introduction 1
HILLARY BURLOCK AND ROBIN EAGLES

2 Bath Assembly Rooms and Its Subscribers 15
TIMOTHY MOORE AND RUPERT GOULDING

**3 'Solemn yet Sumptuous': Robert Adam's Designs for an
Alternative Assembly Room in Bath** 39
AMY FROST

**4 'I am a Sort of Prisoner here': Elite Performance and Bath
Society in the Eighteenth Century** 57
JEMIMA HUBBERSTEY

**5 Not Just Suitors, Balls, and Proposals: The Late
Eighteenth-Century Bath Marriage Mart Reassessed** 78
RACHEL BYNOTH

**6 Rauzzini and the Upper Assembly Rooms Subscription
Concert Series: The First Five Years** 96
BRIANNA E. ROBERTSON-KIRKLAND

vi *Contents*

7 Two Kingdoms: Masters of Ceremonies at Bath and
Tunbridge Wells, 1735–*c*.1801   116
RACHAEL JOHNSON

8 Electing the *Arbiter Elegantiarum* in Bath and Beyond:
Power, Politics, and the 1769 Bath Contest   139
HILLARY BURLOCK

9 The Undertakers of Eighteenth-Century Bath   162
DAN O'BRIEN

10 British Female Hospitality and Fashionable Society in
Eighteenth-Century Nice, 1769–92   182
ISABELLE EVE CARLOTTI-DAVIER

11 The 'Bath Revolution'? Musical *Distractions* in French
Spas, *Cercles*, and *Salons*   202
PHIL BONJOUR

12 Bath, Abroad: How British American Colonists Imagined
and Encountered the Famed Spa City   224
VAUGHN SCRIBNER

13 Bath Assembly Rooms: Then, Now, and Next   247
TATJANA LEBOFF

Appendices   *251*
Index   *256*

Figures

2.1 The 'Articles of Agreement' for the Bath Assembly Rooms, with the signatures of the original 63 subscribers. 16

2.2 Thomas Hudson (attr.), *Henry Arthur Herbert, 1st earl of Powis (2nd creation)*, c.1740, oil on canvas, National Trust, Powis Castle and Garden, 86064. 20

2.3 James Watson, *Sir William Robinson, 2nd bt.*, c.1777, mezzotint, 37.7 × 27.9 cm. 21

2.4 William Hoare, *Daniel Danvers*, 1780, painting, 13.2 × 10.6 cm. 24

2.5 Thomas Gainsborough, *Philip Dehany and his wife Margaret, and their daughter Mary*, c.1761–2, oil on canvas, 238.5 × 147 cm. 31

3.1 Office of Robert Adam, *Design for a Ball and Concert Room at Bath* [Elevation], pen and wash, 175.9 × 57.2 cm. 40

3.2 Robert Adam, *A plan for an unknown building, attributed to either one seen by Adam on his Grand Tour*, c.1755–6, or to a preliminary design for the Concert and Ball Room proposals for Bath, c.1768. pen and pencil, 25.7 × 20.3 cm. 46

3.3 Office of Robert Adam, *Plan of the Ball and Concert Rooms at Bath*, pen and wash, 87.9 × 63.7 cm, Sir John Soane's Museum, SM Adam vol 28/49. 47

3.4 Office of Robert Adam, *Section through the Ball & Concert Room at Bath* [transverse section], pen and wash, 125.1 × 55.8 cm. 47

3.5 Office of Robert Adam, *Section through the Ball and Concert Room at Bath* (longitudinal section), pen and wash, 170.4 × 55.5 cm. 48

3.6 After Charles-Louis Clérisseau, *Peristyle of the Diocletian palace in Split*, from Robert Adam's *Ruins of the Palace of the Emperor Diocletian at Spalatro in Dalmatia*, 1764, line engraving, Yale Center for British Art, Paul Mellon Collection, L 1.37 Copy 1 (Folio A). 49

viii *Figures*

3.7 Antonio Lafreri, *Plan of the Baths of Diocletian, Rome*, from *Speculum Romanae Magnificentiae*, 1546–90, line engraving, Yale Center for British Art, Paul Mellon Collection B1974.12.1476. 50

3.8 Office of Robert Adam, *Plan of the New Town at Bath*, 1777, pen and wash, 48.5 × 32.2 cm, Sir John Soane's Museum, SM Adam vol 38/6. 52

4.1 Allan Ramsay, *Lady Jemima Campbell, Marchioness Grey, Countess of Hardwicke*, 1741, oil on canvas, 172 × 134 cm, National Trust, Wimpole Hall, 17243. 61

4.2 Thomas Hudson, *Lady Elizabeth Yorke, Lady Anson*, 1751, oil on canvas, 110.5 × 85.7 cm, National Trust, Shugborough, 1291188. 62

4.3 Jemima Hubberstey, *North Parade, Bath*, 2023, photograph. 64

4.4 Jemima Hubberstey, *View of the River Avon from the North Parade, Bath*, 2023, photograph. 64

7.1 J. Badslade, *Tunbridge Wells, Kent: bird's eye view*, undated, etching with engraving, 35.3 × 43.3 cm, Wellcome Collection, 22970i. 120

8.1 *Female Intrepidity, or the Battle of the Belles on ye Election of a King of Bath*, 1769, etching, 11.9 × 17.5 cm, Lewis Walpole Library, 769.05.00.01 Impression 1. 151

8.2 *The Brentford Election*, 1768, etching, 11 × 18 cm, Lewis Walpole Library, 768.12.00.01 Impression 1. 152

10.1 Richard Purcell, *Penelope Rivers (née Atkins), Lady Rivers when Mrs Pitt*, c.1746, mezzotint, 35.1 × 25.1 cm, National Portrait Gallery, NPG D40255. 188

10.2 The different areas of residency of British female travellers in late eighteenth-century Nice. Joseph Rosalinde, *Carte topographique de la ville et de la campagne de Nice*, 1825, lithograph, Bibliothèque Nationale de France/GALLICA, GE F CARTE-5616. Courtesy of the Bibliothèque Nationale de France. 188

10.3 The main points of interest in late eighteenth-century Nice. Joseph Rosalinde Rancher, *Detail of the map of the town of Nice*, in *Guide des étrangers à Nice*, 1825, lithograph, Bibliothèque Nationale de France/GALLICA, GE F CARTE-5616. Annotated by the author:
A: the 'Grande Place'
B: Cathedral and Bishop's Palace
C: Governor's house (Royal Palace)
D: the Senate of Nice
E: Theatre Royale (now the Opéra de Nice)

	F: the 'Terrace'	
	G: the 'Cours' (Corso)	
	H: Héraud Palace ('Hôtel d'Angleterre' and the consul's house in 1792)	189

11.1 Simon Levy, *Valses favorites du cercle d'Aix les bains. Nouveau recueil suivi d'un galop pour le piano avec accompagnement de violon, flûte ou flageolet ad libitum composé et dédié à son ami Strauss, artiste du Théâtre des Italiens et directeur des Concerts d'Aix par Simon Lévy*, undated, In-fol. oblong, Bibliothèque Nnationale de France, VM12 G-8320 [*Favourite waltzes from the Aix les bains circle. New collection followed by a galop for piano with accompaniment by violin, flute, or flageolet ad libitum composed and dedicated to his friend Strauss, artist at the Théâtre des Italiens and director of the Concerts d'Aix by Simon Lévy*]. 206

11.2 Martin Cadenat d'après Sorrieu, *Souvenir d'Aix-les-bains. Sale [sic] de danse du casino* [Casino Ballroom], in *Journal d'Aix-les-Bains*, 1853, lithograph, Bibliothèque Nationale de France, JO-7116. 207

Contributors

Tom Boden has worked in heritage for 18 years and is General Manager for the National Trust's Bath Portfolio (UK), looking after Bath Assembly Rooms, Dyrham Park, Prior Park Landscape Garden, the Bath Skyline and Bathampton Meadows. He began his career as a history teacher and is passionate about bringing history to life for everyone.

Phil Bonjour is a PhD candidate at the University of Limerick (Ireland) in the Centre for the Study of Popular Music and Popular Culture. He is a graduate of the Paris Conservatory in musicology (history of music and musical culture) and of the École des Hautes Études en Sciences Sociales in sociology.

Hillary Burlock is a British Academy Postdoctoral Fellow at the University of Liverpool (UK), working on the development of British assembly rooms. Her recently completed thesis explored the intersections between dance and political cultures in late Georgian Britain. She works on eighteenth-century histories of dance, sociability, performance, and politics from 1700 to 1832.

Rachel Bynoth is a lecturer in Historical and Critical Studies (Design) at Bath Spa University (UK). Her recently completed doctoral thesis examined expressions of anxiety in the Canning family letter network 1760 to 1830 to understand what it tells us about remote relationships in the long eighteenth century. She works on histories of emotions, gender, politics, family, and distant communications from 1700 to 1945.

Isabelle Eve Carlotti-Davier obtained her PhD in modern history from the University of Paris-Cité (France), where she is now based in the Department of Identités, Cultures, Territoires. Her research focuses on British female travel in eighteenth-century Italy. She has published on the social and cultural aspects of hospitality through British women's experiences in Nice and at the court of Savoy.

Contributors xi

Robin Eagles is Editor of the House of Lords 1660–1832 section at the History of Parliament (UK). His publications include *Francophilia in English Society* (2000), an edition of the *Diaries of John Wilkes* (2014), and, most recently, a biography of Wilkes, *Champion of English Freedom: The Life of John Wilkes, MP and Lord Mayor of London* (2024).

Amy Frost is the Senior Curator of Bath Preservation Trust (UK) and specialises in British architecture of the eighteenth and early nineteenth centuries. She is an expert on the British collector, writer, and owner of enslaved people William Beckford (1760–1844) and lectures at the University of Bath, School of Architecture.

Rupert Goulding, FSA, is Head of Curatorship at the National Trust (UK), and previously the regional curator with responsibility for the Bath Assembly Rooms.

Jemima Hubberstey completed her PhD at the University of Oxford and English Heritage, examining literary coteries and garden design in the eighteenth century. She was subsequently a postdoctoral research fellow at the University of Oxford, exploring the intellectual lives of elite Georgian women. She now works for Historic Royal Palaces (UK).

Rachael Johnson, based at the University for the Creative Arts (UK), focuses on the social, cultural, and medical life of England's spas and seaside resorts during the long eighteenth century. Rachael has published a number of pieces on her research, looking primarily at the Kentish resorts of Tunbridge Wells and Margate.

Tatjana LeBoff is the Project Curator for the National Trust at the Bath Assembly Rooms (UK), where she is working on the development of a new visitor offer which will explore the Georgian social heyday of the Rooms. Her curatorial practice is centred around bringing heritage, social history, and contemporary art together through dynamic exhibitions and programming.

Timothy Moore is a social and literary historian of the eighteenth and nineteenth centuries. He is a lecturer in literary history at Regent's Park College, University of Oxford; a curator for the Bath Assembly Rooms at the National Trust; and an associate curator at Jane Austen's House Museum (UK).

Dan O'Brien is Visiting Research Fellow at the Centre for Death and Society, University of Bath (UK), and Associate Fellow of the Royal Historical Society. His research focuses on the undertaking trade and the organisation of funerals in eighteenth-century England. He also seeks to understand how the undertakers and their goods were perceived by society.

xii *Contributors*

Brianna E. Robertson-Kirkland is a lecturer in historical musicology at The Royal Conservatoire of Scotland (UK), and her most recent publications include *Venanzio Rauzzini and the Birth of a New Style in English Singing Scandalous Lessons* (2022), and *Allan Ramsay's The Tea Table Miscellany* co-edited with Professor Murray Pittock (2023).

Vaughn Scribner, based at the University of Central Arkansas (USA), is the author of *Under Alien Skies: Environment, Suffering, and the Defeat of the British Military in Revolutionary America* (2024), *Merpeople: A Human History* (2020), and *Inn Civility: Urban Taverns and Early American Civil Society*, in addition to numerous articles and book chapters.

Foreword

Bath has a global reputation for being one of the most beautiful cities in the world, with two World Heritage Site inscriptions affirming the significance of its Georgian architecture and urban design. Bath was transformed during the eighteenth century, from a small, overcrowded city within its medieval walls to an expansive succession of terraces, squares, and crescents in the fashionable Palladian style, with a range of facilities including the baths, Pump Room, shops, and entertainments to cater for all the needs of its visitors. This was the deliberate creation of a beautiful city, designed to attract high society for the season, as epitomised in the creation of the Upper Assembly Rooms designed by John Wood the Younger to be the preeminent social venue. This building is now looked after by the National Trust.

For many years, popular understanding of the Georgians that created this city of pleasure focused on polite society with the emphasis on genteel activities such as dancing, music-making, promenading, and taking tea, as represented in numerous adaptations of period novels. Georgian Bath was therefore seen as the stage where such activities could play out, governed by the 'Rules of Bath' as set out by 'Beau' Nash, the city's most famous Master of Ceremonies. While this was undoubtedly the case, such a focus tended to overlook crucial factors that enabled newly enriched upper ranks of society to enjoy the 'Comforts of Bath',[1] including where the money came from, who worked in the city, and what was the hidden human cost behind such lives of luxury.

Over recent decades, much research has been undertaken to provide a richer and more nuanced understanding of the city's history. Locally, the work of the History of Bath Research Group and the peer-reviewed *Bath History Journal* has provided an important space to showcase the work of researchers uncovering new perspectives. Combined with a wealth of local history publications and academic research, there is a growing interest in aspects of Georgian society that move beyond the 'polite' facade.

xiv *Foreword*

For example, much recent work has focused on uncovering the wealth that flowed into Bath via fortunes made through the trade and exploitation of enslaved Africans on colonial plantations in the Caribbean and North America. The construction of the beautiful Georgian city as a pleasure ground for the upper ranks in society required the enormous injection of wealth generated by an economy built by the nexus of empire, military power, and the industrial revolution. The Bath and Colonialism Archive Project is one example of recent activity in this space, and institutions such as Beckford's Tower, Bath Abbey, and the Holburne Museum, alongside the National Trust, are committed to understanding and sharing their historic connections to colonialism. Alongside this, recent research has also uncovered a greater understanding of Black presence in Georgian Bath. This includes the celebrated performances of George Bridgetower at the Bath Assembly Rooms in December 1789, as well as the career of William Hamlet whose life transitioned from runaway slave to portrait maker for royalty.

Other recent publications include a focus on Bath's Georgian pleasure gardens, which were outdoor counterparts to the assembly rooms of the city. These explore the rivalry between different promoters, the competition to secure the most celebrated musicians, and the precarious financial position of many of the proprietors, all of which find echoes in the research into Bath Assembly Rooms.

Georgian Bath was renowned as a place of opportunity, where the aspiring middling sort could encounter the nobility and anyone who could afford a ticket could come to the balls at Bath Assembly Rooms, the height of the social season. The recent 2021 inscription of the Great Spas Towns of Europe (including Bath) as a World Heritage Site recognises the importance of European spa culture that led to the creation of grand international resorts. Alongside a focus on health and wellbeing, these new leisure destinations promoted new social interactions and supported cultural activities. Bath was the leading spa that influenced the development of many counterparts in Europe and beyond, and so understanding the opportunities and limitations created by the Georgian spa city can provide insight into wider social changes of the period.

This book brings together a brilliant array of chapters that explore themes ranging from the musicians who performed at Bath Assembly Rooms, to the subscribers that funded the building, and the undertakers whose businesses were thriving in eighteenth-century Bath. The book represents the output of a conference held in 2021 to mark the 250th anniversary of the opening of Bath Assembly Rooms. For the National Trust, this was an opportunity to connect with academics to bring together current research in these themes. All of this research will be used to underpin our creation of a new experience for visitors to Bath Assembly Rooms, bringing

Foreword xv

to life a richer understanding of the Georgian city through an immersive experience in the rooms where 'all the world assemble'.[2]

But Bath is not a museum; it is a living city, and we want the Bath Assembly Rooms to continue to play a central role in the social and cultural life of its denizens. Alongside a new experience for visitors to Bath Assembly Rooms during the day, we are working with a range of partners and community groups to develop an active programme throughout the year, enabling people to come together for different occasions. Since taking on direct management of Bath Assembly Rooms in March 2023, the National Trust has hosted concerts, balls, festivals, a Wikithon, and a lion dance for Chinese New Year, and we will continue this tradition into the future, finding ways to broaden relevance and reach new and more diverse audiences.

Understanding Bath's rich history, with all its contradictions and complexity, is key to considering how we can best work together for a brighter future. Knowing that this was a city built on the proceeds of empire, yet led the way as a welcoming place for a broader and more diverse society, gives me hope that Bath can continue to be outward facing, inclusive, and welcoming to all in the twenty-first century.

Tom Boden, National Trust

Notes

1 This phrase references the title to the satirical print series 'The Comforts of Bath' created by Thomas Rowlandson in 1798.
2 Charles Molloy Westmacott, *The English Spy (1825)* (Sherwood, Gilbert, and Piper, 1907), ii, 306.

Acknowledgements

Bath and Beyond has been a collaborative effort from the start of this project, manifesting in a conference and reception to mark the 250th anniversary of the opening of the Upper Assembly Rooms in Bath in 2021. The interdisciplinary conference was organised by Elaine Chalus (University of Liverpool), Oliver Cox (University of Oxford), Robin Eagles (History of Parliament Trust), Rupert Goulding (National Trust), and Hillary Burlock (Queen Mary University of London). This event was jointly sponsored by the Royal Historical Society, British Society for Eighteenth-Century Studies, and the Early Dance Circle (notably Barbara Segal, Bill Tuck, Sharon Butler, and Paul Cooper), and supported by the History of Parliament Trust and the National Trust. We would like to thank them for their generous support of these commemorative events.

We are also grateful to all those who spoke (and performed) at the conference and reception, particularly for the interdisciplinary spirit they brought, and to the fascinating conversations and collaborations that arose from this international event. Beyond the authors to this book, we would like to thank the Bath Minuet Company, Rhian Davies, Maximilian Ehrhardt, Jonathan Foyle, Hannah Greig, Kevin Grieves, Ann Hinchliffe, David Hughes, Rose McCormack, Michael McMullen, Ellis Naylor, Olivette Otele, James Peate, Mark Philp, Steve Poole, Kim Simpson, Cathryn Spence, Matthew Spring, and Sophie Vasset. The Bath 250 conference brought together academics, heritage professionals, independent scholars, dancers, and musicians working on leisure culture, imperialism and colonialism, tradespeople and industry, architecture, literature and satire, and politics. Together, we shone a new light on the complex communities forged in Bath by its fashionable residents and visitors, by industrial and entrepreneurial tradespeople, and by the city's iconic architecture. We would also like to thank those who attended the virtual conference and the reception at the Bath Assembly Rooms from all around the world, including Wera Hobhouse, MP for Bath; Councillor Lisa O'Brien, Chair of the Bath and North East Somerset Council; and Tom Boden from the National Trust.

Acknowledgements   xvii

From that conference, the conversations continued, coalescing into this edited collection. This book owes a huge amount to the work of Peter Borsay and aims in some small way to add to his groundbreaking research. We are indebted to the mentorship and guidance of Debbi Simonton and Elaine Chalus as editors of the Routledge Studies in Eighteenth-Century Cultures and Societies, and Louise Ingham from Routledge for her support and advice. And finally, we would like to thank our families for their love, patience, and support during this collaborative process.

Abbreviations

BCL	Bath Central Library
BL	British Library
BLARS	Bedfordshire and Luton Archives and Record Service
BNF	Bibliothèque Nationale de France
BRO	Bath Record Office
Huntington Lib.	Huntington Library
LBS	Legacies of British Slavery Database, University College London
NLW	National Library of Wales
ODNB	Oxford Dictionary of National Biography
RCT	Royal Collection Trust
SCA	Sheffield City Archives
SHC	Somerset Heritage Centre
Staffs. RO	Staffordshire Record Office
TNA	The National Archives, Kew
VAM	Victoria and Albert Museum
WYAS	West Yorkshire Archive Service

1 Introduction

Hillary Burlock and Robin Eagles

On the evening of 30 September 1771, Bath's Upper Assembly Rooms opened with a magnificent ridotto.[1] Design, planning, and construction of the building took two years from 1769 to the grand opening of one of Britain's most iconic institutions for dancing and entertainments. Officers in scarlet and navy-blue wool coats could be seen mingling with ladies in sack-back gowns trimmed with lace, frills, and furbelows. The event was marked by actor-impresario (and politician) Richard Brinsley Sheridan in his poem 'The Ridotto of Bath', told from the perspective of Timothy Screw, 'Underserver', to confectioners Khuff and Fitzwater:

> But here I must mention the best thing of all,
> And what I'm inform'd ever marks a Bath ball;
> The Variety 'tis which so reign'd in the crew,
> That turn where one would the classes were new;
> For here no dull level of rank and degrees,
> No uniform mode, that shews all are at ease;
> But like a chess table, part black and part white,
> 'Twas a delicate checker of low and polite.[2]

According to Sheridan, tradespeople were seen sharing the space with lords and ladies and elegant young misses. Sheridan's poem derided guests wearing paste and 'Bristol-stone diamonds' (quartz) instead of parures of precious gemstones.[3] As such, he echoed what Tobias Smollett observed of Bath society in the same year, through the character of Squire Bramble in *Humphry Clinker*, who had been dismayed at the prospect of 'a very inconsiderable proportion of genteel people . . . lost in a mob of impudent plebeians'.[4]

At nine o'clock in the evening, the sideboards in the Tea Room were opened to ball attendees, providing a profusion of confections for the company's delectation. The refreshments provided in Bath in 1771 included viands which 'went off at such a rate', jellies, biscuits, macaroons, fruit,

DOI: 10.4324/9781003393856-1

2 Bath and Beyond

sweetmeats, and wine.[5] Following the refreshments, dancing commenced in the Ball Room. Days before the ridotto, the *Bath Chronicle and Weekly Gazette* announced, 'There will be minuets, country dances, cotillions &c in the several rooms, as may be agreeable to the company'.[6] The ridotto ended at 11 o'clock in the evening according to the rules established by Master of Ceremonies William Wade.[7] They indicated that, upon a signal from the Master of Ceremonies, the dancing was to conclude exactly at that time, even mid-dance, with sedan chairs and carriages ready to whisk guests home to their lodgings.

On 30 September 2021, 250 years to the day after the Upper Assembly Rooms opened, a reception with lectures and eighteenth-century dancing was held to mark the close of the 'Bath 250' conference.[8] Historians of eighteenth-century Britain with close interests in the history of Bath were keen to mark the anniversary with a high-profile event involving key figures working on Bath's history and heritage, with Bath Assembly Rooms as the focus. The virtual conference and in-person reception attracted over 800 participants worldwide, demonstrating Bath's continuing global appeal and influence. The conference fostered discussion around architecture, leisure and entertainment; Bath's tradespeople and class; political manoeuvring; health; and embodiment: much broader themes than this book is able to cover. The conference was also an opportunity to pay tribute to the late Professor Peter Borsay, who was one of the most important recent commentators on Georgian Bath and who researched the development of assembly rooms across Great Britain in his seminal work *English Urban Renaissance, 1660–1770*.[9] Through a series of chapters, this book underpins the influence of Bath's assembly and spa culture in a wider, global context.

Situated within a growing literature on eighteenth-century sociability, as evidenced by the *Digital Encyclopedia of British Sociability in the Long Eighteenth Century*, this book seeks to provide new insights into the cultural contributions of the Bath Assembly Rooms.[10] Through chapters examining the trope of the marriage market to the underexplored roles of the Master of Ceremonies, this collection examines the nuanced and multifaceted experiences of Bath's inhabitants and visitors. Bath may have been just one of many spa and watering towns to experience a rapid growth in popularity in the mid-eighteenth century thanks to what Paul Langford has described as a 'rage for spa water and sea water', but it provided the template in Britain and beyond for other towns and cities with spas and assembly rooms to emulate.[11] As such, it rapidly overtook earlier rivals like Epsom and Scarborough in influence and popularity. During the eighteenth century, as well as a place where people sought to recover their health, Bath was also a sociable place—a location where soft power was exerted and where arts and performance were fostered. The social season in the spa town created spaces for political actors (men and women) taking a break from their duties. It was thus a place both of retirement and of lively social, political, and cultural discourse.

This book seeks to re-examine spa and assembly culture, key venues for sociability in the long eighteenth·century. Recent publications such as Sophie Vasset's *Murky Waters: British Spas in Eighteenth-Century Medicine and Literature*, Liesbeth Corens's article 'Seasonable Coexistence: Temporality, Health Care and Confessional Relations in Spa, *c.*1648–1740', and Topi Artukka's chapter 'Space, Sociability and Daily Life in Early Nineteenth-Century Finnish Polite Society' have pointed to renewed interest in spa and assembly culture in Britain and Europe.[12] There has also been important work on reconsidering what it meant to be a 'leisure town' by Leonard Schwarz and John Stobart.[13] Relatively little work, however, has focused on assembly rooms in their own right, the most significant contribution being Peter Borsay's *English Urban Renaissance, 1660–1770*.[14] Exploring the social and cultural history of these spaces extends beyond Borsay's book, which catalogued early assembly room construction across England selectively. Helen Berry and Angela Dain have analysed individual and regional case studies in Newcastle and East Anglia.[15] While their micro-historical approaches highlight the value of assembly rooms in their local communities, as yet no study on the cultural influence of British assembly rooms has been undertaken. This book on the cultural influence of arguably the most famous assembly room, the iconic Upper Assembly Rooms in Bath, takes an important step towards understanding the influence of this significant cultural institution in the city, across England, and more broadly, into Europe and North America.

Prior to the conceptualisation of the assembly room, sociability and entertainments took place in private houses, as well as gatherings in inns and churches. The assembly room became a focal point for socialising within the community in the eighteenth century. The term 'assembly' was defined by Edward Philips in 1720 as 'a Concourse, or Meeting of People', a definition which emerged when early assembly rooms were constructed across Britain in the 1710s and 1720s.[16] On the one hand, Ephraim Chambers's 1741 *Cyclopaedia* expanded upon Philips's definition, outlining the audience and purpose of the assembly as 'a stated and general meeting of the polite persons of both sexes; for the sake of conversation, gallantry, news, and play'.[17] Dr Johnson, on the other hand, later defined it rather more concisely as 'a company met together', referencing Shakespeare's *Henry VIII*.[18] Assembly rooms were multi-purpose spaces for balls, concerts, card parties, and other entertainments in which any 'polite' community could gather. By 1795, the word 'assembly' was specifically linked with the activity of dancing in John Ash's *New and Complete Dictionary*

4 Bath and Beyond

of the English Language, defining the term as 'a company of people met together, a ball or genteel entertainment'.[19]

Assembly rooms proliferated across the British Isles, in spa, market, county, port, and industrial towns and cities. The second half of the seventeenth century saw new forms of sociability emerge in London, from the flowering of pleasure gardens and an abundance of theatres, coffee-houses, clubs, libraries, and public parks. By the early eighteenth century, the so-called provincial 'urban renaissance' saw the rise of polite venues in market and spa towns the length and breadth of England, Scotland, Wales, Ireland, and the Channel Islands.[20] The quintessential polite entertainment was that which took place in purpose-built assembly rooms, providing a designated public space in which sociability, politeness, and politics were enacted. The assembly room was a public venue with a wider demographic crossing its threshold than the court at St James's Palace or elite London residences. When the Upper Assembly Rooms opened in 1771, there were two other assembly rooms operating within Bath's lower town, known as Gyde's Rooms and Simpson's Rooms (named after the proprietors at the time). Once the Upper Assembly Rooms were opened, Gyde's Rooms closed, and Mr Simpson retired, prompting Mr Gyde to take over the management of the remaining assembly room on Terrace Walk.[21] The two remaining assembly rooms became known as the Upper and Lower Rooms, sparking competition between the two sociable venues.

While assembly rooms came to be synonymous with the activity of dancing, this activity is notably absent from this book. Some discussion of the importance of dancing minuets, country dances, and cotillions features in Rachel Bynoth's exploration of the marriage market in Bath and its assembly rooms. Bath and Beyond does, however, dance peripherally around this activity through exploring vital figures like the Master of Ceremonies, one of whose functions was to regulate dancing in the assembly rooms. Greater social mixing within assembly rooms was expected due to their need to be commercially viable; however, it was also a space in which the movement of bodies within the ballroom was heavily regulated and made exclusive by the need to pay subscription fees and for subscribers to vouch for the respectability of new members.[22] Dance was much more than entertainment; it was a physical and aesthetic accomplishment to be acquired, polished, and displayed. It is perhaps worth noting that when the future George III's household, as the Prince of Wales, was established in 1751, his educational establishment included both a dancing master and an assistant dancing master, along with writing masters and language coaches.[23] That said, not everyone appreciated the highly regulated nature of a Bath ball. Paul Langford drew attention to the experience of the marquis de Bombelles at one ball he attended at Bath in 1784 where he was disappointed to find the women sitting 'in three rows, like the Fathers at the Council of

Constance'.[24] The radical MP, John Wilkes, staying in Bath over Christmas 1777, noted of one ball that 'no female danced half so well as the little Grace of Prince's Court': his daughter, Polly.[25]

The influence of Bath and its ballrooms was weighty in Georgian society, adding a lustre to social debuts and dance treatises. Bath's reputation for girls' schools was a notable draw for proficient dancing teachers (male and female). Having learned from the famed Gaetan Vestris in London, Lucy de Rossi's dancing school and curriculum was later endorsed by the 'God of Dance' in the *Bath Chronicle and Weekly Gazette*. He vouched: 'I do certify to have instructed Madame de Rossi in the Art of Dancing, and that she is perfectly capable to teach Dancing in an excellent manner, and with effect'.[26] An almost verbatim announcement had been carried by the *Morning Chronicle* a few days earlier, though there Vestris had asserted de Rossi's capacity to teach 'Town Dancing'.[27] De Rossi opened her own school in Margaret Buildings (equidistant between fashionable residences in the Royal Crescent and The Circus, and just a short distance from the Upper Assembly Rooms) in 1790. Also operating in the city in the 1790s were two sisters, Anna and Catherine Fleming, whose father 'led the Pump-Room Band during the memorable supremacy of Beau Nash'.[28] The connection of the Fleming sisters to Nash, and later the Upper Assembly Rooms, likely helped them to establish their dancing schools in the latter decades of the century. Anna Fleming's pupils included political hostesses such as Georgiana, duchess of Devonshire, and her sister Henrietta, countess of Bessborough, as well as pupils attending numerous girls' boarding schools in Bath.[29]

Bath's influence in Georgian dance culture was further demonstrated in the publication of hundreds of annual collections of country dances by music publishers including Cahusac, Thompson, Fentum, and many more. For instance, Thomas and William Cahusac's *Annual Collection of Twenty-four Favorite Country Dances for the Year 1800* published the latest fashionable tunes and accompanying choreographies, which claimed to come from 'Court, Bath, & all Public Assemblies'.[30] Referencing Bath and its assembly rooms was a significant marketing tool to encourage young men and women to purchase their collections. As a result, claiming authenticity to tunes and choreographies, as 'danced at Bath', turned Bath and its assembly rooms into a cultural touchstone for fashionable dance trends, shaping the popularity of the tunes performed elsewhere.[31] The musicians, dancing masters, and music publishers underpinning the sale of these collections formed only a small segment of tradespeople and professionals supporting the Bath Assembly Rooms. Maids assisted ladies in changing their hoops between minuets and country dances. Confectioners provided delicacies at the weekly assemblies during the season, while chandlers produced and sold spermaceti candles to light the 10 lead crystal chandeliers

6   Bath and Beyond

hanging in the Assembly Rooms. This is an important reminder that while assembly rooms were an exclusive space for fashionables to mingle, they were underpinned and maintained by a network of professionals in the city, not least the chairmen who carried participants to and from the rooms.

As well as being an important spa and leisure town, Bath was also an important point of focus politically, not least because it was one of the seven parliamentary boroughs within Somerset, giving it significant weight within the locality. William Pitt the Elder (later earl of Chatham) was one of its most prominent residents in the 1750s and 1760s as well as being one of its Members of Parliament (MPs). Indeed, there seems to have been a clear sense of Bath being a place that attracted more than its fair share of high-profile parliamentarians. Prior to Pitt's election in 1757, the city's MPs included the prominent soldiers, Field Marshal George Wade and Sir John (later Lord) Ligonier, as well as Robert Henley, subsequently Lord Chancellor and promoted to the House of Lords as earl of Northington. A later MP, Lord Powerscourt, gained notoriety for the worst of reasons after being involved in a high-profile duel, with his activities attracting the public condemnation of the local clergy.[32] Most of Bath's residents, however, had no formal say in who represented them. At the beginning of the eighteenth century the population stood at around 3,000, but by the beginning of the nineteenth century this had increased more than tenfold,[33] and as Penelope Corfield has pointed out, by 1801 '61 per cent of the city's population of 34,000 were women'.[34] The voting population, though, was restricted to just 30 members of the corporation, with the influential postmaster, Ralph Allen, based at nearby Prior Park, exercising a disproportionately large role in selecting candidates during the 1740s and 1750s.

It was not just its position as a parliamentary borough that made Bath important politically though. As a spa town where members of the elite congregated in substantial numbers, it became one of several informal centres of political discourse. As Langford has observed, members of both the House of Lords and Commons, along with their associates, punctuated their residences at Westminster with tours of 'running from spa to bathing place, and from horse-race to bathing place again'.[35] Early in the reign of George I the 3rd earl of Sunderland, effectively premier minister, spent long stints at Bath for his health. It was plain, though, that he was not able to cast off the burdens of office while he was there and continued to manage his portfolio from afar. Just how important Bath could be as a place for politicking away from the capital is indicated by the fact that plotting for the new Chatham administration took place at a 'congress' held in Bath in advance of the new 1766 parliamentary session. According to Lord George Sackville, this was productive not only of intercourse between Chatham and the duke of Bedford, but of proposals for 'taking in some of his Grace's friends'.[36]

Introduction 7

Just over a decade later, John Wilkes arrived in Bath for a brief visit during the Christmas recess, in the course of which he was honoured with assisting Master of Ceremonies William Dawson at a ball in the Upper Assembly Rooms.[37] He may have been the greatest curiosity (he certainly liked to think he was), but he was far from being the only high-profile figure taking advantage of the place at the time. He noted the presence of Lord Kellie, the earl (and countess) of Coventry, former MP Edward Willes (by then a judge), and Lord Dillon and that Lord George Germain (the former Lord George Sackville) was expected the same day, though this was someone 'with whom I shall not chat'.[38] If he was hoping for respite from politics, he had come to the wrong place and on 7 January 1778, he reported: 'The rage of politics is, I think, more violent at Bath than even at London, and nothing is talked of but America.'[39] As Vaughan Scribner notes in his chapter, many visitors from the Thirteen Colonies congregated in Bath, and he recounts an interaction involving one such and the Anglo-Irish MP, Isaac Barré, and their disagreement over Barré's most recent actions in Parliament relating to America. Of course, it was not just high politics that preoccupied such elite visitors. On one of his subsequent visits in 1784, Wilkes attended 'a grand rout' hosted by Lady Conyngham, though he reported to his daughter that such events 'bid fair to ruin Bath as a public place'.[40]

One thing worth observing is that being forced to abide by the rules of the Upper Assembly Rooms meant that rival politicians were, for a while, regulated by Bath's determining culture rather than their own political exigencies. This did not mean, of course, that Bath (and other places) was immune to greater national issues. It is striking, as Hillary Burlock notes in her chapter, that the lively contest for the role of Master of Ceremonies in Bath in 1769 coincided with an election year, marked by agitation arising from the Wilkes affair. It is a feature that is deserving of further research: the extent to which elections to institutions beyond Parliament or local corporations reflected such national tensions. That Bath was not alone in being employed as a political centre is also apparent from Phil Bonjour and Isabelle Eve Carlotti-Davier's chapters. Both indicate the way in which Nice and French spa towns were also used as places for political and diplomatic scheming.

According to John Brewer, Bath 'was a city of quackery, leisure and intrigue',[41] while Paul Langford characterised it as 'a gigantic pleasure garden for propertied society'.[42] Perhaps most importantly, it was a city that underwent important transformation in the eighteenth century. As Rosemary Sweet has demonstrated, in a period when interest in the antique was growing, 'Bath's origin as a Roman city was an obvious asset in enhancing its cachet'.[43] As noted earlier, the population boomed and this was accompanied by a series of high-profile building developments, many of

8   Bath and Beyond

them, such as Queen Square, undertaken by John Wood the Elder.[44] Wood's son was then responsible for further building works, but as Amy Frost shows, the new Upper Assembly Rooms completed by Wood the Younger in 1771 might have looked very different if another scheme had been taken up instead. Frost examines the plans for an alternative set of rooms by the Adam brothers, designed shortly before those of Wood the Younger. Possibly, these were merely speculative designs, such as those drafted by Adam for a new Palace of Westminster, or perhaps they were intended for a different location within Bath. Significantly, given Bath's Roman origins, they drew upon Adam's experiences on the continent, inspired in large part by the Baths of Diocletian. They were not to be, very likely as a result of the prohibitive costs involved.[45] Planning, designing, and funding the rooms were vital to the financial success of the Bath Assembly Rooms. Timothy Moore and Rupert Goulding detail the subscription of early investing subscribers and their relationships to the creation and management of the Assembly Rooms. The shareholding proprietors largely hailed from Bath itself, but some were based further afield. Many investors were connected through marriage and kinship, and included both men and women. They represented a largely exclusive coterie of local landowners, clerics, professionals, doctors, MPs, and military figures. Significantly, some owed their wealth to profits from plantations, meaning that the development of Bath stemmed directly from the exploitation of enslaved people.

Bath's assembly rooms, from the older Mr Gyde and Mr Simpson's Rooms near the River Avon to the Upper Assembly Rooms, were all governed by the central figure of the Master of Ceremonies. The role was created by Richard 'Beau' Nash, who ruled Bath society as 'King' for 56 years.[46] Rachael Johnson investigates the early connection between Bath and Tunbridge Wells as two 'kingdoms' ruled by Nash and other successive Masters of Ceremonies. Though this arrangement would last almost unbroken until 1801, Johnson considers how sharing a Master of Ceremonies created dissatisfaction among the visitors to both spas. Moreover, the selection of a new Master of Ceremonies in Bath and beyond, elected by the subscribers, could prove contentious. Hillary Burlock argues that the election of a Master of Ceremonies paralleled parliamentary elections, including enfranchisement, canvassing, and formal polling through a case study of the particularly heated electoral contest for the position in 1769, a year marked by nationwide disruption following Wilkes's repeated efforts to be recognised as MP for Middlesex.

Alongside the permanent population of Bath was the no less (and in some ways more) important transient population of tourists and temporary residents taking advantage of cheap lodgings: possibly as many as 12,000 in any one season.[47] Not all of them looked forward to a trip to Bath. Gertrude Savile, aunt of the prominent reforming politician Sir George Savile, confided to her diary in advance of one visit that she arrived in Bath 'with little hopes of pleasure, nay, with the greatest dread and horror'.[48] Jane Austen's heroine, Anne Elliot, evinced similar unease at the prospect of residence in Bath, though in her case it was more to do with her father's unwillingness to economise. Her father, Sir Walter, though, was convinced the city promised him the prospect of being 'important at comparatively little expense'.[49] Jemima Hubberstey examines the complicated relationship aristocratic families had with Bath, as a place which demanded consummate elite performances. Through the correspondence of Elizabeth, Lady Anson and Jemima, Marchioness Grey, Hubberstey explores the tensions between their private interests and the expectations of fashionable Bath society. Rachel Bynoth, by contrast, approaches Bath through the lens of the history of emotions, exploring how the city's marriage mart was experienced by young women at the end of the eighteenth century. She demonstrates how letters could be duplicitous, how they were often used by mothers to check up on their daughters' prospects and discern which feelings and emotions were expressed about the place, its society, and practices.

As a cultural hub, Bath proved of enormous importance to artists and musicians. John Brewer has emphasised that the city was home to renowned portraitists such as William Hoare and later to Thomas Gainsborough, who were benefited from wealthy residents willing to take advantage of enforced leisure time to sit for their portraits.[50] Bath was also a centre of musical excellence, even if one visitor, Revd John Penrose, complained of a concert in the Pump Room that there was so much 'prating' that he could not hear the music.[51] The Upper Assembly Rooms became home to a vibrant, international musical community and the creative domain of the Italian castrato, Venanzio Rauzzini. As Brianna E. Robertson-Kirkland demonstrates, Rauzzini, the musical director responsible for its subscription concert series, experimented with the format, programming, and pricing, weaving his students into the series as leading performers. The musical experience of those attending spas on the continent is considered by Phil Bonjour, examining the contrasting spa towns of Évian, Vichy, and Aix-les-Bains. Bonjour explores the creation of new spaces to deliver packed programmes of musical entertainments, uncovering the motivations and commercial strategies of the entrepreneurs behind the French musical *distractions* sector.

Bath and its assembly rooms were influential throughout the Western hemisphere. As Vaughn Scribner demonstrates, Bath's influence resonated in the hearts and minds of American colonists both before and after the American Revolution. He shows that Bath held sway over the colonial mindset, whether in a Virginia spa or rubbing shoulders with the elite in the assembly rooms. Similarly, Isabelle Eve Carlotti-Davier shows how the patronage of a relatively small number of English expats, boosted by the patronage of members of the British royal family, helped transform Nice

10 Bath and Beyond

into a fashionable health resort for the *beau monde* in search of diversion from mental and bodily ills.

Of course, for some a visit to a spa presaged their ultimate journey. Not everyone seeking a cure found one, thus turning Bath and other spas into their final residences. Dan O'Brien considers this aspect of the Bath experience through the medium of a late eighteenth-century comedy *Better Late Than Never*, which depicts three quarrelsome undertakers, named (appropriately enough) Finis, Coffin, and Grimly. From this starting point, O'Brien examines the background, development, and competitive behaviour of Bath's undertaking businesses. Many had diverse interests as the profession of undertaker developed in the period. To succeed, they showed entrepreneurial flair in promoting their businesses, using advertising and other ways of promoting their trade.

This book is in many ways intended as a starting point for further research. Much more needs to be said about the development of Bath alongside other fashionable resorts, as well as the reason for Bath's success while other earlier locales, like Scarborough, were unable to keep up. In 1778 Frederick (Fritz) Robinson wrote to his brother, Lord Grantham, from Brighton, noting how the town had grown and boasted a new assembly room.[52] In 1788, Cheltenham received a boost to its reputation by the visit of George III, on the brink of his long period of illness, while in the 1790s Weymouth was also to benefit from regular visits by the king and royal family.[53] Yet through all these developments, Bath remained a touchstone, very much the *cordon bleu* in the world of the spa town, and an inspiration to spa towns and assembly rooms in Britain and beyond.

Notes

1 Throughout this book, the National Trust's Bath Assembly Rooms will be referred to as the 'Upper Assembly Rooms' or 'Bath Assembly Rooms', in comparison with discussions of the 'assembly rooms' as an institution.
2 Richard Brinsley Sheridan, *The Ridotto of Bath, a Panegyrick; Written by a Gentleman, Resident in That City: Being an Epistle from TIMOTHY SCREW. Under-Server to Mesrs. Kuhf and Fitzwater to His Brother HENRY, Waiter, at Almack's* (Bath 1771).
3 Sheridan, *Ridotto.*
4 Tobias Smollett, *Humphry Clinker* (New York: The Century Co., 1967), 66, quoted in Paul Langford, *A Polite and Commercial People: England 1727–1783* (Oxford: Oxford University Press, 1989), 107.
5 Sheridan, *Ridotto.*
6 *Bath Chronicle and Weekly Gazette*, September 26, 1771.
7 R. Cruttwell, *The Strangers' Assistant and Guide to Bath* (Bath, 1773), 34.
8 The 'Bath 250' conference was organised by Elaine Chalus (University of Liverpool), Robin Eagles (History of Parliament), Rupert Goulding (National Trust), Oliver Cox (University of Oxford), and Hillary Burlock (Queen Mary, University of London). The conference received funding support from the Royal Historical Society, British Society for Eighteenth-Century Studies, and Early Dance Circle.

Introduction 11

9 Peter Borsay, *The Image of Georgian Bath, 1700–2000* (Oxford: Oxford University Press, 2000); Peter Borsay, *The English Urban Renaissance: Culture and Society in the Provincial Town, 1660–1770* (Oxford: Oxford University Press, 1989); Peter Borsay, *A History of Leisure: The British Experience Since 1500* (Basingstoke: Palgrave Macmillan, 2006).

10 DIGIT.EN.S. [Online], "DIGIT.EN.S.: The Digital Encyclopedia of British Sociability in the Long Eighteenth Century," accessed March 6, 2024, www.digitens.org/en.

11 Langford, *A Polite and Commercial People*, 102.

12 Sophie Vasset, *Murky Waters: British Spas in Eighteenth-Century Medicine and Literature* (Manchester: Manchester University Press, 2022); Liesbeth Corens, "Seasonable Coexistence: Temporality, Health Care and Confessional Relations in Spa, *c.*1648–1740," *Past & Present* cclvi (2022): 129–64; Topi Artukka, "Space, Sociability and Daily Life in Early Nineteenth-Century Finnish Polite Society," in *Daily Lives and Daily Routines in the Long Eighteenth Century*, ed. Gudrun Andersson and Jon Stobart (Abingdon: Routledge, 2021).

13 Jon Stobart and Leonard Schwarz, "Leisure, Luxury and Urban Specialization in the Eighteenth Century," *Urban History* xxxv (2008): 216–36.

14 Borsay, *English Urban Renaissance*.

15 Helen Berry, "Creating Polite Space: The Organisation and Social Function of the Newcastle Assembly Rooms," in *Creating and Consuming Culture in North-East England, 1660–1830*, ed. H. Berry and J. Gregory (London: Routledge, 2004), 120–40; Angela Dain, "Assemblies and Politeness, 1660–1840" (PhD diss., University of East Anglia, 2000).

16 Edward Philips, *The New World of English Words, or, a General Dictionary* (London, 1720), 62; Borsay, *English Urban Renaissance*, 336–49.

17 Ephraim Chambers, *Cyclopaedia: Or an Universal Dictionary of Arts and Sciences*, 2 vols. (1741), i, np.

18 Samuel Johnson's Dictionary [Online], "ASSE'MBLY," accessed February 17, 2024. https://johnsonsdictionaryonline.com/views/search.php?term=assembly.

19 John Ash, *The New and Complete Dictionary of the English Language* (London, 1795), 65.

20 Borsay, *English Urban Renaissance*.

21 Trevor Fawcett, *Bath Entertain'd: Amusements, Recreation and Gambling at the 18th-Century Spa* (Bath, 1998), 8.

22 Jane Austen, *Persuasion (1817)*, ed. James Kinsley (Oxford: Oxford University Press, 2004), 219.

23 R. O. Bucholz, "The Database of Court Officers: 1660–1837," Household of George, Prince of Wales (Future George III) (1738–1760), accessed March 15, 2024, https://courtofficers.ctsdh.luc.edu/.

24 Paul Langford, *Englishness Identified: Manners and Character 1650–1850* (Oxford: Oxford University Press, 2000), 60–61.

25 John Wilkes, *Letters from the Year 1774 of John Wilkes, Esq. Addressed to His Daughter, the Late Miss Wilkes* (London, 1805), i, 51.

26 *Bath Chronicle and Weekly Gazette*, July 21, 1791.

27 *Morning Chronicle*, July 16, 1791.

28 *Bath Chronicle and Weekly Gazette*, February 13, 1823.

29 *Bath Chronicle and Weekly Gazette*, July 21, 1796, February 13, 1823.

30 Thomas Cahusac and William Cahusac, *Cahusac's Annual Collection of Twenty-Four Favorite Country Dances for the Year 1800* (London, 1800), titlepage.

31 *A Second Set of Elegant Minuets Danc'd at Bath, Adapted for Harpsichord or Piano* (Bath, 1790).

12 Bath and Beyond

32 Stephen Banks, *A Polite Exchange of Bullets: The Duel and the English Gentleman 1750–1850* (Woodbridge: Boydell Press, 2010), 212–13.
33 Langford, *A Polite and Commercial People*, 106.
34 Penelope J. Corfield, *The Georgians: The Deeds & Misdeeds of 18th-Century Britain* (London and New Haven: Yale University Press, 2022), 271.
35 Paul Langford, *Public Life and the Propertied Englishman 1689–1798* (Oxford: Clarendon Press, 1991), 378–79.
36 *HMC Stopford Sackville*, i, 114.
37 *Letters from the Year 1774*, i, 54.
38 *Letters from the Year 1774*, i, 51.
39 *Letters from the Year 1774*, i, 69.
40 *Letters from the Year 1774*, iii, 122.
41 John Brewer, *The Pleasures of the Imagination: English Culture in the Eighteenth Century* (London: Routledge, 1997), 299.
42 Langford, *Public Life and the Propertied Englishman*, 379.
43 Rosemary Sweet, *Antiquaries: The Discovery of the Past in Eighteenth-Century Britain* (London: A&C Black, 2004), 184.
44 Langford, *A Polite and Commercial People*, 106.
45 R. S. Neale, *Bath 1680–1850: A Social History or a Valley of Pleasure, Yet a Sink of Iniquity* (Abingdon: Routledge, 1981), 221.
46 John Eglin, *The Imaginary Autocrat: Beau Nash and the Invention of Bath* (London: Profile, 2005).
47 Langford, *A Polite and Commercial People*, 106.
48 Alan Saville, *Secret Comment: The Diaries of Gertrude Savile 1721–57*, ed. Alan Saville (Devon: Kingsbridge Historical Society, 1997), 1.
49 Austen, *Persuasion (1817)*; Jane Austen, *The Complete Novels of Jane Austen*, ed. Karen Joy Fowler (London: Penguin, 2006), 1099.
50 Brewer, *Pleasures of the Imagination*, 299–300.
51 John Penrose, *Letters from Bath 1766–1767: By the Rev. John Penrose*, ed. B. Mitchell and H. Penrose (London: A. Sutton, 1983), 55.
52 BLARS, L 30/14/333/110: F. Robinson to Grantham, July 1, 1778.
53 Michael Kassler, *Memoirs of the Court of George III, vol. iv. The Diary of Queen Charlotte, 1789–1794*, ed. Michael Kassler, 5 vols. (London: Routledge, 2015), iv, 236–68.

Bibliography

Manuscript Sources

Bedfordshire and Luton Archives and Record Service

L 30/14/333/110, Wrest Park Papers

Primary and Secondary Sources

Artukka, Topi. "Space, Sociability and Daily Life in Early Nineteenth-Century Finnish Polite Society." In *Daily Lives and Daily Routines in the Long Eighteenth Century*, edited by Gudrun Andersson and Jon Stobart. Abingdon: Routledge, 2021.

Ash, John. *The New and Complete Dictionary of the English Language*. London, 1795.

Austen, Jane. *The Complete Novels of Jane Austen*. Edited by Karen Joy Fowler. London: Penguin, 2006.

Austen, Jane. *Persuasion*. Edited by James Kinsley. Oxford: Oxford University Press, 2004.

Banks, Stephen. *A Polite Exchange of Bullets: The Duel and the English Gentleman 1750–1850*. Woodbridge: Boydell Press, 2010.

"Bath." *Bath Chronicle and Weekly Gazette*, July 21, 1796.

"Bath." *Morning Post*, July 16, 1791.

"Bath. Wednesday, September 15." *Bath Chronicle and Weekly Gazette*, September 26, 1771.

Berry, Helen. "Creating Polite Space: The Organisation and Social Function of the Newcastle Assembly Rooms." In *Creating and Consuming Culture in North-East England, 1660–1830*, edited by H. Berry and J. Gregory, 120–40. London: Routledge, 2004.

Borsay, Peter. *The English Urban Renaissance: Culture and Society in the Provincial Town, 1660–1770*. Oxford: Clarendon Press, 1989.

Borsay, Peter. *A History of Leisure: The British Experience Since 1500*. Basingstoke: Palgrave Macmillan, 2006.

Borsay, Peter. *The Image of Georgian Bath, 1700–2000*. Oxford: Oxford University Press, 2000.

Brewer, John. *The Pleasures of the Imagination: English Culture in the Eighteenth Century*, 299. London: Routledge, 1997.

Bucholz, R. O. "The Database of Court Officers: 1660–1837." Accessed March 15, 2024. https://courtofficers.ctsdh.luc.edu/.

Cahusac, Thomas, and William Cahusac. *Cahusac's Annual Collection of Twenty-Four Favorite Country Dances for the Year 1800*. London, 1800.

Chambers, Ephraim. *Cyclopaedia: Or an Universal Dictionary of Arts and Sciences*. London, 1741.

Corens, Liesbeth. "Seasonable Coexistence: Temporality, Health Care and Confessional Relations in Spa, *c*.1648–1740." *Past & Present* 256, no. 1 (August 2022): 129–64. https://doi.org/10.1093/pastj/gtab018.

Corfield, Penelope. *The Georgians: The Deeds & Misdeeds of 18th-Century Britain*. New Haven: Yale University Press, 2022.

Cruttwell, R. *The Strangers' Assistant and Guide to Bath*. Bath, 1773.

Dain, Angela. "Assemblies and Politeness, 1660–1840." PhD diss., University of East Anglia, 2000.

DIGIT.EN.S. "DIGIT.EN.S.: The Digital Encyclopedia of British Sociability in the Long Eighteenth Century." Accessed March 6, 2024. www.digitens.org/en.

Eglin, John. *The Imaginary Autocrat: Beau Nash and the Invention of Bath*. London: Profile Books, 2005.

Fawcett, Trevor. *Bath Entertain'd: Amusements, Recreation and Gambling at the 18th-Century Spa*. Bath: Ruton, 1998.

Historical Manuscripts Commission. *Report of the Manuscripts of Mrs. Stopford-Sackville, of Drayton House, Northamptonshire*. Hereford: Historical Manuscripts Commission, 1910.

Kassler, Michael, ed. *Memoirs of the Court of George III. Vol. IV: The Diary of Queen Charlotte, 1789–1794*. London: Routledge, 2015.

Langford, Paul. *Englishness Identified: Manners and Character 1650–1850*. Oxford: Oxford University Press, 2000.

14 Bath and Beyond

Langford, Paul. *A Polite and Commercial People: England 1727–1783*. Oxford: Clarendon Press, 1989.

Langford, Paul. *Public Life and the Propertied Englishman 1689–1798*. Oxford: Clarendon Press, 1991.

"Madame de Rossi." *Bath Chronicle and Weekly Gazette*, July 21, 1791.

Neale, R. S. *Bath 1680–1850: A Social History or a Valley of Pleasure, Yet a Sink of Iniquity*. London: Routledge, 1981.

Penrose, John. *Letters from Bath 1766–1767: By the Rev. John Penrose*. Edited by B. Mitchell and H. Penrose. London: A. Sutton, 1983.

Philips, Edward. *The New World of English Words, or, a General Dictionary*. London, 1720.

Samuel Johnson's Dictionary. "ASSE'MBLY." Accessed February 17, 2024. https://johnsonsdictionaryonline.com/views/search.php?term=assembly.

Savile, Gertrude. *Secret Comment: The Diaries of Gertrude Savile 1721–57*. Edited by Alan Saville. Devon: Kingsbridge Historical Society, 1997.

A Second Set of Elegant Minuets Danc'd at Bath, Adapted for Harpsichord or Piano. Bath, 1790.

Sheridan, Richard. *The Ridotto of Bath, a Panegyrick; Written by a Gentleman, Resident in that City: Being an Epistle from TIMOTHY SCREW. Under-Server to Mesrs. Kuhf and Fitzwater to His Brother HENRY, Waiter, at Almack's*. Bath, 1771.

Smollett, Tobias. *The Expedition of Humphry Clinker*. London: Penguin Books, 1967.

Stobart, Jon, and Leonard Schwarz. "Leisure, Luxury and Urban Specialization in the Eighteenth Century." *Urban History* 35, no. 2 (August 2008): 216–36. https://doi.org/10.1017/S0963926808005464.

Sweet, Rosemary. *Antiquaries: The Discovery of the Past in Eighteenth-Century Britain*. London: A&C Black, 2004.

"Upper Assembly Rooms." *Bath Chronicle and Weekly Gazette*, February 13, 1823.

Vasset, Sophie. *Murky Waters: British Spas in Eighteenth-Century Medicine and Literature*. Manchester: Manchester University Press, 2022.

Wilkes, John. *Letters from the Year 1774 of John Wilkes, Esq. Addressed to His Daughter, the Late Miss Wilkes*. London, 1805.

2 Bath Assembly Rooms and Its Subscribers

Timothy Moore and Rupert Goulding

Around midday on 1 May 1769, a legal clerk left the Black Bear Inn in Bath with a list of over 60 names and addresses to begin what would become a protracted series of afternoon calls. These were not social visits; he carried with him a piece of parchment containing legal articles and space for 70 signatures (Figure 2.1). This parchment, and the 63 signatures that he eventually collected, became the foundational document for Bath's newest and most important gathering space. It was the 'Articles of Agreement' for the city's 'New' or 'Upper' Assembly Rooms, and its signatories were the people whose subscriptions then constituted the biggest investment in a single building in the history of Bath (Appendix 1).[1] This chapter examines these investing subscribers and explores the sometimes-unexpected nature of their relationships, social demographics, and sources of income. Far from revealing an elite group who invested in the project for purposes of further self-aggrandisement, the subscribers prove to be a surprisingly mixed group of people, consisting of a variety of ages, origins, professions, and levels of socio-economic status.[2]

The conceptualisation of the New Assembly Rooms (now simply the 'Bath Assembly Rooms', after outlasting both its rivals) was developed over decades. The building was originally the brainchild of John Wood the Elder (1704–54), master architect of Bath and designer of Queen Square and the Circus. Disliking the city's existing culture of class-based exclusivity, Wood praised the city's first assembly rooms for providing an early prototype of an environment where 'Rank began to be laid aside, and all Degrees of People . . . united in Society with one another'. But, according to Wood, this inclusivity project could '[not] be called . . . compleat'. Desirous to take the idea to a new level, he opined that a much bigger, more 'capacious and convenient Structure for People to Assemble is highly necessary: Such a House I have, for many Years back, had a View of Building'.[3] It was not until 1765, however, that his son, John Wood the Younger (1728–1782), first attempted to transform his father's vision into a reality.

DOI: 10.4324/9781003393856-2

16 *Bath and Beyond*

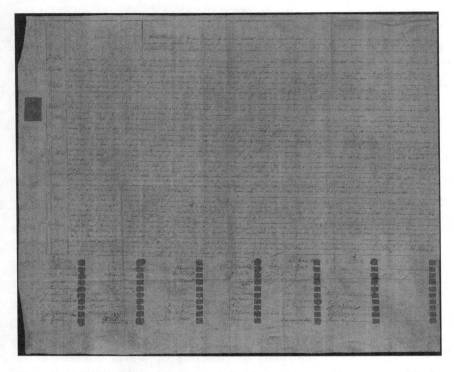

Figure 2.1 The 'Articles of Agreement' for the Bath Assembly Rooms, with the signatures of the original 63 subscribers. Courtesy of Bath Record Office: Archives and Local Studies.

After an initial proposed scheme for a new set of assembly rooms in Queen Square failed to succeed, a second scheme in 1768 fixed on an empty plot on the east side of the Circus as the site for the new assembly space. Prospective investors were invited to meet with Wood at his house, 6 Brock Street, 'to explain the Plans to any Gentleman who will do him the honour of calling on him for that purpose'. Seventy shares at £200 each were made available, and within just five months, 68 shares were bought by 63 people. The first stone was laid by Wood on 24 May 1769, where 'a band of music attended, and great ceremony was observed on the occasion'.[4] Just two years later, the works were completed, and the opening night was celebrated with a grand ridotto ball on 30 September 1771.

True to the spirit of Wood the Elder's original conception, the Upper Assembly Rooms initially functioned as a space of welcome for a surprisingly large range of visitors from across the social spectrum. With a popularity that far surpassed its competitors (the Lower Rooms and Gyde's

Rooms on the Gravel and Terrace Walks, respectively), the Upper Assembly Rooms catered to the widest range of Bath's society yet and initially admitted anyone who could pay for a ticket. This inclusivity was originally praised: 'Ceremony beyond the essential rules of politeness is totally exploded; everyone mixes in the Rooms upon an equality', gushed the *New Bath Guide* in 1788.[5] However, its progressiveness was soon after mocked by critics who feared that the admittance of tradespeople compromised the respectability of the space. In the same year as the building opened in 1771, complaints were already made that 'a very inconsiderable proportion of genteel people are lost in a mob of impudent plebeians', and assemblies in the New Rooms became a favourite target for satirists.[6] These critiques gradually took their toll, and the climate of the New Rooms became steadily more exclusive. By 1816, a committee of the subscribers 'unanimously resolved' that no tradespeople or other 'improper persons' should be admitted to its famous assemblies.[7]

As the rules for assemblies changed, so too did the subscribers who funded and managed the Upper Assembly Rooms. In fact, by the year 1814, only one of the original 63 subscribers still retained their shareholding.[8] Much of this change was occasioned by the deaths of original subscribers, whose shares in the Rooms were then transferred or sold as part of the division of their estates. However, the movement of shares was also occasioned by other causes. Some were transferred voluntarily by their shareholders; others were transferred automatically through marriage or inheritance. Some were even forfeited because the original shareholder was unable to keep up with its associated payments, or because they lost confidence in the venture's potential for financial return. Certain shareholders began with one share but subsequently became owner of two or more; conversely, others began with multiple shares but ultimately ended up with one or none. Tracing the journey of these shares thus raises interesting questions about the original 63 subscribers themselves, including their biographies, social demographics, and sources of income. This chapter explores these issues by focusing on three specific case groups of subscribers: first, those who sat on the range of committees formed to institute the Bath Assembly Rooms; secondly, those subscribers who were women, and thirdly, those subscribers who funded their investment in the Upper Assembly Rooms through profits derived from the labour of enslaved populations in the Caribbean.

The Original Subscribers

As a group, the original 63 subscribers of the Bath Assembly Rooms had a wide range of ages, professions, and family backgrounds, as well as varying levels of social ties to the city. The youngest was Christopher Talbot (1751–75), aged only 20 at the Rooms' opening, while several others were

18 *Bath and Beyond*

in their 60s. Some subscribers were established Bath residents with long-standing familial ties to the city; others were from regions as far away as the East or West Indies, or those who visited Bath from more established residences elsewhere in Britain. Their economic and social capital also ranged enormously. Although some were wealthy or well-known figures who featured regularly in Bath's annals of fashionable society, others are harder to identify and study.

The vast majority of the subscribers were members of the gentry and were either established Bath residents or those who visited the city primarily for leisure trips made during the social season (typically October to May).[9] Some subscribers took temporary lodgings for the occasion, but a significant number maintained permanent houses in Bath in addition to their primary residences. Over a third of the original subscribers owned either two or more properties and often lived at the most fashionable Bath addresses. For instance, at least 10 original subscribers either owned or stayed in properties on the Royal Crescent or the Circus.[10] However, a small number also seemed to have lived in slightly less desirable locations. At least five subscribers lived on either Queen Square or in the Westgate buildings—locations that were already in perceived decline by the 1770s and were mocked by Jane Austen and her characters after her first visits to the city in the 1790s.[11]

Many of the original subscribers funded their investments in the Bath Assembly Rooms through inherited wealth or through profits derived from established portfolios of assets. However, some had to work to afford their investment. Of these, most were involved in the so-called 'respectable' professions, whose work did not compromise their status among the gentry. Subscribers in these categories included doctors, lawyers, bankers, clergy, and officers in the army or navy. At least five were (or had been) provincial MPs, and three—William Street (*c.*1727–85), Francis Bennett (1712–90), and Walter Wiltshire (1719–99)—served as the sometime mayor of Bath.[12] Certain shareholders also had investments or management positions in other civic institutions, such as the Bath Fire Insurance corporation or the city's various hospitals.

Subscribers associated with supposedly less respectable professions, or work that was more closely linked to trade, included Francis Bennett, a linen draper, and Samuel Roffey (1706–1813), originally a gin distiller. However, as Francis Bennett became mayor, these associations were not necessarily a barrier to respectability and Bennett was clearly an important member of Bath's corporation. At least four subscribers were apothecaries, and at least three were merchants or traders, or involved in the East India Company.[13] Other lines of business were potentially even more disreputable: Walter Wiltshire, originally a carrier, later became the proprietor of a suite of gambling rooms and was at one point taken to court and fined

Bath Assembly Rooms and Its Subscribers 19

£500 (nearly £100,000 today).[14] Wiltshire was by no means the only subscriber to find himself or a family member to be the subject of a legal or parliamentary inquiry.[15]

While only a minority of the subscribers were involved in trade, this did not prevent the reputability of the Upper Assembly Rooms' shareholders from being targeted. As the shareholders had direct control over the proceedings of balls and concerts, the supposed ignobility of certain subscribers was weaponised by critics who objected to the management of Bath's social schedule by those they denigrated as 'a parcel of shopkeepers'.[16] As early as 1774, one commentator in *The Rival Ballrooms* went so far as to describe the 'two sorts of persons' that had come to be associated with the subscribers of the New Rooms. The first sort were sneeringly described as '[local] Proprietors, who have houses, &c. near the Rooms, and whose small fortunes make the interest from their shares a matter of importance'. The second group were described even more derogatorily: they were 'low and ignorant persons', described as worth a mere '2 or 300*l*. per year fortune':

> who have settled here lately; . . . and being admitted occasionally into better company, they presently forget themselves; and begin to suppose, from being suffered in the company of their superiors, that they are really persons of consequence. These are the people who perhaps may sneak out one guinea . . . or half a guinea for the use of the rooms, fire, candles, tea and cotillon from October to May, supported by strangers' subscriptions. These are the people who go to the balls and concerts with the strangers' tickets after they have left the place. . . . It is to be hoped, however, that they will in future . . . decently retire to some cheap place, where they may strut and swell . . . without disturbing the peace of this loved city, or . . . the first people of distinction in this kingdom who resort here.[17]

These accusations suggest that money-conscious shareholders took advantage of their position by gaining free admittance to the assemblies. By reusing the tickets of those who had a subscription for the season but who had left the city early, frugal subscribers could thereby 'sneak out' an extra guinea. The specific reference to 'the use of the rooms' for 'fire' and 'candles' further suggests that some subscribers spent additional time using the facilities at the Upper Assembly Rooms to reduce the personal expense of maintaining fires and candles in their own homes. Between the dining facilities of the coffee room, the leisure facilities of the billiards room and reading room, and the health and promenading opportunities of the cold bath and ballrooms, it would certainly have been possible to while away a full day at the Upper Assembly Rooms.[18]

Figure 2.2 Thomas Hudson (attr.), *Henry Arthur Herbert, 1st earl of Powis (2nd creation)*, c.1740, oil on canvas, National Trust, Powis Castle and Garden, 86064. ©National Trust Images/John Hammond.

Despite this possibility, it was not very fair of critics to divide the subscribers of the Upper Assembly Rooms into only 'two sorts of persons'. As an anonymous contemporary pointed out, the subscribers more accurately comprised at least 'one Nobleman, two or three Baronets, several Ladies, between thirty and forty Gentlemen (chiefly of rank and fortune)' and only 'six or seven of the principal traders of Bath'.[19] Although the wealth and status of the subscribers did vary enormously, working subscribers would have formed only a small minority of the wider group. Moreover, the attempted division of the subscribers into only two sorts of persons conveniently ignored those subscribers who were themselves members of the landed gentry, and who would certainly have considered themselves to be among 'first people of distinction in this kingdom'. For instance, subscriber Sir William St Quintin (1729–95, 5th baronet of Harpham), whose father was high sheriff of Yorkshire, was a member of an old and established family. St Quintin visited Bath only infrequently and managed his investment in the Upper Assembly Rooms remotely from the family seat in Scampston, perhaps partly to better oversee the ongoing redevelopment of the estate by Capability Brown.[20] At least four other original subscribers—Henry Herbert, 1st earl of Powis (1703–72; Figure 2.2); Sir Peter Denis

Figure 2.3 James Watson, *Sir William Robinson, 2nd bt.*, c.1777, mezzotint, 37.7 × 27.9 cm, National Portrait Gallery, D39808. © National Portrait Gallery, London.

(1713–78), Sir Philip Frances (1740–1818), and (later) Sir William Robinson (Figure 2.3)—moved in high social circles both within and without the context of the Bath season. However, the shares owned by the social elite changed hands just as equally and often as those of the other subscribers, and the shareholders soon included new subscribers of title, including Lord Clive (1725–74) and Sir Bourchier Wrey (1715–84, 6th baronet). Although these instances were not direct exchanges, these titled subscribers did seem to have certain unique relationships and connections with each other that set them apart from the other subscribers.[21]

The subscribers thus formed a dense web of interconnections. Many of the initial 63 subscribers knew each other outside the context of their shared investment in the Upper Assembly Rooms, either through existing relationships to family or friends or through expanding social or professional networks facilitated by Bath's fashionable society. Yet it is also possible to further divide the subscribers by other shared characteristics. The remainder of this chapter examines various examples of such subgroups: namely, those subscribers who were members of the Assembly Room's

22 Bath and Beyond

management committees; those subscribers who were women; and those subscribers with links to colonialism or the labour of enslaved peoples.

Management Committees

The *Journal of the Proceedings of the Subscribers to a New Set of Assembly Rooms* charted the decisions made at general meetings of the shareholders from their first gathering on 27 April 1769 to the last entry on 14 May 1772 at the end of the inaugural season.[22] One of the first resolutions was to form working groups as constituted in the 'Articles of Agreement', endorsed by all investors. These included the formation of a 'Committee for the Conveyances and Law' who were responsible for acquiring the site, and a 'Committee for inspecting and Directing the [said] Buildings' to oversee construction.[23]

The Law Committee initially consisted of Jonathan Morton Pleydell, John Charnock, Walter Bennett, John Williams, and Edward Daniel, with any three members making a quorum.[24] Four of the committee had legal expertise. John Charnock (1721–1809) was a barrister of the Inner Temple and from Barbados (see section "Colonial Links").[25] Jonathan Morton Pleydell (1725–97) was of Lincoln's Inn and lived in Bathford, Teignmouth in Devon, before moving to Rochestown, Dublin, in the 1780s. His older brother, Edmund Morton Pleydell (1724–94), inherited the family estates of Milborne and Whatcombe in Dorset, while Jonathan inherited his father's Irish estates in counties Cavan and Meath.[26] John Williams (*d*.1803) was an attorney of Trowbridge, Wiltshire, who practised in property law around Bath.[27] Edward Daniel (*d*.1819) was from a legal family based in Bath and Bristol.[28] Walter Bennett has yet to be identified, though it seems plausible that he was related to the shareholder and future mayor Francis Bennett.[29] The *Journal from the General Meetings* records that Morton Pleydell, Williams, and Daniel disposed of their shareholdings within months, although it does not explain why.[30]

The land purchase was completed on 13 October 1769 when the Law Committee members purchased the site in trust from John Wood the Younger and his business partner, property developer Andrew Sproule (1720–94).[31] The signatories to the transaction were Jonathan Morton Pleydell and two non-shareholders with close familial connections to the project. Joseph Colborne (1715–81) of Hardenhuish, Wiltshire, was a sibling of three shareholders: the apothecaries Benjamin and William Colborne, and Elizabeth Towers. All three brothers are interred in the family crypt at St Nicholas Hardenhuish, Chippenham, built in 1779 by John Wood the Younger.[32] Dr Henry Harrington (1727–1816) was the other signatory, a leading medic in the city, as well as an author and composer, and the second son of an established family from nearby Kelston,

Somerset. He moved to the city in 1762 and in the next year became the governor of the General Hospital; in 1770 he became a councilman and then mayor in 1793.[33] He was a cousin of another original shareholder William Harrington (1705–80), who was a landowner and coal works proprietor from Newton St Loe and Corston, and, according to the *Bath Chronicle*, was both a doctor and the recipient of a £10,000 lottery prize in 1778.[34]

Once the land was acquired, a new Building Committee managed the construction. It consisted of Walter Bennett and shareholders Richard Salter, William Adams, John Wood, Benjamin Colborne, William Greenwood, Daniel Danvers, William Street, and Revd Arthur Cookson. The quorum was four, and Colborne was the chairman when present, holding the deciding vote.[35]

William Adams (*d*.1777) lived in the Walcot area of Bath and was buried at the parish church of St Swithin's. He was related to the Hoare banking family through marriage; his wife Mary (1714–67) was granddaughter of Sir Richard Hoare (1648–1719) and cousin of Henry Hoare 'the Magnificent' (1705–85), builder of the Stourhead landscape gardens.[36] Adams's will reveals much about his social network and includes gifts of books, plate, and artworks to several friends and associates involved in the Upper Assembly Rooms, such as Dr Henry Harrington, the artist William Hoare and his wife Mary, and Mrs Edward Drax—wife of his fellow Management Committee member.[37]

Benjamin Colborne (1716–93) was a prominent Bath figure, an apothecary, and a substantial London landowner.[38] He was highly active in Bath society and held roles such as turnpike commissioner, vice president of the Bath Agricultural Society, and trustee and co-treasurer of the Bath General Hospital. He lived in the Circus and was neighbour to the artist Thomas Gainsborough; it is likely that they exchanged ideas as Colborne was considered a 'well wisher to all artists' and they both developed similar paper varnish techniques at the same time.[39] Colborne also sat on the Furnishing Committee, which was responsible for both commissioning Edmund Garvey (*c*.1740–1813) to paint decorative blinds in the Ballroom and accepting Gainsborough's gift of a portrait of Master of Ceremonies Captain William Wade (1734–1809).[40]

Captain William Greenwood (*d*.1796) was a partner and shareholder of the Bath Fire Office (established 1767), a turnpike commissioner, and likely a resident in Bladud's Buildings.[41] His son, Revd William Greenwood, installed a memorial to his parents in St Michael's Extra Muros, inscribed in Latin 'GUL GREENWOOD Navis bellicæ Præfect' (roughly meaning 'leader of naval ships'), indicating his father's naval career, which encompassed tours to the East Indies and several campaigns in the Caribbean during the Seven Years' War.[42]

24 Bath and Beyond

Figure 2.4 William Hoare, *Daniel Danvers*, 1780, painting, 13.2 × 10.6 cm. Portrait is courtesy of Bath in Time, and owned by the Royal United Hospitals Bath NHS Trust, located in the RNHRD & Brownsword Therapies Centre.

Daniel Danvers (*d*.1779; Figure 2.4) established the Cam, Clutterbuck, Whitehead, Danvers & Phillott partnership in 1768, trading as the Bath Bank from Trim Street. They were the first bank in the city and provided credit to the working committees of the Upper Assembly Rooms.[43] William Hoare presented Danvers's portrait posthumously to the Bath General Hospital in 1780 to commemorate his term as treasurer; it was hung in the board room.[44]

William Street was married to Elizabeth Wood, sister of architect John Wood the Younger; therefore, his influential role in the Upper Assembly Rooms is not surprising. Street was a highly successful apothecary with both local and wholesale trade who formed the Horlock, Mortimer, Atwood, Anderdon, Goldney & Street partnership trading as the Bath & Somerset Bank (1775). He was first elected to the city council in 1763, gaining successive offices and sitting on multiple sub-committees for development projects, such as the new Guildhall, Paragon, and Octagon Chapel—the latter particularly beneficial as its site was on his land. During the development of the Upper Assembly Rooms, Street acquired Lyncombe Spa, which initially provided smallpox inoculation and hospital recuperation to Bathonians and visitors before being converted into his country residence; the inclusion of a cold bath at Lyncombe might point towards the enthusiasm for installing a similar facility at the Upper Assembly Rooms. Street died in office as mayor in 1785.[45]

Revd Arthur Cookson (1720–81) was the youngest son of Alderman William Cookson (d. 1743), three times mayor of Leeds; his brother, also William (1710–79), was twice mayor of Hull. Arthur studied at Cambridge before entering the clergy and taking up a teaching post at St Peter's, now Leeds Minster. By 1765 he was resident in Bath and married to Anne (née du Prat), a woman of Huguenot descent and widow of Huguenot soldier Colonel Charles de Rambouillet. Cookson's stepdaughter Margaret Rambouillet (d.1806) was one of the female investors in the Upper Assembly Rooms, with her will making specific mention of her shareholding.[46]

A new sub-committee was established in early 1771 'for Furnishing' the Upper Assembly Rooms, funded by a dedicated shareholding.[47] The first proper meeting was held on 2 April 1771, with membership drawn from all those on the Building Committee, excepting Walter Bennett and two additional fellow shareholders, William Robinson (Figure 2.3) and Robert Sutton. The meetings were typically held at the Trim Street home of William Kingston, John Wood's clerk-of-works, before moving to the Upper Assembly Rooms as they neared completion.[48] The journal's last entry was on 7 May 1772, after which the committee's responsibilities were adopted by the more enduring 'Committee for Managing and Conducting the Affairs'. This was constituted by the proprietors of the Upper Assembly Rooms at their General Meeting of 14 May 1771.[49] This committee managed expenditure and appointed operational staff, with their journal running until December 1775, just one month after the operation of the Upper Assembly Rooms was leased out entirely to their former clerk, Robert Hayward (d.1779).[50]

The original committee members were Benjamin Colborne, Robert Sutton, William Adams, Edward Drax (see section "Colonial Links"), William Robinson, David Nagle, and Daniel Danvers. Of these, Robert Sutton (c.1726–75) of Scofton Hall, Nottinghamshire, was educated at Westminster and Cambridge and embarked on a Grand Tour 1753–54.[51] In letters to the 3rd duke of Portland in the 1760s, he discussed severe and repeated attacks of gout, difficulty walking, and his intention to move to Bath.[52] Sutton married Elizabeth Ducarel in Bath in 1762, and died aged 49 in the city, leaving a poetic memorial in Bath Abbey praising his polished manners and inflexible integrity.[53] William Robinson (1704–85) was another Grand Tourist attracted to Bath due to his health. He later inherited a baronetcy from his elder brother (Thomas Robinson of Rokeby,

26   Bath and Beyond

former MP for Morpeth and governor of Barbados) in 1777.[54] David Nagle (1719–1800), on the other hand, was a member of the Irish Catholic gentry. A kinsman of philosopher and Bristol MP Edmund Burke, he came from a leading Catholic land-owning family in Ballygriffin, near Cork, and had grown up with brandy distiller Richard Hennessy. His sister, Nano Nagle (c.1718–84), founded seven schools or almshouses for women, and in 1771 an Ursuline convent; in 2013 she was declared Venerable by the Roman Catholic Church.[55] He moved to Bath with his brother Joseph in 1762, likely after a substantial inheritance from his uncle (d.1757),[56] and invested widely in Bath. In 1777, he publicly subscribed to a new Catholic chapel for the city, though it was irreparably damaged in the Gordon Riots of 1780.[57] He lived at No.1 the Circus and subscribed to their central garden's refurbishment in 1799.

Thus, in total, 22 men were involved in the creation of the Upper Assembly Rooms, from securing land ownership, through construction and furnishing, to operation. Most were shareholders, and of this number eight were involved in two or more committees; three (Adams, Benjamin Colborne, and Danvers) were involved in three committees as the scheme's most committed proponents. There were clear clusters of relationships with overlapping participants: a group of Bath property developers (Bennett, Kingston, Robinson, Sproule, Street, and Wood) and lawyers who facilitated their transactions (Charnock, Daniel, Danvers, Morton Pleydell, and Williams). There were members of Bath's mercantile and civic elite, especially those from the dominant apothecary and medicinal trade (Colborne(s), Harrington, and Street). A notable group were Irish, owned Irish lands, or worked in Ireland (Morton Pleydell, Nagle, Omer, and Sproule).[58] Finally, there was a cluster of visiting investors who were drawn to Bath, albeit due to ill health, or attracted to the city's sociability (Adams, Cookson, Drax, Greenwood, Nagle, Robinson, Salter, and Sutton).

Women Subscribers

Although the subscribers involved in the management of the Upper Assembly Rooms were all men, women also made up an important part of the shareholders from the outset of the enterprise. When the articles were signed in 1769, 11 of the original 63 subscribers were women, representing 19 per cent of the total shareholding.[59] However, by 1780, this number rose to 19, a third of the total shareholding.[60] Although these women represented different life stages and marital status, their demographics are surprisingly homogenous. Only one of the original 11 women subscribers (Margaret Smith) was married at the time of investment. Two were widowed (Sarah Snee and Elizabeth Towers); the rest were all wealthy, unmarried women of independent means. At least three (Elizabeth Towers, Margaret Rambouillet, and Jane Denis) probably purchased shares in connection with male siblings or relatives who were themselves subscribers. These shares may have been recommended or gifted to female relations to add to their independence or supplement their potential dowries. However, the rest were adult, independent women, of a range of ages, who considered the Upper Assembly Rooms a worthwhile investment, obtaining shares on their own behalf and for personal reasons of their own.

Three of the women subscribers were sisters: Margaret (1708–80), Alice (1710–72), and Jane (1718–95) Horsman were three of four daughters. The Horsmans were a wealthy family, and the erstwhile death of the mother had provided each daughter with lucrative shares and arrears from numerous properties. They had enough financial independence to remain single if they wished, and only Margaret, the eldest of the sisters, chose to get married. Following this event, the four sisters took up residence in Queen Square, and Margaret, Jane and Alice were all present to sign the *Articles* in 1769. It remains unclear why Ann Horsman, the remaining sister, abstained from the opportunity in contrast to her sisters. However, apparently the three subscribing sisters retained some of Ann's doubts about the merits of the investment. Within a year, Alice had assigned her share to a third party, and in a subscriber's meeting of 1770, the minutes note that 'it was unanimously agreed that Mrs Magt Smith & Mrs Jane Horsman have forfeited their Respective Shares by not paying their Last payment in according to Notice in pursuance of the Articles'.[61] Given the sisters' lucrative property portfolio, it is unlikely that they were unable to afford this payment; perhaps all three sisters decided to withdraw from the scheme voluntarily, but only Alice was able to find a replacement shareholder. Demonstrably, not all subscribers remained satisfied with their investment, and were quite willing to forfeit their shares if necessary.

Katherine Wright (*d.*1804) was another female subscriber who lost her share, although for a quite different reason. Not much is known about her early life, and this lack of available information, coupled with her status as one of the rare subscribers living in the non-glamorous Westgate Buildings, suggests that Katherine was not from a wealthy or well-known family. Why an unmarried woman of this profile invested in the Upper Assembly Rooms is unclear; she was not, however, a subscriber for very long. By 1771, her name was crossed out of the subscribers' book and noted to be 'now the property of . . . Capn Fraine'.[62] Katherine Wright married Captain Joseph Fraine in Bath Abbey on Monday, 20 May 1771; Fraine (1724–1802) was a commanding officer in the navy with an illustrious career that spanned 15 years. Significantly, although Fraine left his wife a large amount of money upon his death, he did not return her the share in the Assembly Rooms, gifting it to a male friend instead.[63] Katherine Wright

28   Bath and Beyond

was by no means the only woman over the years whose share was permanently transferred away from her.

One notable woman more successful at retaining her shareholding was Elizabeth Towers (1718–1803), sister of Benjamin and William Colborne, who lived with the former in his house on the Circus. Brought up in Bath and Chippenham, Elizabeth married Revd Samuel Towers in 1754, but upon his death three years later inherited a significant portfolio of property in Hertfordshire and Middlesex. Opting to return to Bath to be close to her brothers, she further secured her independence by investing in mortgages (a common staple for widows at the time). Presumably, she did so under her brothers' guidance; like Benjamin and William, many of her clients were prominent Bathonian property developers and several of the indentures that she was party to were witnessed by William Colborne. One of her tenants was commercial gardener William McPherson, who in 1799 hosted Mr Cross's collection of wild animals, including lions and an elephant, in 'McPherson's Gardens' at the bottom of Orchard Street. In 1771, Elizabeth further expanded her property portfolio by purchasing ground rents worth £18,626 15s. from John Wood, who was attempting to clear debts related to expenses associated with the Upper Assembly Rooms. By her death in 1803, her will listed a host of 'moneys, mortgages, estate in mortgage, in stock, funds and other securities', and included properties in North Parade, South Parade, Queens Parade, Duke Street, and Pierrepont Street.[64] As a wealthy woman without a husband, Towers thus represented a group of women subscribers who (with only a few exceptions) remained unmarried and who used their investment as an opportunity to join an expanding female network of like-minded, independent individuals.

Colonial Links

Georgian Bath and its citizens profited richly from the wealth accumulated by colonial expansion and the triangular trade, and the city became a hub for plantation owners.[65] At least eight of the original subscribers (13 per cent) funded their investment in the Upper Assembly Rooms through wealth directly or indirectly derived from either expansionist colonial enterprise or the labour or trade of enslaved peoples.[66] In the case of Charles Mein (d.1774), only a minimal fraction of his own wealth consisted of the generational profits accumulated by his grandfather, Patrick Mein, during the latter's seat on the Barbados Island Council.[67] However, in other cases, the subscribers' involvement was much more direct. Sir Philip Francis (1740–1818) was so actively involved in the East India Company that he sat on its Supreme Council by 1773, and at least four other subscribers were either first-hand owners of, or gained direct profit from, the labour or trade of enslaved workers on Caribbean plantations.[68]

Bath Assembly Rooms and Its Subscribers 29

One of the most prominent examples of these was Edward Drax, former MP for Wareham (1726–91). Drax was an important figure within the Management Committee and sometimes hosted meetings at his house on Queen's Parade. Drax belonged to an old plantation-owning family who were among the first English colonisers of the Caribbean; the Drax Hall estate became the property of Edward when he outlived his elder brother and inherited it in 1789.[69] Although this was some time after his subscription to the Upper Assembly Rooms, Drax already had practical experience running the family plantations, and even co-authored a publication on the management of enslaved workers three years before inheriting Drax Hall.[70]

Another notable subscriber with colonial assets (and who also later sat on the Management Committee) was James Leigh-Perrot (1735–1817), Jane Austen's uncle. Originally born into a middling gentry family, Leigh-Perrot inherited the estate of a distant relative at the age of 16, but soon gained additional wealth by marrying an heiress of considerable fortune. Jane Cholmeley (1746–1836) was born in Barbados to planter Robert Cholmeley, and later became sister-in-law to the governor of Barbados, William Spry.[71] In addition to inheriting the assets of her father, Jane is also believed to have had inheritances through her mother's second marriage to another planter, Thomas Workman of Barbados.[72] As both the Cholmeley and Workman estates in St Michael have not been traced, it has been presumed that they were sold by the Leigh-Perrots.[73] Certainly, they were extremely wealthy, as Leigh-Perrot's will provided his wife with £10,000 and houses in Great Pulteney Street, Bath and Scarletts, Berkshire, not to mention gifts of £6,000 to his nieces and nephews—including Jane Austen. Presumably at least some of this wealth was also used to fund the Leigh-Perrots's house on the Paragon, where Austen stayed when she first visited Bath—and where their colonial associations may also have been present in their servant Frank, who Austen seemingly identified as 'black' in her correspondence.[74]

Another subscriber in one of the management committees with a Barbados connection was John Charnock, described in his will as 'a native of Barbados but at this time resident in Bath'.[75] The nature of John Charnock's connections to the Charnock plantations in Barbados and Jamaica remains difficult to verify. One generation earlier, the Barbados plantation was reported to have been conveyed in trust by one Benjamin Charnock, presumably to settle debts accrued by the estate; it is possible that it was these familial debts which were later related to John Charnock's eventual dismissal from the subscribers in 1772 due to his pecuniary difficulties (the meeting recorded that it was 'unamiously [sic] agreed that . . . Jno Wood & Jno Charnock Esqrs have forfeited [sic] their Respective Shares by not haveing [sic] made good their Payments [sic]').[76] However, by 1778, Charnock

30 Bath and Beyond

seemed to live quite comfortably at No.13 in the newly completed Royal Crescent, and upon his death in 1809 was able to leave substantial assets to his executors John Wood Nelson and Benjamin Adam, who ran an established West India merchant partnership from London. He did not use his return to wealth to re-invest in the Upper Assembly Rooms, making him one of only four of the original 63 subscribers to have permanently lost their share through forfeiture.

Two other subscribers with known links to plantations were also related to each other through marriage. Richard Salter (d.1776) was from an established plantation-owning family in Barbados (as was his wife Margaret, who was also born on the island), and Salter served as the island senator and magistrate.[77] Although living at Bladud's Buildings in 1768 when writing his will, he was in Barbados when he died in 1776, and his monument remains in the cathedral church of St George, Bridgetown.[78] Upon his death, the Salter plantation passed to his daughter Margaret, and thence, through her marriage, to another subscriber Philip Dehany (1720–1809) (Figure 2.5). Philip was the son of David Dehany, a Bristol planter whose estate comprised over 4,000 acres of land in Hanover, Jamaica.[79] Upon the death of his father, Philip Dehany (later MP for St Ives) inherited not just his father's estates but also all 'the works, negroes, cattle and stock' thereon, as well as various other associated 'parcels of land' and 'houses and stores' (Philip's mother was also gifted '3 enslaved people').[80] Philip's marriage into the Salter family only added to this asset portfolio, and left Dehany associated with at least five separate Caribbean plantations (the Barbican, Kew, Point, Paradise, and Salter estates). The profits from these estates enabled Dehany not only to maintain his country mansion of Farleigh Wallop near Bath but also to build an entirely new one (Kempshott Manor, Hampshire) and keep a town house in London, in addition to investing in side-schemes such as the Upper Assembly Rooms.

After the 68 shares of the original 63 subscribers began changing hands, later subscribers brought new connections to the labour of enslaved people and the expansion of colonial enterprises. For instance, in 1771, Lord Clive ('Clive of India'), known today as one of the most controversial figures in the management of colonial Bengal and its associated Great Famine, took over the forfeited share of Margaret Smith and retained it until his death.[81] Continuing research is needed to further examine these kinds of colonial connections to the subscribers. While later uses of the Upper Assembly Rooms transformed the building into an abolitionist hub and served as a platform for the likes of William Wilberforce, it remains pertinent to acknowledge plantation-based income streams from certain of the building's early investors, and the complex way in which their colonial connections interact with the formation and early history of the Bath Assembly Rooms.[82]

Figure 2.5 Thomas Gainsborough, *Philip Dehany and his wife Margaret, and their daughter Mary*, c.1761–2, oil on canvas, 238.5 × 147 cm, Sotheby's, Inc. Photograph courtesy of Sotheby's, Inc. © 2024.

Conclusion

This preliminary investigation into the founding investors in the Upper Assembly Rooms has provided a glimpse of the city's socio-economic structure, one built upon the intersecting interests of commerce, health, and sociability. Shareholders sufficiently motivated to fund the creation of the largest realised Georgian public building came from different geographic, social, and economic positions, but they shared the same desire for a financial return alongside glittering cultural entertainment. Bath's burghers were invested financially and reputationally in the city's aggrandisement, alongside tourists and invalids with portable economic and social capital who came to Bath for the company or recuperation. Investments came through independent women, from the Caribbean, India, Ireland, landed estates and urban rents, legal incomes, and the profits of carriers, apothecaries, and drapers. Though it seems likely that not every shareholder knew all the others, there were evidently significant clusters of kith and kinship, which

32   Bath and Beyond

only grew as the shares changed hands. This preliminary study points towards the value of a future macro study of all the shareholders as these networks developed over time, as a case study of not only the development of Bath but also Georgian society more widely.

Notes

1 Ronald Stanley Neale, *Bath, 1680–1850: A Social History* (London: Routledge, 1981), 221.
2 This chapter is part of ongoing research, providing a snapshot of our understanding of the original subscribers as of February 2024.
3 John Wood, *A Description of Bath* (London, 1765), ii, 320, 411.
4 R. W. M. Wright, *Assembly Rooms, Bath, a Souvenir Booklet to Commemorate the Re-Opening* (Bath: Mendip Press, 1938), 22.
5 *The New Bath Guide; or, Useful Pocket Companion* (Bath, 1788), 25.
6 Notable examples include depictions in Thomas Rowlandson's *The Comforts of Bath* (1798); Robert Cruikshank, *The English Spy* (London, 1824).
7 Pierce Egan, *Walks Through Bath* (Bath, 1819), 133.
8 The sole surviving example of the original 63 subscribers in 1814 was James Leigh-Perrot.
9 *The Rival Ballrooms* (Bath, 1774), 34.
10 Other addresses include residences on Brock Street, the Paragon, Bladud's Buildings, Milsom Street, Gay Street, and Trim Street.
11 Jane Austen, *Persuasion (1819)*, ed. J. Kinsley (Oxford: Oxford University Press, 2004), 39, 127–28.
12 Subscribers who were (or had been) MPs included Henry Herbert (Bletchingley and Ludlow), Peter Denis (Hedon), Philip Dehany (St Ives), Philip Francis (Appleby), and Edward Drax (Wareham). Many subsequent shareholders were also MPs (or had been). For their parliamentary biographies, see "The History of Parliament," accessed February 6, 2024, www.historyofparlia mentonline.org/volume/1715-1754/member/herbert-henry-arthur-1703-72; www.historyofparliamentonline.org/volume/1754-1790/member/ denis-peter-1713-78; www.historyofparliamentonline.org/volume/1754-1790/ member/dehany-philip-1720-1809; www.historyofparliamentonline.org/volume/ 1790-1820/member/francis-philip-1740-1818 and www.historyofparliamen tonline.org/volume/1754-1790/member/drax-edward-1726-91.
13 Subscribers associated with the apothecary trade included Thomas Haviland, William Street, and the Colborne brothers; subscribers involved in the merchant trade or the East India Company included Joseph Salvador, Jonathan Charnock, and Philip Francis.
14 Godfrey Laurence, *Bathford Past and Present*, ed. David Howells (Corsham: Bathford Society, 2010), 62. There are different ways of calculating estimations of historic sums in today's worth, from pure monetary inflation to changes in costs of goods and labour. This chapter has drawn from MeasuringWorth.com, providing an estimate of £80,000 according to the real price.
15 Perhaps two of the most memorable examples of this are Lord Clive, whose conduct in India became the subject of a parliamentary enquiry in 1772, and Jane Leigh-Perrot (wife of James Leigh-Perrot and aunt of Jane Austen), who was charged (and acquitted) for Grand Larceny in 1800.
16 *Rival Ballrooms* (Bath, 1774), 51.

17 *Rival Ballrooms*, 33–34.
18 *New Bath Guide*, 22.
19 *New Bath Guide*, 55.
20 Historic Houses Association [Online], "Capability Brown at Scampston," accessed December 12, 2023, www.capabilitybrown.org.uk/sites/default/files/capability_brown_at_scampston_leaflet.pdf.
21 For instance, when Lord Powis moved to Powis Castle (the seat of the earldom), he sold his former country estate to fellow subscriber Lord Clive.
22 BRO, 0028A/4: Journal of Proceedings of Shareholders, 1769–1772.
23 BRO, 0028A/4; 0028A/1: Tontine Agreement for the New Assembly Rooms, May 1, 1769.
24 BRO, 0028A/4: Journal of Proceedings of Shareholders.
25 A memorial to John's wife Frances (*d*.1808) in All Saints, Chingford, London, describes his legal career (though both were buried in St James's, Bath), as does a memorial to their only son also John (*d*.1807) at St Margaret's, Lee; Walter Scott, *The Antiquary* (1873), 287; Kent Archaeology [Online], *Lee Churchyard. Leland Duncan's sketches of heraldic coats of arms etc on gravestones*, accessed December 12, 2023, www.kentarchaeology.org.uk/research/monumental-inscriptions/lee.
26 Joseph Foster, *Alumni Oxonienses: The Members of the University of Oxford, 1715–1886: Their Parentage, Birthplace, and Year of Birth, with a Record of Their Degrees*, 4 vols. (Oxford: Parker & Co., 1888–1891), iii, 1122; Plymouth Archives, The Box, 69/P/1/4: Pleydell Estate papers, appointment; Landed Estates: Ireland's Landed Estates and Historic Houses, *c*.1700–1914, "Pleydell (Wilton, Somerset)," accessed December 12, 2023 https://landedestates.ie/estate/3982.
27 *Bath Chronicle*, May 9, 1799.
28 BRO, BC/6/2/9/2382/8: Attested copy conveyance, December 28, 1771; TNA, PROB 11/1621/220; Edward Yescombe, '"Hazardous and Scanty Securitys": The Career of William Yescombe, Bath Attorney, 1760–1774', *Bath History* x (2005): 97–120.
29 In the same year, Walter Bennett advertised a house on the Vineyards and in May 1770 was described in the subscribers' journal as being 'out of the kingdom'. *Bath Chronicle*, March 21, 1771.
30 BRO, 0028A/4: Journal of Proceedings of Shareholders, June 24, 1769, November 14, 1769.
31 Little is known of Sproule's biography. He may have been Irish, though he developed many houses in Bath, including five on the Circus (his tenants included the duke of Bedford and Lord Clive) and five houses on Brock Street, one let to the artist Joseph Wright of Derby. He also built Stacie's Hotel and Assembly Room in Weymouth, opening 1773, reflecting the emergent interest in sea bathing.
32 TNA, PROB 11/1077/310; Greenways Group of Churches [Online], "Burials 'C'," accessed December 12, 2023, https://harnish.org.uk/gravec.htm.
33 Trevor Fawcett, "Bath City Council Members, 1700–1835," accessed December 12, 2023, https://historyofbath.org/FawcettPapers/FawcettPapers; ODNB, accessed November 15, 2023, www.oxforddnb.com; s.v. Harrington, Henry.
34 TNA, PROB 11/1066/335; Ian Grimble, *The Harington Family* (New York: St Martin's Press, 1957), 219; BRO [Online], "Corston," accessed December 12, 2023 www.batharchives.co.uk/cemeteries/corston; Somerset Heritage Centre

34   *Bath and Beyond*

[SHC], DD/GL/138: Newton St Loe coal works etc. deed, 1768; *Bath Chronicle*, May 18, 1780.
35 BRO, 0028A/4: Journal of Proceedings of Shareholders.
36 Betty Rizzo, "Two Versions of Community: Montagu and Scott," *Huntington Library Quarterly* lxv (2002): 193–214; Edward Hoare, *Some Account of the Early History and Genealogy, with Pedigrees from 1330, Unbroken to the Present Time, of the Families of Hore and Hoare* (London: Alfred Russell Smith, 1883), 46.
37 TNA, PROB 11/1035/246.
38 TNA, PROB 11/1238/131; his will made extensive provision for his daughter Lady Sarah Ridley's second son, if he took his name.
39 Susan Sloman, *Gainsborough in Bath* (New Haven: Paul Mellon Centre for Studies in British Art, 2002), 111–12.
40 Sloman, *Gainsborough*, 126–27.
41 SHC, DD/BK/3/19: Indenture of Transfer, February 12, 1801; *Bath Chronicle*, December 12, 1793; *Bath Chronicle*, April 9, 1789.
42 Translation: William Greenwood Ship of War Commander; Three Decks [Online], "William Greenwood (c.1720–1796)," accessed December 12, 2023, https:// threedecks.org/chicago-il/index.php?display_type=show_crewman&id=7402.
43 Stephen Clews, "Banking in Bath in the Reign of George III," *Bath History* v (1994): 104–24.
44 Royal National Hospital for Rheumatic Diseases, RNHRD3; Randle Falconer and Anthony Brabazon, *History of the Royal Mineral Water Hospital, Bath*, 3rd ed. (Bath: Charles Hallett, 1888), 44.
45 Trevor Fawcett, History of Bath [Online], "William Street: An Apothecary's Progress," accessed December 12, 2023, https://historyofbath.org/FawcettPapers/ FawcettPapers.
46 Arthur and Anne Cookson (*d.*1789), with Margaret Rambouillet, are buried in All Saints, Weston; Joseph Howard and Frederick Crisp, *Visitation of England and Wales Notes*, 14 vols. (London: Heritage Books, 1896–1921), v, 32, 35; TNA, PROB/11/1442/98.
47 BRO, 0028A/3: List of Subscribers to the New Assembly Rooms, 1769–1814.
48 Walter Ison, *The Georgian Buildings of Bath 1700–1830* (London: Faber & Faber, 1948), 233.
49 BRO, 0028A/6: Minutes of the Management Committee, The New Assembly Rooms, 1771–1775.
50 Trevor Fawcett, "The Upper Assembly Rooms at Bath in the 1770s: Private Property or Public Amenity?," *The Regional Historian* xxiv (2012): 19.
51 His father was also Robert Sutton (1699–1776) who sat for Joseph Wright of Derby.
52 University of Nottingham, Pw F 8645: Robert Sutton to W.H.C. Cavendish-Bentinck, June 29, 1769.
53 Sheffield Archives, ACM/W/170: Chancery case of Sutton v. Sutton, February 10, 1778; Hugh Belsey, *Thomas Gainsborough, the Portraits, Fancy Pictures and Copies After Old Masters* (New Haven: Yale University Press, 2019), 795; Bath Abbey [Online], "Sutton, Robert," accessed December 12, 2023, www.bathab beymemorials.org.uk/person/sutton-robert.
54 Elizabeth Montagu Correspondence [Online], "William Robinson, 2nd Baronet Robinson," accessed December 12, 2023, https://emco.swansea.ac.uk/ emco/person/682/.
55 International Presentation Association [Online], "Venerable Nano Nagle," accessed January 14, 2024, https://globalpres.org/nano-nagle/.

56 Presentation Sisters Union [Online], "Bath," accessed December 12, 2023, https://pbvm.org/who-we-are/archives/bath/; Nano Nagle Place [Online], "The Story of Nano Nagle," accessed December 12, 2023, https://nanonagleplace.ie/the-story-of-nano-nagle/; Jessie Castle and Gillian O'Brien, "'I am Building a House': Nano Nagle's Georgian Convents," *Irish Architectural and Decorative Studies* xix (2016): 54–75.

57 J. A. Williams, ed., *Catholic Records Society Records: Post Reformation Catholicism in Bath*, vol. 1, 79 vols. (London: Catholic Record Society, 1905–2006), lxv, 105.

58 This is perhaps not surprising as Bath was described by John Beresford in 1795 as a 'little Dublin' to an Irishman, quoted in Castle and O'Brien, 'I am Building a House'.

59 Jane Denis, Elizabeth Towers, Margaret Rambouillet, Margaret Smith, Alice Horsman, Jane Horsman, Miss Coward, Katherine Wright, Dyonisia Thresher, Margaret Gordon, and Sarah Snee.

60 Because certain women owned more than one share, these percentages are calculated by the total amount of shares owned by women (12 and 21, respectively) as opposed to the total amount of women shareholders (11 and 19, respectively).

61 BRO, 0028A/4: Journal of Proceedings of Shareholders, March 27, 1770.

62 BRO, 0028A/3: List of Subscribers to the New Assembly Rooms.

63 Devon Record Office, 1142B/FW50: Will of Joseph Fraine, October 3, 1801. A transcription by Jonathan Frayne can be found at GEN UKI [Online], "Will of Joseph Fraine (1801)," accessed February 6, 2024, www.genuki.org.uk/big/eng/DEV/Barnstaple/JosephFraine1801.

64 TNA, PROB 11/1396/240.

65 See, for example, Smollett's comments in *Humphrey Clinker*: 'Every upstart of fortune, harnessed in the trappings of the mode, presents himself at Bath . . . Clerks and factors from the East Indies, loaded with the spoil of plundered provinces; planters, negro-drivers, and hucksters from our American plantations . . . f[i]nd themselves suddenly translated into a state of affluence . . . and all of them hurry to Bath, because here, without any further qualification, they can mingle with the princes and nobles of the land'. Tobias Smollett, *The Expedition of Humphrey Clinker (1771)*, ed. L. M. Knapp (Oxford: Oxford University Press, 1966), 36–37.

66 Edward Drax, Philip Dehany, Charles Mein, Joseph Salvador, Richard Salter, Jonathan Charnock, Philip Francis, and James Leigh-Perrot.

67 K. H. Ledward, ed., *Journals of the Board of Trade and Plantations*, 14 vols. (London: HMSO, 1920), i, 281–85.

68 Drax, Dehany, Salter, and Leigh-Perrot.

69 Matthew Parker, *The Sugar Barons: Family, Corruption, Empire and War* (London: Hutchinson, 2011); Centre for the Study of the Legacies of British Slavery [LBS [Online], "Edward Drax," accessed February 6, 2024, www.ucl.ac.uk/lbs/person/view/2146643067.

70 Edward Drax et al., *Instructions for the Management of a Plantation in Barbados and for the Treatment of Negroes* (Boston: D. Fowle, 1786).

71 Deirdre Le Faye, *Jane Austen's Letters* (Oxford: Oxford University Press, 2011), 506, 583.

72 LBS [Online], "Thomas Workman of Barbados," accessed February 6, 2024, www.ucl.ac.uk/lbs/person/view/2146667067.

73 LBS [Online], "Jane Leigh Perrot (née Cholmeley)," accessed December 12, 2023, https://wwwdepts-live.ucl.ac.uk/lbs/person/view/2146660413.

36 *Bath and Beyond*

74 Austen identifies the Leigh-Perrot's servant Frank by his 'black head . . . waiting in the hall window'. It is possible that this could simply mean that his hair was black, but the fact that he is only ever called by his Christian name (when all the other Leigh-Perrot servants were referred to by the last names) is suggestive of the fact that he himself was black and that he did not have a Christian surname: Le Faye, *Letters*, 81.
75 TNA, PROB 11/1501/256.
76 BRO, 0028A/4: Journal of Proceedings of Shareholders, February 11, 1772.
77 LBS [Online], "Richard Salter," accessed February 6, 2024, www.ucl.ac.uk/lbs/person/view/2146665833.
78 Designed by Joseph Nollekens, the preparatory concept design of the piece can be found in the collections of the Victoria and Albert Museum (VAM, E.472–2010).
79 TNA, CO 142/31: List of landholders and their holdings, 1754, s.v. 'Dehany'; LBS [Online], "David Dehany (Senior)," accessed February 6, 2024, www.ucl.ac.uk/lbs/person/view/2146645677.
80 Vere Langford Oliver, *Caribbeana, Being Miscellaneous Papers Relating to the History, Genealogy, Topography, and Antiquities of the British West Indies*, 8 vols. (London: Mitchell Hughes & Clarke, 1910–1919), iii, 289; LBS [Online], "Philip Dehany," accessed February 6, 2024, www.ucl.ac.uk/lbs/person/view/2146638189.
81 BRO, 0028A/4: Journal of Proceedings of Shareholders, May 14, 1771.
82 Roger Holly, "The Anti-Slavery Movement in Bath," *Bath History* xiv (2016): 81.

Bibliography

Manuscript Sources

Bath Record Office

0028A: Early Records of the Upper Assembly Rooms 1769–1814

Plymouth Archives, The Box

69/P/1/4: Pleydell Estate papers, appointment

Printed Primary and Secondary Sources

Austen, Jane. *Persuasion*. Edited by J. Kinsley. Oxford: Oxford University Press, 2004.
Barker, Elizabeth. "Documents Relating to Joseph Wright 'of Derby' (1734–97)." *The Volume of the Walpole Society* 71 (2009): 1–216.
"Bath." Presentation Sisters Union. Accessed December 12, 2023. https://pbvm.org/who-we-are/archives/bath/.
The Bath Chronicle.
Belsey, Hugh. *Thomas Gainsborough: The Portraits, Fancy Pictures and Copies After Old Masters*. New Haven: Yale University Press, 2019.
"Burials 'C'." Greenways Group of Churches. Accessed December 12, 2023. https://harnish.org.uk/gravec.htm.

"Capability Brown at Scampston." Historic Houses Association. Accessed December 12, 2023. www.capabilitybrown.org.uk/sites/default/files/capability_brown_at_scampston_leaflet.pdf.

Casey, Christine. "Testaments to Craftsmanship: in Pursuit of Digital Records." Accessed December 12, 2023. https://craftvalue.org/blog/testaments-to-crafts manship/.

Castle, J., and G. O'Brien. "'I am Building a House': Nano Nagle's Georgian Convents." *Irish Architectural and Decorative Studies* 19 (2016): 54–75.

"Centre for the Study of the Legacies of British Slavery (LBS)." Accessed February 6, 2024. www.ucl.ac.uk/lbs.

Clews, Stephen. "Banking in Bath in the Reign of George III." *Bath History* 5 (1994): 104–24.

Cruikshank, Robert. *The English Spy*. London, 1824.

Drax, Edmund et al. *Instructions for the Management of a Plantation in Barbados and for the Treatment of Negroes*. Boston: D. Fowle, 1786.

Egan, Pierce. *Walks Through Bath*. Bath, 1819.

Falconer, R., and A. Brabazon. *History of the Royal Mineral Water Hospital, Bath*. Bath: Charles Hallett, 1888.

Fawcett, Trevor. "Bath City Council Members, 1700–1835." History of Bath. Accessed December 12, 2023. https://historyofbath.org/FawcettPapers/Fawcett Papers.

Fawcett, Trevor. "The Upper Assembly Rooms at Bath in the 1770s: Private Property or Public Amenity?" *The Regional Historian* 24 (2012): 14–20.

Fawcett, Trevor. "William Street: An Apothecary's Progress." History of Bath. Accessed December 12, 2023. https://historyofbath.org/FawcettPapers/Fawcett Papers.

Foster, Joseph. *Alumni Oxonienses: The Members of the University of Oxford, 1715–1886: Their Parentage, Birthplace, and Year of Birth, with a Record of Their Degrees*. Oxford: Parker & Co., 1888–1891.

Grimble, Ian. *The Harington Family*. New York: St Martin's Press, 1957.

"The History of Parliament Online." Accessed February 6, 2024. www.historyof parliamentonline.org/.

Hoare, Edward. *Some Account of the Early History and Genealogy, with Pedigrees from 1330, Unbroken to the Present Time, of the Families of Hore and Hoare*. London: Alfred Russell Smith, 1883.

Holly, Roger. "The Anti-Slavery Movement in Bath." *Bath History* 14 (2016): 79–87.

Howard, J., and F. Crisp. *Visitation of England and Wales Notes*. London: Heritage Books, 1896–1921.

Huggins, Mike. "Racing Culture, Betting, and Sporting Protomodernity: The 1750 Newmarket Carriage Match." *Journal of Sport History* 42, no. 3 (2015): 322–39. https://doi.org/10.5406/jsporthistory.42.3.0322.

Ison, Walter. *The Georgian Buildings of Bath*. Bath: Kingsmead Press, 1980.

Laurence, Godfrey. *Bathford: Past and Present*. Edited by D. Howells. Corsham: Bathford Local History Society, 2010.

Ledward, K. H., ed. *Journals of the Board of Trade and Plantations*. London: HMSO, 1920.

"Lee Churchyard. Leland Duncan's Sketches of Heraldic Coats of Arms etc on Gravestones." Kent Archaeology. Accessed December 12, 2023. www.kent archaeology.org.uk/research/monumental-inscriptions/lee.

Le Faye, Deirdre. *Jane Austen's Letters*. Oxford: Oxford University Press, 2011.

38 Bath and Beyond

Neale, Ronald S. *Bath, 1680–1850: A Social History*. London: Routledge, 1981.
The New Bath Guide; or, Useful Pocket Companion. Bath, 1788.
Oliver, V. L. *Caribbeana, Being Miscellaneous Papers Relating to the History, Genealogy, Topography, and Antiquities of the British West Indies*. London: Mitchell Hughes & Clarke, 1910–1919.
"Omer, Thomas." Dictionary of Irish Architects. Accessed December 12, 2023. www.dia.ie/architects/view/4177/OMER-THOMAS.
Parker, Matthew. *The Sugar Barons: Family, Corruption, Empire and War*. London: Hutchinson, 2011.
The Rival Ballrooms. Bath, 1774.
Rizzo, Betty. "Two Versions of Community: Montagu and Scott." *Huntington Library Quarterly* 65, no. 1–2 (2002): 193–214.
Scott, Walter. *The Antiquary*. London: A. & C. Black, 1873.
Sloman, Susan. *Gainsborough in Bath*. New Haven: Paul Mellon Centre for Studies in British Art, 2002.
Smollett, Tobias. *The Expedition of Humphrey Clinker*. Edited by L. M. Knapp. Oxford: Oxford University Press, 1966.
Sproule, Anna. *Lost Houses of Britain*. North Pomfret, VT: David & Charles, 1982.
"The Story of Nano Nagle." Nano Nagle Place. Accessed December 12, 2023. https://nanonagleplace.ie/the-story-of-nano-nagle/.
"Sutton, Robert." Bath Abbey. Accessed December 12, 2023. www.bathabbeymemorials.org.uk/person/sutton-robert.
"Venerable Nano Nagle." International Presentation Association. Accessed January 14, 2024. https://globalpres.org/nano-nagle/.
"William Robinson, 2nd Baronet Robinson." Elizabeth Montagu Correspondence. Accessed December 12, 2023. https://emco.swansea.ac.uk/emco/person/682/.
Williams, J. A., ed. *Catholic Records Society Records: Post Reformation Catholicism in Bath*. London: Catholic Record Society, 1905–2006.
Wood, John. *A Description of Bath*. London, 1765.
Wright, R. W. M. *Assembly Rooms, Bath, a Souvenir Booklet to Commemorate the Re-Opening*. Bath: Mendip Press, 1938.
Yescombe, Edward. "'Hazardous and Scanty Securitys': The Career of William Yescombe, Bath Attorney, 1760–1774." *Bath History* 10 (2005): 97–120.

3 'Solemn yet Sumptuous'

Robert Adam's Designs for an Alternative Assembly Room in Bath

Amy Frost

The language of Classicism defined the architecture of Britain and its colonial expansion in the eighteenth century. Within the exploration of that language there were shifts in style as architects experimented with vocabulary, seeking to adapt and innovate it to suit contemporary design and new building types. The 1760s saw the fading of Palladianism as the dominant architectural style in Britain. Instead, architects had increasingly started to look directly to Ancient Greece and Rome for inspiration, rather than to the architecture of the Italian Renaissance that had defined Palladianism. This shift in style towards Neoclassicism was led by the work of Scottish architect Robert Adam (1728–92). His interest in Ancient Roman structure, plan form, and decoration led to the popularity of a distinct 'Adam Style' that was widely imitated in architecture, interiors, and furniture design. In Bath, it was John Wood the Younger (1728–82) who instigated the shift between styles through his designs for the Royal Crescent (1767–75) and Bath Assembly Rooms (1769–71).

The Royal Crescent, in particular, transitioned the architecture of Bath away from the Palladianism that Wood's father, John Wood the Elder (1704–54), had made the dominant style in the city through buildings such as Queen Square (1727–34) and the Circus (1754–67). Neither the Royal Crescent nor the Bath Assembly Rooms ever quite crossed the line into fully fledged Neoclassicism, but both buildings exemplify the stylistic innovation Wood the Younger was trying to achieve. Wood was not the only architect to explore the new style in Bath during the 1760 and 1770s. Thomas Warr Atwood (*c*.1733–75) was working in parallel, yet his design for The Paragon (1768–75), though an extraordinary essay in structure, lacks the charisma of Wood's Palladian-Neoclassical style. Thomas Baldwin (*c*.1750–1820) would also soon follow with his Adam-infused designs for the Guildhall (1775–78) and Northumberland Buildings (1778), and then John Palmer (*c*.1738–1817) with an Adam-esque lightness of style at St James Square (1790–93).[1] At the time of the building of Bath Assembly

DOI: 10.4324/9781003393856-3

Rooms however, there was no Bath-based architect who could stylistically rival Wood the Younger in the city.

It was perhaps for that reason that Robert Adam, the creator of the freshest and most fashionable architectural style in the country, was commissioned in 1767–68 (as this chapter argues), a year before Wood's building, to design a 'Ball and Concert Room' in Bath. Although never referred to as being a design for assembly rooms, the Ball and Concert Room proposed by Adam was clearly intended to function as such, and can be seen as a more grandiose, and more overtly Roman, alternative to the Bath Assembly Rooms by Wood.[2] With an 11-bay concave Corinthian colonnaded entrance front, had it been built, Adam's proposed building would have dominated its surroundings, and a journey through its interiors would have been a visual feast, inspired in plan form by the thermal baths of Ancient Rome. The dating of the Adam proposal is key, however, to understanding whether or not the Adam assembly room designs were presented as an alternative to John Wood's Bath Assembly Rooms, or actually intended as a competitor.

This chapter seeks to unpick the dating and creation of Adam's Ball and Concert Rooms designs, examining whether the intended location was the same as Wood's constructed Bath Assembly Rooms or actually part of a grandiose scheme the Adam Brothers designed for elsewhere in the city. Through examination of the drawings for the Adam project this chapter will then show how the most ambitiously 'Roman' of any Georgian building in Bath were the assembly rooms that were never built.

Robert Adam's Ball and Concert Room design is for a large and imposing building, with a grand concave colonnaded entrance behind which sits a ballroom and concert room flanking a corridor leading to a large domed rotunda (Figure 3.1). The design is illustrated across five finished ink and wash drawings held in the Sir John Soane's Museum collection.[3] They are

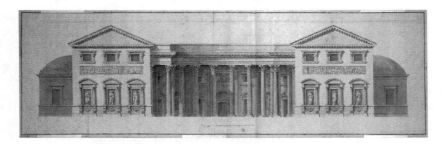

Figure 3.1 Office of Robert Adam, *Design for a Ball and Concert Room at Bath* [Elevation], pen and wash, 175.9 × 57.2 cm, Sir John Soane's Museum, SM Adam vol 28/45. © Sir John Soane's Museum, London.

frustratingly undated, and the drawings are unattributed to any specific draughtsman's hand, although the overall project is attributed to Robert Adam as the principal designer. A further eight pencil and pen preliminary sketches also illustrate the project, of which some have been identified as being drawn by either Robert or James Adam.[4] There is equally frustratingly little further evidence of the project either in the Soane's Museum's Adam collection or in the Pulteney Estate papers deposited in the Bath Record Office.

The Bath Ball and Concert Room drawings sit among a wider collection of Adam designs for Bath relating to commissions for William Johnstone Pulteney and the Bathwick Estate—600 acres of land on the east side of the River Avon, today centred around the wide promenade of Great Pulteney Street. The Adam drawings for Bath include a series of masterplans for the creation of a large extension to the city across the Bathwick Estate (1777–82), designs for a prison (1771), and the designs for one of Bath's most well-known landmarks, Pulteney Bridge (1769–74).[5] With the exception of Pulteney Bridge, these grand and elaborate plans by Adam for a vison of Bath on a monumental Roman scale were never realised. The development and construction of Pulteney Bridge is the most well documented through the Pulteney Estate Papers, being the only executed building, and one where the involvement of the Bath Corporation was essential due to the necessity for an act of Parliament to construct it.[6] The prison intended for Grove Street, too, is referenced in the city records and there is a small but significant reference to the Adam masterplans for the Bathwick Estate within the Pulteney papers.[7] Any documentary reference to Adam's designing a Ball and Concert Room, however, remains undiscovered. Unpicking the mystery around the Adam designs therefore relies upon a series of assumptions, the first having already been referenced, that the proposed Ball and Concert Rooms were intended to present the city of Bath with a new set of assembly rooms.

Dating Adam's Assembly Rooms

In order to unravel the dating of the Adam assembly room designs, what and who brought the Adam brothers to Bath must first be understood. William Johnstone was an Edinburgh solicitor who in 1760 married Frances Pulteney. In 1767, Frances inherited the Bathwick Estate from her cousin General Harry Pulteney, who had in turn inherited from his brother, William Pulteney, earl of Bath, in 1764.[8] After taking his wife's surname, William Johnstone Pulteney immediately looked to maximise the potential of Frances's newly inherited property through development, including expanding the city across the river.[9] Pulteney is often referred to as a friend of the Adam brothers, an assumption generally made due to their shared

42 Bath and Beyond

Scottish heritage and possible acquaintance while students in Edinburgh in the mid-1740s. An assumed friendship was reinforced by evidence naming Pulteney as a pallbearer at Robert Adam's funeral in 1792.[10] The earliest evidence currently known for the involvement of the Adams brothers with William Johnstone Pulteney's vision for Bath is a letter to him from James Adam concerning Pulteney Bridge in 1770.[11] There is, however, evidence that shows the Adams's connection with the Pulteney family was in place earlier than that. Prior to his death, the earl of Bath had commissioned plans from Robert Adam for a mansion house on his estate at Eyton-on-Severn in Shropshire, which Gareth Williams has dated c.1758–64.[12] The assumption that could be made is that this commission from the earl of Bath was perhaps following an introduction made through William Johnstone (Pulteney) after his marriage to Frances in 1760. The Eyton-on-Severn mansion was never built, but Adam returned to the Pulteney Shropshire estate when William Johnstone Pulteney commissioned him to undertake alterations to Shrewsbury Castle from c.1768, contemporaneous to when the Adams's involvement in Bath seems to have begun.[13]

In August 1769, William Johnstone Pulteney was using designs by John Paty for the new bridge over the river to Bathwick. The fact that Pulteney was already considering shops at the ends of the bridge suggests the influence of Adam from earlier in 1769, or feasibly even mid-to-late 1768.[14] Even if they had not actually met in Scotland, it is safe to assume that a man in Pulteney's position with architectural ambitions was aware of the Adams's work in London after he moved there in 1759. Knowledge of the Adams's plans for the Adelphi scheme in London (1768–75) and its riverside location would certainly have resonated with Pulteney and his vison for Bathwick, and perhaps influenced him in inviting Adam to draw up plans for the estate. Putting aside the unknown start date of any personal connection between the men, the start of the professional Pulteney-Adams-Bath relationship was probably no earlier than October 1767 when Frances Pulteney, and therefore William Johnstone Pulteney, took control of the Bathwick Estate and its wealth.

It has generally always been assumed that the Adam assembly room designs were presented as an alternative to those of John Wood, and therefore intended to be built on the same site where Wood's Upper Assembly Rooms now stand. It is this which has led to the Adam drawings being dated previously c.1765–68. It is a strong possibility, but one where the understanding of when the Adam brothers first became involved with Pulteney's plans for Bath becomes an important factor. If the Adam assembly room designs were proposed as an alternative to Wood's plans, it would reaffirm the work of the Adams in Bath as starting earlier than the documented 1770 date. The dating of the drawings themselves can, however, be narrowed down further, when pursuing this theory. Previously dated

'Solemn yet Sumptuous' 43

as c.1765–68, it is actually unlikely that the Adam designs are from earlier than October 1767, both due to when Pulteney took control of the Bathwick Estate and that (if they are an alternative to Wood's design) they appear to have been created during a key moment in the evolution of Adam's assembly rooms project.

John Wood's proposal for assembly rooms to the northwest of Queen Square was first advertised in November 1764, but had, by 1766, faltered in part due to a dispute over the land ownership.[15] By the time it was resolved in 1768, Wood had relocated his proposed rooms to the upper town, to the site northeast of his development at the Circus, with the subscriptions opening on 29 November 1768.[16] There was, therefore, a two-year hiatus in Wood's scheme, during which the Adam designs could have been potentially put forward. This would date the Adam designs more firmly as being made between October 1767 and November 1768. It could also suggest a loss of confidence in Wood's ability to deliver a new building, which Pulteney took advantage of by presenting attractive and elaborate plans by a well-established London architect as an alternative. The Adam designs reached finished drawing stage, suggesting they were presentation drawings for a client or funder. Whether they were prepared and seen just by Pulteney himself, or if they were ever disseminated further by him to a wider group of stakeholders in the city, is unfortunately unknown.

What if, however, Adam's assembly room designs were never actually intended to be for the same location as Wood's? Both the initial Queen Square location and the final Circus location of John Wood's Bath Assembly Rooms were closely linked with wider developments for a network of streets designed by him and his father before him. It would have been a bold move from Pulteney and Adam to put forward their proposal for a site so closely linked to the speculative plans of another designer and developer, or land to which that developer had already laid claim. So, it is perhaps more likely, therefore, that the Adam proposal was for a site elsewhere in the city. The other alternative that must be considered is that they were designed to be built on the Bathwick Estate itself, and therefore as a competitor to those assembly rooms, both existing and Wood's newly proposed.

However, the earliest recorded date for Adam having undertaken town planning designs for Pulteney is c.1770–73, when the Adams were paid £163 9s. 0d. for 'a plan of the Streets Buildings and Squares of a New Town on the Bathwick side of the River'.[17] They were however, clearly involved in ideas for the laying out of the estate prior to that, and as has already been established, potentially as early as October 1767. The Adam assembly room designs, therefore, could also be feasibly dated to a later period, even as late as the last dated plan for Bathwick by Adam in 1782.[18] None of the Adam Bathwick Estate plans, however, have any indication of

44 *Bath and Beyond*

a single detached building of the scale of the assembly room designs drawn on them. Therefore, the intended location for these grand and imperial rooms by Adam in Bath remains a matter of speculation.

This is a very elongated way of arriving at the most important aspect of the Adam designs for assembly rooms in Bath—which is that, almost irrespective of why and for what site they were made, they hold a significant place in the development of Adam's modern architectural expression of Western classical antiquity.

The Influence of Rome

The Adam assembly room designs are, as stated by Alastair Rowan, 'one of the most remarkable and distinguished designs produced by Adam soon after his return from Rome'.[19] In 1758, Robert Adam returned from an extensive European Grand Tour spent primarily in Rome, and he was infusing his work with the impact that his knowledge and understanding of the structures he had surveyed there provided. It resulted in his work of the 1760s being particularly Roman in scale and detailing. The 'solemn yet sumptuous' Bath designs offer an 'antique gravitas' that was not as apparent in Adam's work before his Grand Tour.[20] It is this rigorous use of Roman forms and motifs that reinforce the dating of the Adam assembly room designs to *c.*1768 as forming part of his immediate post-Rome body of work.

Fundamental to the Adam assembly room designs is a sense of scale, or greatness, that presents a monumentality which will define the ideas of Neoclassicism in British architecture from the 1760s onwards. This monumentality, combined with a balance of simplicity and complexity in form and decoration, was Robert Adam's interpretation of Roman architecture innovated for eighteenth-century Britain. It was wholly appropriate then for designing in the Roman city of Bath—even if the city at that date had little evidence of its Roman architectural heritage on show.[21]

So how do the designs for the assembly rooms illustrate this new confidence in Roman forms from Adam? The elevation has a concave colonnade made up of 10 giant Corinthian columns with corresponding pilasters on the wall that sits behind, between which sit four pedimented doorways (Figure 3.1). The outer two doorways lead into small triangular rooms, perhaps functioning as footman or watchman's spaces. The inner two doors flank the central entrance, where two Ionic columns support a thermal, or Diocletian, window above. The concave form of this entrance is a clever conceit. Rather than a projecting portico, the curved entrance forms a courtyard space and draws anyone approaching it into the body of the building, making it both an imposing and welcoming space. It is possible to imagine the crowds attending subscription balls or concerts flooding

'Solemn yet Sumptuous' 45

into that space, funnelling in through the main and two side doors, while also having a degree of shelter for themselves and any attendants under the long colonnade.

Flanking the entrance are two three-bay pedimented wings housing the ballroom and concert room. Their elevations are articulated with pedimented niches with large statues of figures inspired by classical antiquity, above which are large carved friezes and windows taken, as noted by Rowan, from Michelangelo's St Peter's Basilica, Vatican City.[22] This principal elevation is largely blind, with the small windows in the attic storey bringing in little natural light, corresponding to the internal spaces, as the principal function of the rooms was for use at night and would therefore be artificially lit. It both reduces the need to take up wall space with window openings and maximises the ability to articulate internal wall space with other forms of decoration. It is a familiar arrangement when looking at other examples of the Georgian assembly room building typology, from the earl of Burlington's first model assembly room design for York (1730–35) back to a key influence upon them, the Egyptian Halls as described and illustrated in 1570 by Andrea Palladio in *I quattro libri dell'architecturra* (*The Four Books of Architecture*), and one that John Wood employs in his own plans for the executed Bath Assembly Rooms.

An early sketched plan for a building annotated by Robert Adam in French has been attributed as being both an influence upon the Bath designs and a preliminary sketch for them (Figure 3.2).[23] It is potentially of a building Adam visited and recorded while on his travels (and therefore dated to *c*.1755–56), or alternatively an early design for the assembly rooms (making it *c*.1767–68). As the online catalogue entry for this design, written by Frances Sands, notes, both explanations make it a key source for the initial ideas of the assembly rooms, as it shows a building with a concave colonnaded entrance flanked by projecting wings with a central salon.[24] On either side of this central axis sit rectangular rooms, on the left side a ballroom and on the right a concert room. The similarities with the finished plan of the assembly rooms are clear (Figure 3.3). After moving in from the main entrance, what in the early sketch is a central salon with side apses, in the later Bath plan becomes a plainer rectangular hall space. The reasoning behind this reduction of detail being that rather than leading into a grand single staircase as seen in the early sketch, in the Bath plan the space functions as an anteroom or hallway opening into the large rotunda behind, which sits at the heart of the building. The staircase in the finished Bath plan is reduced in significance, split into two simpler access routes flanking the rotunda, highlighting that the upper floor is of secondary importance to the principal rooms on the ground floor.

The most apparent shift between the sketch (irrespective of whether it dates from either *c*.1755–56 or *c*.1767–68) and the finished Bath plan is

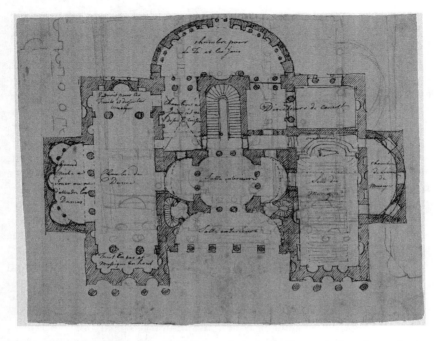

Figure 3.2 Robert Adam, *A plan for an unknown building, attributed to either one seen by Adam on his Grand Tour, c.1755–6, or to a preliminary design for the Concert and Ball Room proposals for Bath, c.1768*. pen and pencil, 25.7 × 20.3 cm, Sir John Soane's Museum, SM Adam vol.55/173 verso. © Sir John Soane's Museum, London.

the increase in complexity of the interior architecture of the building. The finished assembly rooms plan shows a profusion of projections, recessions, columns, niches, and apses, in the ballroom, concert room, and in what can be assumed to be the tearoom in the rotunda. It all combines to form elaborate interiors that are fully illustrated in the finished section drawings for the project.

A Procession Through Antiquity

The transverse section of the Adam assembly room design shows the transition from the large open entrance into the small plain hall in more detail and highlights the impact that moving from that small and tight space into the large volume of the rotunda would have had on the visitor (Figure 3.4). Stepping into the rotunda during the day, when the room, assuming it functioned as the tea and coffee room, would have been used more than

'Solemn yet Sumptuous' 47

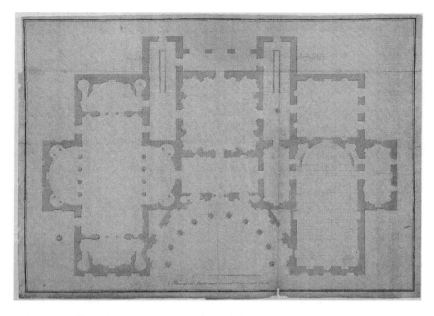

Figure 3.3 Office of Robert Adam, *Plan of the Ball and Concert Rooms at Bath*, pen and wash, 87.9 × 63.7 cm, Sir John Soane's Museum, SM Adam vol 28/49. © Sir John Soane's Museum, London.

Figure 3.4 Office of Robert Adam, *Section through the Ball & Concert Room at Bath* [transverse section], pen and wash, 125.1 × 55.8 cm, Sir John Soane's Museum, SM Adam vol 28/47. © Sir John Soane's Museum, London.

48 Bath and Beyond

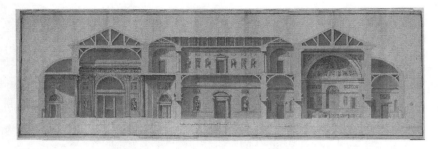

Figure 3.5 Office of Robert Adam, *Section through the Ball and Concert Room at Bath* (longitudinal section), pen and wash, 170.4 × 55.5 cm, Sir John Soane's Museum, SM Adam vol 28/48. The ball room sits to the left of the central space, the concert room to the right. © Sir John Soane's Museum, London.

the ball or concert rooms. Natural light would have filtered in from the central oculus and that transition from the dark low space of the hall into the large lit open space would have had significant impact. At night when the rooms were in full use, it would have been lit by candelabra or torches on stands, although Adam does not draw in any apparent lighting in any of the designs. The influence of the Pantheon in Rome on the rotunda design is clear, in particular in the coffering of the domed ceiling, and can be related to the design by Adam for the rotunda at Kedleston Hall, Derbyshire, from 1760.[25]

A smaller, yet more elaborate coffered domed ceiling is seen in the assembly rooms' concert room, illustrated in the longitudinal section (Figure 3.5). The apse at the far end of the concert room, where the performers would have been located behind a small balustrade, is decorated with coffering that was intended to have detailed scenes and buildings from classical antiquity illustrated in them.[26] Imagine the fashionable 'Company' of Bath promenading through these rooms, passing from one space into another, each space having a different character and form, and surrounded by the plaster reliefs, statues, and decoration that is Adam's interpretation of ancient Rome. It would have been a movement or procession through antiquity re-imagined for eighteenth-century Bath.

This interior architecture by Adam, full of detailing and movement, was particularly influenced by his experience walking the ruins of Roman buildings while on his Grand Tour. Anyone visiting Adam's proposed assembly rooms would have stepped beyond the colonnaded entrance under the Diocletian window, through the plain rectangular hall and into the circular rotunda in a journey that connects the designs to some of the most influential sources for Adam's ideas at this time. These being namely the structures

'Solemn yet Sumptuous' 49

Figure 3.6 After Charles-Louis Clérisseau, *Peristyle of the Diocletian palace in Split*, from Robert Adam's *Ruins of the Palace of the Emperor Diocletian at Spalatro in Dalmatia*, 1764, line engraving, Yale Center for British Art, Paul Mellon Collection, L 1.37 Copy 1 (Folio A). Courtesy of Yale Center for British Art, Paul Mellon Collection.

created for the Emperor Diocletian, the Baths of Diocletian in Rome, and Diocletian's Palace in Split in Croatia, which Adam surveyed and published in his book *The Ruins of the Palace of the Emperor Diocletian at Spalatro in Dalmatia* in 1764 (Figure 3.6). Adam is known to have spent time recording Roman bath complexes, including the baths of Diocletian and Caracalla in Rome and those at Tivoli, for a revision of A.B. Desgodetz's 1682 publication *Les Édifices Antiques de Rome* [The Ancient Buildings of Rome], although the drawings Adam made for this before he left Rome are now lost.[27] A series of surviving drawings by Adam records the plan of a Roman bath complex, possibly the Baths at Tivoli, the finished version of which shows a large public building comprising a courtyard with bay ends, surrounding a central structure, the walls of the whole complex being articulated with multiple colonnades and recesses.[28] The influence of this structure, and other such Roman Thermae or baths complexes, in the arrangement of the three principal assembly rooms' spaces and the progression of a visitor through them, is clear in the Adam designs. The plan of the Baths of Diocletian, for example, relates closely to Adam's assembly room plan, with the central axis of entrance, hall, and rotunda (and what appears to be a rear portico behind it) reflecting the movement through the

50   Bath and Beyond

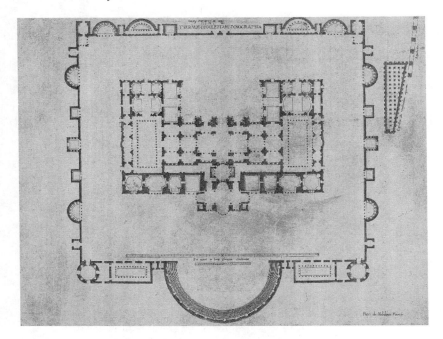

Figure 3.7 Antonio Lafreri, *Plan of the Baths of Diocletian, Rome*, from *Speculum Romanae Magnificentiae*, 1546–90, line engraving, Yale Center for British Art, Paul Mellon Collection B1974.12.1476. Courtesy of Yale Center for British Art, Paul Mellon Collection.

Tepidarium [warm room], *Frigidarium* [cold room], and *Natatio* [swimming pool] of the Roman Thermae (Figure 3.7). While the flanking ball and concert rooms reflect the location of the flanking *Palaestra* (courts for exercise) in the plan of Diocletian's Baths, Adam's Bath ballroom follows a form similar to the plan of the Caldarium at the Diocletian baths but is relocated from the end of the central axis to the left flanking Palaestra position.

These Ancient Roman buildings clearly had a lasting impact on Adam in all aspects of design, influencing plan, form, scale, and decoration. Roman Baths were an acknowledged influence upon the 3rd earl of Burlington's assembly room designs in York, as he too drew upon the Roman heritage of the city he was designing for as inspiration, and Adam himself sought Burlington's book on the Baths of Diocletian and Caracalla.[29] The extent to which Adam infuses his assembly room design for Bath with the forms of antique Roman Bath structures is heightened by his knowledge of the city's own Roman history. Although he would not have had first-hand knowledge of the full extent of the ancient Roman baths and temple complex

'Solemn yet Sumptuous' 51

in Bath, the idea of its possible architectural heritage would have been a strong influence. Visually linking the modern building to the history of the city would also have been a useful tool in selling the designs to prospective investors, even if most would have probably only recognised the connection through the decoration and language of classicism, and not through an understanding of influences upon the plan form. In comparison, Adam's designs for Exeter's assembly rooms, which are dated c.1768 and therefore contemporaneous to the Bath designs, are far more modest in scale and although some elements of the plan, and the use of the Diocletian window, can be matched between the two schemes, the prestige of the Bath proposal clearly reflects the greater wealth and social position of Bath and the marketability of its Roman inheritance in comparison to its Devon counterpart.[30]

A study of John Wood's plan of the executed Bath Assembly Rooms shows a similar arrangement in spaces to Adam's, and therefore suggests an equally similar inspiration from knowledge of Roman Thermae complexes.[31] It is unknown whether John Wood ever visited Rome himself, although he owned several publications illustrating its ancient and Renaissance buildings, including Adam's *Ruins of the Palace of the Emperor Diocletian at Spalatro in Dalmatia*.[32] Adam's knowledge and experience of these same Roman buildings was undoubtedly greater than Wood's, however, and it is tempting to suggest that Wood was using Adam's plan for assembly rooms as a source when designing his own. Of course, this would have been dependent on Adam's plan having been shared outside of just Pulteney and his associates working on the Bathwick Estate.

An Unbuilt Vision for Bath

The final question over the Adam designs for assembly rooms in Bath is therefore, why were they never built? Walter Ison posited that Adam's design was never built because 'the committee decided to accept the less ambitious plans which Wood proposed of the same site'.[33] However, no evidence corresponds with any committee ever actually having seen the Adam plans, and the 'committee' for the new rooms was instigated as a speculation by Wood himself, so the possibility of him having shown them the plans of a rival designer seems unlikely. It also works on the assumption that the Adam designs were for the site northeast of the Circus. However, even if the alternative location of it being a proposal for somewhere on the Bathwick Estate were to be considered, the explanation for it remaining unexecuted was likely the same—that Adam's Roman grandeur and gravitas was simply too expensive to realise.

This explanation is reinforced by the failure of any of the Adam plans for the Bathwick Estate to be executed, with the exception of Pulteney Bridge. The earliest surviving plan for Bathwick by Adam dates from 1777

52 Bath and Beyond

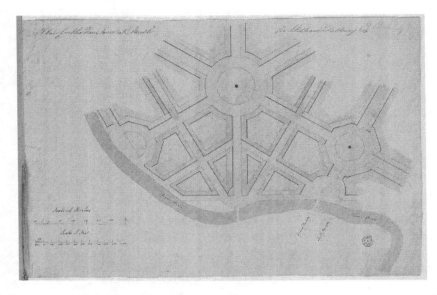

Figure 3.8 Office of Robert Adam, *Plan of the New Town at Bath*, 1777, pen and wash, 48.5 × 32.2 cm, Sir John Soane's Museum, SM Adam vol 38/6. © Sir John Soane's Museum, London.

(although as noted earlier, the office was paid for plans in 1770–73) and proposes a 'New Town' made up of large streets radiating out from the east end of Pulteney Bridge and connecting riverside crescents to a central circus (Figure 3.8). Elevations for the buildings stretching along the riverside show a series of river gates and terraces of townhouses on a scale far greater than anything built by the two John Woods.[34]

Had it been constructed, Adam's vision for Bath would have radically changed the scale, and our understanding, of the city we know today.[35] As Ison noted in 1948, when the Adam designs for Bath were published in a book on Bath for the first time, it would have required the financial resources of 'an absolute monarch', which, following the large expense of constructing Pulteney Bridge, even Pulteney and his wife did not possess.[36] The Adam vision was diluted into the plans for Bathwick executed by Thomas Baldwin and continued by John Pinch, resulting in the laying out of Great Pulteney Street (1788–95), Sydney Place (1792–6), and (New) Sydney Place (1804–1808). The vista of Great Pulteney Street is now seen as one of the crowning moments in Bath's Georgian town planning glory, but imagine it being just a tributary road of a far larger and more monumental design.

'Solemn yet Sumptuous' 53

With that thought in mind, imagine Adam's designs for the assembly rooms having been constructed instead of John Wood's. The intended site becomes almost irrelevant, as wherever it could have been located, Robert Adam's vison for the assembly rooms, a grand ball and concert room infused by the 'solemn and sumptuous' scale and imagery of ancient Rome, would have been an 'heroic space', a building unlike anything else the city of Bath had to offer, either then or now.[37]

Notes

1 For an overview of the work of Atwood, Baldwin, and Palmer working in Bath contemporary to Wood see Michael Forsyth, *Bath* (New Haven and London: Yale University Press, 2003).
2 The author is grateful to Dr Frances Sands and David Hughes for their insight and advice regarding the Adam designs for Assembly Rooms at Bath. Throughout this chapter, John Wood the Younger's design will be referred to as the Upper or Bath Assembly Rooms, in contrast with the Adam assembly room designs.
3 The finished Adam drawings held at the Sir John Soane's Museum are: *Plan of the Ball and Concert Rooms at Bath*, SM Adam, vol. 28/49; *Design for a Ball and Concert Room at Bath* [Elevation] SM Adam, vol. 28/45; *Section through the Ball & Concert Room at Bath* [transverse section] SM Adam, vol. 28/47; *Section through the Ball and Concert Room at Bath* [longitudinal section] SM Adam, vol. 28/48; *Section through the Ball and Concert Room at Bath* [ballroom section] SM Adam vol 28/48. The annotating of each drawing has been identified as the hand of William Adam. For an overview of all the Adam designs for Bath see David King, *The Complete Works of Robert and James Adam, and Unbuilt Adam* (Oxford: Architectural Press, 2002).
4 The preliminary drawings held at the Sir John Soane's Museum are SM Adam, vol. 1/1, 1/3, 1/4, 2/115, 21/61, 27/50, and 27/54. See also SM Adam, vol. 55/173 verso. For the reattribution of some of these preliminary sketches see Sir John Soane's Museum Catalogue [Online], "Upper Assembly Rooms, Bennett Street, Bath: Unexecuted Designs for the Building, c.1765–68 (14)," accessed September 30, 2023, https://collections.soane.org/THES95130 and https://collections.soane.org/THES95134.
5 For the Bathwick Estate plans see Sir John Soane's Museum Catalogue [Online], New Town, Bath, "Somerset: Unexecuted Street Scheme Commissioned by William Pulteney, 1777–82," accessed September 30, 2023, https://collections.soane.org/SCHEME1219. The drawings are Sir John Soane's Museum SM Adam, vol. 38/1, 38/6–9, and 10/79–81. For the Prison design see Sir John Soane's Museum Catalogue [Online], "Bath Prison, Grove Street, Bath, Somerset, unexecuted designs commissioned by William Pulteney, 1771," accessed September 30, 2023, https://collections.soane.org/SCHEME1217. The drawings are SM Adam, vol. 38/10–11.
6 Jean Manco, "Pulteney Bridge," *Architectural History* xxxviii (1995): 129–45.
7 For the Prison see BRO, BC/2/1/1/9: Bath Corporation Minutes, Book 9, 102–3, 150. For the reference to the Bathwick masterplans see endnote 15.
8 See Oxford Dictionary of National Biography [Online], M. J. Rowe and W. H. McBryde, "Pulteney [Formerly Johnstone] Sir William, Fifth Baronet

54   Bath and Beyond

(1729–1805)," accessed September 30, 2023, www.oxforddnb.com/display/ 10.1093/ref:odnb/9780198614128.001.0001/odnb-9780198614128- e-56208.

9 For the Pulteney Estate and its development see W. H. McBryde and M. J. Rowe, *Beyond Mr Pulteney's Bridge* (Bath: Bath Preservation Trust, 1987).

10 *Caledonian Mercury*, March 15, 1792.

11 Huntington Lib., mssPU-5: James Adam to William Johnstone Pulteney, August 24, 1770.

12 Gareth Williams, "The Hidden Hand of Genius: Robert Adam and the Pulteney Estate in Shropshire," *The Georgian Group Journal* xxiv (2016): 65–80.

13 Williams, "The Hidden Hand of Genius." For the Shrewsbury Castle Adam drawings see Sir John Soane's Museum Catalogue [Online], "Shrewsbury Castle, Shropshire: Designs for Interior Decoration for Sir William Pulteney," accessed September 30, 2023, https://collections.soane.org/SCHEME1162.

14 For Paty designs and the influence of Adam on the addition of shops see Manco, "Pulteney Bridge."

15 The first advert for a 'Complete set of Assembly Rooms' by John Wood was dated November 17, 1764 published in the *Bath Chronicle and Weekly Gazette*. A receipt by John Burge for money paid by Sir William Yea for the intended Assembly Rooms at Queen Square, Walcot dated June 16, 1766 appears to be the last documentation for the Queen Square Assembly Rooms, SHC DD/ WO/58/10/2, with thanks to David Hughes for providing this reference.

16 The opening of subscriptions for the Wood designed Assembly Rooms was advertised in the *Bath Chronicle and Weekly Gazette* on December 1, 1768. For the early records of the subscriptions and Tontine, see BRO, 0028A.

17 The payment for the plans to Mr Adam is listed in two versions of the *General Accounts for the building of Pulteney Bridge* in the BRO, Pulteney Estate Papers. The first PUL Mss 1811 and then again in PUL Mss 1818, and its duplicate 1818 (2), list the Adam payment for plans as having been deducted. Although these are undated, they correspond to PUL Mss 1820 The *State of the Artificers Bills* for building Pulteney Bridge where the town plans are not listed (having been deducted earlier), and which notes that the received bills date between August 11, 1770 and March 27, 1773.

18 SM Adam, vol. 38/8 and 10/81.

19 Alistair Rowan, *Bob the Roman: Heroic Antiquity and the Architecture of Robert Adam* (London: Sir John Soane's Museum, 2003), 27.

20 Rowan, *Bob the Roman*, 27.

21 It is worth reminding readers that the Roman Baths and Temple Complex in Bath were not fully discovered and excavated until the second half of the nineteenth century. Knowledge of the city's bath complex from the mid-eighteenth century came from the discovery of the east end of the baths during the demolition of the Old Abbey House to make way for foundations for the duke of Kingston's Baths. So, while the Roman history of the bath complex was understood during the second half of the eighteenth century, the built heritage that evidenced it was far less apparent than what the city shows today.

22 Rowan, *Bob the Roman*, 27.

23 The drawing [SM Adam, vol. 55/173 verso] has been attributed by Alan Tait as one of the Adam Grand Tour drawings dating it *c.*1755–56 and by Alistair Rowan as a preliminary Bath drawing *c.*1765–68. See Sir John Soane's Museum Catalogue [Online], accessed September 30, 2023, https://collections. soane.org/THES95126. The drawing annotations are in French, and Rowan has suggested this was for the convenience of one of the foreign draughtsmen in

the Adam office who would have translated the sketch into a finished drawing. Rowan, *Bob the Roman*, 29.

24 Sir John Soane's Museum Catalogue [Online], accessed September 30, 2023, https://collections.soane.org/drawings?ci_search_type=ARCI&mi_search_type=adv&sort=7&t=THES95125

25 King, *Unbuilt Adam*, 29.

26 The detailed design for the coffering in the concert room can be seen in two of the preliminary drawings at the Sir John Soane's Museum, SM Adam, vol. 27/51 and 1/3.

27 Rowan, *Bob the Roman*, 20–21.

28 See Sir John Soane's Museum Catalogue [Online], accessed September 30, 2023, https://collections.soane.org/OBJECT955 and A. A. Tait, *Robert Adam, the Creative Mind: From the Sketch to the Finished Drawing* (London: Sir John Soane's Museum, 1996), 13.

29 Tait, *Robert Adam*, 13. For Burlington's York Assembly Rooms see Pamela D. Kingsbury, *Lord Burlington's Town Architecture* (London: RIBA Heinz Gallery, 1995), 42–58.

30 The Adam Exeter Assembly Rooms were unexecuted; for the designs see Sir John Soane's Museum, SM Adam, vol. 44/109–12. Adam also designed Assembly Rooms in Glasgow (1791) and alterations to Edinburgh Assembly Rooms (1791).

31 The influence of the Baths of Caracalla in particular has been identified as a possible source for John Wood. See "Bath Assembly Rooms: Statement of Significance for the National Trust," Unpublished report, Donald Insall Associates (December 2021), 100–2. Access to this report is courtesy of the National Trust.

32 Adam's book is Lot 45, first day of sale, June 8, *Catalogue of a Valuable and Select Collection of Books of Antiquities, Architecture, Etc . . . of Mr Wood Architect*, Christie's, June 8–9, 1795, photocopy in Museum of Bath Architecture Collection.

33 Walter Ison, *The Georgian Buildings of Bath 1700–1830* (London: Faber & Faber, 1948), 51.

34 Although not designed, when John Wood the Elder's plans for the Royal Forum are considered. Timothy Mowl, Brian Earnshaw and Cathryn Spence, *Architect of Obsession: John Wood and the Creation of Georgian Bath*, 2nd ed. (Bradford on Avon: Stephen Morris, 2022), 159–76; Amy Frost, Cathryn Spence, and Timothy Mowl, *Obsession: John Wood and the Creation of Georgian Bath* (Bath: Building of Bath Museum, 2004), 92–94.

35 For the Adam plans for Bathwick see note 3, and, also Alistair Rowan, *Vaulting Ambition: The Adam Brothers Contractors to the Metropolis in the Reign of George III* (London: Sir John Soane's Museum, 2007), 68–69.

36 Ison, *Georgian Buildings of Bath*, 199–201.

37 Rowan, *Bob the Roman*, 11, 27.

Bibliography

Cunliffe, Barry. *The City of Bath*. Stroud: Alan Sutton, 1986.

Forsyth, Michael. *Bath*. New Haven and London: Yale University Press, 2003.

Frost, Amy, Cathryn Spence, and Timothy Mowl. *Obsession: John Wood and the Creation of Georgian Bath*. Bath: Building of Bath Museum, 2004.

Ison, Walter. *The Georgian Buildings of Bath 1700–1830*. London: Faber & Faber, 1948.

56 Bath and Beyond

King, David. *The Complete Works of Robert and James Adam, and Unbuilt Adam.* Oxford: Architectural Press, 2002.

Manco, Jean. "Pulteney Bridge." *Architectural History* 38 (1995): 129–45.

McBryde, W. H., and M. J. Rowe. *Beyond Mr Pulteney's Bridge.* Bath: Bath Preservation Trust, 1987.

Mowl, Timothy, Brian Earnshaw, and Cathryn Spence. *Architect of Obsession: John Wood and the Creation of Georgian Bath.* Bradford on Avon: Stephen Morris, 2022.

Rowan, Alistair. *Bob the Roman: Heroic Antiquity and the Architecture of Robert Adam.* London: Sir John Soane's Museum, 2003.

Rowan, Alistair. *Vaulting Ambition: The Adam Brothers Contractors to the Metropolis in the Reign of George III.* London: Sir John Soane's Museum, 2007.

Tait, A. A. *Robert Adam, the Creative Mind: From the Sketch to the Finished Drawing.* London: Sir John Soane's Museum, 1996.

4 'I am a Sort of Prisoner here'

Elite Performance and Bath Society in the Eighteenth Century

Jemima Hubberstey

Bath was one of the most frequented spa towns in the eighteenth century, designed to cater to all the needs of the Georgian elite. Today, we are perhaps most familiar with literary depictions of Bath and might expect that its Georgian visitors should, like Jane Austen's Catherine Morland, have been 'all eager delight . . . as they approached its fine and striking environs', or, like Frances Burney's Evelina, found that 'the charming city . . . answered all my expectations'.[1] It might, therefore, seem surprising to find accounts of Georgian women who were not so enchanted with the fashionable metropolis. In 1740, Elizabeth Montagu, 'Queen of the Bluestockings', famously wrote to the duchess of Portland of her boredom at Bath, commenting that the city 'affords no inspiration' and that no other place 'stands in greater need of something to enliven the brain and inspire the imagination'.[2] As a writer and scholar in her own right, Montagu was disappointed that Bath offered little intellectual stimulation. Yet as recent studies have shown, both the literary culture and the burgeoning print trade in Bath should have provided plenty to satisfy the intellectually curious.[3] We might consider that her unhappiness came about, not necessarily due to the lack of literary resources or intellectual society at Bath, but rather by the prohibitive expectations of elite society which dictated the behaviours and activities of upper-class women.

This tension is particularly acute in the accounts of Jemima, Marchioness Grey (1722–97), and her sister-in-law, Elizabeth, Lady Anson (1725–60), when they visited Bath in October 1749. Though these women are not as well documented as some of their contemporaries, their accounts of Bath offer important insights into how elite women negotiated the expectations of fashionable society with their own interests and inclinations, which was particularly acute in a setting like Bath. Soile Ylivuori has argued that politeness was effectively a disciplinary power that produced docile bodies, a concept this chapter will adopt and expand through considering the role that environment played in enforcing and controlling elite women's behaviour.[4] Of course, for members of the elite, performing social rituals

DOI: 10.4324/9781003393856-4

58 *Bath and Beyond*

was a key part of attesting their positions and would have applied regardless of setting.[5] However, there is a clear difference in how polite identity is interpreted and performed in different environments and contexts. Within Grey's ancestral home at Wrest Park in Bedfordshire, where she and her husband hosted their own literary circle, they operated through what we might term an intellectual polite sociability, in which both sexes would improve the other through learned conversation. By contrast, in the fashionable worlds of both London and Bath, Grey made a point of hiding her intellectual interests and was far more prone to self-censorship. As Katherine Glover and other scholars have shown, while academic learning was, in many respects, a marker of social progress and civilisation, women had to be careful not to be seen to transgress the model of normative feminine behaviour, for so doing could 'be perceived as an attack on society itself'.[6]

At Bath in particular, with its dances, card evenings, and bathing rituals, polite feminine performance was an essential way of life for aristocratic women like Grey and Anson, and subject to surveillance by fashionable society.[7] Through their letters, we are afforded a window into the thoughts they concealed from the outside world as they disclosed the personal difficulty of reconciling themselves to the lifestyle at Bath. In fact, this chapter considers the way in which their letters provide a space for subversive performance, especially given the common medical advice that water-drinkers should avoid letter-writing.[8] Their letters, in many respects, are both playful and performative, sometimes professing to reveal an inner truth that has been carefully concealed from the surveillance of society, and at other times deliberately masking the self as the authors ostensibly submit to the social performances expected of them. As Patricia Spack observes, a letter might 'on occasion purport to reveal the heart, but also . . . it more often constructed a social mask'.[9] Overall, this chapter argues that by highlighting the contrasts between the expectations of fashionable performance and their own personal grievances, Grey and Anson's letters created space for self-expression against the backdrop of highly ritualised and enforced social activity at Bath.

Polite Sociability and Intellectual Culture at Wrest Park

Understanding the intellectual environment that Grey and her husband, Philip Yorke (1720–90), cultivated at Wrest Park is important to appreciate the role that environment played in enforcing different modes of polite behaviour. Grey and Yorke were married on 22 May 1740, when she was 17 and her husband, the eldest son of Lord Chancellor Hardwicke, was 20. The marriage was primarily arranged as a mutually beneficial political union: for the ambitious, newly risen Lord Chancellor, it was an opportunity to establish his family within the upper echelons of society, while for Grey's family, the wealthy and politically influential Yorkes made for

'I am a Sort of Prisoner here' 59

powerful allies. However, despite the obvious advantages of the union, it was predominantly a marriage of minds. The couple shared interests in literature, history, and politics, which provided a solid foundation for an affectionate and intellectually fulfilling marriage. This no doubt allowed a considerable amount of cerebral freedom at Wrest Park too: in the early years of her marriage, Grey described how she and her husband spent their days studying together in the library 'with a competent Quantity of Books & Candles, and looking most profoundly wise'.[10]

It was not only in her husband that Grey found an academic companion. His siblings, particularly Charles, Elizabeth (later Anson), and Margaret (later Heathcote), regularly visited Wrest Park and formed a part of the literary circle that met there in the summer months. Members of this circle also included the Yorkes's cousin, John Lawry; the antiquary, Daniel Wray; the historian, Thomas Birch; the poet and garden designer, Thomas Edwards; and Grey's childhood friend, and later Bluestocking, Catherine Talbot. Like the Bluestocking salon, the Wrest Circle afforded women equal respect as intellectuals, and the men within the circle even came to prefer the heterosocial environment at Wrest. Upon returning to the University of Cambridge after a stay at Wrest Park in 1742, Daniel Wray wrote to Yorke:

> I know not, whether I ought to thank the ladys for the pleasure I received in their consideration; since they have given me a most inconvenient taste and I shall hereafter despise those male-companys, among which I constantly live, as extremely imperfect, & wanting not only that variety, but that elegance & delicacy, which a mixture of sensible women introduces.[11]

This comment suggests how far the coterie adhered to ideals of polite sociability, that is to say, a belief that men and women complemented and improved the other through conversation. This concept also characterises the group's private *Wrestiana* manuscript; in 'Epistle from Wrest to the Ingenious Philemon', the ladies and gentlemen provide different and yet complementary responses to Henry Coventry's *Philemon to Hydaspes*. The ladies, 'more poetically inventive', respond creatively to the poetry translations, while the men, 'upon comparing them with the Greek', praise their accuracy.[12] It is likely that the Yorke siblings had been raised in a similar environment. They were an intellectual family, and while the two eldest boys were encouraged from a young age to write philosophical essays in a family manuscript, the *Triumvirate*, the girls were also encouraged to develop interests in literature, philosophy, and the arts. Anson was even tutored privately in mathematics by the land surveyor and school master, John Dougharty, where 'she made a progress in that science beyond what the sex in general are thought capable of'.[13] However, even their home

60 *Bath and Beyond*

environment did not offer the same stimulation as Wrest. After her visit in 1744, Anson wrote to Grey:

> I do not as yet very well know where I am, for I expect to go to billiards after dinner; to hear some tunes on the harpsicord, doubt whether we shall drink tea at the Pavilion, or Bowling Green, do not know what object to look for in the prospect . . . can't guess what book you and I shall read next, miss the terrestrial maps extremely, the agreable [*sic*] companies of my walk & much more, & was vastly disappointed last night, on asking at nine o'clock what star that was, [that] shone so bright on the left hand of the north window in the library, to find the person I addressed, knew neither the star, nor the place; in short, as I am *tombe de mon haut*, I have prudently resolved, not to guess at any thing we are to do, nor to ask any questions, without saying to my self, this is not Rest.[14]

Of course, the activities she describes, attending private musical performances at home and drinking tea, were in themselves social rituals in which polite rules and behaviours would have been observed. Yet, intellectual activities are also infused into this environment: analysing landscapes, reading, surveying, and astronomy. Thus, while Yorke and Grey maintained elite performances in their own country house, there was an unusual level of intellectual permissiveness that allowed the women in particular a freedom they did not have elsewhere. Indeed, the women in the coterie frequently replicated this space of polite, intellectual sociability in their letters to one another.[15]

Jemima Grey and Elizabeth Anson developed a close relationship, and Grey even came to regard Anson as an 'additional sister'.[16] In her teenage years, Anson was an active member of the 'Society at Wrest', as she referred to the coterie, contributing several compositions to *Wrestiana*.[17] The two women grew particularly close following Anson's marriage in 1748 to the celebrated naval commander, George Anson, spending much time together in London.[18] Anson especially valued the quiet, intellectual camaraderie in her friendship with Grey, writing that she particularly missed being 'Quiet & Clever Together' in the library at Wrest.[19] Yet, as prominent members of the country's social and political elite, both women were compelled to perform in accordance with the expectations of their class, which was particularly heightened in a setting like Bath.

'The Prospect of Going to Bath Is, I Must Own, Very Unpleasing to Me'

Bath, claimed as a fashionable resort for the *beau monde*, stood in stark contrast to the permissive, intimate, and intellectually stimulating environment

'I am a Sort of Prisoner here'   61

Figure 4.1 Allan Ramsay, *Lady Jemima Campbell, Marchioness Grey, Countess of Hardwicke*, 1741, oil on canvas, 172 × 134 cm, National Trust, Wimpole Hall, 17243. ©National Trust Images/Roy Fox.

at Wrest Park.[20] The excursion to Bath seems to have been motivated primarily by Anson's health, with Grey coming along, albeit 'much pressed to it', to keep Anson company.[21] Anson was often in poor health, and letters between family members often refer to her 'complaint' though it is unclear what this was exactly.[22] In any case, in 1749, Anson resolved to try spas across the country, visiting Tunbridge Wells before Bath for its medicinal powers. On 9 August, she remarked to Grey:

> The prospect of going to Bath is, I must own, very unpleasing to me, and nothing renders it tolerable but the thoughts of being with your ladyship, and of leaving this place, wch is as disagreeable to me as possible, having met with no opportunity of contracting new acquaintance to make me remember it with pleasure; however if the waters prove beneficial, and I really think, notwithstanding the little rub I mentioned, that they agree very well, I shall, with great pleasure, retain a <u>distant respect</u> for it, as well as your ladyship (emphasis in original).[23]

Figure 4.2 Thomas Hudson, Lady Elizabeth Yorke, Lady Anson, 1751, oil on canvas, 110.5 × 85.7 cm, National Trust, Shugborough, 1291188. ©National Trust Images/John Hammond.

Anson's emphasis on the possibility of 'contracting new acquaintance' shows there was an expectation of increasing one's social circle during such visits. Philip Yorke similarly emphasises Bath's sociable potential in his letter to Grey, suggesting she might 'form some acquaintance, wch you wd be glad to keep up afterwards'.[24] In fact, Grey's response suggests this was a maxim she had been frequently told, and when she arrived at Bath, one she realised failed to hold true:

> Was it not enough to be told from . . . every other part of the globe we conversed with that, to be sure, with the company & diversions of this Place we must pass our time very agreeably here . . . but even from Paris I must hear the same repeated with the addition of a prophecy, that we may form new acquaintance here one may like to keep afterwards—I assure you that necessary animal the confidante has not walked the parade yet.[25]

Evidently, Bath's reputation for company and diversions meant that Georgian visitors arrived with high expectations, which in this case only added to Grey and Anson's disappointment when such a prophecy was never fulfilled. Anson was particularly delighted that her husband made no mention in his letter of the 'company & diversions here', adding that 'all other Letters to Lady Grey, or me, have supposed us to be highly delighted with [them]'.[26] It is perhaps no surprise that the ladies, finding no like-minded acquaintances in the city, quickly became disillusioned with the fashionable resort.

Despite their elevated status, neither Anson nor Grey was familiar with the social scene at Bath, relying on friends and acquaintances to determine when the season even started.[27] Unsure when they should time their journeys, their travel plans too were chaotic, so that while Grey had already made her way to Bath, Anson was still in Staffordshire, staying with her brother-in-law at Shugborough and taking in the races at Lichfield. Even before her arrival at Bath, Grey was out of humour. She wrote bitterly to her husband that 'I must make two tedious days of travelling by my self, & may be some days alone I suppose in quite a strange place to me before they [Lord and Lady Anson] arrive'.[28] Anson too seemed to dread the prospect of yet another spa town, writing to Grey:

> I feel for the disagreeable situation you must be in, in being alone at so odious a place as my imagination represents Bath to be, upon the strength of what I found Tunbridge:—the idea of it spoils any pleasure I might have in staying a few days longer here [at Shugborough].[29]

Despite the encouragement of their family and friends, neither Anson nor Grey relished the prospect of Bath, especially when it meant leaving their country residences. It would be easy to attribute their disenchantment with Bath to the early mismanagement of their affairs, but it was not the city itself, but rather the fashionable culture of Bath and the lack of intellectual stimulation itself that became a source of tension.

'I Have Been Forced to Stand and Eye the Prospect Like a Bird in a Cage'

Bath certainly stood in stark contrast to Grey's family home at Wrest Park with its extensive gardens and libraries.[30] Although there were booksellers in Bath, they did not satiate the appetites of more discerning readers like Grey, and she was dismayed to find that one bookseller 'has really no books that give one the least curiosity'.[31] However, for Grey, the city's one redeeming feature was the surrounding scenery. She had arranged to stay in half the end house of the North Parade, recently built by John Wood the Elder in 1741 (Figure 4.3).[32] On the outskirts of the city, it offered extensive views and overlooked the promenade along the river Avon (Figure 4.4). Ever an enthusiast of the countryside, Grey at once took delight in the

Figure 4.3 Jemima Hubberstey, *North Parade, Bath*, 2023, photograph. Credit: the author.

Figure 4.4 Jemima Hubberstey, *View of the River Avon from the North Parade, Bath*, 2023, photograph. Credit: the author.

'I am a Sort of Prisoner here' 65

verdurous prospects. She enthused to her husband that her situation was 'really vastly pleasant, which . . . is quite out of the town & sees no more of it than what adorns the prospect, as indeed the view of the hills all round you & of the river below them is a very beautiful country scene'.[33] Grey was an adroit travel correspondent, and her extensive descriptions of gardens, landscapes, and country scenes reveal her insightful engagement with landscape aesthetics as well as practical understanding of gardens.[34] Her friends certainly deferred to her judgment in these matters, and before her tour of Staffordshire in 1748, Daniel Wray wrote to her husband, 'Lady Grey's picturesque eye will discover many particulars worthy of your Travelling Pocket-Book'.[35] With a keen practical interest in gardens, Grey was not averse to rambling over rough terrain to inspect the latest improvements, and later recalled when she was visiting the Ansons at Moor Park, newly landscaped by Lancelot 'Capability' Brown, how she had 'got herself knee deep in a bank of new made Earth, but . . . saved her Shoes at last'.[36]

At Bath, there was no risk of Grey losing her shoes on a ramble. There were promenades in the city, and Grey described her amusement as she looked out from her window and saw 'various fine Sunday folk' on a stroll, 'pretty <u>ge'mmen</u> in lac'd hats, & pretty misses in gauze capuchins'.[37] Yet for Grey, the true temptation lay in exploring the countryside, a pleasure she denied herself for fear of being seen. She describes her disappointment to Catherine Talbot:

> The only temptation I have had has been to take some long walk. It looked as if . . . we might discover many pretty paths in the fields, & even scramble up to the downs so high above us.—But Alas! Alas! . . . walking alone in this place is impossible. So I have been forc'd to stand & eye the prospect like a bird in its cage. . . . Besides, I have been considering that for a fine lady who designs shortly to make a figure in the rooms & at public breakfasts, to be seen <u>walking</u> up & down styles, or trudging about with her petticoats shortened, & her leathern shoes . . . one cannot (as your good folks say), away with (emphasis in original).[38]

Grey depicts the expectations of the fashionable world as a metaphorical 'cage' that 'forces' her to adhere to prescribed behaviours. Her description effectively conveys the contrasts between her natural inclinations and the manners and fashions expected in Bath; the verbs 'scramble' and 'trudge' comically contrast the unrefined, physical efforts of outdoor exploration and the polished manners expected of a 'Fine Lady'. Indeed, the practicalities of walking stand in stark contrast to fashionable dress and behaviour, and her reference to 'petticoats shorten'd & leathern shoes' is the antithesis of the fine figures promenading along the river with their 'gauze capuchins'.[39] It is not to be forgotten that dress and appearance were carefully scrutinised at Bath. Infamously, at the Bath assembly, the Master of Ceremonies, Beau Nash, harbouring 'the strongest aversion to a white

66 Bath and Beyond

apron', tore one off the duchess of Queensberry, remarking 'none but *Abigails* appeared in white aprons' (emphasis in original).[40] Evidently, Grey was not prepared to scandalise Bath society even further by appearing in leather shoes and shortened petticoats, and her account shows how far she self-censored her behaviour, imagining the possibility of outsider scrutiny and observation.

This is not the only time Grey self-censored. On another occasion, she was mortified that while drinking tea with 'fine gem'men' in her London home, she had been forced to admit she was reading Horace and fled the room in horror, remarking to Talbot that 'an old Latin poet . . . by no means belongs to a fine London lady'.[41] Her husband's friend, Daniel Wray, was oblivious to Grey's embarrassment on this occasion, and while she was trying to make her excuses, he 'found nothing better to talk of but electrical experiments, & appointing a day for me to go . . . to see them'.[42] An interesting tension emerges: while, according to ideals of polite sociability, women's education was a necessary part of the civilising process, there was clearly a line that could not be crossed in fashionable society.[43] After confessing that she read Horace, Grey was convinced that she would be ridiculed as a 'femme scavante [*sic*]'.[44] The men within the Wrest Circle actively encouraged female learning; Wray once expressed his admiration for Grey and his disappointment that 'she will not oftener exert her good sense & excellent taste, instead of patiently attending to our prattle!', but this view did not extend to the 'fine gem'men' Grey was entertaining.[45] This incident reveals how far educated, elite women actively hid their intellect in order to conform to the ideals of the *beau monde*, which was heightened in fashionable urban settings; Grey evidently felt she must conform to both the society and the place in becoming a 'fine London lady'.

Yet elite women could also be criticised as frivolous for adhering to the behaviours expected of the *beau monde*. Although recent studies have started to regard fashion as evidence of women's creativity and agency, contemporary literature nonetheless depicted the frivolities of dress in direct contrast to the serious business of learning.[46] Joseph Addison remarked that women's 'toilet is their great scene of business' and promoted his *Spectator* to 'divert the minds of my female readers from greater trifles'.[47] An interest in fashion could be therefore used by critics to undermine women's serious intellectual or political endeavours, and this is certainly the case with Elizabeth Anson. Anson was intelligent, artistic, and politically savvy, but, more so than Grey, took a clear interest in fashion. Catherine Talbot once remarked that 'you can scarce keep clear of one or other of her numberless gowns', though she and Grey often called upon Anson for fashion advice.[48] Yet Anson's fashionable appearance was used by her critics to undermine her intellect and even suggest a vacuous and artificial character. Upon seeing Anson at Bath on 17 November 1755 (Anson made frequent visits owing to her and her husband's health), Mary Delaney remarked, 'Lady Anson began the last ball in a green damask sack, trimmed very full with blond lace and lappets: I was much entertained with her airs', and elsewhere remarked that she was 'coxcombical, and affects to be learned'.[49] The figure of the fine lady with intellectual aspirations could easily make her a figure of mockery, and Horace Walpole, envious of the Yorkes after his father's political fall, did not hesitate to criticise Anson for the 'profusion of absurdities that she utters'.[50] While these waspish comments were written in private correspondence, they do reveal that aristocratic women were subjected to constant surveillance and judgement from both sides. Appear too learned and they might appear too intellectual for the fashionable world; appear too interested in fashion and they might come across as vacuous. For women like Grey and Anson, it is no surprise that this brought about an anxiety in how they presented themselves before fashionable society as well as how they were perceived by their peers.[51]

Writing Medicinal Bath

If it was frowned upon for fine ladies to be seen trudging around fields, it was certainly expected that they should partake in the medicinal and social rituals at Bath. Yet these could also denote a bathetic shift from the glamorous to the ridiculous, especially as the desire for sociability and amusement jarred against the city's dual purpose to serve as a spa and cure illness. As David Cottom observes, Bath made 'strange bedfellows of medicine and fashion'.[52] In this respect, letters, offering a more confidential space for dissent, provide an ideal vehicle to satirise a city that made fashionable pursuits out of illness. It was after all through her letter to the duchess of Portland that Elizabeth Montagu famously remarked:

> we hear of nothing but Mr. Such a one is not abroad to-day: Oh no says another poor gentleman he died to day, then another crys my party was made for quadrille to night but one of the gentlemen has had a second stroke of the palsey, and cannot come out. There is no depending on people, no body minds engagements.[53]

Anson was similarly dismayed to find herself without companions when her friends, including Grey, fell ill. She wrote to her husband,

> I have indeed been three mornings at the Pump-Room, from whence I have returned home between my glasses, not being able to stay in that croud [sic] alone, for Lady Grey has never ventured & Lady Portland has had a cold wch has confined her ever since Sunday so that she has not been able to escort me.[54]

68   *Bath and Beyond*

Paradoxically, although Bath was supposed to cater to the medicinal needs of the elite, those very illnesses proved inimical to the fashionable social scene there.

Yet, as historians observe, illnesses could be fashionable if they presented their victims in a positive light, 'bestowing heightened creativity, greater emotional sensitivity, or finer social discrimination'.[55] In most cases, this manifested through hypochondrial distempers or a delicate constitution, but in Bath, exclusive sites like the baths and the Pump Room encouraged the elite to make a performance of their treatments. As Joanne Edwards states, they became spaces 'to be seen performing your correct, societal role'.[56] But Grey and Anson's letters create a caricature of these treatments, and thereby articulate their resistance to the demands of fine society. When Grey visited the Cross Bath, she could not reconcile herself with the experience. Though the Cross Bath was one of the oldest and most prestigious baths, before its reconstruction in 1784 it had fallen into considerable decay; one commentator observed that the dressing rooms were 'dark as dungeons' and the baths more like 'open unseemly ponds'.[57] Grey had little more to say in its praise:

> I have bathed once [at The Cross], & am sorry to say I dislike it more than anything that I ever did; not only the ceremonial is the most marvellously strange & disagreeable that can be, but the bathing itself I found vastly unpleasant . . . the only ideas I could distinctly settle in the Bath were,—that of all deaths I should not like drowning.[58]

Her caricature of the baths as a place of danger undermines the medicinal benefits. Her focus on the 'ceremonial' aspect of bathing shows her criticism is levelled not just at the unpleasant sensation of the water but also bathing rituals as a conspicuous performance.

Anson similarly satirises the baths, using a culinary metaphor to describe that she had been 'this morning . . . in the <u>Stew-pan</u> for the third time, which makes me very stupid for a great part of the day: (and Lady Grey having also been parboiled to-day)' (emphasis in original).[59] If fashionable illness was supposed to showcase enhanced creativity, Anson suggests it rather dulls her faculties. She seems to have trialled many treatments for her health, including sea-bathing at Southampton in the summer of 1751. Her account is similarly mocking as she draws attention to the discrepancy between bathing in fiction and reality:

> I have long known that poetry & painting are very deceitful arts . . . but I could scarce have imagined any fairy-tale so void of resemblance to something or other in nature as all the elegant descriptions and representations of baths, and nymphs diverting themselves in the water are.—and I do from henceforward declare absolute war to all pictures

of <u>Diane</u> (whom I do not wonder at for her severity to <u>Acteon</u>) & her nymphs bathing, &c, &c, unless in burlesque by Mr. Hogarth, who, if he would promise to leave me out of it, I could furnish with a good figure or two for such a design (emphasis in original).[60]

Contemporary sources were quick to emphasise the historical and classical precedent for bathing, even elevating it to an activity of the gods, but Anson deliberately disrupts these associations.[61] Using her own classical knowledge to interject in the story of Diana and Actaeon, in which Actaeon is transfigured into a stag as a punishment for watching Diana while bathing, Anson undermines bathing as a conspicuous 'ceremonial' performance by challenging the gaze of any viewers. Her suggestion of a scene 'in burlesque' by William Hogarth not only allows her to rid bathing of its glamorous associations, but by depicting herself in alliance with the famous satirist, she resists becoming the object of observation herself. Thus, applying her own intellectual background in her letter allows Anson to renegotiate the relationship between observed and observer.

Grey similarly uses her learning to reconfigure the medicinal world of Bath, but this time, she draws on her literary knowledge to eschew the medicinal discourses of Bath and reframe physicians with their potions and cures into fictional villains. This is especially significant considering that her own illness at Bath, a sudden Quartan ague, had left her at the mercy of her physicians and arguably with little agency as she submitted to different treatments. Grey underplayed the illness in her letters, perhaps not allowing it to claim her entirely, writing to Yorke that it was merely a 'slight sort of ague & a cold'.[62] Anson was rather more anxious, writing to her husband that the physician 'has ordered a vomit [for Grey], wch she has taken & is gone to Bed, & to-morrow begins the bark', adding her concern that 'disorders of this kind do not usually yield to remedies so easily'.[63] However, in her own letters, Grey's allusion to James Thomson's *Castle of Indolence* (1748) creates a virtual space for the sort of literary playfulness that characterised the circle at Wrest Park. In this respect, she takes on the role of literary hostess rather than invalid. Insisting that her husband should rescue her, she writes:

It would be the most becoming gallantry in a knight just come from Paris to succour a pair of innocent forlorn damsels that wicked enchanters in the form of physicians have placed there *pour s'ennuyer a la mort*, at least perswade [*sic*] Lord Anson to hasten his return to comfort my lady who is quite as much out of sorts as your humble servant.[64]

Thomson's *Castle of Indolence* satirises the idle, country house lifestyle, as an evil wizard entices the inhabitants into a state of idleness until the Knight of Arts and Industry breaks the enchantment. Grey's letter playfully

70   *Bath and Beyond*

casts her husband as the knight who might rescue her from the indolent lifestyle at Bath, and indicates that the only real danger is not illness, but rather that physicians might bore them to death. Yet on a personal level, this literary joke also alludes to their own literary lifestyle at Wrest Park. Grey's literary circle had been reading Thomson's poem there the previous summer and Grey drew parallels between their own lifestyle in the country and the *Castle of Indolence*, writing to her aunt that the descriptions were 'quite enchanting' and 'I should have borne no good will to the busy meddling Knight that had disenchanted me' for 'I really think it dangerous to read in the country where your inclinations are so tranquillised & so averse to business & interruptions'.[65] Grey's allusion to the *Castle of Indolence* therefore shows a clear difference between literary retreat and escape at Wrest Park, and Bath, which she configures as a place of imprisonment, danger, and (perhaps worst of all for her active mind) boredom.

Epistolary Performances

Evidently, the letter provided a virtual space for dissent and satire, but this final section will consider how letters also constitute an epistolary performance. Scholars have argued how far aristocrats' letters already constitute a performance of elite identity, but it is significant that Anson and Grey's letters are not simply a straightforward performance or vehicle for self-expression but a virtual space for role play.[66] Towards the end of her stay at Bath, Grey's letters take on a distinctly coquettish tone as she tries to encourage her husband to make haste and visit her, hinting that after all her complaints, she and her sister-in-law might at last be tempted by the fashionable gallantry of the *beau monde*. She remarks:

> Lady Anson goes every morning to the Pump Room and gets a circle of *beaux esprits* about her, has the finest things said to her in the finest style by the finest speakers (lamentations without end that we so seldom make them happy by appearing amongst them) and in consequence . . . who do you think . . . sat an hour with us? Even the great Mr Pitt himself. Now judge how our opinion of Bath must be changed, whether we don't prefer it to all other places, & indeed whether you will be able to get us from it at all.[67]

Grey's letter is undoubtedly tongue-in-cheek, but her avowal that 'we don't prefer [Bath] to all other places' is a marked shift from her earlier letters, and we might consider it a performance in which she pretends to adhere to the fashionable politeness expected in Bath. There were certainly advantages to socialising among the elite, and Grey's pointed reference to William Pitt the Elder hints at the opportunity for political networking.

Yet her account also insinuates a more dangerous element of fashionable society, that these rituals of courtship and gallantry offer seductive possibilities. The reported voices of the *beaux esprits*, though banished behind parenthesis, are not entirely hidden, and make a teasing appearance in this letter. Though Grey's account is intended to be humorous, it does reveal a culture within fashionable Bath society where women expect to be courted. Courtship could be innocent, but as Laura L. Runge and Jenny Davidson observe, while gallantry ostensibly referred to the refined courtship of women, the term was loaded with connotations of lewd seduction.[68] As Grey's letter suggests, Bath offered dangerous potential to be seduced both by the company and by the place. She adds a playful warning, 'I advise you & Lord Anson to come down quickly & take some care of your wives, or I don't know how this state of liberty you leave them in, so flattered & courted as they are, may end'.[69] As contentedly married women, it is unlikely that either seriously considered taking full advantage of their 'liberty', but Grey nonetheless uses her letter to perform the behaviour of the fashionable *beau monde* at Bath as a warning that she may no longer privately resist, but rather submit to Bath's pleasure-seeking society.

Nor is Grey the only one to use her letter for a playful performance of fashionable society. For most of Grey's stay in Bath, Yorke was abroad in Paris. This adds a particularly interesting dynamic to their correspondence as he and Grey discuss and compare the *beau monde* of the two cities. In fact, Grey teasingly suggests that while she has become accustomed to country life at Wrest, Yorke might have succumbed to French manners, remarking 'alas alas what will you do with such a mere country animal after *la conversation fine & delicate des belles de Paris*'.[70] Yet Yorke's letters also constitute a performance of fine society. Positioning himself as a gallant with his '*fleurettes*' [amorous talk] for Grey, his 'Belle', he writes, 'you will not be surprised, if I shd *en pur gallanterie*, throw myself into your arms out of a postchaise when you least expect it, & think me perhaps a *conterdis fleurettes* to some <u>Belle</u> on this side of the Water' (emphasis in original).[71] Here, Yorke's letter becomes role play, especially as the figure of the gallant was supposed, in the words of Henrietta Howard, countess of Suffolk, to 'say tender things to every lady he meets' yet 'must have the spirit to be inconstant—for he loses the title of gallantry the minute he becomes a downright lover'.[72] To adopt the role of gallant, Yorke imagines that he and his wife are romantic strangers rather than a loyally married couple of almost 10 years. His view of marriage within the *beau monde* is cynical at best, and in another letter, he suggests the hypocritical performance of affection between married couples; 'how many fine ladys wd be sorry to be taken at their words when they press their dears return, & how many fine gentlemen wd have the most ingenious excuses for deferring it with all the affectionate reluctance imaginable'.[73] Yet he sees himself and

72 Bath and Beyond

Grey as distinct from the fine world of fashion, adding 'but *comme nous ne sommes ni l'un ni autre sur se pied la*, I have the pleasure of acquainting you . . . I will hasten down to you without loss of time'.[74]

In the couple's correspondence, there is a mutual satisfaction that neither quite conforms to the fashionable worlds they occupy. Following Yorke's return to England, Grey suggested that travelling had little effect on him, writing to Talbot that: 'we don't think him so entirely changed, but that we should have guessed at him even in the midst of a Bath crowd, nor that our English friend is quite lost in the Frenchman'.[75] In these instances, the performance within the letter goes as far as showing an understanding, and indeed, a role play of the *beau monde*, while also making a point of distancing from it, or at least, never quite fully allowing it to subsume their identities. While they can perform the roles expected of them, they dictate their own terms in private. Responding to Grey's 'threats' that he was to make haste to Bath, Yorke joked that he would comply but keep her demands a secret, 'lest I shd be considered as under petticoat government, & that of a wife too, wch in this refined age is not the most readily submitted to'.[76] While Yorke reveals his awareness of social expectations in 'this refined age' he nonetheless readily complies with the demands of the 'petticoat government'.

Conclusion

Though literary tropes have conditioned us to expect glamorous depictions of eighteenth-century Bath, Grey and Anson's letters give us greater insight into the reality for members of the elite as they occupied a world in which the inhabitants were both observers and the observed. In close-reading their letters, this chapter has explored the way in which both women resisted prevailing narratives of Bath and exposed fashionable society through satirical epistolary performances. This is not to argue that they attempted to eschew politeness altogether: politeness was inevitably an important marker of distinction for the upper classes and would have applied in any setting. But there needs to be greater discernment between the more intellectual polite sociability that characterised the literary circle at Wrest Park, and the more fashionable polite sociability that dictated behaviour of the *beau monde* in settings such as Bath. This is a difference that Grey felt particularly when she was forced 'like a bird in a cage' to monitor her behaviour, aware of the constant possibility of surveillance. Yet we might argue that in a place where ill health and conspicuous medicinal treatments dictated their lifestyles and their bodies through ritual and regulation, letter writing allows Grey and Anson to create their own spaces for resistance, satire, and intellectual agency. As their letters make clear, if they conform to the expectations of the *beau monde*, then it is through parody and role play, and it is nonetheless a performance, rather than a true expression of the self. Their letters from Bath, therefore, become important vehicles to express their sense of self in an environment that simultaneously threatens to erode it.

Notes

1 Jane Austen, *Northanger Abbey: And Persuasion*, 4 vols. (1818), i, 16; Frances Burney, *Evelina, or, the History of a Young Lady's Entrance into the World*, ed. Margaret Anne Doody (W.W. Norton, 1994), 436.

2 Huntington Lib., MO 288 A: Elizabeth Montagu to Margaret Cavendish Bentinck, January 4, 1740.

3 Elizabeth Child, "'To Sing the Town': Women, Place, and Print Culture in Eighteenth-Century Bath," *Eighteenth Century Culture* xxviii (1999): 155–72; Rose McCormark, "Leisured Women and the English Spa Town in the Long Eighteenth Century" (PhD diss., Aberystwyth University, 2015).

4 Soile Ylivuori, "A Polite Foucault? Eighteenth-Century Politeness as a Disciplinary System and Practice of the Self," *Cultural History* iii (2014), 170–89, 171.

5 Patricia Spacks, *Privacy: Concealing the Eighteenth-Century Self* (Chicago: The University of Chicago Press, 2003), 88; Ingrid Tague, *Women of Quality* (Cambridge: Cambridge University Press, 2002), 162–93.

6 Katharine Glover, *Elite Women and Polite Society in Eighteenth-Century Scotland* (Woodbridge: Boydell, 2011), 44–45; Bridget Hill, *Women Alone: Spinsters in England 1600–1850* (New Haven: Yale University Press, 2001), 83; Felicity Nussbaum, *The Autobiographical Subject: Gender and Ideology in Eighteenth-Century England* (Baltimore: John Hopkins University Press, 1989).

7 Ylivuori, "A Polite Foucault?," 173.

8 Alain Kerherve, "Writing Letters from Georgian Spas: The Impressions of a Few English Ladies," in *Spas in Britain and in France in the Eighteenth and Nineteenth Centuries*, ed. Annick Cossic and Patrick Galliou (Newcastle: Cambridge Scholars Publishing, 2006), 263–96, 264.

9 Spacks, *Privacy*, 12.

10 BLARS, L30/9a/4, f. 14: Jemima Grey to Catherine Talbot, October 26, 1744.

11 BL, Add. MS 35401, f. 15v: Daniel Wray to Philip Yorke, August 11, 1742.

12 Private collection, "Epistle from Wrest to the Ingenious Philemon," *Wrestiana*, ff. 20–21: signed 'P.W.L.' for Philip Yorke, Daniel Wray, and John Lawry.

13 Richard Cooksey, *Essay on the Life and Character of John Lord Somers, Baron of Evesham: also Sketches of an Essay on the Life and Character of Philip Earl of Hardwicke* (1791), 32–41.

14 BLARS, L30/9/102/1: Elizabeth Yorke to Jemima Grey, 1744. 'Rest' is a deliberate pun, referring to Wrest Park as the family's summer retreat.

15 Leonie Hannan, *Women of Letters: Gender, Writing, and the Life of the Mind in Early Modern England* (Manchester: Manchester University Press, 2016); James Daybell, *Early Modern Women's Letter Writing, 1450–1700* (Basingstoke: Palgrave Macmillan, 2001). For letters as a polite act, see Tague, *Women of Quality*, 165.

16 BLARS, L30/9a/3, f. 37: Jemima Grey to Mary Gregory, June 3, 1760.

17 BLARS, L30 9/3/3, p. 157: Elizabeth Anson to Jemima Grey, July 1748.

18 BLARS, L30/9a/3, f. 37: Jemima Grey to Mary Gregory, June 3, 1760.

19 BLARS, L30/9/3/25, p. 225: Elizabeth Anson to Jemima Grey, November 3, 1750.

74 *Bath and Beyond*

20 Hannah Greig, *The Beau Monde* (Oxford: Oxford University Press, 2013), 24.
21 BLARS, L30/9/113, f. 25: Philip Yorke to Jemima Grey, September 17, 1749.
22 BL, Add. MS 34351, f. 164: Philip Yorke to Chancellor Hardwicke, October 20, 1748.
23 BLARS, L30/9/3/11, p. 180: Elizabeth Anson to Jemima Grey, August 9, 1749.
24 BLARS, L30/9/113 f. 28: Philip Yorke to Jemima Grey, October 7, 1749.
25 BL, Add. MS 35376, f. 29v: Jemima Grey to Philip Yorke, October 10, 1749.
26 Staffs. RO, D615/P (S) 1/1/5: Elizabeth Anson to George Anson, October 12, 1749.
27 BLARS, L30/9/3/12, f.183: Elizabeth Anson to Jemima Grey, August 30, 1749. In this letter, Anson first informs Grey that 'at the Bath itself the proper season for wch. Dr Wilmot told me yesterday was not "till the end of September", adding by postscript at the end that "I am told one should take Lodgings at the Bath by the tenth of September".'
28 BL, Add. MS 35376, f. 26: Jemima Grey to Philip Yorke, September 13, 1749.
29 BLARS, L30/9/3/14, p. 188: Elizabeth Anson to Jemima Grey, September 23, 1749.
30 BLARS, L30/9a/5, f. 153: Jemima Grey to Catherine Talbot, October 3, 1749.
31 BLARS, L30/9a/5, f. 153: Jemima Grey to Catherine Talbot, October 3, 1749.
32 BLARS, L30/8/3/12, p. 185: Elizabeth Anson to Jemima Grey, September 9, 1749. Anson had seen Grey's stepmother at Lichfield races, who recommended that 'the North Parade was the pleasantest, and the best part of town.'
33 BL, Add. MS 35376, f. 28: Jemima Grey to Philip Yorke, September 13, 1749.
34 Andrew Hann, "A Tale of Two Advisors: Jemima, Marchioness Grey and the Improvement of the Gardens at Wrest Park in the Mid-Eighteenth Century," *Women's History* ii (2019): 5–14.
35 BL, Add. MS 35401, f. 67v: Daniel Wray to Philip Yorke, August 5, 1748.
36 BLARS, L30/11/123, f. 29: Mary Jemima Grey to Amabel Polwarth, November 23, 1774.
37 BLARS, L30/9a/5, f. 145: Jemima Grey to Catherine Talbot, September 24, 1749.
38 BLARS, L30/9a/5, f. 148: Jemima Grey to Catherine Talbot, September 24, 1749.
39 Greig, *Beau Monde*, 3.
40 Oliver Goldsmith, *The Life of Richard Nash, Esq; Late Master of the Ceremonies at Bath* (1762), 37.
41 BLARS, L30/9a/4, ff. 30–32: Jemima Grey to Catherine Talbot, January 18, 1744/5.
42 BLARS, L30/9a/4, ff. 30–32: Jemima Grey to Catherine Talbot, January 18, 1744/5.
43 Glover, *Elite Women,* 167.
44 Glover, *Elite Women,* 167.
45 BL, Add. MS. 35401, f. 116: Daniel Wray to Philip Yorke, August 19, 1749.
46 Serena Dyer, *Material Lives: Women Makers and Consumer Culture in the 18th Century* (London: Bloomsbury, 2021); Serena Dyer and Chloe Wigston Smith, eds., *Material Literacy in Eighteenth-Century Britain: A Nation of Makers* (London: Bloomsbury, 2020).
47 Joseph Addison, *The Spectator No. 10* (Monday, March 12, 1711).
48 BLARS, CRT 190/45/43 (1), p. 253: Catherine Talbot to Jemima Grey, June 9, 1752.
49 Mary Delaney, *The Autobiography and Correspondence of Mary Granville, Mrs. Delaney,* ed. Lady Llanover, 3 vols. (1861), iii, 367.
50 Horace Walpole, *The Yale Edition of Horace Walpole's Correspondence,* ed. W. S. Lewis, 48 vols. (New Haven: Yale University Press, 1937), ix, 89.

'I am a Sort of Prisoner here' 75

51 See Elizabeth Montagu's similar negotiation of self in relation to fashionable society, in Stephen Bending, *Green Retreats: Women, Gardens, and Eighteenth-Century Culture* (Cambridge: Cambridge University Press, 2013), 139.
52 Daniel Cottom, "In the Bowels of the Novel: The Exchange of Fluids in the Beau Monde," *NOVEL: A Forum on Fiction* xxxii (1999): 157–86, 158.
53 Huntington Lib., MO 288 A: Elizabeth Montagu to Margaret Cavendish Bentinck, January 4, 1740.
54 Staffs. RO, D615/P (S) 1/1/13: Elizabeth Anson to George Anson, October 12, 1749.
55 David E. Shuttleton, "The Fashioning of Fashionable Diseases in the Eighteenth Century," *Literature and Medicine* xxxv (2017): 270–91, 273.
56 British Library [Online], Joanne Edwards, "Jane Austen and the Georgian Social Whirl of Bath," accessed August 11, 2023, https://blogs.bl.uk/english-and-drama/2023/04/jane-austen-bath.html.
57 Andrew R. Boucher, Richard K. Morriss, and Simon R. Mayes, "An Architectural Analysis of the Hot Bath and Cross Bath, Bath, 1997–2003," *Post-Medieval Archaeology* xlvii (2013): 164–94, 185; Alexander Sutherland, *Attempts to Revive Medical Doctrines* (1763), 11.
58 BLARS, L30/9a/5, f. 149: Jemima Grey to Catherine Talbot, September 24, 1749.
59 Staffs. RO, D615/P (S) 1/1/13: Elizabeth Anson to George Anson, October 12, 1749.
60 BLARS, L30/9/3 p. 27: Elizabeth Anson to Jemima Grey, August 7, 1751.
61 John Floyer, *The Ancient Psychrolousia Revived* (1702), 1–30.
62 BL, Add. MS 35376, f. 29: Jemima Grey to Philip Yorke, October 10, 1749.
63 Staffs. RO, D615/P (S) 1/1/14: Elizabeth Anson to George Anson, October 3, 1749.
64 BL, Add. MS 35376, f. 29: Jemima Grey to Philip Yorke, October 10, 1749.
65 BLARS, L30/9a/1 f. 162: Jemima Grey to Mary Gregory, June 1748.
66 Ruth Larsen, "An Archaeology of Letter Writing: The Correspondence of Aristocratic Women in Late Eighteenth-and Early Nineteenth-Century England," in *Pen, Print and Communication in the Eighteenth Century*, ed. Caroline Archer-Parré and Malcolm Dick (Liverpool: University of Liverpool Press, 2020), 75–88.
67 BL, Add. MS 35376, f. 31: Jemima Grey to Philip Yorke, October 14, 1749.
68 Laura L. Runge, "Beauty and Gallantry: A Model of Polite Conversation," *Eighteenth-Century Life* xxv (2001): 43–63, 44; Jenny Davidson, "Gallantry, Adultery and the Principles of Politeness," in *Hypocrisy and the Politics of Politeness: Manners and Morals from Locke to Austen* (Cambridge: Cambridge University Press, 2009), 46–75, 46–47.
69 BL, Add. MS 35376, f. 31: Jemima Grey to Philip Yorke, October 14, 1749.
70 BL, Add. MS 35376, f. 24: Jemima Grey to Philip Yorke, September 13, 1749.
71 BLARS, L30/9/113 p. 25: Philip Yorke to Jemima Grey, September 16–17, 1749.
72 Henrietta Howard, *Letters to and from Henrietta Countess of Suffolk and Her Second Husband, the Honourable George Berkeley,* ed. John Wilson Croker, 2 vols. (1824), i, 134.
73 BLARS, L30/9/113, p. 28: Philip Yorke to Jemima Grey, October 7, 1749.
74 BLARS, L30/9/113, p. 28: Philip Yorke to Jemima Grey, October 7, 1749.
75 BLARS, L30/9a/5, f. 159: Jemima Grey to Catherine Talbot, October 21, 1749.
76 BLARS, L30/9/113, p. 30: Philip Yorke to Jemima Grey, October 14, 1749.

76 *Bath and Beyond*

Bibliography

Bending, Stephen. *Green Retreats: Women, Gardens, and Eighteenth-Century Culture*. Cambridge: Cambridge University Press, 2013.

Boucher, Andrew R., Richard K. Morriss, and Simon R. Mayes. "An Architectural Analysis of the Hot Bath and Cross Bath, Bath, 1997–2003." *Post-Medieval Archaeology* 47, no. 1 (2013): 164–94. https://doi.org/10.1179/0079423613Z.00000000030.

Child, Elizabeth. "'To Sing the Town': Women, Place, and Print Culture in Eighteenth-Century Bath." *Studies in Eighteenth-Century Culture* 28 (1999): 155–72. https://doi.org/10.1353/sec.2010.0340.

Cottom, Daniel. "In the Bowels of the Novel: The Exchange of Fluids in the Beau Monde." *NOVEL: A Forum on Fiction* 32, no. 2 (1999): 157–86. https://doi.org/10.2307/1346221.

Davidson, Jenny. *Hypocrisy and the Politics of Politeness: Manners and Morals from Locke to Austen*. Cambridge: Cambridge University Press, 2009.

Daybell, James. *Early Modern Women's Letter Writing, 1450–1700*. Basingstoke: Palgrave Macmillan, 2001.

Dyer, Serena. *Material Lives: Women Makers and Consumer Culture in the 18th Century*. London: Bloomsbury, 2021.

Dyer, Serena, and Chloe Wigston Smith, eds. *Material Literacy in Eighteenth-Century Britain: A Nation of Makers*. London: Bloomsbury, 2020.

Edwards, Joanne. "Jane Austen and the Georgian Social Whirl of Bath." *British Library*. Accessed April 27, 2023. https://blogs.bl.uk/english-and-drama/2023/04/jane-austen-bath.html.

Glover, Katharine. *Elite Women and Polite Society in Eighteenth-Century Scotland*. Woodbridge: Boydell & Brewer, 2011.

Greig, Hannah. *The Beau Monde*. Oxford: Oxford University Press, 2013.

Hann, Andrew. "A Tale of Two Advisors: Jemima, Marchioness Grey and the Improvement of the Gardens at Wrest Park in the Mid-Eighteenth Century." *Women's History* 2, no. 13 (Summer 2019): 5–14.

Hannan, Leonie. *Women of Letters: Gender, Writing, and the Life of the Mind in Early Modern England*. Manchester: Manchester University Press, 2016.

Hill, Bridget. *Women Alone: Spinsters in England 1600–1850*. New Haven: Yale University Press, 2001.

Kerherve, Alain. "Writing Letters from Georgian Spas: The Impressions of a Few English Ladies." In *Spas in Britain and in France in the Eighteenth and Nineteenth Centuries*, edited by Annick Cossic and Patrick Galliou, 263–96. Newcastle: Cambridge Scholars Publishing, 2006.

Larsen, Ruth. "An Archaeology of Letter Writing: The Correspondence of Aristocratic Women in Late Eighteenth-and Early Nineteenth-Century England." In *Pen, Print and Communication in the Eighteenth Century*, edited by Caroline Archer-Parré and Malcolm Dick, 75–88. Liverpool: University of Liverpool Press, 2020.

McCormark, Rose. "Leisured Women and the English Spa Town in the Long Eighteenth Century." PhD diss., Aberystwyth University, 2015.

Nussbaum, Felicity. *The Autobiographical Subject: Gender and Ideology in Eighteenth-Century England*. Baltimore: John Hopkins University Press, 1989.

Runge, Laura L. "Beauty and Gallantry: A Model of Polite Conversation." *Eighteenth-Century Life* 25, no. 1 (2001): 43–63. https://doi.org/10.1215/00982601-25-1-43.

Shuttleton, David E. "The Fashioning of Fashionable Diseases in the Eighteenth Century." *Literature and Medicine* 35, no. 2 (2017): 270–91. https://doi.org/10.1353/lm.2017.0012.

Spacks, Patricia. *Privacy: Concealing the Eighteenth-Century Self.* Chicago: The University of Chicago Press, 2003.

Tague, Ingrid. *Women of Quality.* Cambridge: Cambridge University Press, 2002.

Ylivuori, Soile. "A Polite Foucault? Eighteenth-Century Politeness as a Disciplinary System and Practice of the Self." *Cultural History* 3, no. 2 (2014): 170–89. https://doi.org/10.3366/cult.2014.0069.

5 Not Just Suitors, Balls, and Proposals

The Late Eighteenth-Century Bath Marriage Mart Reassessed

Rachel Bynoth

As Catherine Morland in Jane Austen's *Northanger Abbey* said, 'Oh, who could ever be tired of Bath?'[1] For a young woman like her, eighteenth-century Bath was all balls, promenading, and socialising. The goal: to find a husband. Catherine's situation highlights some of the discomforts of this process, and a few of the dangers, but ends in a typical Austen happy ending in the form of Catherine's marriage to Henry Tilney.[2] Though historians such as Peter Borsay, John Eglin, Paul Langford, and Katharine Glover have uncovered what happened in Bath during the Season—its delights, its status, and its facades—there is ample room for further discussion on how contemporaries experienced one aspect of Bath: the marriage market.[3] Many discussions rely heavily on Jane Austen's *Northanger Abbey* as the central source for information. Given that Austen herself was allegedly not fond of Bath, this chapter argues that additional contemporary experiences are required to construct a more nuanced and detailed picture of the experiences of the marriage market in Bath at the end of the eighteenth century.

The decision of who to marry, if one was to marry at all, was central to a woman's future. Writers like Eliza Haywood stressed that marriage was 'the business on which our all depends' as it irrevocably affected financial security, familial and societal roles, and one's happiness.[4] Conduct literature of the period gave various pieces of advice for women seeking husbands and while all agreed that a companionate marriage was the ideal, all gave differing and sometimes conflicting advice on behaviours, manners, and expectations for courtship and marriage.[5] There were also other factors, such as any familial, social, or dynastic expectations, which stressed the importance of performing well within the Bath social scene. Indeed, Bath was like a shop window, with each woman provided the space to demonstrate her worth as a marriage prospect, in the hopes that she could catch a matrimonially minded man's attention. Many respectable young women might also find that this was their first proper outing into society, as Bath was seen as an excellent space for a young woman's debut.[6] It is

DOI: 10.4324/9781003393856-5

Not Just Suitors, Balls, and Proposals 79

therefore unsurprising that a woman taking part in the Bath marriage mart could feel anxiety and pressure to succeed, in more ways than one.

This chapter considers how people expressed their feelings on visiting Bath and taking part in the marriage market towards the end of the eighteenth century. It will consider the perspectives of a debutante, chaperone, and even distant stakeholders, such as parents overseeing their daughters' progress from afar, through the letters of two young eighteenth-century women: Bess Canning and Betsy Sheridan. This chapter does not profess to represent all young women through their perspectives, but rather seeks to highlight the multiplicity of viewpoints of trying to find a husband through the Bath marriage market in the later eighteenth century. Through analysing their letters, this chapter will demonstrate how letters could be duplicitous in their dealings with Bath and how letters were often used by mothers to check up on their daughter's prospects. It discerns which feelings and emotions were expressed and shared about Bath, and why. It goes beyond the dancing and the card games to consider the delights, emotions, and pressures for young women entering the marriage market in late eighteenth-century Bath.

The Marriage Market in Bath

If you visit the Pump Rooms in Bath today, you can see a statue of a man standing in a central alcove in the wall. That man, Richard 'Beau' Nash, was the Master of Ceremonies, known as the 'King of Bath'.[7] Bath was already a prolific spa town, known for its royal patronage, when Nash arrived there just after the turn of the eighteenth century, but it was his influence in forming and overseeing the social routines and rules of Bath that led to Bath's reputation as a fashionable centre for pleasure, sociability, and spouse-hunting. Most work on Nash focuses on his influence on Bath as a centre for pleasure, and in creating and managing the 'Company', those fashionable individuals who adhered to Nash's social routines.[8] These routines were so set that they, along with Nash's rules (and later his successors variations), were printed in the *Bath Guide* every year.[9] Mornings saw a visit to the Pump Rooms, often to view the subscription book to note who was in town and who had left. Afterwards came what John Eglin calls a 'lengthy walking route', which provided not only exercise but also ample opportunities to be seen by other members of the Company. This might involve a trip to Parade Gardens, later Great Pulteney Street, or shopping in Milson Street. Afternoons might be spent calling on people and taking tea, or hosting visitors before a ball or the theatre would round out the day. Small private social gatherings became more popular towards the end of the century.[10]

80 Bath and Beyond

However, Nash was also instrumental in creating Bath's reputation as a marriage market, for it was this structured routine of sociability and amusements that allowed people to see and be seen by other members of the Company, which in turn made Bath an excellent place to go spouse-hunting. This routine was presented as particularly conducive to making matches with *The Historic and Local New Bath Guide* of 1812 presenting Bath as a 'vortex of amusement' where ladies and gentlemen are 'entertained with a Breakfast, a Concert, and a Dance', but a sense of exclusivity comes with the added note that '1000 only can be admitted'.[11] This is particularly the case towards the latter end of the eighteenth century, after Nash's death.

Nash himself was particularly central in facilitating the marriage mart, as he used his influence and position to broker matches or ward ladies away from unsuitable partners. Surviving letters note that he advised figures such as the 6th duke of Somerset on the matrimonial prospects of young women, such as the two Finch sisters.[12] He was also at 'the service of the fair sex' through his role as Master of Ceremonies, making it his business to know about all Bath's visitors' reputations, social standings, and fortunes. His position as a respectable and well-connected man made him an excellent confidant to a young miss, for he was not seen as a threat to her reputation and his opinion was trusted.[13] While subsequent Masters of Ceremonies did not hold such a position of confidence with the young ladies, Nash's prominence in this role aided Bath's reputation as a marriage mart long after he had died in the 1760s.

This was partially due to the rise of print media and newspapers. Starting in Nash's day, and continuing into the early nineteenth century, the *Bath Chronicle* listed all the recent arrivals into Bath alongside the latest births, deaths, and marriages, news of the subscription balls at the Upper Assembly Rooms, and theatre gossip. The *Times* and the *Bath Chronicle*, amongst others, aided the reputation of Bath as the place to visit for 'company continue flowing in here from all Quarters'.[14] Thus, print media was a key tool for continuing sociability and the prospect to see and be seen in Bath, key requisites for the marriage market.[15] Beyond this, the newspapers also kept up with the latest gossip on engagements, marriages, divorces, and scandals, noting in 1787 that in Bath there was one elopement, three 'flipped ankles', and two pregnancies, but also that the young ladies were also becoming wiser to the charms of the fortune hunter, for 'not one *lucky bit* in this way has yet taken place' (emphasis in original).[16] Part of this gossip included reports of groups or societies of 'fortune hunters' such as one noted in the *Bath Chronicle* from August 1800. They allegedly sought heiresses for wives at Bath, treating the search for a wife as a game, with a prize to be won. If a member of the group was successful, he was 'firmly *held and bound* to pay so many thousands if he gets the heiress by the funds of the Club' (emphasis in original).[17]

Other infrastructural developments, such as the building of the Upper Assembly Rooms (opened in 1771), Great Pultney Street (completed in 1789), and Sydney Gardens (opened in 1795), show that Bath's reputation as a space of sociability and pleasure was still strong enough in the latter quarter of the eighteenth century to warrant further building works. Cynthia Hammond has noted that Sydney Gardens embodied 'all that [Jane Austen] disliked about Bath's social whirl and frivolity', suggesting that Bath was still a place for pleasure and entertainment, as it had been in the earlier part of the century.[18] However, Bath's clientele had changed. As the century wore on, the city's clientele shifted from aristocratic and upper-class circles to a broader social mixture, with more middling gentry and professional middle classes joining in the social rounds by the end of the century.[19] The two young ladies discussed in this chapter were part of these social circles, respectable but not aristocratic, though both associated with aristocratic acquaintances, largely due to their family's Whig politics. Nevertheless, Bath's reputation as a marriage market remained. Indeed, so prolific was Bath's reputation as a marriage market throughout the eighteenth century that historian Eglin suggests 'Bath was to matrimony what Newmarket was to horses and Billingsgate was to fish'.[20] Though, as we shall so see, navigating the Bath marriage market was no easy task.

Bess Canning: A Lack of Suitors

While Austen's Catherine Morland represents the teenage debutante entering society for the first time at the end of the eighteenth century, 1792 found 16-year-old Bess Canning recounting her first social season in Bath. This section draws on Bess's two visits to Bath in 1792–1793 and 1798 to consider the anxieties connected with not only trying to obtain a husband but also the difficulties of finding a dance partner, especially during a period of war. This is first viewed from Bess's mother, Hitty's, perspective, before considering Bess's viewpoint itself, to demonstrate how both mothers and daughters felt about the Bath marriage mart experience.

Bess Canning was the only child of Stratford and Mehitabel 'Hitty' Canning, a respectable middle-class Anglo-Irish family who rubbed shoulders with the elite in Whig political society, such as the duchess of Devonshire, Charles James Fox, Elizabeth Sheridan, and Lady Duncannon. However, these connections had lapsed after the death of Elizabeth Sheridan a few months before Bess's debut in Bath and her venture into the marriage market. Thus, while Bess was known in elite circles, she had little dowry; nor did her mother chaperone her on either of her trips to Bath as Bess stayed with her aunt and uncle Leigh. This, however, did not indicate a lack of interest in her marriage prospects. Like Mrs Bennet, from Austen's *Pride and Prejudice*, Hitty's business in life was to see Bess married and starting

82 Bath and Beyond

her own family and household. She had been training Bess for this since she was a young adolescent.[21] A daughter's success in society reflected on her mother, who handled her education and her upbringing. Hitty's own concern and devotion to her children were also key to her societal reputation as a mother. Letters allowed Hitty to continuing rearing her younger children at home, while remaining an anxious mother, because she was physically absent from Bess at an important milestone in Bess's life: her formal entrance into society.[22] Thus, Hitty had a lot emotionally invested in Bess's trips to Bath for the Season, which accounts for her anxious need to know everything that was going on and her desire to monitor her daughter's every move through their correspondence.

Bess visited Bath twice. She was 16 on her first visit to Bath in November 1792, but she also returned in 1798, when she was 22. Throughout her correspondence with her mother, in both 1792 and 1798, Bess's marriage prospects occupied a great deal of space and indicate that the aim of both trips to Bath was to find a suitable husband. In 1798, for example, her aunt and uncle went as far as to write poetry about her suitability to become a wife to a lucky man. These poems focus on her accomplishments, her beauty, and her companionship.[23] However, Bess failed to find a husband until 1805, when she was 29 years old.

Due to the ongoing wars, there was a shortage of men of marriageable age and, by the early nineteenth century, this was particularly exacerbated. Those who were considered marriageable were often fighting overseas, which made finding a marriage partner, an already anxiety-inducing task, ever harder.[24] Austen herself subtly notes this in *Pride and Prejudice*, when heroine Elizabeth Bennet sits down at the Meryton Ball for want of a partner.[25] Although the war factored into the struggles for Bess to secure a match, Hitty appeared more anxious about this than Bess herself. While it is unclear how the lack of men influenced Hitty's letters to her daughter when she was in Bath in both 1792 and 1798, they do provide an insight into the types of anxieties which a mother had about her daughter coming out into society at the time.

Remaining at the family home in Wanstead, London, Hitty's letters depict her micro-management of her daughter. Older or married women, often relatives, would act as chaperones for visits such as this one to Bath, and played a key role in safeguarding the young woman's reputation, as well as helping her make social connections and, where necessary, instructing her in social behaviour.[26] On both her visits to Bath, Bess was accompanied by her aunt Leigh, and her cousins, Letitia Perceval, 15 in 1792 and Bess Leigh, 7 in 1792, though Bess Leigh did not partake in the dancing. As Hitty was not going to be physically monitoring her daughter herself, she 'demanded' in her 'two or three last letters' that Bess tell her about her social behaviour: 'whether I <u>be</u> a silent, or a talkative miss when I am dancing, or on what topicks [*sic*], I touch' (emphasis in original).[27] While the language here reflects Bess's interpretation, Hitty's behaviour suggests that she was anxious for good news regarding Bess's social performance in Bath. This reflects a point in earlier letters to her daughter in 1789, when she was 13 and learning to enter society, when Hitty noted that 'many Eyes are upon us + all our actions will be well scrutinised'.[28] Hitty wanted her daughter to succeed in the 'Eyes' of the watching Bath assembly.

While the letters allowed for Hitty's concerns to be placated, Hitty's demands also caused tension between her and her daughter. There are a total of 54 surviving letters from their correspondence, covering both the 1792–1793 season and the 1798 season, of which 47 are from Bess. This suggests that Bess had to write frequently to her mother about her daily activities. In one such instance, in 1793, Bess expressed frustration in her reply to Hitty's requests:

> on those occasions: look in the <u>newspapers</u> for such <u>information</u>; the first time you read of a certain, young lady now at Bath, the <u>admiration</u> of the ballrooms &cc&cc, you may see, I make no doubt, will fully satisfy your curiosity, and will convince you that my <u>beauty</u>, <u>elegance</u>, <u>grace, and uncommon wit</u> is not to be surpassed.[29]

At 16, Bess's thoughts were less on marriage than on enjoying the sights and sounds of Bath. Mother and daughter had different aims of the trip and it was Hitty who was anxious for Bess's prospects.

Hitty's uneasiness regarding Bess's experiences in Bath were also evident in Bess's second visit in 1798, when Bess was 22, were evident enough for Bess to reassure her in her very first letter home. She wrote of her '[t]ran-scendent good fortune—surely nothing was ever half so lucky, or half so well timed', and that she was 'in a <u>Whirlwind</u> of <u>felicity</u>'.[30] However, in the same sentence she quickly turned to her mother's feelings:

> pray feel no anxieties about me Mrs Leigh considers of everything for me & takes as much care & looks after me just as if I were her own. I make no doubt all will go on exactly as you could wish, tell my dear little P—I shall be quite angry with her if she anticipates anything but <u>good.</u> . . . Do not suffer the least apprehensions about my dress & so forth—you know Mrs Leigh's attention and Joanna does everything for me. If possible I shall try to get a few Lessons in dancing—I must make Hay while the <u>Sun shines</u> if possible & I would have you to know I never looked half so well.[31]

Whether Bess was prompted by the likelihood of Hitty's advice potentially cutting though her joy, or genuine anticipation of Hitty's worries,

84   *Bath and Beyond*

is difficult to ascertain. What Bess's letters do communicate is that Bess saw this as a positive experience which she was prepared for and ready to undertake in both 1792 and 1798, even without her mother by her side. Excitement, hope, and joy fill Bess's pages, communicating that while Hitty was anxious about her daughter's prospects, Bess herself was not. The marriage market was less a time of anxiety for debutantes and more one of excitement. It held discomfort for their mothers and chaperones as they navigated the events, the shopping, and the choices of the current Season to try to secure a coveted match.

This excitement is seen in many of Bess's 1792 and 1798 letters, including her opening letter detailing her first ball in 1792. It reads more like the excitement shown by Catherine Morland in *Northanger Abbey*. Her rushed tone denotes her excitement:

I was dressed (for I suppose you like to hear everything) in my [illegible word] petticoat (with everything proper <u>underneath</u>) with a jacket made of the pink poplin and a white sash, and half sleeves of lawn and a muslin handkerchief put on very nicely. Parsley dressed my hair very well, and on it I wore a wreath of red roses; now don't you think I was <u>mighty</u> smart? . . . Well, then to the rooms we went about half past seven, and got very good places in the best part of the room, and all that you know. So then the dancing began and I wondered what my fate would be for though I suspected that the kind Mrs Leigh, had been her interest for me the day before, yet—I could not be certain; well the first dance was finished when I heard Mr Leigh say 'I wish your partner was come,' ho!ho! thinks I, I smoke something, lo, in after moments after in came Mr Terringhm and he came up to us, he says to me, 'shall you like to dance?' . . . I got up and danced like a pea upon a Trencher. My partner, I assure you, was something very smart not to say handsome, and danced very well and was very good natured when this dance was over, the cotillions began; Mr Terringham took to another partner, when one cotillion was danced we went to tea, and after tea there was another which took up so long a time that we were in a fright least my partner should forget me in the interim, and leave me in the <u>lurch</u> so the old aunts so settled it with Mr Bleaney Rofrer that if my partner did not come back to me, that he should dance with me, so I had <u>two</u> strings to my bow: which how ever we found unnecessary for as soon as the cotillion was over, Mr Terringham came to me, and took me out and I danced again. Bess was afraid to look at me the first time, but now she and Aunt Fan so <u>perched</u> themselves on a bench that to my great <u>annoyance</u> they saw everything I did. However, I had the satisfaction to hear from them since that I performed very well. When I began the first dance I was in a <u>terrible</u> fright but afterwards I felt quite at my ease, the last dance was very very pleasant.[32]

Not Just Suitors, Balls, and Proposals 85

This lengthy letter almost reads quite breathlessly, with few pauses and no paragraphing. Bess's letters from her 1792–1793 Bath visit often read like this, as she continually apologises for hurrying to finish writing before attending the next ball, concert, or home visit. Her letter also shows the importance of chaperones in securing dance partners for young ladies, as the Leighs play a pivotal role in Bess's success in securing two partners, though she only went with one for the evening. Bess's detailed description appears to have satisfied Hitty. Indeed, the detail here suggests that Bess paid great attention to her surroundings and the experience, a reflection of the observant nature of others in a Georgian ballroom. Bess herself noted that her aunt and cousin 'saw everything I did' and her own 'fright' at being observed, but the success of the evening meant that Hitty received an excited letter detailing Bess's triumph.

However, Bess was less successful in finding a partner for the next ball, despite efforts to assist her from the Leighs and George Canning. The opening to her letter immediately notes the lack of suitors as a 'Mr Badcock . . . was obliged to stand up with seven, or eight ladies successively' for the opening minuets.[33] Bess's letter suggests that not just any partner would do, as she turned down a boy of 15:

> the old aunts were aghast at the idea of my making my first essay with a dump of a boy so Mrs Leigh in her cunning little manner, made a pretty little speech to the gentlemen, such as 'Miss Canning was not sure that she could dance at all, but if she did, Mr Leigh had engaged a partner for her'.[34]

Despite Mr Leigh's efforts, no further suitors could be found, and Bess noted to her mother that 'the next time I go to a Ball, now that I know the manoeuvres of it, I shall get them to look out for a partner earlier in the evening, and then I shall have a better chance'.[35] It appears that there was an art to securing a dance partner, especially amongst a scarcity of men. In late 1792, drafting had already begun for the Revolutionary Wars and so the lack of *Beaus* in the room is likely a reflection of the beginning of the war effort.[36]

Despite her positivity in her letter from 30 December 1792, when she was unable to secure a partner, she 'begun in a very bad way', at a ball on 2 January 1793, despite the efforts of her cousin, George Canning, to try to secure her a partner.[37] However, through their connections, a partner was found:

> Mr Foster (husband to Miss Rebeccah Mcchuse) who is a goodnatured [*sic*], genteel sort of man, said he was acquainted with several gentlemen, who that moment seeing one of them, he brought him by the nape of the neck to me and introduced him, by the name of T, I, P, P, I, N,

86 *Bath and Beyond*

<u>Tippin</u> Mr. Tippin—how should you like your daughter <u>Tippin</u>? I assure you he is a very smart little man, and as they like me descended from the <u>ancient</u> family of <u>Tippin</u>, very great people in the kingdom of Ireland, but let it be great or little, I never saw a pea upon a Trencher, dance better than my <u>little</u> partner, we danced three dances together very briskly, really I never saw such a civil, good natured creature.—Mr Leigh asked him if he liked music? To which reason they gave him an invitation to the party on Tuesday.[38]

Bess's letters to her mother recount her feelings of disappointment and fear, for she opened the letter by saying that she 'was very much <u>affeared</u>, that I should not get a partner', but her tone changed once she secured a *Beau* for the evening. Her letter becomes excited, fast-paced, and detailed once more, informing her mother once again of her success. Her letters are a vessel to communicate her achievements to her mother, whom she wanted to please.

Bess Canning: The Pressures of the Dance

After one managed to find a dance partner, there was the dance itself. Dancing was part of the wider social culture of Bath where 'appearances meant everything'.[39] Individuals were constantly on show, with the social spaces such as the Pump Room, theatre, and promenades all designed for displaying oneself and scrutinising others. As Francis Lambert noted in his *Treatise on Dancing*:

the object of learning to dance is not to acquire the most difficult movements of the feet . . . . The object to be attained is an easy carriage of the body, and a graceful management of the arms and head. . . . A person that dances well in this respect will be graceful in a room, and will be distinguished upon all occasions.[40]

It is unsurprising then that the *Bath Chronicle* advertised space to practise dancing at the Upper Assembly Rooms as late as 1800.[41]

Dancing was not just a series of steps, but an essential ritual in displaying one's grace and deportment.[42] It was so important that children were schooled in it from a young age. Bess's letters note that she enrolled in dance lessons throughout her adolescence, and she attended a ball at Mrs Curtis's prior to her debut in Bath society.[43] In her memoirs of her childhood in the 1790s, Susan Sibbald noted that 'Wednesday was dancing day' at her school in Bath. Mademoiselle Le Mercier taught the 'positions and steps' with Miss Fleming, the main dance mistress teaching the 'Minuetts [*sic*], and figure dances', implying that more than just the steps were taught

Not Just Suitors, Balls, and Proposals   87

during these dances to the young ladies.[44] Sibbald's school held a dance at the Upper Assembly Rooms every three years, in front of 'the Grown Ups', led by the Master of Ceremonies, to show off the 'Leevites', as the school pupils were known. Thus, the pressure to perform and 'do credit to Bath' is evident in her memoirs, especially when Susan was presented with a different wreath, and she should 'fear every one would be looking at my conspicuous head'. However, when the dancing was a success, there were rewards: Susan's sister's 'dancing was so much noticed that the Duchess of York spoke to her and kissed her'.[45]

While there were several styles of dance, it was the minuet which particularly showed off a dancer's poise and control, due to its slow pace. Usually the first dance to open a ball, the minuet was a French dance, traditionally danced by a single pair, but was danced by many pairs in a row by the end of the eighteenth century. Indeed, minuets were performed 'from the court of St James's Palace to the homes of nobility and gentry in London and the assembly rooms of Great Britain'.[46] In particular, the minuets were danced by young ladies searching for a husband, and as such, it was a dance which was studied by every eye in the room. Lord Chesterfield once commented upon the minuets danced at Bath:

> You would laugh if you were to see the dancing in the ball rooms, where of twenty minuets there are at least nineteen ridiculous ones, performed by people who had either very bad dancing masters, or who were so invincibly awkward as to baffle the care and pains of the best.[47]

Bess's cousin 'Letitia danced a minuet but did not perform quite as well as was expected, but she was a good deal frightened', whereas Bess 'got off dancing the Cottilion [*sic*], not choosing to exhibit before so many people who were watching the steps of every miss with criticising eyes'.[48] This is despite a previous letter of Bess's to her mother, before her trip to Bath, stating that she had been taking dancing lessons, and that she could 'now dance a minuet with *pas grave* pretty bobbish', suggesting that she felt her dancing of the minuet had greatly improved.[49] The pressures of the Bath ballroom and Letitia's less favourable experience clearly influenced Bess's decision not to dance a minuet in Bath. After all, 'appearances meant everything in a city like Bath', and Bess's decision suggests she felt it was better not to try than fail to impress with a minuet.[50]

During Bess's second visit to Bath, in 1798, it becomes apparent that Bess was not making much progress in her search for a husband. Hitty commented on this in her letters to Bess, writing that 'the Girls ought all to pray for a Peace, for till that much desired Blessing arrives, it is in vain for them to crop, and dress and go to Public Places—Poor little P-s chops feel considerably yesterday, on hearing of the terrible scarcity of Beaux at

88 Bath and Beyond

Bath'.[51] Hitty's letter once again suggests that attempting to find a husband in Bath during the Revolutionary Wars was 'in vain', and that Bess was unlikely to find a husband through the usual route of attending balls and performances. Indeed, Bess confirmed Hitty's suspicions, reporting that the gatherings were 'defective in the same respect . . . all Women & no Men'.[52]

For Bess's part, she displayed more boredom than anxiety in her later 1798 letters. She wrote that she 'was forced to flirt a little with [Lady Mary Anne's son] for want of something better to do'.[53] The anxiety of the marriage market appears to have primarily lay with the parents in its early stages rather than the daughters. However, as the 1798 letters continue, a sense of uneasiness creeps into Bess's vivid descriptions of the lack of men in Bath. Bess wrote that 'a kind of fatality seems to attend all my Beaux—not that I wish to be melancholic just now'.[54] While concerns of finding a suitable husband are evident across many eras of history, this particular example typifies the anxieties of trying to secure a match during times of war, when there were few men available and a shortage of men for a generation due to death in battle. Bess and her mother's correspondence reveals both the difficulties of the marriage market for young ladies at the end of the eighteenth century, and also the behaviours of chaperones and parents in trying to secure their daughters a match.

Betsy Sheridan: Tiredness, Loneliness, and Boredom

Bess was a young woman during her forays into Bath's social scene, but Betsy Sheridan was 27 when she entered the Bath marriage market in April 1785—the same age as Anne Elliot in Austen's *Persuasion*—and would have been considered old to be looking for her first husband. Her letters speak of her tiredness: she had just come from a full season in London.[55] However, her relocation to Bath was as much for her father's ill health, as for her to find a future husband. Thus, historians need to be mindful of the context for young women entering the marriage market. Not all of them were optimistic first timers, in awe of all the new sights and sounds which were on offer; for many, Bath offered simply another round of socialising and balls.

Betsy's letters express low spirits and a disengagement with the events going on around her. Interestingly, a letter to her married sister, Alicia Le Fanu in 1785, suggests that she was annoyed by her family's expectations:

> to look out for a young Batchelor here—and Harry *says nothing* about coming home. I see how it is, I am thrown off and you are keeping him for someone else, but to be even with you I am determined not to accept of one of the numerous offers which I shall certainly meet with here (emphasis in original).[56]

Not Just Suitors, Balls, and Proposals 89

Betsy's letter suggests that she too saw Bath as a space where attachments were formed, and proposals made. Yet her letter intimates that she was interested in marrying Harry, presumably Alicia's brother-in-law, Harry Le Fanu, whom she did marry in 1791. Betsy may have already been in love with him, or he may simply have been an excuse. Either way, Betsy clearly expressed that she did not wish to engage with the marriage market in Bath. This disinterest is often conveyed through a sense of repetition, and with this, boredom. She highlights that she was living 'the same old life—Airing—home and cards, not very enchanting but to say the truth I am not in spirits to enjoy any other'.[57] On another occasion, she met a Miss Brook whose company she enjoyed 'more than all the amusements of Bath put together'.[58] With such a prescribed routine, John Eglin notes that boredom was registered by several guests visiting Bath.[59] Indeed, Rachael Johnson's discussion on Tunbridge Wells's spa society in the 1790s, and Jemima Hubbertsey's examination of Jemima Grey and Elizabeth Anston's visit to Bath in 1749, also attest to this.[60] They could, like Betsy, have come straight from the London Season, with its own routine of balls, concerts, and spouse-hunting, and been exasperated by the repetitive nature of Bath's social scene.[61]

Furthermore, expressing boredom could also be an example of what Elena Carrera calls 'social acts of communication', that is that boredom could be a way of communicating other feelings or thoughts.[62] Betsy might have been hiding a sense of shame at her lack of ability to find a husband, or her secret love of the humdrum routine that she denounced. Indeed, her comments might reflect the late eighteenth-century fashion for boredom, often equated with the French *ennui*. Both terms can denote several different emotional states, such as 'annoyance, worry, frustration and even impotence'.[63] Thus, Betsy's 'boredom' was possibly much more complex than the result of enacting a repetitive daily routine.

However, letters could also be an important space to articulate feelings which could not be displayed publicly, or even to other family members. Writing again to her sister, Alicia Le Fanu, Betsy noted that her father 'has insisted on subscribing me to the Cotillion Balls which are on Thursdays so I am fairly in for a round of hurry'.[64] This visit records the usual attendance of balls, and that Betsy 'saunter'd about Pump Room, Libraries etc. in short spent a true Bath morning, I should not chuse to spend many such'.[65] To highlight the routineness of Bath's social scene, Betsy's next entry also mentioned a Pump Room visit: 'I went with the same Lady to the Octagon Chapel and afterwards like a fool let myself be dragg'd to the Pump Room, Parades etc in the heat of the day'.[66] This resulted in fatigue fever, what could possibly be heat exhaustion, but the term 'fatigue' suggests another hidden meaning beyond the medical, to denote tiredness and ennui with the regular social pattern of Bath. There is a sense that Betsy

90   Bath and Beyond

endured Bath's social rounds for her father, who appeared to be unaware of her true feelings.

Indeed, Betsy noted that she did not feel like she belonged in Bath and its social world, suggesting that worry, frustration, and even loneliness were underlying her expressions of boredom. She wrote that in the gardens, when she was walking with her father, a friend came and stopped to talk to him. However, 'as I was unemploy'd I felt rather awkward standing by a set of People who honor'd me with no other notice than an impertinent Stare'.[67] Her use of the phrase 'set of People' denotes distance and unfamiliarity— Betsy was informing her sister that she was not part of this 'set'. Her use of the term 'awkward' communicates the opposite of the desired poise, grace, and self-control expected of young ladies seeking to show off their wifely qualities to potential spouses and their families. Yet, it was Betsy who judged the 'set'—deeming their 'Stare' was impolite and uncalled for. Bess being exposed to the scrutiny of those socialising in Bath, the entry exposes eighteenth-century Bath's sometimes-uncomfortable nature.

This discussion of not belonging adds to a sense of loneliness in Betsy's letters, despite being surrounded by people in Bath society. Writing to her sister, Betsy 'wish[ed] for money every day, for certainly it could procure me the highest gratification I can taste in this world—the society of the few I truly love'.[68] Here, loneliness is perceived as the absence of loved ones. Betsy's experiences of the Company of Bath were 'lacking or deficient' in forming relationships that resulted in feelings of belonging, happiness, and meaning—feelings she attributed to her relationship with her sister.[69] Her mention of money could be for two reasons: either she could not afford to visit her sister, or she believed that money would eliminate the need to find a husband and give her the freedom to spend her days in the company of those she loved. Either way, Bath did not provide Betsy with the amusements displayed in either Catherine Morland's account or Bess Canning's letters. Importantly, Betsy's letter suggests that writing letters to her sister was not enough: it was physical presence that she craved, likely because she wished to leave the performance arena of Bath.

Part of Betsy's boredom likely stemmed from her desire to remain single, at least while in Bath. Her ambitions for her time in Bath were clearly different from her father's, as on her next visit to Bath in 1786, Betsy's letter notes her promise to her father:

> to dance this Evening as my Father says he don't understand my turning Old Woman; and our young Oxonian Mr Drake is to have the honour of my hand. I do as I am bid on this occasion but to say the truth I am surprised to find how very indifferent I am grown to those sort of amusements, but in my present situation I think it is a duty to struggle with that indifference, as it would exclude me from the society I must mix with, and indulging my feelings will not restore me to that I have lost.[70]

Not Just Suitors, Balls, and Proposals 91

Once again, Betsy used her letter to communicate her distance from the company that she kept in Bath. In so doing she also reflected the tensions of her role in society, particularly where her wishes clashed with those of her father, and especially as they kept her from her beloved sister. The reference to age communicates that Betsy's actions were more in line with that of an older woman, not a young lady seeking a marriage match. While Betsy revealed that she was 'indifferent' to 'those sort of amusements', it was 'her duty to struggle with that indifference' so that she could please her father and try to find a husband. As with Bess Canning's letters, there is a sense in Betsy's letters that parents were highly influential in the experiences of the marriage market: they too highlight the tensions between personal feelings and a sense of familial duty.

Both the correspondences of Bess Canning and Betsy Sheridan nuance the more typical viewpoint of the excited Bath debutante portrayed in *Northanger Abbey*. Their letters present anxious chaperones and bored young ladies with many mixed feelings about Bath's social scene and crucially also allude to the difficulties faced by young women entering the marriage market at a time of war. The letters themselves are part of the shaping of these emotions and experiences, whether as hurried scribbles to record as many details as possible of a triumph in the ballroom, or as spaces to convey notions of affection to a dearly missed sister. Each young woman in Bath's ballrooms had their own contexts, which fashioned their Bath experiences.

Notes

1 Jane Austen, *Northanger Abbey (1803/1817)* (London: Penguin, 2008), 82.
2 See Hazel Jones, *Jane Austen and Marriage* (London: Continuum, 2009) for a more comprehensive discussion on marriage in Jane Austen's novels.
3 Peter Borsay, *The English Urban Renaissance: Culture and Society in the Provincial Town 1660–1770* (Oxford: Clarendon Press, 1989); John Eglin, *The Imaginary Autocrat: Beau Nash and the Invention of Bath* (London: Profile Books, 2005); Paul Langford, *A Polite and Commercial People* (Oxford: Clarendon Press, 1989); Katharine Glover, *Elite Women and Polite Society in Eighteenth-Century Scotland* (Woodbridge: Boydell & Brewer, 2011).
4 Mira [Eliza Haywood], *The Wife* (London: T. Gardener, 1756), 6.
5 Rachel Bynoth, "Anxious Expressions: Remote Relationships in the Canning Correspondence Network, 1760–1830" (PhD diss., Bath Spa University, 2024), chap. 1; Jones, *Jane Austen and Marriage*, 2–3.
6 Eglin, *Imaginary Autocrat*, 92–93.
7 Eglin, *Imaginary Autocrat*, 5–7.
8 Examples include Eglin, *Imaginary Autocrat*; Borsay, *English Urban Renaissance*; Graham Davis and Penny Bonsall, *A History of Bath: Image and Reality* (Lancaster: Carnegie Publishing, 2007); R.S. Neale, *Bath: A Social History, 1680–1850 or a Valley of Pleasure, Yet a Sink of Iniquity* (Abingdon: Routledge, 1981).
9 Some of the numerous examples of later Bath Guides with Nash's rules include *The New Bath Guide, Or Pocket Companion* (Bath, 1662), 24–25; *New Bath*

92 *Bath and Beyond*

Guide (Bath: R. Cruttwell, 1785), 20–21; and for one with his successors version of his rules see *New Bath Guide, or Useful Pocket Companion* (Bath, 1799), 21–26.

10 Eglin, *Imaginary Autocrat*, 56–57, 60–61.

11 *The Historic and Local New Bath Guide* (Bath, 1812), 112.

12 Eglin, *Imaginary Autocrat*, 91.

13 Eglin, *Imaginary Autocrat*, 97–98.

14 *The Times*, January 16, 1787.

15 *Bath Chronicle*, October 29, 1789.

16 *The Times*, January 16, 1787.

17 *The Times*, August 6, 1800.

18 Cynthia Imogen Hammond, " 'The Gardens Will Be Illuminated': Gendered and Georgian Pleasures in Sydney Gardens," *Bath History* xi (2019): 9.

19 Graham Davis and Penny Bonsall, *Bath: A New History* (Keele: Keele University Press, 1996), 44.

20 Eglin, *Imaginary Autocrat*, 90.

21 Jane Austen, *Pride and Prejudice (1813)* (Cambridge: Cambridge University Press, 2006), 5; Rachel Bynoth, "A Mother Educating Her Daughter Remotely Through Familial Correspondence: The Letter as a Form of Distance Education," *History* cvi (2021): 727–50.

22 Bynoth, "A Mother Educating Her Daughter Remotely."

23 BRO, fl2111–2308: Elizabeth Canning to Mehitabel Canning, July 7, 1798.

24 Roy Adkins and Lesley Adkins, *Eavesdropping on Jane Austen's England* (St Ives: Little, Brown, 2013), 4–5.

25 Austen, *Pride and Prejudice*, 11.

26 Jones, *Jane Austen and Marriage*, 46.

27 BRO, fl2111–2308: Elizabeth Canning to Mehitabel Canning, January 22, 1793.

28 Bynoth, "A Mother Educating Her Daughter Remotely," 738–40, 749–50; WYAS WYL888/LC02169 [Accession 2169]. Mehitabel Canning to Elizabeth Canning, February 17, 1789.

29 BRO, fl2111–2308: Elizabeth Canning to Mehitabel Canning, January 22, 1793.

30 BRO, fl2111–2308: Elizabeth Canning to Mehitabel Canning, November 4, 1798.

31 BRO, fl2111–2308: Elizabeth Canning to Mehitabel Canning, November 4, 1798.

32 BRO, fl2111–2308: Elizabeth Canning to Mehitabel Canning, November 28, 1792.

33 BRO, fl2111–2308: Elizabeth Canning to Mehitabel Canning, December 30, 1792.

34 BRO, fl2111–2308: Elizabeth Canning to Mehitabel Canning, December 30, 1792.

35 BRO, fl2111–2308: Elizabeth Canning to Mehitabel Canning, December 30, 1792.

36 Atle L. Wold, *Scotland and the French Revolutionary Wars, 1792–1802* (Edinburgh: Edinburgh University Press, 2017), chap. 3.

37 BRO, fl2111–2308: Elizabeth Canning to Mehitabel Canning, January 2, 1793.

38 BRO, fl2111–2308: Elizabeth Canning to Mehitabel Canning, January 2, 1793.

39 Trevor Fawcett, "Dance and Teachers of Dance in Eighteenth-Century Bath," *Bath History* ii (1988): 28.

40 Francis Lambert, *Treatise on Dancing* (Norwich, 1815), 2–3.

41 *Bath Chronicle*, November 20, 1800.

42 See Hillary Burlock, "Politics and Pirouettes: The Intersection of Politics and Social Dance in Late Georgian Britain" (PhD diss., Queen Mary University, 2022).

Not Just Suitors, Balls, and Proposals 93

43 BRO, fl2111–2308: Elizabeth Canning to Mehitabel Canning, May 23, 1792.
44 Susan Sibbald, *The Memoirs of Susan Sibbald (1783–1812)*, ed. Francis Paget Hett (Whitefish, Montana: Kessinger Publishing, 2010), 44–45.
45 Sibbald, *Memoirs of Sisan Sibbald*, 58–60.
46 Hillary Burlock, "'Tumbling into the Lap of Majesty': Minuets at the Court of George III," *Journal of Eighteenth-Century Studies* xviv (2021): 205.
47 Lord Chesterfield, *The Letters of Lord Chesterfield*, ed. Bonamy Dobrée, 6 vols. (London: Eyre & Spottiswoode, 1932), vi, 2895.
48 BRO, fl2111–2308: Elizabeth Canning to Mehitabel Canning, January 12, 1793.
49 BRO, fl2111–2308: Elizabeth Canning to Mehitabel Canning, May 23, 1792.
50 Fawcett, "Dance and Teachers of Dance," 28.
51 WYAS WYL888/LC02169 [Accession 2169]: Mehitabel Canning to Elizabeth Canning, November 1798 (full date missing due to ripped seal).
52 BRO, fl2111–2308: Elizabeth Canning to Mehitabel Canning, November 12, 1798.
53 BRO, fl2111–2308: Elizabeth Canning to Mehitabel Canning, October 18, 1798.
54 BRO, fl2111–2308: Elizabeth Canning to Mehitabel Canning, November 19, 1798.
55 Elizabeth Sheridan, *Betsy Sheridan's Journal: Letters from Sheridan's Sister 1784–1786 & 1788–1790*, ed. William Le Fanu (London: Eyre and Spottiswoode, 1960), April 1985–May 1985, 23–52.
56 Sheridan, *Betsy Sheridan's Journal*, April 25–May 3, 1785, 45.
57 Sheridan, *Betsy Sheridan's Journal*, April 25–May 3, 1785, 45.
58 Sheridan, *Betsy Sheridan's Journal*, April 25–May 3, 1785, 46.
59 Eglin, *Imaginary Autocrat*, 55–56.
60 See Chapters by Rachael Johnson, "Two Kingdoms: Masters of Ceremonies at Bath and Tunbridge Wells, 1735–c.1801"; Jemima Hubbertsey, "'I am a Sort of Prisoner Here': Elite Performance and Bath Society in the Eighteenth Century," in this book.
61 Hannah Greig, *The Beau Monde* (Oxford: Oxford University Press, 2013).
62 Elena Carrera, *Boredom* (Cambridge: Cambridge University Press, 2023), 2.
63 Carrera, *Boredom*, 3.
64 Sheridan, *Betsy Sheridan's Journal*, May 8–10, 1786, 82.
65 Sheridan, *Betsy Sheridan's Journal*, June 1, 1786, 84–85.
66 Sheridan, *Betsy Sheridan's Journal*, June 1, 1786, 85.
67 Sheridan, *Betsy Sheridan's Journal*, July 1–7, 1786, 91.
68 Sheridan, *Betsy Sheridan's Journal*, April 25–May 3, 1785, 47.
69 Katie Barclay, Elaine Chalus, and Deborah Simonton, "Introduction," in *The Routledge History of Loneliness*, ed. Katie Barclay, Elaine Chalus, and Deborah Simonton (Abingdon: Routledge, 2023), 2–3.
70 Sheridan, *Betsy Sheridan's Journal*, May 8–10, 1786, 82.

Bibliography

Manuscript Sources

Bath Record Office

   fl2111–2308: Family Correspondence of Mrs Stratford Canning.

West Yorkshire Archive Service

   WYL888/LC02169 [Accession 2169] George Canning Letters to his Aunt Mrs Canning and to her daughter, Elizabeth (Lady Barnett), 1788–1827.

94 Bath and Beyond

Printed Primary and Secondary Sources

Adkins, Roy, and Lesley Adkins. *Eavesdropping on Jane Austen's England*. St Ives: Little, Brown, 2013.

Austen, Jane. *Northanger Abbey*. London: Penguin, 2008.

Austen, Jane. *Pride and Prejudice*. Cambridge: Cambridge University Press, 2006.

Barclay, Katie, Elaine Chalus, and Deborah Simonton. "Introduction." In *The Routledge History of Loneliness*, edited by Katie Barclay, Elaine Chalus, and Deborah Simonton, 1–13. Abingdon: Routledge, 2023.

"Bath." *The Times*, January 16, 1787.

Borsay, Peter. *The English Urban Renaissance: Culture and Society in the Provincial Town, 1660–1770*. Oxford: Clarendon Press, 1989.

Burlock, Hillary. "'Tumbling into the Lap of Majesty': Minuets at the Court of George III." *Journal of Eighteenth-Century Studies* 44, no. 2 (June 2021): 205–24.

Bynoth, Rachel. "Anxious Expressions: Remote Relationships in the Canning Correspondence Network, 1760–1830." PhD diss., Bath Spa University, 2024.

Bynoth, Rachel. "A Mother Educating Her Daughter Remotely Through Familial Correspondence: The Letter as a Form of Distance Education in the Eighteenth Century." *History* 106, no. 373 (December 2021): 727–50.

Carrera, Elena. *Boredom*. Cambridge: Cambridge University Press, 2023.

"A Curious and We Trust Untrue Report Is in Circulation." *The Times*, August 6, 1800.

Davis, Graham, and Penny Bonsall. *A History of Bath: Image and Reality*. Lancaster: Carnegie Publishing, 2007.

Eglin, John. *The Imaginary Autocrat: Beau Nash and the Invention of Bath*. London: Profile Books, 2005.

Fawcett, Trevor. "Dance and Teachers of Dance in Eighteenth-Century Bath." *Bath History* II (1988): 27–48.

Glover, Katherine. *Elite Women and Polite Society in Eighteenth-Century Scotland*. Woodbridge: Boydell, 2011.

Greig, Hannah. *The Beau Monde*. Oxford: Oxford University Press, 2013.

Hammond, Cynthia Imogen. "'The Gardens Will Be Illuminated': Gendered and Georgian Pleasures in Sydney Gardens." *Bath History* XI (2019): 8–30.

The Historic and Local New Bath Guide, 1812.

Jones, Hazel. *Jane Austen and Marriage*. London: Continuum, 2009.

Lambert, Francis. *A Treatise on Dancing*. Norwich, 1815.

Langford, Paul. *A Polite and Commercial People: England 1727–1783*. Oxford: Oxford University Press, 1998.

Lord Chesterfield. *The Letters of Lord Chesterfield*. Edited by Bonamy Dobrée. London: Eyre & Spottiswoode, 1932.

Mira [Eliza Haywood]. *The Wife*. London: T. Gardener, 1756.

Neale, R. S. *Bath: A Social History, 1680–1850 or a Valley of Pleasure, Yet a Sink of Iniquity*. Abingdon: Routledge, 1981.

The New Bath Guide. Bath: R. Cruttwell, 1785.

The New Bath Guide, or Pocket Companion. Bath: C. Pope, 1762.

The New Bath Guide, or Useful Pocket Companion. Bath: R. Cruttwell, 1799.

"News." *The Bath Chronicle*, October 29, 1789.

"Notice." *The Bath Chronicle*, November 20, 1800.

Sheridan, Elizabeth. *Betsy Sheridan's Journal: Letters from Sheridan's Sister 1784–1786 & 1788–1790*. Edited by William Le Fanu. London: Eyre and Spottiswoode, 1960.

Sibbald, Susan. *The Memoirs of Susan Sibbald (1783–1812)*. Edited by her Great-Grandson Frances Paget Hett. Whitefish, Montana: Kessinger Publishing, 2010.

Wold, Atle L. *Scotland and the French Revolutionary War, 1792–1803*. Edinburgh: Edinburgh University Press, 2015.

6 Rauzzini and the Upper Assembly Rooms Subscription Concert Series

The First Five Years

Brianna E. Robertson-Kirkland

Musical entertainment was an important part of Bath life throughout the eighteenth century, with two key venues hosting fashionable concert series that attracted the most affluent members of Bath society. The old assembly rooms were initially the primary concert venue for the city, and though they were positioned in a prime location at North Parade, as the century progressed and Bath greatly expanded, the New Assembly Rooms were built in the upper part of the city. Designed by John Wood the Younger (1728–82), the Upper Assembly Rooms became the principal concert venue, although the older assembly rooms would continue to host some concerts until they were lost to a fire in the 1820s. Nicknamed the Lower Assembly Rooms and Upper Assembly Rooms, these two venues represented the division between the old, lower part of the city and the fashionable, new, upper section. It was in these two venues that the Italian castrato singer Venanzio Rauzzini (1746–1810) established himself as one of the most successful musical directors in Bath. Indeed, his name became synonymous with Bath concerts at the turn of the nineteenth century. Rauzzini attracted the most celebrated singers and instrumentalists in the country to perform for him, including English operatic stars who built prominent careers on the European continent such as Elizabeth Billington (1765–1818), Anna Selina Storace (1765–1817), John Braham (*c.*1774–1856), and international celebrities including German singer Gertrud Mara (1749–1833), Polish violin virtuoso Feliks Janiewicz (1762–1848), and the Polish-British child prodigy of African descent George Bridgetower (1778–1860). While the previous director of subscription concert series, Thomas Linley the Elder (1733–1795), had attracted some international talent, it was through Rauzzini that both established and up-and-coming English and European talent came together to showcase Bath as a prominent city for musical activity.

During the 1778–1779 season, Rauzzini and his co-director, Flemish violinist Franz La Motte (*c.*1751–80), took over the organisation of the Upper Assembly Room subscription concert series. Together they produced

DOI: 10.4324/9781003393856-6

two seasons, with Rauzzini becoming sole director of the 1780–1781 season following La Motte's death. For the next 30 years, Rauzzini was an important figure in the city, diligently organising the winter subscription concert series, then later a spring series, and multiple other concerts around the city. It was only with his death in 1810 that a new musical director, his close friend Andrew Ashe (c.1758–1838), took over the position. Rauzzini's memory as the foremost musical director was not easily replaced, however. On 25 October 1810, five months after Rauzzini's passing, Ashe publicly praised him, noting that he had been at 'the very head of his profession, and father of most of the best singers of the present day, who gratefully assisted at his Concerts on terms that no successor can have any pretensions to expect'.[1] The new musical director clearly felt that key to Rauzzini's success had been the singers who came to perform in the concerts. As discussed in *Venanzio Rauzzini and the Birth of a New Style in English Singing: Scandalous Lessons*, it was his ability to foster long-term friendships with his students, many of whom would emerge as celebrity singers, that also enabled the success of the Upper Assembly Rooms subscription concert series and the other musical events the castrato organised in the city.[2]

However, the previous study did not examine the amount of time it took Rauzzini to build a roster of students who were ready to perform in professional concerts. Indeed, even more time was needed for those students to emerge as celebrities, which would further entice concert audiences to see them perform. While Rauzzini had already been working as a singing master from the moment he arrived in Britain to take up the position as *primo uomo* at the King's Theatre in London in 1774, the number of students under his tuition was relatively few and remained so until after his retirement from the stage. It was only once he was well established in Bath that the number of aspiring professional students increased to the point that he could regularly call upon them to perform at his concert series. But this prompts the question: if Rauzzini would come to rely on students to sing at his later concerts, what did he do in his early years as musical director of the Upper Assembly Rooms subscription concerts—and is there evidence of struggle, including financial, repertoire programming, and securing singers during this time?

Paul F. Rice argues that Rauzzini was successful right from the moment he took over the concert series, in part because he inherited an effective model from his years as co-director with La Motte.[3] However, even Rice notes in an overview of the concert series in 1781–1783, and 1784–1786, that Rauzzini often struggled to make the series profitable.[4] The Upper Assembly Rooms concert series had been financially funded via subscription since the Rooms opened, with audience attendees typically subscribing to attend the whole series of concerts at the start of the season. As for

98   Bath and Beyond

the concerts themselves, Linley, the former musical director, had established a regular weekly slot for performances, with each concert scheduled to take place at 6.30pm on Wednesday evenings from late October to January.[5] The weekly concert was only occasionally interrupted to accommodate individually ticketed benefit concerts.[6] Programming for both the subscription concert series and benefit concerts consisted of miscellaneous repertoire, including beloved favourites well known to audiences; signature arias, songs, and instrumental pieces performed by celebrated musicians; and new compositions. Linley the Elder's format was not at all original: the Upper Assembly Rooms subscription concert series was clearly inspired by the first subscription concert series established in London in 1765 by Johann Christian Bach (1736–1782) and Carl Friedrich Abel (1723–1787). Known as the Bach-Abel concert series, they recruited celebrity singers and instrumentalists to come and perform in weekly concerts that typically took place every Wednesday evening from January to May.[7] When La Motte and Rauzzini took over as musical directors, they maintained the same model, but by the time Rauzzini became sole director, he had instigated several small but significant changes that shaped the series overall. While Rice has provided a useful overview of Rauzzini's first five years as sole musical director, he does not provide a detailed examination of the multiple changes that Rauzzini attempted. The subscription concert series advertisements, published in the Bath newspapers throughout 1780–1786, reveal intriguing details, showing that his tenure as musical director was not built on solid foundations, nor was the format of the series fixed. It was only once Rauzzini experimented with the format and pricing, and started to weave his students into the concert series as leading performers, that he hit his stride as musical director.

As such, this chapter provides a detailed examination of the first five years of Rauzzini's tenure as musical director of the Upper Assembly Rooms winter subscription concert series, noting the changes he implemented during this time, and what ultimately led Rauzzini to secure the longevity of the series. It builds on Rice's existing work, by further expanding upon the research on the Upper Assembly Rooms subscription concerts and events undertaken by him and others, including Kenneth James and Peter Borsay.[8] Indeed, it is fitting in an edited collection dedicated to celebrating 250 years since the opening of the Upper Assembly Rooms that this chapter should delve deeper into the subscription concert series, which, as Rice pointed out in 2014, has been somewhat neglected by scholarship.[9] It should also be noted that Rice published a useful record of the 1786–1810 subscription concerts, including the names of performers and repertoire performed, as an appendix to his monograph. This chapter complements that study by adding to the record and including similar information for the 1780–1786 concerts as an appendix to this chapter (Appendix 2).

Unfortunately, Rauzzini did not advertise all the repertoire performed, and so the appendix is not a comprehensive repertoire list for each concert. However, analysing the evolution of the concerts in Rauzzini's first five years as sole director, and completing the record to include the number of concerts, dates, names of performers, and pricing information, will prove useful to current and future scholars.

1777–1780 Series: A Musical Partnership

A professional Italian singer and composer, Rauzzini came to Britain in 1774, and after singing for three seasons at the King's Theatre, he started working with Flemish violinist and composer La Motte, co-directing a series of eight concerts at the Lower Assembly Rooms in Bath, from November 1777 to January 1778. Initially, the pair were contracted for four concerts, but owing to their success, a further four were announced on 11 December 1777.[10] These concerts reportedly rivalled Linley's subscription concert series at the Upper Assembly Rooms, with the London newspaper *The Morning Chronicle* stating, 'A rival concert, indeed, has made some noise, and carried (oh wonderful!) Many of the upper town down to the lower rooms, to hear La Motte and Rauzzini'.[11]

Division between the Upper and Lower Assembly Rooms had already been the talk of Bath after the resignation of William Wade in 1777 prompted the establishment of two Masters of Ceremonies. William Dawson was Master of Ceremonies at the Upper Assembly Rooms from 1777 to 1785, while William Brereton was Master of Ceremonies at the Lower Assembly Rooms from 1777 to 1780. While Masters of Ceremonies were responsible for managing assembly rooms, as Hillary Bulock and Rachael Johnson discuss in this book, La Motte and Rauzzini had a great deal of freedom to choose their performers and repertoire, thus allowing them to showcase their abilities as concert directors. Rice explains that the Upper Assembly Rooms subscription concert series had 'lost some of its prestige' due to Linley's absence during the previous season. By the latter half of the 1770s, the Linley family had a growing number of opportunities in London that forced Linley to divide his time between the two cities.[12] By 1778, and following the death of Thomas Linley the Younger, the family made London their permanent home, thus leaving the Upper Assembly Rooms without a musical director. La Motte and Rauzzini stepped in to fill the vacant position, further cementing their collaborative relationship, which, in addition to the Bath concerts, had also resulted in a successful concert series at the Hanover Square Rooms in London in the spring of 1778 and 1779. While the pair were in partnership, it was La Motte who typically directed the instrumentalists, while Rauzzini sang. Thus, La Motte and Rauzzini could rely on each other to fulfil fundamental roles necessary to make a

100 *Bath and Beyond*

concert successful—an instrumental lead and a vocal star. Rauzzini's role would significantly change once he was sole director.

For the 1778–1779 Upper Assembly Rooms subscription concert series, La Motte and Rauzzini offered 10 concerts between 4 November and 6 January, with additional concerts performed on 24 December 1778 and 13 January 1779. The latter concert was described as 'the last in the season' but not billed as a subscription concert despite utilising the same singers and instrumentalists.[13] Rather these were additional events over and above the subscription concerts and demonstrate that there was more than enough of an appetite for concerts throughout the winter season in Bath. The singer secured for the 1778–1779 season, in addition to Rauzzini, was Maria Prudom (*d*.1783), an English singer who performed at the King's Theatre and Drury Lane from 1776 to 1782. While no programmes were published in the newspaper that indicate the kind of repertoire performed, securing a prominent opera singer to sing alongside Rauzzini was an attractive draw for audiences. For the 1779–1780 series, La Motte and Rauzzini secured Irish singer Mary Madden (1760–1856), who was not a theatre singer, though she and her sister, Lucretia, were clearly vocally talented and highly thought of by Bath audiences. Together, they performed (alongside La Motte and Rauzzini) a concert specifically for Miss Mary Madden on 22 January 1780, which was 'By particular Desire of several of the Nobility and Gentry'.[14] At this stage, Rauzzini and La Motte were relying on talent already based in England, rather than inviting international celebrities to come and perform. Their reputations as talented musicians were certainly known on the Continent, but, as directors they still need to prove their abilities beyond Bath and London.

There were two different ways that audiences could attend concerts in Bath. They could purchase a subscription at the start of the season, for the sum of £2 2*s*. for gentlemen, and £1 1*s*. for ladies,[15] or non-subscribers could purchase individual concert tickets at the cost of 7*s*. 6*d*. for gentlemen, or 5*s*. for ladies.[16] After Rauzzini took over as sole director, the ticket and subscription costs would fluctuate, as will be discussed later in this chapter. As for the series format, the non-subscription ticket and subscription price and structure all remained the same, with 10 concerts planned for performance between 10 November 1779 and 25 January 1780, though the final concert was delayed until 28 January 1780 on account of La Motte's 'indisposition'.[17] This was the last concert series La Motte ever organised.

1780–1781 Series: Rauzzini as Sole Director

The 1780–1781 series consisted of 10 concerts, with the final concert initially planned for Wednesday 24 January, but delayed because fellow

Rauzzini and the Upper Assembly Rooms   101

Italian castrato and one of the leading singers for the series, Giusto Fernando Tenducci (*c.*1735–90), was engaged to sing at the Bach-Abel concert series in London.[18] This was a recurring issue, with Tenducci engaged to sing at both the Bath and London subscription concert series from 1780 to 1783. By the following season, Rauzzini tried to find solutions to ensure his concert series was not significantly impacted by Tenducci's absence.

Though an Italian castrato who had trained in Naples, Tenducci had spent much time in England, having arrived in 1758 to sing at the King's Theatre, London. He was appointed second man for the 1758–1759 and 1759–1760 King's Theatre seasons, before financial difficulties landed him in debtors' prison for eight months in June 1760.[19] Such a scandal did not destroy his career, and by 1764, Tenducci had returned to sing at the King's Theatre before being contracted to sing at Smock Alley Theatre, Dublin, the following season. He returned to Britain in 1768 and became a prominent concert singer, often appearing in Edinburgh and London. Recruiting such a fashionable vocalist was lucrative for Rauzzini, since it undoubtedly guaranteed that audiences would attend to hear the castrato, although it meant that he had to work around Tenducci's challenging schedule. Furthermore, Tenducci's appearance added an air of internationalism, with his Italian heritage often highlighted in advertisements for the Bath concerts, which described him as 'Signor Tenducci'.[20] As such, Rauzzini was able to expand the talent of his concert series to include an Italian singer without the expense of attracting one who primarily lived and worked on the Continent.

Tenducci's appointment also meant that Rauzzini did not have to be both leading singer and sole director for the whole series. Indeed, a review published in the *London Courant* on 28 January 1782 revealed that '[Rauzzini] had not exerted himself a single song these two years'.[21] Even during the La Motte-Rauzzini concert series, he was not the only performing singer, but once he was sole director, he often tried to recruit at least two additional singers, if not more. Unfortunately, the financial success of the previous series determined just how many singers he could recruit, and, as will be shown, during his first five years, there were times when he was forced to restrict hires to only one other singer, while taking more of a prominent performance role himself.

Additional concerts that permeated the subscription series schedule were benefits, including one for Rauzzini's keyboard pupil, Jane Mary Guest (*c.*1762–1846), on 6 December 1780.[22] Guest was not listed as a performer for the series, though the same vocalists and instrumentalists all performed for her benefit concert. As she joined the subscription series the very next season, it is possible this benefit was a trial run, testing her abilities to perform in public with the subscription concert players. Evidently, she was already considered a regular of the concerts by March 1781, as she

102 *Bath and Beyond*

was directly mentioned in a suggestive poem by an anonymous 'Gentleman at Bath, to his Friend at Stow':

> For at Bath it is not very easy to tell
> A male from a female, a *Beau* from a *Belle*:
> The from the crown of the head, quite down to the waste,
> Our Beaux, and our Belles, are equally chaste:
> Of what sex the *thing is*, when he meets a *B — n*.
> But a Monday night's ball, is the thing of all things,—
> Except a full concert, when Rauzzini sings;
> Or GUEST, with her *forte piano* soft touches,
> Plays in time to the clapper of canes and of crutches;
> Or when Fischer's sweet Oboe, a Ballad conveys:
> While the whisper goes round, that '*I know what it says* . . .' (emphasis in original)[23]

Guest's appearance was the first example of Rauzzini integrating his students into the concert series, a useful tactic he would continue to build upon throughout his years of directing.

1781–1782 Series: Adjusting the Schedule and Prices

For the 1781–1782 series, though the number of concerts remained the same, with 10 concerts performed throughout the winter season, Rauzzini increased the cost of subscriptions to two guineas for gentlemen and one guinea for ladies.[24] Conversely the non-subscriber tickets remained the same, though Rauzzini made sure to publicise the rules for transferring tickets, noting that a gentleman's ticket could admit two ladies. He also noted that only subscribers would be permitted to attend rehearsals.[25] Rules that dictated one's behaviour at the Upper Assembly Rooms had been commonplace since Richard 'Beau' Nash (1674–1761) served as Master of Ceremonies, so explicit instructions of this kind were not uncommon. However, that did not prevent audiences from misbehaving, with Ian Bradley pointing out that 'Fighting among servants trying to secure the best seats for their employers led eventually to a ban on the reserving of seats'.[26]

The increase in costs could perhaps be explained by the increase in the number of billed leading singers who performed at the first four concerts. Tenducci returned to perform for the series. Joining him were Rauzzini's pupil English singer Maria Storer (*d.*1795) and Italian singer Francesca Corri (*c.*1750–1802), who had moved to Edinburgh in 1771 following her recruitment to perform as leading singer for the Edinburgh Musical Society.[27] Once again, Rauzzini was able to capitalise on an Italian singer already resident in Britain, though she was only able to commit to performing 'for

Rauzzini and the Upper Assembly Rooms 103

the first four nights'.[28] As always, Rauzzini was also listed as a leading singer, but only performed twice in January 1782, the first time at Tenducci's benefit concert, where the second half consisted of a performance of Leonard Leo's *Miserere* arranged by Rauzzini. At this performance, he sang a solo air and a duet with Tenducci from the *Miserere* that 'yielded every thing that superb taste, and sound-judgement, with every power of execution, could possibly produce'.[29] Information regarding previous repertoire selections prior to this concert is extremely limited, so it is unclear if Rauzzini adopted the model of programming miscellaneous selections in the first half followed by a larger sacred work in the second half earlier than December 1781. By the 1782–1783 season, Rauzzini would try to give the concerts more of a structure, by programming large-scale sacred works advertised in advance, though, as this chapter will later show, the venture was not entirely successful.

The second time Rauzzini performed was at a concert on 23 January when Tenducci had, once again, left to perform at the Bach-Abel subscription concert series in London.[30] At this concert, Storer performed one of Rauzzini's compositions that was intended for Tenducci, a sonnet, with the first line 'From place to place forlorn I go'. Despite receiving praise for her performance, with a reviewer noting it was performed 'most enchantingly', she was not mentioned on the title page of the published song.[31] Instead, Tenducci was credited as the singer, having performed it 'with universal applause', an understandable marketing tactic since buyers were often attracted to purchase songs based on the famous singer associated with it.[32]

In addition to the ticket price increase, the season also started earlier, with the first concert taking place on 24 October. The series technically concluded on 2 January 1782, though Rauzzini went on to announce two additional subscription concerts for the 16 and 23 January, with Rice suggesting that these were intended to 'recoup some of the losses' from the principal series of concerts.[33] If this was Rauzzini's plan, then it was a complete failure, with the castrato stating in the *Bath Journal*,

> Mr. RAUZZINI thinks it is his DUTY to signify his grateful Thanks with those subscribers who have express'd their wishes to give up the second and last Subscription CONCERT with a view to lessening the loss which he has suffer'd from the concerts during the course of the season.[34]

The final concert on 23 January did take place, but only because Rauzzini felt he needed to 'fulfil an engagement' promised to the public.[35]

Why did Rauzzini commence and conclude the principal subscription series sooner than previous seasons? There are a few potential factors. Firstly, Corri's time was limited, and secondly, there was a slight overlap between the added subscription concerts that took place on 16 and

104   *Bath and Beyond*

23 January and the first concerts performed in Abel's subscription concert series in London. This was the last concert series Abel directed, following the death of his long-term partner Johann Christian Bach on 1 January 1782. Simply put, it was good planning on Rauzzini's part to schedule his initial run of concerts, so they did not conflict with Abel's series, especially since Tenducci was engaged to sing for both. However, if Rice is correct, and the series was at a financial loss by early January, Rauzzini perhaps felt compelled to add the additional concerts, knowing the final one would take place with himself as the only principal male singer. While these are pragmatic reasons as to why Rauzzini would change aspects of the series, he also experimented with other minor changes, including starting the first three concerts at the slightly later time of 7pm.[36] It is possible the later start time was also to accommodate one of the performers, but Rauzzini continued to experiment with a 7pm start throughout the following season. Perhaps, he thought a slightly later time would better serve his audience.

Rauzzini was faced with several issues that required solutions, while also trying to identify the most effective way of securing more ticket sales. Ultimately, the Season was unsuccessful, forcing Rauzzini to implement further changes ahead of the following season in the hopes of bolstering ticket and subscription sales, and offset the losses of the 1781–1782 series.

1782–1783 Series: Further Adjustments

The 1782–1783 season consisted of eight concerts, commencing on 30 October, and concluding on 1 January.[37] Subscription rates were lowered for gentlemen to one guinea, but raised for ladies, also to one guinea. Despite the subscription cost for ladies and gentlemen being the same, a lady's ticket was only permitted for another lady, while a gentleman's ticket could be transferred to a lady or a gentleman. Non-subscriber tickets were also lowered to 5s., regardless of gender.[38] Such changes suggest that Rauzzini was attempting to capitalise on women attending the concerts. However, toward the end of the season, Rauzzini advertised another pricing structure, stating that 'The Subscription for the above and two remaining concerts will be, for Ladies and Gentlemen, *Half a Guinea* each'.[39] Rauzzini was financially desperate. A review of Guest's benefit published on 24 December commented: 'The disproportion between the goodness of the present season and the last, rendered it impossible for the meeting to be so extremely crowded as it was last year, but it was exceedingly brilliant, and furnished the great ball-room very well'.[40] Even with changes that the reviewer deemed to be improvements, it was not enough to entice some audience members back to the concerts.

Rauzzini and the Upper Assembly Rooms   105

Both Tenducci and Storer returned to perform for the season, with Rauzzini increasing the number of leading singers by the sixth concert. English singer Ann Cantelo (1766–1831) was initially advertised as performing 'for that night only', though she returned to perform at the seventh concert, and at 'Mr Rauzzini's Concert Night' that took place on 24 December.[41] Cantelo was previously apprenticed to Johann Christian Bach, but following his death sought vocal instruction from Rauzzini. Following his typical model for ensuring his students gained experience on the performance platform as well as in the music room, Rauzzini quickly made her one of the leading singers in the subscription concert series. She was his third student to take a leading role in the concerts, following Guest and Storer.

Further changes included concerts commencing at the later start time of 7pm, and Rauzzini publishing some of the larger-scale repertoire he planned to perform. The advertisement for the first subscription concert of the series stated, 'In the course of the Concert will be performed the celebrated Orfeo by Gluck; Amintas, an English Opera, and several Cantatas by the most eminent composers'.[42] The two named operas were deliberately chosen to highlight Tenducci, since he had performed the two title roles previously. Moreover, *Orfeo* was familiar to London audiences, having had its premiere in London in 1770, though the title role was sung by Gaetano Guadagni (1728–92), not Tenducci. He would not perform the role until 1771, when he sang it in Florence.[43] Arias from *Orfeo* had also been performed at London concerts, and in *pasticcio* operas throughout the 1770s and 1780s, with Tenducci then becoming more associated with the opera following the publication of his translated libretto in 1785.[44] He also played the title role of Amintas at Covent Garden in 1769 and Haymarket in May 1770, the latter of which was his benefit concert.[45]

Gluck's *Orfeo* was performed on 13 November at the Upper Assembly Rooms subscription concert series, followed by Johann Christian Bach's *Serenata of Aurora* on 20 November. *Orpheus*, likely Gluck's *Orfeo* since it was 'at the particular desire of the Subscribers', was performed again at the fifth concert on 27 November, with Johann Christian Bach's *Rinaldo and Amida* performed on 4 December and repeated on 18 December at Guest's benefit concert. Cantelo replaced Storer in this concert, performing the role of Armida, alongside Tenducci who sang Rinaldo. *Rinaldo and Armida* perfectly showcased Tenducci, who had already performed the role in 1778 for Signora Balconi's benefit concert, and Cantelo who likely was familiar with the work given that Bach was her former master.[46] A review from 24 December stated that her 'performance . . . proved her to possess very extensive powers, and a voice uncommonly sweet'.[47]

106 *Bath and Beyond*

Storer's absence, reportedly due to ill-health, foreshadowed her departure from Bath in 1782. A notice published in the *Bath Chronicle and Weekly Gazette* that also advertised her final concert prior to leaving the city stated:

> The very ill state of health which Miss Storer has long laboured under, obliging her to try the air of a more southern climate, she flatters herself that her *friends*, sensible of the necessity there is for such a step will honour her on this occasion with their accustomed patronage, trusting at her return she will be the better enabled to gratify the first wish of her heart, in the exertion of her talents for their entertainment (emphasis in original).[48]

A warmer climate would certainly help Storer recover from illness, particularly if it was affecting her voice. The sentiment also aligns with advice Rauzzini gave many of his students, including Anna Selina Storace and Michael Kelly (1762–1826), to whom he recommended they go to Italy to receive further instruction.[49] From the statement, Storer seemed determined to improve her voice and return to Bath, though she ultimately never returned to the British stage. She moved to America where her sisters were already performing, married John Henry (*d.*1794), manager of the Old American Company, and found fame as the 'first prima donna on the American stage'.[50] As such, she is another of Rauzzini's celebrity singers and was his first student to gain international success outside of Europe.

Returning to the programming for the 1782–1783 series, Rauzzini advertised that he would sing one of the named, secondary roles within the larger works, with Tenducci, Storer, and Cantelo performing the leading parts. This was in addition to him conducting the instrumentalists, which he did 'with infinite credit to himself, and satisfaction to the company'.[51] Rice comments on the minor criticism Rauzzini received during his first two seasons as sole director, suggesting this prompted him to take a prominent singing role.[52] While this might be the case, by the 1783–1784 series, he only had the assistance of Cantelo, requiring him to continue both singing and directing. Otherwise, every concert would only have consisted of solo singing by Cantelo and instrumental numbers. Though Rauzzini was compelled by audiences to sing more regularly, his decision might also have been financially influenced.

Despite carefully choosing large-scale repertoire that suited his singers, advertising the works in advance, and performing the most popular works again at the request of his audience, the series was not as successful as Rauzzini had hoped. By the seventh concert, he had returned to a programme of miscellaneous repertoire, and would maintain this structure for the 1783–1784 series.

1783 Series: Rework and Return

Just as the previous season, only eight concerts were performed with the series commencing on 5 November and concluding on 24 December 1783. The exact reason as to why Rauzzini, once again, opted to conclude the series early is unknown. He was not under pressure to avoid conflicting with Abel's concert series, as he had returned to the Continent in 1782.[53] Considering the financial losses Rauzzini incurred in previous seasons, he may have feared further losses by mounting too many concerts. Indeed, he even reduced the number of leading singers to one—Cantelo—in addition to himself, who was usually named as a leading performer. It is telling that this series lacked an international name, but Rauzzini's financial situation restricted his options.

Prices remained the same, only now the cost for subscribers was one guinea, and non-subscriber tickets were 5s., regardless of gender.[54] There was also no clarification regarding the transference of tickets, indicating that ladies and gentlemen could gift tickets to each other and be admitted without issue. The advertisement also noted that for those ladies who wished to sit in the Gallery it had been 'fitted up for their reception', suggesting that the gallery space had undergone some redecoration to make it more comfortable.[55]

Other changes Rauzzini had instigated the previous season were reversed, with the start time of concerts returning to 6.30pm. Also returning was a programme of miscellaneous repertoire. Rauzzini advertised the programme of the first concert in the *Bath Chronicle and Weekly Gazette* in advance of the concert, perhaps as a way of enticing subscribers:

Act I. New Overture, Haydn; Song, Miss Cantelo, Sarti; Concerto Flute, Mr. Decamp; Duetto Miss Cantelo and Mr. Rauzzini; Concerto Violin, Mr Pieltain.

Act II. Overture, la Buona Gigliola, by particular desire; Concerto Piano Forte, Miss Guest; Song, Miss Cantelo, Kozeluck [Koželuch], (accompanied on the Violin by Mr. Pieltain, and on the Piano Forte by Miss Guest) Concerto Oboe, Fischer; Song, (Queen Mary's Lamentation) Miss Cantelo; Full Piece.[56]

There are few details as to exactly what was performed, with Rauzzini rarely noting the titles of instrumental or vocal numbers. What was more crucial was advertising the names of composers, all of whom were living and producing popular new works. This was also perhaps a way of showcasing international connections, as no European singers beyond Rauzzini were able to appear.

Though Haydn did not come to London until 1791, his music was already well known in London, having been performed regularly at the Bach-Abel

108 *Bath and Beyond*

subscription concert series. David Wyn Jones states that 'Haydn's music came to dominate concert life in London where he was, effectively, resident composer *in absentia*'.[57] Opening the series with a Haydn overture likely encouraged audience members to attend. As for the other composers mentioned, Giuseppe Sarti (1729–1802) was a successful Italian composer who composed several operas, sacred, and instrumental works in his lifetime, many of which were performed in London. *Alessandro E Timoteo*, a serious opera first performed in Parma on 6 April 1782, was presented just a couple weeks later at the King's Theatre, London, on 15 April.[58] Czech composer Leopold Koželuch (1747–1818) was a rising star, having succeeded Mozart as court organist at Salzburg in 1781. He would later go on to establish his own publishing house. While his music was not as well known as Sarti in 1783–1784, he went on to work with the important music publisher George Thomson (1757–1851), who produced the popular, multivolume collection *A Select Collection of Original Scottish Airs*, published between 1793 and 1841.[59] As part of this collection, not only was Koželuch given the opportunity to set the works of Robert Burns (1759–1796), but his name also appeared alongside celebrated European composers including Haydn and Ludwig van Beethoven (1770–1827).

Two other pieces were named in the programme: the overture to *La buona figliuola* by Niccolò Piccinni (1728–1800), and *Queen Mary's Lamentation* with the lyrics by Anne Hunter (1742–1841) and music by Tommaso Giordani (*c*.1730–1806).[60] *La buona figliuola* had been performed regularly in London since its premier on 13 March 1770. As such, the overture was a familiar favourite for audiences. *Queen Mary's Lamentation*, a song in the style of a traditional Scottish air, was performed by Tenducci at Abel's final concert series in 1782. The song was published in the same year, and proved popular, being republished many times throughout the 1780s and 1790s. Such repertoire choices proved that Rauzzini was aware of what audiences deemed entertaining and fashionable. He did not entirely rely on miscellaneous repertoire for the whole season, however. For the final concert, he mounted a performance of the ever-popular *Messiah* by Handel, a work that he typically performed for his own benefit. Considering the series ended late in December, it seemed an appropriate seasonal choice to include as part of the principal series.

1784–1785 Series: A Working Formula

By the 1784–1785 season, Rauzzini finally found a formula that appeared to satisfy audiences, insofar as he would repeat the same pricing structure, programming, and number of concerts without significant alteration for many seasons to come. The series consisted of eight concerts, priced at one guinea for subscribers and 5s. for non-subscribers. Rauzzini had requested an alteration to the pricing, though this was denied in an advertisement:

Rauzzini and the Upper Assembly Rooms 109

RAUZZINI having been informed that the alteration he proposed is not agreeable to the Company, takes this method respectfully to acquaint them that his utmost wish is to give general satisfaction; therefore Gentlemen's Tickets will be transferrable to Ladies or Gentlemen as usual.[61]

In previous seasons, Rauzzini had made several alterations to the rules for transferring tickets, and this advert suggests he was still dissatisfied with the process. Regardless, the company had spoken, and previous processes upheld. Throughout his career in Bath, it was regularly commented that Rauzzini organised his concerts with much 'liberality', with William Meyler stating in his *Poetical Amusement on the Journey of Life* 'The liberality of Mr. Rauzzini, in conducting the Bath Concerts, was ever conspicuous—and several seasons the Receipts were inadequate to the expenses'.[62] Such a comment suggests that many felt Rauzzini exercised freedom in selecting the performers and repertoire and, as such, the blame for exceeding his budget was on him, with attempts to raise subscription prices often thwarted.

Cantelo returned to perform for the season alongside Marie Chanu (*d*.1793), who gained more prominence as a British concert singer throughout the 1780s following her marriage to Dieudonné-Pascal Pieltain (1754–1833). Indeed, her future husband held the position of first violinist at the Upper Assembly Rooms subscription concert series.[63] Rauzzini did not publish the programmes in advance of the concerts, but did note by the fourth concert,

Mr. RAUZZINI, anxiously willing to oblige those Ladies and Gentlemen who honor him with their Company at the Concerts most respectfully begs leave to inform them that the First Act this Evening will consist of *Ancient Music only*, the Second as usual.[64]

Every concert thereafter was noted to 'consist of both *Ancient* and *Modern Musick*'.[65] Rauzzini finally managed to identify a programming formula that worked. From this point on, the concerts consisted of both ancient and modern music, typically split into two acts.[66]

While he did not publish the programme for the principal series in advance, the programme for Cantelo's benefit concert on 19 January 1785 provides some insight into the type of repertoire performed. It should be noted, however, that Cantelo did not adopt the ancient-modern programme structure:

Act I: Overture, Haydn. Quartetto, Clarionet, Mr Mahon, [Charles Frederick] Baumgarten. Song, Miss Chanu, [Carl Philipp] Stamitz. Concerto, [Francesco] Germiniani. New Song, Miss Cantelo, Rauzzini. Concerto, Flute, [Tebaldo] Monzani.
Act II. Concerto Violin, Pieltain. Song, Rauzzini, Rauzzini. Sonata, Piano-Forte, Miss Guest, [Muzio] Clementi. Song, Miss Cantelo, Mr. Rauzzini, Handel. Full Piece, Bach.[67]

110　*Bath and Beyond*

Handel and Germiniani (1697–1762) were the only already deceased composers featured in the concert, though both were firm favourites with British audiences. Also featured were two songs composed by Rauzzini, one performed by himself and the other by Cantelo. Rauzzini had grown his reputation as a composer over the last five years, with several of his compositions published in London, and four of his operas staged at the King's Theatre, notably *L'ali d'amore* (staged 1776, 1777, and 1778), *L'eroe cinese* (staged 1782), *Creusa in Delfo* (staged 1783), and *Alina ossia La Regina di Golconda* (staged 1784). As time progressed, more of his song compositions would feature in the concert series, particularly as he engaged more of his students to perform. Rauzzini already had a track record of programming repertoire that would showcase his leading singers at their best. However, as he worked with more students, he made sure to compose new material specifically for them, and programme it in the concert series. As such, he ensured they performed repertoire that was vocally suited to them, while also showcasing himself as a leading, fashionable composer, particularly since he went on to publish much of this repertoire. For example, he published 'The Village Maid: a Favorite Song, Sung by MISS CANTELO with the greatest applause at the CONCERTS, BATH',[68] and while the publication was prepared for the public, and as such, does not provide an exact transcription of Cantelo's performance, the song was very clearly associated with her. A melancholic song about a woman jilted by her lover, Henry, it is not especially difficult. Marked 'Larghetto', the compass of the song is an octave, with simple ornaments and a cadenza, as was the typical style for the period. *The Village Maid* is very similar in style to another song regularly performed by Cantelo, *Auld Robin Gray*. Rauzzini was certainly aware of Cantelo's rendition, having heard her perform *Auld Robin Gray* at a concert in Southampton in 1782 where they were performing together.[69] There were two versions of *Auld Robin Gray* in circulation in the latter half of the eighteenth century. Musical entrepreneur and friend of Rauzzini, Domenico Corri (1746–1825), printed both versions in his 1788 collection *A New & Complete Collection of the Most Favourite Scots Songs*.[70] As such, it is difficult to ascertain the exact version Cantelo performed, though 'New Sett [*sic*] of AULD ROBIN GRAY' seems the most likely, since it is the more melancholic of the two, describing a woman who settled to marry Robin Gray, despite the fact she was in love with a sailor called Jamie, who she thought had died in a shipwreck. Cantelo clearly had a fondness for sorrowful works, even publishing her own song setting, entitled 'Werter's Sonnet', that similarly centred on heartbreak and despair—another example of how Rauzzini's singers expanded their talents beyond singing and Bath.[71]

Rauzzini and the Upper Assembly Rooms 111

1785–1786 Series (and Beyond)

Having established a structure for the series that worked effectively, this series consisted of eight concerts, all beginning at 6.30pm. The pricing structure remained the same as had been in place since the 1782–1783 season. Cantelo returned to sing with Rauzzini, with the advertisement stating: 'Principal Vocal PERFORMERS, Miss CANTELO, Signor RAUZZINI, *etc*'. Cantelo appeared to prove popular enough with audiences that he did not need the draw of international singers to bolster attendance.

The concert structure included mostly modern music in the first half and ancient music in the second, with the first concert programme as advertised:

Act 1. New Overture, Haydn. Rondo, Miss Cantelo, [Giambattista] Martini. Concerto Violin, Pieltain. Duetto, Miss Cantelo and Signor Rauzzini. Concerto Oboe, Mr. Fisher. Chorus, *The Lord shall reign for ever and ever–from Israel in Egypt*. Handel (emphasis in original).
Act II. Selected from Handel's Music. Second Hautboy Concerto. Chorus, *The many rend the Skies*, Alexander's Feast. Song, Sig. Rauzzini, *Pious Orgies*, Judas Maccabeus. First Grand Concerto on the Organ, Miss Guest. Song, Miss Cantelo, *Thou shalt bring them in Israel in Egypt*. Coronation Anthem, *Zadok the Priest*.[72]

The miscellaneous nature of the concerts allowed Rauzzini to feature new compositions, alongside beloved older repertoire, which audiences clearly found more enticing than regular performances of large-scale works. Indeed, Rauzzini demonstrated his confidence in this structure for the concert (and in the abilities of his keyboard student, Jane Guest) by purchasing an organ for the Upper Assembly Rooms, noting that he considered it as 'necessary to do justice to the beauties of Mr Handel's Compositions'.[73] Although the performance of *Messiah* remained a staple, with it frequently performed as a benefit concert for Rauzzini, it was an exception to the now, normal structure of the subscription concerts.

Rauzzini featured his students in the Upper Assembly Rooms subscription concerts from the 1781–1782 series, with both Guest and Cantelo establishing themselves as long-standing performers from 1781 and 1782 onwards. By 1786–1787, two more students, Maria Poole (*c.*1775–1833) and English singer Charles Incledon (1763–1826), joined the roster, with Rauzzini composing repertoire for them to perform. Unfortunately, many of Poole's songs were not specified, but the castrato published several songs composed for Incledon including, *Cynthia, Gentle Anna's Love*, and *The Topsail Fills, the Waving Bark Unmoors*.[74]

112 *Bath and Beyond*

More of Rauzzini's students featured in the concerts throughout his tenure, allowing him to maintain variety in the concerts, and removing the pressure to sing himself. Overall, hiring students was much more cost-effective, since they were already in Bath to obtain lessons from Rauzzini, and they gained valuable performance opportunities by singing in the series. Hiring star singers was riskier and more costly, since they could be tempted to sing elsewhere without the promise of a lucrative fee. Rauzzini had already experienced this with Tenducci, and while there was no apparent animosity between them, Tenducci's absence required changes to be made to the structure of the series that shaped audience attendance. While star singers performed for Rauzzini between 1786 and 1810, he generally became less reliant on recruiting them, and instead built a network of students, current and former, that he could slot into the format and rhythm of the series.

Conclusion

What this chapter demonstrates is that Rauzzini faced a myriad of difficulties when he became sole director of the Upper Assembly Rooms subscription concert series. He had two years of working alongside fellow co-director, La Motte, and much experience as a singer on the Continent and in Britain, but this did not guarantee success for his concert series. Likewise, having had an established concert series in the Upper Assembly Rooms did not mean that Bath residents and visitors would continue supporting it in the long term. Rauzzini had to balance hires, as well as identify a pricing structure, regular date and time slot, and programme repertoire to encourage audience members to support the series. The advertisements for the concerts from 1786 to 1810 reveal a remarkable consistency in his approach to programming. Haydn and Johann Christian Bach regularly featured in the modern music side of the concert (along with his own compositions), while Handel repertoire, a firm favourite with British audiences throughout the eighteenth and nineteenth centuries, dominated the act featuring ancient music. It took Rauzzini five years to identify a workable formula that allowed him to maintain a long-term concert series. As his reputation as a singing master, composer, and musical director grew, he unified his skillset, drawing on his network of singers and former students, many of whom would become international stars, to perform for him. As such, Rauzzini established the Upper Assembly Rooms subscription concert series as a desirable and fundamental aspect of Bath life for the next 25 years.

Notes

1 *Bath Chronicle and Weekly Gazette*, October 25, 1810.
2 Brianna E. Robertson-Kirkland, *Venanzio Rauzzini and the Birth of a New Style in English Singing Scandalous Lessons* (Abingdon: Routledge, 2022), 45.

3 Paul F. Rice, *Venanzio Rauzzini in Britain: Castrato, Composer, and Cultural Leader* (New York: University of Rochester Press, 2015), 204.

4 Rice, *Venanzio Rauzzini in Britain*, 212–21.

5 In the *Bath Chronicle and Weekly Gazette* on October 9, 1777, an advertisement outlines the typical, weekly schedule for the Upper Assembly Rooms, stating: 'The First Subscription Ball for the Winter Season, at the New Assembly Rooms, will be on Monday the 13th of October. | And the First Cotillon Ball at the New Rooms on Thursday 17th of October. | The First Subscription Concert, under the direction of Mr. Linley, on Wednesday the 29th of October'.

6 Paul Rice, "Venanzio Rauzzini: An Italian Musician in Britain," *Lumen* xxxiii (2014): 101–21.

7 David Wyn Jones, *The Life of Haydn* (Cambridge: Cambridge University Press, 2009), 125.

8 Rice, "Venanzio Rauzzini: An Italian Musician in Britain"; Rice, *Venanzio Rauzzini in Britain*; Kenneth James, "Concert Life in Eighteenth-Century Bath" (PhD diss., Royal Holloway, University of London, 1987); Kenneth James, "Venanzio Rauzzini and the Search for Musical Perfection," *Bath History* iii (1990): 90–114; Peter Borsay, "Concert Topography and Provincial Towns in Eighteenth-Century England," in *Concert Life in Eighteenth-Century Britain*, ed. Susan Wollenberg and Simon McVeigh (Abingdon: Routledge, 2017), 35–50.

9 Rice, "Venanzio Rauzzini: An Italian Musician in Britain," 110.

10 *Bath Chronicle and Weekly Gazette*, December 11, 1777.

11 *The Morning Chronicle*, November 15, 1777.

12 Rice, *Venanzio Rauzzini in Britain*, 79.

13 *Bath Chronicle and Weekly Gazette*, January 14, 1779.

14 *Bath Chronicle and Weekly Gazette*, January 6, 1780.

15 *Bath Chronicle and Weekly Gazette*, November 4, 1779.

16 *Bath Chronicle and Weekly Gazette*, January 7, 1779.

17 Rice, *Venanzio Rauzzini in Britain*, 85.

18 The original date of the concert (January 24) was advertised in the *Bath Chronicle and Weekly Gazette*, on January 18, 1781, with the new date (January 27) advertised in the *Bath Chronicle and Weekly Gazette,* January 25, 1781.

19 Cheryll Duncan, "'A Debt Contracted in Italy': Ferdinando Tenducci in a London Court and Prison," *Early Music* xlii (2014): 220–21.

20 *Bath Journal,* December 20, 1780; *Bath Chronicle and Weekly Gazette*, December 20, 1781; *Bath Journal,* December 23, 1783.

21 *London Courant Westminster Chronicle and Daily Advertiser*, January 28, 1782.

22 *Bath Chronicle and Weekly Gazette*, November 30, 1780.

23 *Morning Post and Daily Advertiser*, March 10, 1781.

24 *Bath Chronicle and Weekly Gazette*, November 1, 1781.

25 *Bath Chronicle and Weekly Gazette*, November 1, 1781.

26 Ian Bradley, *Water Music: Making Music in the Spas of Europe and North America* (Oxford: Oxford University Press, 2010), 43.

27 Brianna E. Robertson-Kirkland, "Rediscovering Francesca Corri née Bacchelli (*c.*1750–1802)," in *Adventurous Wives,* ed. Alison Daniell and Kim Simpson (Manchester, Forthcoming).

28 Francesca Corri was wrongfully billed as Miss Corri, who strictly speaking was her daughter, Sophia. An advertisement published on November 15, 1781, confirmed the performer was, in fact, Mrs Corri, and not her daughter who, at this point, was only six years old, and likely would have been billed as a child performer had she been at Bath. *Bath Chronicle and Weekly Gazette*, November 1, 1781.

114 Bath and Beyond

29 *Morning Herald and Daily Advertiser*, December 28, 1781.
30 *London Courant*, January 23, 1782.
31 *London Courant Westminster Chronicle and Daily Advertiser,* January 28, 1782.
32 Venanzio Rauzzini, *From Place to Place Forlorn I Go: A Favorite Rondeau Sung with Universal Applause at the Concert at Bath by Mr. Tenducci* (1785).
33 Rice, *Venanzio Rauzzini in Britain*, 214.
34 *Bath Journal*, January 21, 1782.
35 *Bath Journal*, January 21, 1782.
36 *Bath Chronicle and Weekly Gazette*, November 1, 1781. The concerts reverted to the 6.30 pm start time by the fourth concert.
37 *Bath Chronicle and Weekly Gazette*, October 31, 1782; *Bath Chronicle and Weekly Gazette*, December 19, 1782.
38 *Bath Chronicle and Weekly Gazette*, October 31, 1782.
39 *Bath Chronicle and Weekly Gazette*, December 5, 1782.
40 *General Advertiser and Morning Intelligencer,* December 24, 1782.
41 *Bath Chronicle and Weekly Gazette*, December 12, 1782; *Bath Chronicle and Weekly Gazette,* December 19, 1782.
42 *Bath Chronicle and Weekly Gazette*, October 31, 1782.
43 Alfred Loewenberg, "Gluck's 'Orfeo' on the Stage: With Some Notes on Other Orpheus Operas," *The Musical Quarterly* xxvi (1940): 327.
44 William Weber, *The Rise of Musical Classics in Eighteenth-Century England: A Study in Canon, Ritual, and Ideology* (Oxford: Oxford University Press, 1992), 168–97.
45 London Stage Database [Online], "15 December 1769," accessed August 28, 2023, https://londonstagedatabase.uoregon.edu/event.php?id=35041; London Stage Database [Online], "3 May 1770," accessed August 28, 2023, https://londonstagedatabase.uoregon.edu/event.php?id=35312.
46 C. B. Oldman, "Mozart's Scena for Tenducci," *Music & Letters* xlii (1961): 47.
47 *Parker's General Advertiser and Morning Intelligencer*, December 24, 1782.
48 *Bath Chronicle and Weekly Gazette*, March 27, 1783.
49 Robertson-Kirkland, *Venanzio Rauzzini*, 35, 52.
50 Philip H. Highfill, Kalman A. Burnim, Edward A. Langhans, eds., *A Biographical Dictionary of Actors, Actresses, Musicians, Dancers, Managers & Other Stage Personnel in London, 1660–1800*, 16 vols. (Southern Illinois University Press, 1984), ix, 274.
51 *Parker's General Advertiser and Morning Intelligencer*, December 24, 1782.
52 Rice, *Venanzio Rauzzini in Britain,* 217.
53 Murray Charters, "Abel in London," *The Musical Times* cxiv (1973): 1225.
54 *Bath Chronicle and Weekly Gazette*, November 13, 1783.
55 *Bath Chronicle and Weekly Gazette*, November 13, 1783.
56 *Bath Chronicle and Weekly Gazette*, October 30, 1783.
57 Jones, *The Life of Haydn*, 126.
58 London Stage Database [Online], "15 April 1800," accessed August 28, 2023, https://londonstagedatabase.uoregon.edu/event.php?id=52392.
59 George Thomson, *A Select Collection of Original Scottish Airs* (1793–1841).
60 Caroline Grigson, *The Life and Poems of Anne Hunter: Haydn's Tuneful Voice* (Liverpool: Liverpool University Press, 2009), 37.
61 *Bath Chronicle and Weekly Gazette*, November 4, 1784.
62 William Meyler, *Poetical Amusement on the Journey of Life* (1806), 98. 'Liberality' was used in a similar vein by Alexander Stephens, *Public Characters*, 10 vols. (1799), ii, 502; *The Monthly Mirror*, 22 vols. (1803), xvi, 7; *The Improved Bath Guide* (Bath, 1809), 65.

Rauzzini and the Upper Assembly Rooms 115

63 *Bath Chronicle and Weekly Gazette*, November 18, 1784.
64 *Bath Chronicle and Weekly Gazette,* December 2, 1784.
65 *Bath Chronicle and Weekly Gazette,* December 9, 1784; *Bath Chronicle and Weekly Gazette,* December 16, 1784; *Bath Chronicle and Weekly Gazette,* December 23, 1784; *Bath Chronicle and Weekly Gazette,* December 30, 1784; *Bath Chronicle and Weekly Gazette,* January 6, 1785.
66 Rice, *Venanzio Rauzzini in Britain,* 287–353, Appendix A.
67 *Bath Chronicle and Weekly Gazette,* January 13, 1785.
68 Venanzio Rauzzini, *The Village Maid: A Favorite Song Sung by Miss Cantelo with the Greatest Applause at the Concerts, Bath* (1788).
69 *Salisbury and Winchester Journal,* September 2, 1782.
70 Domenico Corri, *A New & Complete Collection of the Most Favourite Scots Songs, Including a Few English & Irish with Proper Graces and Ornaments* (Edinburgh, 1788), 7–8.
71 Ann Cantelo, *Werter's Sonnet* (c.1800).
72 *Bath Chronicle and Weekly Gazette,* November 10, 1785.
73 *Bath Chronicle and Weekly Gazette,* November 3, 1785.
74 Venanzio Rauzzini, *Cynthia* (c.1790); Venanzio Rauzzini, *Gentle Anna's Love* (c.1790); Venanzio Rauzzini, *The Topsail Fills the Waving Bark Unmoors: A Favorite Song Sung by Mr Incledon* (c.1790).

Selected Bibliography

Borsay, Peter. "Concert Topography and Provincial Towns in Eighteenth-Century England." In *Concert Life in Eighteenth-Century Britain,* edited by Susan Wollenberg and Simon McVeigh, 35–50. Abingdon: Routledge, 2017.

Grigson, Caroline. *The Life and Poems of Anne Hunter: Haydn's Tuneful Voice.* Liverpool, Liverpool University Press, 2009.

Highfill, Philip H., Kalman A. Burnim, and Edward A. Langhans. *A Biographical Dictionary of Actors, Actresses, Musicians, Dancers, Managers & Other Stage Personnel in London, 1660–1800.* Southern Illinois University Press, 1984.

James, Kenneth. "Venanzio Rauzzini and the Search for Musical Perfection." *Bath History* 3 (1990): 90–114.

James, Kenneth. "Concert Life in Eighteenth-Century Bath." PhD diss., Royal Holloway, University of London, 1987.

Jones, David Wyn. *The Life of Haydn.* Cambridge: Cambridge University Press, 2009.

Rice, Paul F. *Venanzio Rauzzini in Britain: Castrato, Composer, and Cultural Leader.* New York: University of Rochester Press, 2015.

Rice, Paul F. "Venanzio Rauzzini: An Italian Musician in Britain." *Lumen* 33 (2014). https://doi.org/10.7202/1026567ar.

Robertson-Kirkland, Brianna E. *Venanzio Rauzzini and the Birth of a New Style in English Singing: Scandalous Lessons.* Abingdon: Routledge, 2022.

7 Two Kingdoms

Masters of Ceremonies at Bath and Tunbridge Wells, 1735–*c*.1801

Rachael Johnson

Masters of Ceremonies were charismatic, flamboyant, and often peculiar characters. Appointed during the eighteenth and nineteenth centuries to lead the social life of England's fashionable spas and seaside resorts, they hosted assemblies, made introductions, welcomed visitors on arrival, and guided newcomers in the conventions of polite sociability. The role of Master of Ceremonies was forged primarily by Richard 'Beau' Nash, Bath's second and most famous post-holder, who ruled over society at the spa for more than 56 years. Nash, Peter Borsay argues, was unique in Bath's history, embodying 'both Bath's virtue and its vices', becoming the 'symbol of what the place stood for'.[1] Through the introduction of a series of social rules Nash guided visitors' behaviour at the spa, teaching them how to conduct themselves in an arena in which royalty, aristocracy, and gentry came together in the pursuit of leisure. Nash's rules were so successful that they were implemented at spas across the country, becoming integral to the leisure lives of the Georgian elite.

This chapter will explore one of the lesser known aspects of Nash's reign and legacy. In 1735, while continuing to act as Master of Ceremonies at Bath, Nash proclaimed himself Master of Ceremonies at the spa's leading competitor, Tunbridge Wells. With Bath's winter season firmly established, Nash was free to spend the summer months at Tunbridge Wells, presiding over a season that ran between May and October. Bath and Tunbridge Wells, spas which had competed for elite patronage, were now linked; visitors were encouraged to move between resorts at the change of the season, rather than choose between them. After Nash's death in 1761, Bath and Tunbridge Wells continued to share a Master of Ceremonies: Jacques Collett from 1761 until 1763, then Samuel Derrick until his death in 1769. The connection was temporarily broken in 1769, following the notorious 'Bath Contest'. The Contest's victor, William Wade, chose to sever the link with Tunbridge Wells, instead choosing Brighton, the newly fashionable seaside destination of the elite, as his summer seat. The connection between Bath and Tunbridge Wells was restored, for the final time, by Richard

DOI: 10.4324/9781003393856-7

Two Kingdoms 117

Tyson, who became Master of Ceremonies at both spas in 1780. By the time Tyson retired from Tunbridge Wells in 1801 (he would continue at the Upper Assembly Rooms in Bath until 1805), the Kentish spa was a very different place to that which Nash had first annexed in 1735; eclipsed by the rapidly expanding seaside resorts, Tunbridge Wells had become a centre for genteel residence and would soon have no need for a Master of Ceremonies.

Outside of the Tunbridge Wells guidebooks, the connection between two of Georgian England's leading watering places has been largely overlooked, by both contemporary Bath commentators and modern-day historians. This chapter explores the effect of a shared Master of Ceremonies on Bath and Tunbridge Wells throughout the eighteenth century, considering the careers of individual post-holders and their influence on the social life of each spa. It argues that, while the connection added to the pockets and prestige of individual Masters of Ceremonies, it did not benefit the spas themselves. At Bath, as an examination of the Bath Contest will show, visitors disliked having to share their Master of Ceremonies. At Tunbridge Wells, Nash's annexation proved damaging to the smaller Kentish spa, robbing it of its autonomy and foisting on it a series of somewhat inadequate social rulers. With their attentions focused firmly on Bath, Nash's successors neglected their second kingdom, presiding over its demise as a fashionable watering place.

Beau Nash at Bath

Richard Nash (1674–1761) became Bath's Master of Ceremonies in 1705 after the first post-holder, Captain Webster, was killed in a duel.[2] A flamboyant and charismatic man, Nash was able to mould the role of Master of Ceremonies into one which allowed him to lead, rather than merely organise, the company's amusements. This started with his ostentatious personal appearance, which was designed to stand out in a crowd. Contemporary portraits show him wearing embroidered waistcoats, a lace cravat, and his signature large, white tricorne hat, as seen in his portrait by William Hoare, where it currently hangs in the Pump Rooms. Further adding to this display, Nash was escorted by musicians and driven through town in a carriage drawn by six grey horses. As Pierce Egan noted in 1819, Nash's 'considerable affectation of splendour in his dress and equipage' had been designed to have 'a powerful and visible effect on the largest part of mankind'.[3] His 'excess' of dress, as Peter M. Briggs argues, added to the theatricality of resort life, with Nash as an 'unintentional caricaturist' who legitimated the 'vanities and follies of those around him'.[4]

In the assembly rooms, Nash's power was absolute. After having advertised a ball in the local newspapers and issued tickets, he welcomed

118   *Bath and Beyond*

guests, forbidding entrance to those deemed not of suitable rank, made introductions, and organised the evening's entertainments. In 1742, Nash introduced a set of Rules, 'for the better Government of the Company of the City'.[5] Published in guidebooks and posted prominently in public spaces, these rules, which were compiled with the 'unanimous Consent' of the 'People of Rank and Fashion', governed behaviour and encouraged harmonious relations between visitors. In part, Nash's Rules spoke to the practical management of a busy leisure venue; at the end of a ball, for example, 'Ladies' were exhorted to 'appoint a time for their Footmens [*sic*] . . . to wait on them Home', presumably to prevent crowds jamming up the streets.[6] However most of the Rules guided the minutiae of visitors' interactions. To encourage cohesion, the privileges of rank were not to be insisted upon, with Nash telling visitors first that 'a Visit of Ceremony at coming to BATH, and another at going away, is all that is expected or desired by Ladies of Quality and Fashion—except Impertinents', and later that 'no Gentleman or Lady take it ill that another Dances before them'. Instead, precedence was given to those of marriageable age, with 'Elder Ladies and Children' encouraged to 'be contented with a Second Bench at the Ball'.[7] Nash also attempted to dissuade social rivalries and gossip, which must have been endemic within such a close-knit community, asking that 'no Person take it ill that any one goes to another's Play, or Breakfast, and not to theirs', and warning that 'all Whisperers of Lies and Scandal [would] be taken for their Authors'.[8] Finally, Nash sought to maintain social standards, ordering that 'no Gentleman give his Tickets for the Balls to any but Gentlewomen'.[9]

When writers in the later eighteenth century looked back at Nash's reign as Master of Ceremonies, they saw the implementation of these rules as the cornerstone of his transformation of spa society. In his 1762 biography of Nash, for example, Oliver Goldsmith suggests that, however 'trifling' Nash's life 'may appear to the inattentive . . . the whole kingdom by degrees became more refined by lessons originally derived from him'.[10] Historical interpretations of Nash's importance, however, are mixed. To Peter Briggs, Nash was 'an epitome of a certain moment and milieu in British social history and . . . a focus of . . . conflicting cultural energies'.[11] Graham Davis and Penny Bonsall, meanwhile, argue that 'his role has been greatly exaggerated', while John Eglin 'raises questions about the nature of his contribution, which to the archivally adapted eye appears insubstantial and insignificant' when compared with other key figures in Bath's history, such as Ralph Allen, John Wood, and Jane Austen.[12] Peter Borsay, by contrast, argues that Nash was constructed as a heroic figure who attained 'semi-fictional status' in his own lifetime.[13] Used by contemporaries and subsequent generations for their own ends, he suggests, Nash became an 'evolving myth' used to 'encapsulate' the 'Georgian image of Bath'.[14]

Early Eighteenth-Century Tunbridge Wells

Nash most likely set his sights on Tunbridge Wells in the 1720s, when the relatively small Kentish spa competed with Bath for the patronage of the rich and famous. Having risen to prominence as a courtiers' spa after the Restoration in 1660, Tunbridge Wells was thriving in the early eighteenth century as a centre for fashionable leisure and pleasure. But although the two resorts offered a similar set of social, cultural, and medical facilities, Tunbridge Wells had a very different nature to Bath. When the Tunbridge Wells waters had been discovered in 1606, there was no development around the site of the spring and the nearest town, Tonbridge, was five miles away. Tunbridge Wells thus grew as a new town, responding directly to the demands of its leisured visitors. While Bath began building the grand squares, parades, and crescents for which it became famous, Tunbridge Wells cultivated a distinct rural charm. Indeed, in 1779 Hester Thrale criticised the spa's lack of architectural unity, commenting that the houses were 'scattered about in a strange wild manner, and look as if they had been dropt [*sic*] where they stand by accident, for they formed neither streets nor squares, but seem strewed promiscuously'.[15]

In a 1718 print (Figure 7.1), which shows a bird's eye view of the spa, the triangular structure housing the waters in the centre is apparent. Behind and to the right of this is the chapel of King Charles the Martyr. Leading down from the waters are the Upper and Lower Walks, otherwise known as the 'Pantiles'. They were lined by a covered portico which gave visitors shelter from the elements as they browsed in the book and toy shops; met for refreshments in the tea rooms or coffee houses; and shopped for food, clothes, and trinkets. In the middle of the Walks, on the right-hand side, were the assembly rooms. Visitors' lodgings were built on the four hills surrounding the centre. Notably, the spa had no organisational authority to match the Bath Corporation; indeed, sitting as it did on the boundary between three parishes, Tunbridge Wells developed without the oversight of a governing body.

Nash first visited Tunbridge Wells in 1721 when, on the advice of his Bath physician Dr Pellet, he went to the spa to take the air, though accounts differ over whether his loyalty to Bath actually permitted him to drink the waters. Writers in later eighteenth-century Tunbridge Wells constructed a triumphal narrative of Nash's influence at the spa and its links with Bath. This was led by Thomas Benge Burr, the spa's first historian, who painted a bleak picture of resort society at the beginning of the eighteenth century:

> The company, thus assembled, formed no general society. The amusements of the gentry were few, confined and selfish. The great brought with them all the haughtiness of nobility, and knew not how to let

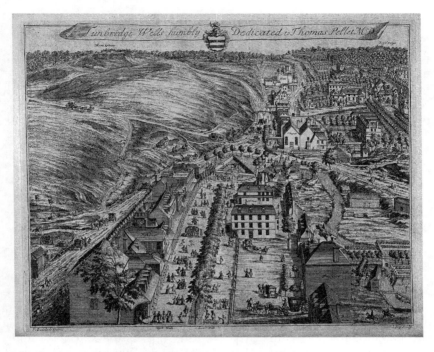

Figure 7.1 J. Badslade, *Tunbridge Wells, Kent: bird's eye view*, undated, etching with engraving, 35.3 × 43.3 cm, Wellcome Collection, 22970i. Courtesy of the Wellcome Collection.

themselves down with grace. In short, delicacy, politeness, and elegant pleasures, were then but just budding forth from amidst the rubbish of Gothic barbarism, and, till these were grown to such a height as to be discernible among us, Tunbridge-Wells was not esteemed a place of pleasure, in which the people of fashion might depend upon being agreeably amused.[16]

Mimicking Oliver Goldsmith, Burr claimed that Nash instigated a transformation. 'Tunbridge-Wells, in common with Bath', he writes, 'owes the present agreeable and judicious regularity of its amusements, to the skilful assiduity of the celebrated Mr Nash'. It was he 'who first taught the people of fashion how to buy their pleasures, and to procure that ease and felicity they sought for, without diminishing the happiness of others'.[17] There is evidence, however, that Nash's annexation of Tunbridge Wells was not welcomed by either residents or visitors. Indeed, it seems that the spa successfully held off Nash for many years.

Prior to Nash, social life at the spa had been run by Bell Causey, one of Tunbridge Wells's most elusive and intriguing figures. Causey ran resort society from the early 1720s until her death in 1734.[18] Historical evidence for her tenure is scant, being drawn primarily from the *Tunbridge Wells Guide*, published by J. Sprange in 1780. The guidebook describes Causey as a 'fine but very large woman' who 'presented as absolute governess at Tunbridge Wells'. She 'directed the company in all their pleasures and amusements,—raised subscriptions for persons in distress, [and] was by a set of geniuses and gamblers allowed two guineas a day to conduct their rooms'.[19] Causey was not an appointed Master of Ceremonies; instead her role, apparently self-appointed, was organisational and opportunistic, drawing on the increasing need to manage the company's entertainments but also exploiting the absence of a governing authority (such as the Bath Corporation) that held the power to make an official appointment.[20]

Later eighteenth-century sources adopt a derogatory tone towards Causey. Instead of presenting Causey's methods as those of a polished, polite social actor, the *Tunbridge Wells Guide* states that 'it was Bell's constant custom to place herself at the top of the steps leading to the Walks, and as the company came from chapel, with her apron spread in both hands, hustle them as they do chickens, to any place, and for any purpose she wanted them for'. The image this concocts is more farmer's wife than Master of Ceremonies. More damning is the *Guide's* opening claim that Causey 'was extremely well known in those days, for attending with her nymphs at the Ring in Hyde-Park, with oranges, nosegays, &c'. This mention of 'nymphs' and orange sellers—a term often used to refer to sex workers—slanders Causey's reputation, implying that outside of the spa season she acted as a brothel-house madam. This depiction is supported by the limited extant sources on Causey, as Sophie Vasset has explored. Most notably, in the *Tunbrigialia* of 1722, a poem 'On B—C' suggests that Causey 'is a go-between at best, a Madam at worst', 'Full many a Maid/Has she lur'd by her Trade/And broke many a Conjugal League'.[21]

Despite these accusations of depravity (it is hard to say with any certainty whether they are true, exaggerated, or entirely fabricated), Causey successfully led the visiting company at Tunbridge Wells for over a decade. Nash's appearance at the first ball of the 1721 season must have been seen as a challenge to Causey's authority, but it seems that Causey was a formidable opponent. According to *The Tunbridge Wells Guide* of 1780, her influence at Tunbridge Wells was so great that 'she would not suffer the great *Beau Nash* to have any power there while she lived, and absolutely kept him from the place till she died'.[22] It was no mean feat for Causey to resist Bath's Master of Ceremonies at the height of his powers. Indeed, the fact that Causey, a woman who did not come from a genteel background, was able to stand up to Nash shows that she must have had significant

122   *Bath and Beyond*

support from Tunbridge Wells's visitors. It may also indicate a level of resistance from the visiting company to Bath's influence; might they have wanted to retain the spa's independence and culture from hostile takeover? If so, this resistance was doomed to fail. When Causey died in 1735, Nash triumphantly stepped in to take her place, arriving into Tunbridge Wells, as Goldsmith reports, 'in a post-chariot and six greys, with out-riders, footmen, *French* horns, and every other appendage of expensive parade'.[23] Whereas at Bath Nash had welcomed visitors with a ringing of the bells, at Tunbridge, it seems, Nash awarded himself a fanfare.

Nash's Second Kingdom

Nash, however, was never so great a man at Tunbridge Wells as he had been at Bath. Older, and lacking the energy of his early years, Nash left the actual day-to-day running of the spa to a deputy, Sarah Porter.[24] Described as 'Queen of the Touters', Porter was appointed by Nash to collect subscriptions from spa visitors.[25] Similar to Causey, Porter appears primarily in Sprange's guidebook of 1780, and supposedly shared many characteristics with her predecessor. Unlike the Master of Ceremonies, Porter seemingly made no claims to gentility, eschewing polite conventions in her interactions with the visiting company. Instead, Sprange's guide describes her as a formidable woman with a 'shrewd memory', who would follow visitors around the assembly rooms until they paid their subscriptions, a method which 'made many of them often very angry'.[26] Though Porter's approach may not have endeared her to visitors (Sprange reports that younger guests 'would often teize [*sic*] her'), it must have been effective, for she remained in post until after Nash's death.[27]

Tunbridge Wells is remarkable, therefore, for being governed primarily by women for around 40 years. Though Porter's authority derived from Nash, both she and Causey effectively managed the practicalities of spa life, using very different techniques from those of official Masters of Ceremonies. Their success testifies to the unique character of Tunbridge Wells; though it now shared a social leader with Bath and advertised its polite credentials, its visiting company continued to accept the directions of a non-genteel woman.

With the day-to-day running of the spa in Porter's safe hands, Nash focused his energies on Tunbridge Wells's famous gaming tables, which were, mostly likely, a significant part of his interest in the spa. Gambling was one of the great passions of the Georgian era. Across the country, vast sums were lost and won on lotteries, betting, and cards, and it was not uncommon for thousands of pounds to be lost in a single night. As Donna Andrew explores, gaming was 'inextricably intertwined with . . .

Two Kingdoms 123

sociability', which helped to make it 'not only the most prevalent but also the most dangerous of the vices'.[28] It also made it particularly well suited to the resort environment. Indeed, gaming was built into the fabric of resort life. Card assemblies were held twice weekly in the assembly rooms at Bath, ensuring that wins and losses at tables were a constant topic of conversation between visitors. Elizabeth Montagu complained of Bath society that 'How dy'e do? is all one hears in the morning, and What is trumps? in the afternoon'.[29] Guidebooks often cautioned visitors of the dangers of the conmen, who preyed on unsuspecting spa-goers, with gamesters and 'sharpers' emerging as stock characters in resort literature.

Goldsmith describes Nash as a talented gamester, suggesting that it was 'by gaming alone . . . [that] he kept up so very genteel an appearance'.[30] Tunbridge Wells, indeed, was well known for its gaming tables. As Thomas Benge Burr described in his 1766 guidebook, 'youth and age, deformity and beauty' joined together to play at 'cards and all sorts of lawful gaming . . . in the great rooms, which are supplied with a proper number of tables, and all necessary accommodations'.[31] Yet Nash's association with the Tunbridge Wells gaming tables would end in disaster. When, in 1739, an Act was passed banning some of the elite's most popular games, gamblers across the country tried to circumvent the rules by devising new ones. At Tunbridge Wells, a man named Cook invented 'Even and Odd' or 'EO', a form of roulette in which letters were substituted for the banned numbers.[32] Nash, seeing a potentially lucrative opportunity, made a deal with Cook and the assembly rooms owner to take a share of the profits. When the game proved successful at Tunbridge Wells, he then brought it to Bath under a similar deal. Nash, however, soon found that his new business associates could not be trusted and, suspecting them of not giving him his true share of the profits, took them to court. This proved a serious mistake. In a devastating move, the courts non-suited him (meaning that his case was dropped), fined one of the Bath proprietors £500 and, in 1748, ruled all play illegal and that no houses could be kept for gambling.[33]

Humiliated and with a main source of his income removed, Nash's finances never recovered. Neither, really, did those of Tunbridge Wells. Whereas at the beginning of the eighteenth century, Tunbridge Wells was one of the country's most fashionable resorts, competing with Bath for the patronage of the fashionable elite, by the time Nash died Goldsmith described the Kentish spa not as Bath's equal, but its 'colony'.[34] Though the spa's literature claims that Nash instigated a positive, polite transformation, this appears unfounded. If, at the beginning of the 1720s, the visiting company and local businesses had indeed supported Bell Causey in preference of Nash, it seems that they had been right to do so.

124   *Bath and Beyond*

Nash's Successors

After Nash died in 1761, Bath and Tunbridge Wells continued to share a Master of Ceremonies. Initially, the connection seems to have continued almost as a matter of course, with Jacques Collet, Nash's deputy, taking up the position in 1761, followed by Samuel Derrick from 1763 to 1769. This arrangement placed the balance of power firmly with Bath. It was at Bath that Collet and Derrick were offered the position of Master of Ceremonies; their appointments were discussed in Bath's assembly rooms and debated in its newspapers.[35] The fact that both Nash's death and Collet's resignation happened during Bath's season exacerbated this; outside of its summer season, there was no real visiting company at Tunbridge Wells to enter an opinion, no central governing organisation to promote the views of its tradespeople, and no newspaper within which the appointment might be debated. Both men, it seems, appeared at Tunbridge Wells at the beginning of the summer, their leadership a *fait accompli*.

Derrick was an unlikely choice for Master of Ceremonies. Born in Dublin, Derrick had been apprenticed to a linen draper before running away to London to seek fame as an actor. Having failed to make his name on the stage, directly before his appointment at Bath, Derrick tried to make a living as a literary man. Scandalously, his greatest success came from his anonymous editorship of *Harris's List of Covent Garden Ladies*, a guide to London's prostitutes that was first published in 1757 and updated throughout the second half of the eighteenth century. Working with Jack Harris, 'the undisputed "Pimp General of all England"', Derrick produced a book which offered 'an exact description of the most celebrated ladies of pleasure to frequent Covent-Garden, and other parts of this metropolis'.[36] With this publication, Derrick was, as Hallie Rubenhold notes, 'skirting the boundaries of complete social disgrace' and in 1762 he relinquished his position as editor.[37] On his appointment as Master of Ceremonies, Derrick proceeded to live a double life and seemed 'determined to establish himself once and for all in the eyes of society as a man of importance and gentility', aiming to 'reset his character and invent a public persona flawless in his knowledge of propriety'.[38] Nonetheless, Derrick's history threatened the reputation of both Bath and Tunbridge Wells and, while new acquaintances may have been convinced, those who knew him apparently 'saw through the transparency of his charade and found it hilarious'.[39]

Derrick used his position as Master of Ceremonies as a launchpad for his literary efforts, publishing in 1767 two volumes of *Letters Written from Leverpoole, Chester, Corke, the Lake of Killarney, Dublin, Tunbridge-Wells, and Bath*. Derrick's description of Bath is exactly what you would expect from its Master of Ceremonies. Bath, he writes, 'is undoubtedly one of the most elegant, pleasant, and convenient spots in

Europe; for you may, in a quarter of an hour, change the most romantic, solitary scene, into croud [*sic*], bustle, splendour, music, dancing, and various amusements'.[40] His account of Tunbridge Wells, however, is mixed. Publishing letters he supposedly wrote in 1762, the year before becoming the spa's Master of Ceremonies, Derrick described his experience of visiting Tunbridge Wells during a bout of ill-health. Of the visiting company, Derrick wrote positively:

> Few places are pleasanter for a couple of months than Tunbridge-Wells. You are here with the most elegant company in Europe, on the easiest terms; and you need be at no loss for a party of Whist or Quadrille with respectable personages, at any price, from a shilling to a guinea to a corner.[41]

Much of his account offered the transparent advertisements that one might expect from the spa's social leader. Yet Derrick's account of Tunbridge Wells was interspersed with derision; he criticised the cost of amenities, quality of provisions, the roads, the touters, musicians, and even the beer. Derrick particularly condemned ironically, given his own literary aspirations, the work of the Tunbridge Wells's water poets, those visitors who traditionally composed verses in honour of the 'beauties' of the walks. 'What they want in wit', he wrote, 'they make up in gross abuse, and bad poetry'.[42] Notably, as author Derrick described himself 'Master of the Ceremonies at BATH', his connection with Tunbridge Wells seemingly dropped.[43]

There are hints, especially after his death, that Derrick had not been popular at Tunbridge Wells. Certainly, historians have seen Derrick's time there as Master of Ceremonies as being of little importance; indeed, he is entirely absent from C.W. Chalklin's otherwise comprehensive study of the spa.[44] Alan Savidge judged him to have been a 'little man, lacking in social presence or dignity, too eager to please' and the 'butt of wites' at Bath, suggesting that 'Nash must have turned in his grave'.[45] Phyllis Hembry likewise summarised him as '"an insignificant puppy" of literary pretensions who was better received at Bath than at Tunbridge Wells, which took umbrage when he attempted to become MC at Brighton'.[46] Though the extant source material is frustratingly silent, it is certainly possible that Derrick fell into a dispute with some of the spa's inhabitants. He was a vain man, who was convinced of his own importance and talents. His private correspondence from earlier in the century shows that this humour could be misjudged, even among his closest friends. It may even be the case that some of the spa's inhabitants discovered Derrick's salacious past, and thus resented his position as *arbiter elegantiarum*. What is clear, however, from what followed Derrick's death, is that his

126 *Bath and Beyond*

failure to unite Bath and Tunbridge Wells would quickly lead to the connection between them being broken.

The Bath Contest

The Bath Contest was a heated and unsavoury dispute which broke out between competing candidates for the post of Master of Ceremonies after Derrick's demise. The Contest led to the connection between Bath and Tunbridge Wells being severed, with the ultimate successor, Captain William Wade, breaking with tradition and choosing Brighton, the new favourite destination of the fashionable elite, as his summer seat. The campaigns of the competing candidates show that Bath's visitors did not appreciate having to share the attention of their Master of Ceremonies, with fealty to Bath emerging as a manifesto promise.

After Derrick's death, the appointment of a new Master of Ceremonies was to be decided by a vote of the subscribers to Bath's assembly rooms. The election, which was fiercely contested by candidates and their supporters, was fought between a number of candidates, including Major William Brereton (Derrick's deputy), Mr Plomer (Master of Ceremonies at the nearby Bristol Hotwells), Charles Jones, and Captain William Wade. Jones and Wade withdrew early in the election process, leaving Plomer and Brereton in an acrimonious conflict which damaged both men's reputations, as explored further in Hillary Burlock's chapter.[47] Bath's newspapers were utilised by both sides to publish statements and denigrate their opponents.

It soon became apparent that neither Plomer nor Brereton would be able to unite Bath's now divided visiting population and Wade was reintroduced as the compromise candidate. Wade was 'mature, tall, handsome, and refined—satisfyingly distinct from the elderly Colet and the diminutive Derrick'.[48] At Bath, he was generally considered a success, yet Wade's ambitions extended beyond the confines of the spa. In June 1769, a month after he was appointed at Bath, the *Bath Chronicle and Weekly Gazette* reported that 'William Wade, Esq; Master of Ceremonies in this city, is appointed to the same honorary office at Brighthelmstone'.[49] The timing of this appointment suggests that Wade, having withdrawn himself from the Bath Contest, had instead looked towards Brighton, continuing with his interest there when his candidature at Bath was resumed. As with Tunbridge Wells, Brighton had an established summer season, which allowed Wade to spend the winter at Bath and the summer at the seaside.

Wade was Brighton's first Master of Ceremonies. Though Scarborough claims the title of England's first seaside resort, Brighton led the field in the second half of the eighteenth century as a fashionable destination for leisure and pleasure. Its rise began in the early 1750s, when Dr Richard Russell,

Two Kingdoms 127

a physician from Lewes in Sussex, brought sea-bathing to the attention of the *beau monde*. His thesis, *A Dissertation Concerning the Use of Seawater in Diseases of the Glands*, first published in Latin in 1750 and in English in 1753, sparked a vogue for sea-bathing which fuelled demand across the country and established Brighton as the country's most fashionable seaside resort. Recognising the opportunity Russell presented, Brighton's resident population, soon joined by outside investors, were quick to meet visitors' needs, first adapting the existing fabric of the town to accommodate guests and then constructing purpose-built facilities. These early seaside resorts consciously mimicked the social, cultural, and medical model that had proven so successful for the inland spas, providing their aristocratic, genteel, and middling-sort visitors with the polite amusements that they had come to expect from a fashionable watering place. By 1769—just 15 years after Russell had opened his practice—a Brighton guidebook boasted that the resort now had two 'neat', 'commodious', and 'elegant' assembly rooms, a parade on which could be found 'a small, but neat orchestra . . . some shops, and the circulating library', as well as a number of bathing machines. Furthermore, it claimed, these new buildings, 'for neatness and elegance, are to be equalled in few towns in this kingdom'.[50] By appointing Wade, Brighton was declaring that it would follow the same social rules that had been established at Bath and hoped to attract much of the same clientele—the fashionable elite.

Where did this leave Tunbridge Wells? The Bath Contest, held just before the start of Tunbridge Wells's summer season, left the Kentish spa without a Master of Ceremonies. Despite their shared history, visitors and tradesmen at Tunbridge Wells were left without a voice in the elections, forced instead to follow events in the newspapers and through personal letters. Tunbridge Wells's guidebooks suggest that Derrick was succeeded by Mr Blake, but contemporary newspapers tell a different story.[51] On 18 May 1769, the *Kentish Gazette* reported, 'The noted Mr Charles Jones, not disheartened with the signal insult put upon him lately at Bath, has offered himself a candidate for the high office of master of the ceremonies at Tunbridge Wells'.[52] Jones seems to have been well received at the spa, for four months later a second report states:

> There has not been for many years, so much genteel company (at this latter end of the season) as is there at present, owing it is thought, to the attendance and particular care of Mr Jones, Master of the Ceremonies, for which the Company, we hear, have presented him with a gold Medal.—Mr Derrick used to quit the Wells about three weeks before this time; it is expected if the weather continues so fine, the season will not be over this month or five weeks.[53]

128 *Bath and Beyond*

There are two things of particular note in this passage, published in September 1769. First, in August, the *Kentish Gazette* had reported that a 'very curious medal . . . ornamented with brilliants' would be made for Wade at Bath.[54] In October, it was reported in the *Kentish Gazette* that Wade had written to the Ladies and Gentlemen of Bath to thank them for presenting him with a gold medallion. By this action, Wade said that he thought himself 'confirmed' in the position of Master of Ceremonies 'by this very honourable testimony of your approbation'.[55] Had Tunbridge Wells, seeing that Wade was to receive a medal, decided to give their own Master of Ceremonies one first in September, in defiance of the man who had snubbed them? Secondly, the passage notes that having a dedicated Master of Ceremonies served to prolong the visiting season, in contrast to Derrick who left for Bath at the end of August.

Despite his success at Tunbridge Wells, Charles Jones was not content with his position at the spa. Just five days after it was reported that Jones applied for the position there, a notice was published stating that he had accepted a position as 'Superintendent and Master of the Ceremonies' at Almack's.[56] Run by elite female patrons, Almack's was one of London's most exclusive venues. The club offered grand assembly rooms for dance and card assemblies at the heart of St. James's, with a subscription system ensuring that only members of the *beau monde* were admitted.[57] As Almack's was opened primarily during the London season (late October till June), Jones was able to hold a position at Almack's and Tunbridge Wells simultaneously. Yet again, Tunbridge Wells had to share its Master of Ceremonies.

Jones only acted as Master of Ceremonies for the spa for a brief period, possibly deciding to devote his attentions exclusively towards the prestigious Almack's. Though it might be assumed that this election for Tunbridge Wells's Master of Ceremonies would be made independently of Bath, it seems that this was not the case. Instead, Wade, still Master of Ceremonies at Bath and Brighton, played a pivotal role. As the *Stamford Mercury* reported in July 1771, 'We hear from Tunbridge Wells, that J. Blake, Esq: of Sevenoaks, having offered himself as Master of the Ceremonies, has been unanimously chosen into that office, in the room of Captain Wade, who presides now only at Brighthelmstone for the summer'.[58] This extract suggests that Wade had been temporarily covering the post of Master of Ceremonies at Tunbridge Wells, alongside adjudicating over the summer season at Brighton. This was an unusual situation, which suggests that Jones left his position abruptly, leaving a void at the heart of the spa's social life that Wade stepped in to fill. After presiding over the election of a new Master of Ceremonies, Wade was free to leave Tunbridge Wells and return to Brighton.

Dissatisfaction at Bath

Though Wade ruled at Brighton until his death in 1809, a period of 40 years, he was forced to resign from his post in Bath in July 1777 after being named in the divorce proceedings of Elizabeth Eustatia and John Hooke Campbell.[59] In the subsequent election, there is evidence that Bath's visitors resented the time that Wade spent at Brighton. As William Brereton declared in the *Bath Chronicle and Weekly Gazette*:

> We have the authority to assure the public, that should Mr Brereton be so happy as to succeed Mr Wade as Master of the Ceremonies, he is determined to make Bath his CONSTANT RESIDENCE; as most people are of the opinion that a city which now abounds with so many families of distinction all the year round, should not be left any part of it, without that power which a Master of Ceremonies is possessed of, as the well-being of the city and its amusements depend upon that order and decency which cannot be supported but by a proper and vested authority in some individual.[60]

Simon Moreau, who would later become Cheltenham's first Master of Ceremonies, offered similar promises: 'should I be so happy to succeed, my whole attention shall be devoted to acquaint myself with that propriety requisite in a situation of such consequence, being determined in such case to make Bath the place of my constant residence';[61] so too did John Donnellan, who promised Bath's visitors that 'my whole time and attention shall be devoted to your service, as the only return I can possibly make for . . . your regard'.[62]

These three candidates—Brereton, Moreau, and Donnellan—actively appealed to those among Bath's leisured population who felt that their Master of Ceremonies should hold just one post. These campaign statements indicate that Bath's visitors had been unhappy about losing their social leader during the summer months, especially as the numbers of leisured visitors residing in Bath long term increased. It is also likely that Wade found his role at Brighton more difficult and time-consuming than he had anticipated. Though ostensibly the role of Master of Ceremonies at the newly emerging seaside resorts was the same as at the spas, in practice they were quite different. This was mainly due to the size and composition of the visiting company. At Bath, it had been possible for Nash to greet each arriving visitor individually; there were fewer visitors, they mostly came from a high social rank, and they often stayed for several months, if not the entire season. At the seaside, however, the size of the visiting company was much larger, and their average length of stay was shorter. Furthermore, Nash's efforts at Bath were facilitated by the centrality of the spa's

130 Bath and Beyond

Pump Room, at which visitors would regularly congregate. At the seaside, by contrast, visitors were encouraged to move away from the resort and explore the shoreline. The challenges this presented are evident in the organisation of assemblies and subscriptions. At Margate, for example, James Walker struggled to cope with the number of visitors seeking tickets for his annual benefit ball in September 1780. This overwhelmed Master of Ceremonies was forced to print a notice in the *Kentish Gazette* apologising to any Ladies and Gentlemen who 'had honoured his Subscription Book with their Names', but had not yet been given a ticket.[63] Embarrassingly, Walker was forced to reprint this notice yearly. Wade would have faced additional pressures at Brighton, which soon became famous as a summer residence of the Prince of Wales; royalty, aristocracy, gentry, and increasing numbers of the middling sort all flocked to the seaside, looking to Wade to provide social cohesion.

Richard Tyson, who became Master of Ceremonies for Bath's Lower Rooms in 1780, made no promises of fealty. Indeed, during the election's initial stage, Tyson suffered from being absent from Bath due to his engagements at Tunbridge Wells, where he had been appointed Master of Ceremonies in 1773.[64] Rumours circulated that he had resigned his candidacy, which Tyson openly rebutted, emphasising through the *Bath Chronicle* that he 'intends to be here [Bath] in a few days, his engagements at Tunbridge-Wells not admitting of his absence from thence sooner'.[65] Tyson's absence from Bath during this crucial stage of the election may have worked against him when it came to the vote.

William Dawson, like Tyson, was not present in Bath when the election was called, having to write from Southampton to express his interest in the post. Dawson, who had been Master of Ceremonies at Southampton since 1770, used his position there as part of his campaign. Stopping short of promising fealty to Bath, Dawson instead hoped that Southampton would support him in taking up a second post. 'The favourable reception my conduct has met with from the public resorting to Southampton', he wrote, 'has encouraged me to hope for their support and protection on the present vacancy'.[66]

The 1777 election had two victors: William Dawson was appointed as Master of Ceremonies for Bath's Upper Assembly Rooms (which opened in 1771), and William Brereton, after years of frustrated ambitions, was appointed to the same position for the Lower Rooms. This reflected the changing axis of Bath's social life as it moved away from the old city to the upper town, but also the ever-growing demands placed on the spa's Master of Ceremonies as the city expanded and visitor numbers increased.[67] Assemblies were held at both rooms each week, led by their respective Master of Ceremonies and both men held an annual benefit ball. The post

Two Kingdoms   131

at the Upper Assembly Rooms was considered superior in rank, with Masters of Ceremonies often serving first in the Lower Rooms before being 'promoted' to the Upper Rooms when a vacancy emerged.

While Brereton was able to dedicate himself to his post in the Lower Rooms, Dawson struggled to meet the demands of both Bath and Southampton. Southampton's residents quickly began to resent the absence of their Master of Ceremonies, and after a few short months, moves were made to remove Dawson from his post. An article in the *Hampshire Chronicle* from January 1778 exhaustively listed Dawson's failings, clearly showing residents' resentment towards their appointed social leader.[68] Of the seven criticisms directed towards Dawson, two accused him of greed, suggesting that Dawson was 'very largely and abundantly provided for by his Appointment to that Office at *Bath*' and that '700*l.* or 800*l.*, *per ann.* is a very ample Endowment' which 'ought to satisfy not only modest, but even ambitious Expectations' (emphasis in original). There was thus no need, they claimed, for one man to hold two posts when he could more than sufficiently support himself with just one. The practicalities of holding two appointments were also questioned. With Southampton now holding assemblies throughout the autumn and winter, as well as during their traditional summer season, it was asserted that 'Mr *Dawson* therefore cannot, consistently with his Duty at *Bath* and *Southampton*, regularly and properly attend'. Finally, while in his election campaign at Bath Dawson had hoped for Southampton's support in his new role, the article claims that his actions made this impossible:

> Because Mr *Dawson's* situation in life being essentially altered to his Advantage since he came here, he cannot, either in common Sense or Justice, be considered as the same Object of our Attention. The Affluence provided for him at *Bath* justifies a transfer of our benevolent and friendly Regard to another; nor will any Mind, wherein Sensibility is accompanied by Reflection, censure or oppose an Endeavour to render publick Munificence as diffusive as possible.[69]

Interestingly, it was not Southampton's visiting company that made such an attack on Dawson, but instead its resident population. Having historically directed assemblies in the town, having raised funds for the refurbishment of the assembly rooms, and having a vested interest in Southampton's prosperity, residents argued that they 'constantly and rightfully possessed the sole Government of this Assembly, and the Appointment of Persons officiating it'.[70]

Despite such vitriolic comments, however, it seems that the majority of Southampton's residents and visitors continued to support Dawson.

132   *Bath and Beyond*

Shortly after Dawson was attacked in print, his supporters published their own newspaper article, pledging their continued support:

> it appears repugnant to our notions of propriety, reason, and justice, to displace from that office a person who has, for so many years, acquitted himself, in all the obligations of it, without reproach, whose general conduct entitles him to that support with which he has hitherto been honoured, and who, we are firmly persuaded, will continue to exert his utmost attention and abilities, in a constant and regular discharge of his duty.[71]

Unlike Dawson's detractors, his supporters were willing to put their names to their show of support. Their backing allowed Dawson to remain as Southampton's Master of Ceremonies until 1784, after which he had just one last winter season at Bath before resigning.

Bath and Tunbridge Wells Reunited

Bath and Tunbridge Wells were reunited in 1780 under the leadership of Richard Tyson. Tyson, described by Phyllis Hembry as 'one of the most competent' Masters of Ceremonies, had presided over Tunbridge Wells for three years before taking up the role at Bath's Lower Rooms.[72] A success at both spas, Tyson seemingly avoided Dawson's difficulties and was promoted to Bath's Upper Rooms in 1785. Tyson's task may have been made easier by Tunbridge Wells's decline as a fashionable centre for leisure and pleasure. Though in the last quarter of the eighteenth-century Tunbridge Wells was still able to attract members of the elite, it had firmly begun its transition to a centre for genteel residence. Rather than shying away from its evolving character, *The Tunbridge Wells Guide* of 1780 described the spa as settled and established, containing all the conveniences visitors would need during their stay.[73]

A letter written by Amabel, dowager Baroness Hume (subsequently countess de Grey) in 1791, at what was supposedly the opening of the spa's summer season, shows the spa's decline and provides an insight into Tyson's life at Tunbridge Wells:

> Though many People are dispers'd about in the different Lodgings yet they hardly meet upon the Walks, & not at all at the Rooms. Mr Tyson who still hobbles on through the very little Business this Place affords, made an Attempt last Night to collect us all together & open the Season with a Public Tea-drinking, but it was very empty & very dull; one little Incident only made us laugh, a Kitten got into the Music-Gallery (where

there was no Music) & set up a most piteous <u>Mewing</u>, & some of the Company clapp'd it as a <u>very fine Italian Singer</u> (emphasis in original).[74]

Though no-doubt-exaggerated for comic affect, this letter suggests that the energy had been drained from Tunbridge Wells's social life. As younger generations of the elite joined the genteel and middling sort at the fast-growing seaside resorts, those that continued to visit Tunbridge Wells seemed to place few demands on Tyson.

Tyson also appears to have been a more skilled organiser than his recent predecessors who, according to some criticisms, were far more concerned with the 'pleasures and enjoyments of the world' than the smooth running of resort life.[75] At both Bath and Tunbridge Wells, Tyson introduced his own set of social rules, which updated those set by Nash earlier in the eighteenth century. Like Nash, Tyson sought to guide the behaviour of the visiting company, but over the course of the eighteenth century, priorities had changed. Speaking to a group now familiar with the social mixing which characterised watering-place society, Tyson did not require equality within his assembly rooms, unlike Nash. Instead, he supported the divisions of social rank, asking those Ladies who had precedence to ensure they claimed it at the start of each dance. Nash's aims of bringing together the nobility and gentry in the shared pursuit of leisure had been achieved at Georgian watering places, and deference had not been so easily overcome. Crucially, Tyson brought stability. This was particularly important at Tunbridge Wells, which, after Nash's death, had hosted four Masters of Ceremonies in 12 years. Tyson, by contrast, stayed at the spa for 28 years until, 'doubtless worn out by his double assignment', he retired from the Kentish spa in 1801. Four years later, he also left his post at Bath.

Conclusion

Tyson was the last Master of Ceremonies to rule at Bath and Tunbridge Wells simultaneously. Few in Bath or Tunbridge Wells would have lamented the demise of this link which had lasted for more than 55 years; though it added to the pockets and prestige of postholders, it did very little to improve the fortunes of either spa. For Bath, their Master of Ceremonies' absence during the summer season became increasingly inconvenient as the city's leisured population expanded. As the election campaigns of 1777 show, the visiting company's discontent had reached such a level that all but two candidates promised to renounce other appointments and make Bath their 'constant residence'. While the building of the Upper Assembly Rooms, which demanded the appointment of two Masters of Ceremonies within Bath, helped to meet the rising year-round demands from

134   Bath and Beyond

visitors, the criticisms levelled at Dawson from Southampton show that dual appointments were unpopular.

At Tunbridge Wells, the connection with Bath was actively detrimental. While the spa's guidebooks may have presented Nash's arrival as heralding the resort's polite transformation, in reality his impact was minimal. Likewise, Nash's successors mostly neglected the smaller spa and, offering little in the way of innovation, presided over its decline. Crucially, during the mid-eighteenth century, Tunbridge Wells lacked a voice in the appointment of its Masters of Ceremonies: elections were fought and decided at Bath, with seemingly little thought given to the preferences of the distant Kentish spa. When Wade snubbed Tunbridge Wells in favour of newly fashionable Brighton, it was a sign that the spa's heyday was well and truly over. If indeed Tunbridge Wells's visiting company had supported Bell Causey to resist Nash's attempts at a takeover early in the eighteenth century, it seems that they were right to do so. Despite these drawbacks, individual Masters of Ceremonies could navigate dual appointments successfully, most notably William Dawson and Richard Tyson. William Wade may also have done so, had he not been forced to resign from Bath due to affairs of the heart. These men were able to gain widespread, long-term support at both their seats; their dual appointments, while not ideal, could be accepted. Indeed, as the role of Master of Ceremonies developed into a profession, dual appointments became increasingly common, especially as the number of seaside resorts continued to rise. Yet, looking back over the history of Bath and Tunbridge Wells, none of the postholders considered here truly took advantage of the connection they represented between two of Georgian England's most fashionable watering places. The spas may have shared a social 'king', but Bath and Tunbridge Wells remained two separate and distinct kingdoms.

Examining the connections forged by Bath's Masters of Ceremonies with spas and seaside resorts across England highlights just one of the ways in which the spa's influence spread beyond the confines of the city. Bath stood confidently at the apogee of a growing hierarchy of watering places and the position of Master of Ceremonies at its Upper Assembly Rooms became the country's most coveted position. By moving between resorts, and especially holding two posts simultaneously, Masters of Ceremonies ensured that England's watering places shared a relatively homogenous culture guided by the conventions established at Bath. As the eighteenth century progressed, the connections made between resorts by these figures became increasingly complex and the expectations of postholders solidified. Perhaps most significantly, the role was quickly masculinised, filled by men from the upper middling or lower genteel classes: Bell Causey's power at Tunbridge Wells would not be replicated elsewhere. When Masters of Ceremonies began to be appointed at the newly emergent seaside resorts, they too followed the

Two Kingdoms 135

pattern established by Nash, ensuring that Bath's pattern of life was embedded in these exciting new leisure arenas from the outset. As the seaside holiday spread across the world, so too did Bath's influence.

Notes

1 Peter Borsay, *The Image of Georgian Bath, 1700–2000: Towns, Heritage and History* (Oxford: Oxford University Press, 2000), 62–63.
2 John Eglin, *The Imaginary Autocrat: Beau Nash and the Invention of Bath* (London: Profile Books, 2005), 36. As Eglin notes, while Captain Webster is included in Goldsmith's and Wood's accounts of Bath, there is no archival evidence for his tenure.
3 Pierce Egan, *Walks Through Bath* (1819), 110–11.
4 Peter M. Briggs, "The Importance of Beau Nash," *Studies in Eighteenth-Century Culture* xxii (1993): 218.
5 John Wood, *An Essay Towards a Description of the City of Bath: In Two Parts*, 2 vols. (1749), ii, 248.
6 Wood, *A Description of the City of Bath*, 249.
7 Wood, *A Description of the City of Bath*, 249.
8 Wood, *A Description of the City of Bath*, 249.
9 Wood, *A Description of the City of Bath*, 249.
10 Oliver Goldsmith, *The Life of Richard Nash Esq; Late Master of the Ceremonies at Bath*, 2nd ed. (1762), vii.
11 Briggs, "The Importance of Beau Nash," 226.
12 Graham Davis and Penny Bonsall, *A History of Bath: Image and* Reality (Lancaster: Lancaster University Press, 2006), 118; Eglin, *Imaginary Autocrat*, 244–45.
13 Peter Borsay, *The Image of Georgian Bath, 1700–2000: Towns, Heritage and History* (Oxford: Oxford University Press, 2000), 58.
14 Borsay, *The Image of Georgian Bath*, 61, 65.
15 Frances Burney, *The Early Journals and Letters of Fanny Burney*, ed. Lars E. Troide, 5 vols. (Oxford: Oxford University Press, 1988–2003), iii, 370.
16 Thomas Benge Burr, *The History of Tunbridge-Wells* (1766), 21–22.
17 Burr, *Tunbridge-Wells*, 112.
18 Sophie Vasset, *Murky Waters: British Spas in Eighteenth-Century Medicine and Literature* (Manchester: Manchester University Press, 2022), 169.
19 *The Tunbridge Wells Guide* (1780), 286.
20 Rachael Johnson, "Spas and Seaside Resorts in Kent, 1660–1820" (PhD diss., University of Leeds, 2014), 124.
21 Vasset, *Murky Waters*, 171.
22 *The Tunbridge Wells Guide* (1780), 288.
23 Goldsmith, *The Life of Richard Nash*, 49.
24 After Bell Causey, it is interesting to note that Nash's manager at Tunbridge Wells was also a woman.
25 *A Description of Tunbridge Wells* (1780), 12.
26 *A Description of Tunbridge Wells* (1780), 13.
27 *A Description of Tunbridge Wells* (1780), 13.
28 Donna T. Andrew, *Aristocratic Vice: The Attack on Duelling, Suicide, Adultery, and Gambling in Eighteenth-Century England* (New Haven: Yale University Press, 2013), 177.

136   *Bath and Beyond*

29 Elizabeth Montagu, *The Letters of Mrs Elizabeth Montagu, with Some Letters of Her Correspondents*, 3 vols. (1809–13), i, 73.
30 Goldsmith, *The Life of Richard Nash*, 50.
31 Burr, *A History of Tunbridge-Wells*, 120.
32 Alan Savidge, *Royal Tunbridge Wells: A History of a Spa Town,* rev. Charlie Bell (Tunbridge Wells: Midas Books, 1995), 75.
33 Savidge, *Royal Tunbridge Wells*, 76.
34 Goldsmith, *The Life of Richard Nash,* 26.
35 Collet's resignation, for example, is reported in the *Bath Chronicle and Weekly Gazette*, February 17, 1763. The same newspaper includes several references to Richard Nash's death, for example, March 19, 1761, when the sale of his effects was advertised.
36 Hallie Rubenhold, *The Covent Garden Ladies: Pimp General Jack & the Extraordinary Story of Harris's List* (Stroud: Tempus Publishing, 2005), 124; Jack Harris, *Harris's List of Covent-Garden Ladies: Or Man of Pleasure's Kalendar, for the Year 1773* (1773), titlepage.
37 Rubenhold, *Covent Garden Ladies*, 127.
38 Rubenhold, *Covent Garden Ladies*, 129.
39 Rubenhold, *Covent Garden Ladies*, 257.
40 Samuel Derrick, *Letters Written from Leverpoole, Chester, Corke, the Lake of Killarney, Dublin, Tunbridge-Wells, and Bath*, 2 vols. (Dublin, 1767), ii.
41 Derrick, *Letters Written from Leverpoole*, 56–57.
42 Derrick, *Letters Written from Leverpoole*, 60.
43 Derrick *Letters Written from Leverpoole*, title page.
44 C. W. Chalklin, *Royal Tunbridge Wells: A History* (Phillimore: The History Press Ltd., 2008).
45 Savidge, *Royal Tunbridge Wells*, 83.
46 Phyllis Hembry, *The English Spa 1560–1815: A Social History* (Farleigh Dickinson, 1990), 138.
47 See Hillary Burlock's chapter 'Electing the Arbiter Elegantiarum in Bath and Beyond: Power, Politics, and the 1769 Bath Contest', which can be found in this book.
48 ODNB, accessed October 31, 2023, www.oxforddnd.com; Wade, William; Carter, Phillip.
49 *Bath Chronicle and Weekly Gazette*, June 1, 1769.
50 *The Brighthelmstone Directory, or Guide to That Place* (1769), 12–13.
51 John Clifford, *The Tunbridge Wells Guide* (Tunbridge Wells, 1825), 55.
52 *The Kentish Gazette*, May 18, 1769.
53 *Kentish Gazette*, September 23, 1769.
54 *Kentish Gazette*, August 16, 1769.
55 *Kentish Gazette*, October 11, 1769.
56 *Bath Chronicle and Weekly Gazette,* May 18, 1769.
57 Jane Rendell, "Almack's Assembly Rooms: A Site of Sexual Pleasure," *Journal of Architectural Education* lv (2002): 136, 142.
58 *Stamford Mercury*, July 18, 1771.
59 ODNB, s.v. Wade, William.
60 *Bath Chronicle and Weekly Gazette*, October 16, 1777.
61 *Bath Chronicle and Weekly Gazette*, October 9, 1777.
62 *Bath Chronicle and Weekly Gazette*, October 9, 1777.
63 *Kentish Gazette*, September 16, 1780.
64 *Hampshire Chronicle*, August 9, 1773.
65 *Bath Chronicle and Weekly Gazette,* October 9, 1777.

66 *Bath Chronicle and Weekly Gazette*, October 9, 1777.
67 Hembry, *The English Spa*, 125.
68 *Hampshire Chronicle*, January 12, 1778.
69 *Hampshire Chronicle*, January 12, 1778.
70 *Hampshire Chronicle*, January 12, 1778.
71 *Hampshire Chronicle*, December 1, 1777.
72 Hembry, *The English Spa*, 236.
73 *The Tunbridge Wells Guide* (Tunbridge Wells, 1780), 44.
74 BLARS, L30/23/97: Amabel Hume-Campbell to Jemima Mary Gregory, June 29, 1791.
75 *Bath Chronicle and Weekly Gazette,* September 25, 1777.

Bibliography

Manuscript Sources

Bedfordshire Archives

L30/23/97: Wrest Park (Lucas) Manuscripts.

Printed Primary and Secondary Sources

Andrew, Donna T. *Aristocratic Vice: The Attack on Duelling, Suicide, Adultery, and Gambling in Eighteenth-Century England*. New Haven: Yale University Press, 2013.
"The Ball on Friday at Tunbridge Wells." *Hampshire Chronicle*, August 9, 1773.
"Bath Election." *Bath Chronicle and Weekly Gazette*, September 25, 1777.
"Bath, June 1." *Bath Chronicle and Weekly Gazette*, June 1, 1769.
"Bath, Wednesday October 8." *Bath Chronicle and Weekly Gazette*, October 9, 1777.
"Bath, Wednesday, October 15." *Bath Chronicle and Weekly Gazette*, October 16, 1777.
Borsay, Peter. *The Image of Georgian Bath, 1700–2000: Towns, Heritage and History*. Oxford: Oxford University Press, 2000.
Briggs, Peter M. "The Importance of Beau Nash." *Studies in Eighteenth-Century Culture* 22 (1993): 208–30.
The Brighthelmstone Directory, or Guide to That Place. Brighton, 1769.
Burney, Frances. *The Early Journal and Letters of Fanny Burney*. Edited by Lars E. Troide. Oxford: Oxford University Press, 1988–2003.
Burr, Thomas Benge. *The History of Tunbridge Wells*. Tunbridge Wells, 1766.
"Candid and Impartial Reasons." *Hampshire Chronicle*, January 12, 1778.
Carter, Philip. "Wade, William (1734/5–1809)." In *Oxford Dictionary of National Biography*. Oxford University Press, 2008. https://doi.org/10.1093/ref:odnb/77016.
Chaklin, C. W. *Royal Tunbridge Wells: A History*. Phillimore: The History Press Ltd., 2008.
Clifford, John. *The Tunbridge Wells Guide*. Tunbridge Wells, 1825.
Davis, Graham, and Penny Bonsall. *A History of Bath: Image and Reality*. Lancaster: Carnegie, 2006.
Derrick, Samuel. *Letters Written from Leverpoole, Chester, Corke, the Lake of Killarney, Dublin, Tunbridge-Wells, and Bath*. Dublin, 1767.
A Description of Tunbridge Wells. Tunbridge Wells, 1780.

138 Bath and Beyond

Egan, Pierce. *Walks Through Bath*. Bath, 1819.

Eglin, John. *The Imaginary Autocrat: Beau Nash and the Invention of Bath*. London: Profile, 2005.

"Extract of a Letter from Tunbridge Wells, Dated, September 23, 1769." *Kentish Gazette*, September 23, 1769.

Goldsmith, Oliver. *The Life Richard Nash Esq; Late Master of the Ceremonies at Bath*. London, 1762.

Harris, Jack. *Harris's List of Covent-Garden Ladies: Or Man of Pleasure's Kalendar, for the Year 1773*. London, 1773.

Hembry, Phyllis. *The English Spa, 1560–1815: A Social History*. London: Athlone Press, 1990.

Johnson, Rachael. "Spas and Seaside Resorts in Kent, 1660–1820." PhD diss., University of Leeds, 2014.

"London." *Kentish Gazette*, May 13, 1769.

"London." *Kentish Gazette*, August 16, 1769.

"London." *Kentish Gazette*, October 11, 1769.

"London, May 16." *Bath Chronicle and Weekly Gazette*, May 18, 1769.

"Margate, Sept. 8." *Kentish Gazette*, September 16, 1780.

Montagu, Elizabeth. *The Letters of Mrs. Montagu, with Some Letters of Her Correspondents*. London: T. Cadell & W. Davies, 1809–13.

Rendell, Jane. "Almack's Assembly Rooms: A Site of Sexual Pleasure." *Journal of Architectural Education* 4 (2002): 136–49.

Rubenhold, Hallie. *The Covent Garden Ladies: Pimp General Jack & the Extraordinary Story of Harris's List*. Stroud: Tempus Publishing, 2005.

Savidge, Alan. *Royal Tunbridge Wells: A History of a Spa Town*. Revised by Charlie Bell. Tunbridge Wells: Midas Books, 1995.

"Southampton, Saturday November 29." *Hampshire Chronicle*, December 1, 1777.

The Tunbridge Wells Guide; or an Account of the Ancient and Present State of That Place. Tunbridge Wells, 1800.

The Tunbridge Wells Guide; or an Account of the Ancient and Present State of That Place. Tunbridge Wells, 1801.

Vasset, Sophie. *Murky Waters: British Spas in Eighteenth-Century Medicine and Literature*. Manchester: Manchester University Press, 2022.

"We Hear from Tunbridge Wells." *Stamford Mercury*, July 18, 1771.

Wood, John. *An Essay Towards a Description of the City of Bath: In Two Parts*. Bath, 1749.

8 Electing the *Arbiter Elegantiarum* in Bath and Beyond

Power, Politics, and the 1769 Bath Contest

Hillary Burlock

Spa towns developed over the course of the seventeenth and eighteenth centuries with some earlier outliers like Bath (*c*.60), including Royal Tunbridge Wells (between 1606 and 1630), Epsom (1621), Harrogate (late seventeenth century), Scarborough (early eighteenth century), Cheltenham (1716), Boston Spa (1744), Buxton (1780), and Royal Leamington Spa (1784), as chalybeate springs were discovered around the country and on the Continent (see Phil Bonjour and Isabelle Eve Carlotti-Davier's chapters).[1] Towns emerged around these natural mineral springs, attracting visitors seeking the benefits of the waters. In order to manage the tourists flocking to these spa towns, Masters of Ceremonies and Lady Directresses were appointed or elected to manage their respective spa towns and public amenities like assembly rooms, where company gathered to dance, take tea, and play cards.

Managing and regulating Bath's assembly rooms was the purview of a Master of Ceremonies, a public role long meriting in-depth analysis of its power in the ballroom and broader society. As an arbiter of social harmony, the Master of Ceremonies facilitated social networking, maintained exclusivity, enforced hierarchical precedence, established and enforced rules of conduct, and arbitrated conflicts. These functions were essential to the smooth and effective running of the assembly room and the enjoyment of its patrons. The Master of Ceremonies was the *arbiter elegantiarum*:

> who directs and superintends the arrangements for the time being, to whom all appeals must be made, whose authority is unquestionable, and decisions final; with such powers as these, it is scarcely necessary to add, he should unite the knowledge of the profession with the manners of a gentleman.[2]

Referred to as 'Kings' in Bath, the Master of Ceremonies' authority in the assembly rooms was akin to a constitutional monarchy.[3] These revered public figures, elected regulators of polite society, were paradoxically

DOI: 10.4324/9781003393856-8

140 *Bath and Beyond*

empowered to dictate and regulate the bodies, movements, and behaviour of the peerage, gentry, and middling sort, while not themselves of noble birth. Richard 'Beau' Nash, Oxford dropout and professional gambler, was the son of a Swansea glassworks owner.[4] Samuel Derrick was formerly a linen draper's apprentice, unsuccessful actor, and Irish author.[5] Captain William Wade of the 73rd Regiment was the great-nephew of Field Marshal George Wade, former MP for Bath.[6] William Brereton was an Irish cavalry Major of the 6th (Inniskilling) Dragoons descended from an old English family from Cheshire.[7] The military was well represented in the ranks of Bath's Masters of Ceremonies; between 1702 and 1865, one-third of them were military men, whose careers accustomed them to issuing orders, following and enforcing rules, and maintaining hierarchy and order. Indeed, it was said of Lieutenant-Colonel William Jervois, James Heaviside's successor as Master of Ceremonies of Bath's Upper Rooms in 1825, that 'his discipline of the ball-room was a subject of admiration', well-fitting him for the role.[8]

Subscribers to the assembly rooms were endowed with the right to elect or appoint their Master of Ceremonies when a vacancy arose. Given the high proportion of women at spas, they were given the same voting rights as their male counterparts. The appointment conferred significant and unusual status and sway to the Master of Ceremonies within the community, stemming from the subscribers' voluntary endowment of authority to the appointee, and their willingness to submit themselves to him. With authority outweighing pedigree, the Master of Ceremonies was imbued with the power and responsibility for defining and enforcing the artifice of a world over which *he* was simultaneously *elevated* as 'King', while associates from the same social stratum could be derided as social inferiors.

When multiple candidates stepped forward following the death or resignation of a Master of Ceremonies, elections were held. It was in this relatively rare contest that specific electoral rules and procedures were broken, debated, or communicated, that the power dynamics between the Master of Ceremonies and subscribers were illuminated. As assembly rooms proliferated across Britain, elections of 'Kings' furnished an established and socially acceptable process for selecting a new incumbent, while satisfying subscribers' desires for a voice in the process. Enfranchised by payment of subscriber fees to the assembly rooms, *de facto*, subscribers paid for the right to vote. An election, with its familiar trappings, conveyed the message that the Master of Ceremonies' power stemmed from 'the people', albeit only those who could afford to subscribe. This chapter suggests that Master of Ceremonies' elections at eighteenth- and early nineteenth-century spas paralleled parliamentary elections—including notions of enfranchisement and familiar practices of canvassing and formal polling. It demonstrates

Electing the Arbiter Elegantiarum in Bath and Beyond 141

how familiarity with eighteenth-century electoral practices was translated into the social arena and used in Bath. 'The Bath Contest', as the heated electoral contest for Bath's Master of Ceremonies in 1769 was remembered, serves as a case study throwing new light on the maintenance of, and challenges to, the authority of the Master of Ceremonies.

Assembly Room Elections

Electoral activities for the position of Master of Ceremonies commenced with community canvassing, mirroring the protocol of parliamentary elections. Canvassing was, according to Frank O'Gorman, the 'critical point of contact' between the voters, candidates, and their committees in Georgian elections.[9] During parliamentary elections, canvassing was crucial to securing promises of votes for particular candidates, and gauging levels of community support, achieved by candidates and their agents soliciting votes. This process was no different for electing Masters of Ceremonies or their female equivalents, Lady Directresses. John Courtney's diary recorded that, in Beverley, Yorkshire, the selection of a Lady Directress was a serious undertaking and canvassing was executed by the female candidates or their male family members. In November 1762, Courtney observed:

> This afternoon Mr Dalacourt came to desire I would give my vote to his wifes [sic] being made mistress of the new Assembly Room; I told him, I imagined Mrs Yates would not stand again, and so then I would vote for Mrs Dalacourt please God I live. In evening Mrs Sally Webster, Mr Bowmans [sic] maid came to ask for my vote, she also being a candidate; I was gone to a concert but they told her I was engaged to Mrs Dalacourt.[10]

Votes were solicited and promises given, generating networks of electoral interest and favour surrounding the management of Britain's assembly rooms.

A clear frontrunner often emerged from among the candidates during the canvass and other candidates might then resign in favour of the person leading the polls. Consequently, community relationships were rarely in danger of fraying. In December 1805, Charles Le Bas was elected Master of Ceremonies for the Lower Rooms in Bath, with Captain D'Arcy withdrawing from the fray the day before the vote.[11] As a result, Le Bas's election was unanimous. On the day of the election, polls were opened and closed in an afternoon, after which the votes were counted and the result announced.[12] In Tunbridge Wells in 1804, three candidates for the role resigned their interest the week before the vote, including Captain Hewetson of the 95th

142   *Bath and Beyond*

Rifles, who bowed out the day before the election, reducing the field from six to two candidates:

> [Hewetson] consolidated his interest with Mr Amsinck. The result of which was, that at the close of the election, at four o'clock this day, the votes were for Mr Amsinck, 64; Mr Fry, 34; upon which Mr Amsinck, was declared the successful candidate . . . Lieut. Col. Cumberland in the chair; and the whole election was conducted with the greatest humour and decorum.[13]

Master of Ceremonies' elections were generally conducted with dignity and propriety, as candidates evinced polite behaviour appropriate to the role sought, winning the approbation of voter-subscribers while following established modes of parliamentary campaigning and polling.

The election of a Master of Ceremonies or Lady Directress attracted the notice and engagement of the whole community, as subscribers had the paradoxically democratic opportunity to elect their 'King'. Bath's election of a Master of Ceremonies amplified this engagement, as Bath attracted visitors from across Great Britain and Europe who were invested in the election's outcome. The business of Bath's election was widespread in the press, with results printed in (among others) the *Saint James's Chronicle, Hampshire Chronicle, Salisbury and Winchester Journal, Hereford Journal,* and *Northampton Mercury,* so critical were the results to visitors to the spa town.[14] Although multiple candidates might vie for the role of Master of Ceremonies in other English towns, it typically did not descend into brutal smear campaigns or violence. However, the prestige of the position in Bath inspired an electoral contest in 1769 that was so unbridled that it was more closely comparable to a hotly contested parliamentary election, with rival candidates campaigning fiercely in person and in print.

The 1769 Contest

In 1769, Bath was at the height of its popularity in Georgian England. Fashionable new residences and public spaces were being constructed, including Queen Square (1727–1734), Gay Street (1735–1750), The Circus (1754–1767), Milsom Street (1762), and Octagon Chapel (1767), accommodating visitors who flocked to the town for its annual winter season from October to May. Samuel Derrick had served as Master of Ceremonies since 1763, but died on 28 March 1769, creating a vacancy for this highly sought-after position. As Derrick died two days before Easter, electioneering would have taken place at a time when Bath's season was very full of company. Public awareness of Derrick's serious illness enabled candidates Charles Jones (possibly M.C. for Scarborough), William Wade (M.C. for Brighton),

Electing the Arbiter Elegantiarum *in Bath and Beyond* 143

R. Plomer (M.C. for Bristol), and Major Brereton (Derrick's deputy) to propose themselves as early as 14 March, with electioneering beginning two weeks before Derrick's death. All four candidates gave speeches and published advertisements in the local newspapers to generate support. Jones and Wade bowed out of the contest early in the campaign, conforming to gentlemanly behaviour and precedent, leaving an impasse between the two main rivals.[15] A heated contest between Brereton and Plomer followed, each candidate amassing factions, and dividing the subscribers in half.[16] For nearly a month, the press was filled with vicious squibs, songs, and advertisements smearing the two main candidates, emulating the practices of heated electoral contests.

Following divisive elections, handbills, advertisements, songs, and satiric squibs were collected from candidates' campaigns and published in squib books, preserving election ephemera that otherwise would have been discarded. They detailed campaign strategising in the press and on the streets, and presented the polling and electoral result. Parliamentary squib books were presented as definitive histories of individual elections, appealing to local constituents and other interested parties. The singularity of Bath's 1769 election is evidenced by the publication of its own squib book, *The Bath Contest: Being a Collection of All the Papers, Advertisements, &c. Published before and since the Death of Mr Derrick, by the Candidates for the Office of Master of the Ceremonies, and Their Friends.* It is a vital source for illuminating the Master of Ceremonies' role, and the dynamic between Master of Ceremonies and subscribers when accepted electoral customs went awry. Its publishers deliberately imitated the function and form of squib books, memorialising the contest between two dogged candidates, Brereton and Plomer. *The Bath Contest* was printed by Archer and Cruttwell, printers of *The Bath Chronicle and Weekly Gazette*, who were well placed to preserve the advertisements from the campaign for future readers, mirroring the compilation, publication, and distribution of squib books.[17] It was inexpensively printed at 1*s.*, enabling wider circulation beyond Bath. The octavo and its supplemental coda, *The Conciliade*, were sold by Archer and Cruttwell in St James's Street, just north of the construction of Bath's new, fashionable Royal Crescent.[18] It was also sold in London, Middlesex; Bristol, Gloucestershire; Sherborne, Dorset; and Taunton, Somerset; confirming the expectation of a wider interest and readership than Bath locals.[19]

Squib books commemorated intense moments of electoral strife, but also celebrated the discharge of civic duty, political engagement, and decorum. In 1769, Bath's assembly rooms represented a microcosm of England's electoral system, becoming a borough in miniature, its male and female subscribers becoming active constituents. This particular electoral contest was not met by Bath's assembly room subscribers with equanimity. The

144 Bath and Beyond

heatedness of the campaigning by candidates and their factions indicates how significant the election of the Master of Ceremonies was to the assembly rooms' constituents.

Bath's civic culture was 'justly famed for its integrity, independence, and zeal for the public good', according to William Pitt the Elder (MP for Bath 1757–1766), making the events of the 1769 contest all the more unusual, as it stirred up animosities between Bath *residents* and *visitors*, and rivalry between Bath and Bristol.[20] As a corporation borough, Bath's franchise for parliamentary and municipal elections was extremely limited, restricted to 30 gentlemen and tradesmen who held their offices in the corporation for life. The Georgian franchise for parliamentary and municipal elections was founded in property ownership, and largely dominated by men. Few women fulfilled the property qualifications in order to vote, and those who did tended to use male proxies to deliver their votes in parliamentary elections.[21] By comparison, the franchise for the Master of Ceremonies' election was much wider, with women guaranteed the same right to cast their votes as men.[22] This was similar to some community franchises which enabled women to vote in parish elections and hold office as sextons, beadles, overseers of the poor, constables, highway surveyors, parish clerks, churchwardens, and headboroughs.[23] Additionally, women also had the right to vote on ballot days as stockholders in the East India Company's General Court of Proprietors, which made 'No distinction exists as to religion, profession, or sex'.[24] In the election of Masters of Ceremonies, women were placed on an equal footing with male subscribers, each given voice to judge the character of the Master of Ceremonies, and choose the assembly rooms' management.

Electoral activity clustered around the Guildhall and Parade, with regular meetings at Simpson and Gyde's Rooms, the Town Hall, the Parade Coffeehouse, and the Bear Inn.[25] Gyde and Simpson had rooms for dancing and card assemblies on opposite sides of Terrace Walk just off the Grand Parade. Gyde's Rooms became the election headquarters for Brereton's faction, while Plomer's supporters regularly met at the Town Hall.[26] In establishing committee rooms like this, the candidates echoed parliamentary election practice. In the afternoon following the 28 March 1769 announcement of Derrick's death, Brereton's faction attempted to hold a snap vote in Simpson's Rooms (later known as the Lower Rooms) because a ball was scheduled for that evening.[27] Some constituents saw a speedy election as desirable. Without a Master of Ceremonies to regulate the dancing and manage disputes and precedence, it was feared the activities of the assembly rooms would have ground to a halt.[28] Further, as Brereton had been deputising for a failing Samuel Derrick over the past year, many assumed that he had earned the right to succeed Derrick and would be a more acceptable candidate than a Bristolian 'interloper'. However, a

Electing the Arbiter Elegantiarum *in Bath and Beyond*   145

speedy election did not sit well with rival candidate Plomer, who wanted out-of-town subscribers, including his Bristol associates, to participate.[29] Consequently, a second election was held at Simpson's Rooms (1 April), with both candidates claiming victory. Two additional weeks of rancorous letter-writing filled Bath's newspapers, with neither faction willing to give way.[30] But what made this election so heated?

The language employed in the squibs of *The Bath Contest* highlights the complex relationship between Bath's 'King' and his subjects. Candidates openly echoed eighteenth-century electioneering practices. When William Wade placed his letters in the *Bath Chronicle*, he modelled his rhetoric upon that of a canvassing MP, soliciting 'the Favour of your Votes and Interest, being determined to make it my Study to execute the Office with the strictest Honour and Impartiality, and my best Endeavours to give general satisfaction'.[31] This rhetorical style was used by political candidates throughout the long eighteenth century, as Lord Milton addressed voters in Leeds in 1807 proclaiming, 'aided by your exertions and enthusiasm, I feel confident that I shall be able to secure your independence, and the honour and credit of the County of York'.[32] By emulating parliamentary candidates, Wade appealed to established electoral customs familiar to Bath's inhabitants and visitors. When subscribers questioned the practice of allowing subscribers to pay the requisite subscription fee on behalf of another person, incensed voters sought to 'assert our Rights, and never suffer ourselves to be thus trodden under Foot', demanding electoral integrity with rules determined in advance of the campaign.[33] Radical rhetoric was also deployed by one of Plomer's campaign committee or supporters in an anonymous squib:

> Write to who you please, subscribe in what Manner you please, or interest yourselves as you please, King [Brereton] and his Council have passed a Law, that you shall *not be allowed to vote*; therefore, (to speak in Royal Language) demean yourselves as our dutiful Subjects peaceably and quietly, on Pain of our Royal Displeasure if you behave otherwise (emphasis in original).[34]

The author invoked the spectre of growing concerns about George III's supposed authoritarianism and the influence of the Crown at the time. The 1769 Bath Contest took place only six years following the resignation of 'authoritarian Tory' Prime Minister Lord Bute.[35] Bute was responsible for the 1763 Cider Tax levied on every hogshead of cider produced to help pay off the National Debt from the Seven Years' War, which sparked outrage in the 'cider counties', of which Somerset was one.[36] Political unrest and opposition was compounded by the similar Stamp Act and Sugar Act (1765), which further fuelled discourse around authoritarian rule in 1769,

146   *Bath and Beyond*

of a monarchical figure bypassing the rights of the citizens and demanding docility and subservience, rather than allowing the subscribers to exercise their right to vote. The squibs and handbills from the Bath Contest reflected a wider awareness of county and national politics within their election of the Master of Ceremonies.

Strife also stemmed from disputes over voter qualification. According to the *Bath Chronicle*, the electorate consisted of assembly room subscribers, but dissent arose around including 'transient visitors' or restricting the franchise to local residents only.[37] Transient visitors were akin to outvoters in parliamentary elections who owned property in another constituency but travelled to cast their votes. The ruling by Plomer that 'Three Days Notice was the shortest period required by the Company to render a Meeting valid or respectful' restricted last-minute strategising by a wily candidate to catch his opponent off guard. It also enabled non-local subscribers to attend meetings and cast votes. In addition to outvoter participation, there was dissent around proxy voting and whether new subscribers could be encouraged to vote and sway the result, as this allowed transient *visitors* to have a greater effect than Bath's *residents*.[38] Precedent was set during this election allowing any previous subscriber to the assembly rooms to cast a vote, regardless of their current subscription status. This precedent was later challenged in 1818, when protests arose over the determination to allow only 'the Residents of Bath, and to those living within three miles of it' to vote, as opposed to 'every eligible Subscriber', which had been followed unwaveringly for decades.[39]

Another issue was the implementation of electoral procedure, which was supposed to be determined by subscribers before the campaign. In practice, the procedure was determined on an *ad hoc* basis, reacting to the actions and declarations of each faction. Brereton's and Plomer's factions were both guilty of agreeing to, and dictating, the procedure for the whole company to follow.[40] However, Bath's subscribers refused to be governed in this way during the election of the Master of Ceremonies. Their stern complaints in the press opined that the rules for this contest ought to have stemmed from the subscribers collectively and been imposed on the candidates and their factions.[41] Indeed, one exasperated subscriber angrily wrote,

> the Publick hath been offended, and the Decencies of private Conversation violated by tales . . . of Malice and Calumny: That Complaints and Reproaches of Irregularity, Precipitation, Injustice, and Invasion of Rights, have been urged with Virulence and Acrimony by both Parties.[42]

The rancour greeting these candidates' presumption indicates that a Master of Ceremonies' power emanated from the collective uniting around a

Electing the Arbiter Elegantiarum in Bath and Beyond   147

'King' who embodied politeness (as demonstrated by previous Masters of Ceremonies), instead of personal interest (as experienced in this election). As power stemmed from the subscribers to dictate and agree upon the rules of the assembly rooms and their elections, the candidates bypassed and wrested this power from their electorate.

Polite and gentlemanly conduct was expected amidst canvassing, as the candidate's character was supposed to be unimpeachable. The Master of Ceremonies' duty to the subscribers required that he be '*Decus et tutamen*', 'an ornament and safeguard', for the community he served.[43] Specifically, he had a duty of pastoral care towards the young ladies and gentlemen, as a protector of 'the Beauty and Virtue, the Youth and Inexperience of both Sexes . . . placed for Protection from Rudeness and Seduction; for Security from Ruin', and to be a 'Guardian of the young People of both Sexes, to keep them out of the Hands of Gamblers and Fortune-Hunters'.[44] He was to be an exemplar of honour, politeness, refinement, and good moral character to foster these qualities in his young subscribers. Yet smear campaigns filled Bath's newspapers with letters and anecdotes besmirching each candidate's character.

Brereton was dubbed a gambler and fortune hunter, the very threats from which Masters of Ceremonies were supposed to shield the assembly. Smear campaigns also targeted his Irish heritage, counterpointed by Plomer's claims of being a true Englishman.[45] The campaign's racialised language impugned Brereton and his subscribers as 'impudent, ignorant Irishmen', foreigners intruding on the management and regulation of an English spa town.[46] A letter published in the press from 31 March indicated that having a 'foreign' Master of Ceremonies was

> A Presumption extremely offensive and disgusting to all modest Persons. As if a few foreign Families, of whatever Nation, coming here from Motives of Health, Pleasure, Interest, or Convenience, have a Right to take the Lead, direct the Amusements, and give Law to the Natives.[47]

This invective racialised and 'othered' Brereton and his supporters. Plomer's xenophobic campaign squibs further charged Brereton's campaign with sole responsibility for electoral irregularities, arguing that, 'Englishmen are above those little sordid, local Partialities which they have in all Places and upon all Occasions to encounter in their ungenerous Neighbours'.[48] Of course, examinations of eighteenth-century English elections nuance the falsity of this claim, as factional partisanship frequently took hold in England's towns and cities, with treating, bribery, and corruption rampant in some boroughs and counties.

Brereton's campaign dubbed Plomer a tallow chandler, cheesemonger, and rope-maker. Although Plomer insisted he had conducted his canvass

148   *Bath and Beyond*

with 'Propriety, Decency, and Moderation, which became a Gentleman', Brereton derided Plomer as no gentleman, a Bristolian tradesman unfit to set foot in Bath.[49] Despite the fundamental commerciality of assembly rooms, overt links with trade were considered unsavoury. Openly associating Plomer with trade tarnished his character and social status, which was in no way aided by a letter from 24 Bristolian tradesmen (including tobacco merchants, cheesemongers, linen merchants, sugar bakers, confectioners, and grocers) defending Plomer's candidacy.[50] The letter stated, 'animated by the Example of our Correspondents in the Metropolis, we have generously resolved to ease you of the Trouble of governing yourselves, by placing at your head our beloved Mr P[lomer]'.[51] This incendiary and crowing missive was not a satiric squib. Indeed, I have been able to verify the names and professions of 50 per cent of the signatories still in business six years later in *Sketchley's Bristol Directory* from 1775.[52] This unwelcome intervention was seen as a condescending intrusion on the rights and voices of Bath's citizens, ratcheting up tensions between Bristolian tradesmen and Bath's fashionable residents and visitors.

The *Bath Contest* and *The Conciliade* make it possible to explore the polling process and results in this election, as they record the poll lists from both election attempts. Formal polling became confused by the uncoordinated votes held by the two factions. Brereton's faction held a vote on the afternoon of 28 March, his poll list indicating a majority of 268 votes. However, another vote was held on 1 April at Simpson's Card Room for four hours, lasting from 11 o'clock in the morning to three o'clock in the afternoon. An advertisement published the previous day indicated the use of pollbooks for subscribers to record their votes formally.[53] These votes would have been voiced publicly and inscribed in the pollbook as a matter of public record. However, it is unclear whether there were separate polling booths set up for each candidate and whether votes were given orally as well, as practised in parliamentary elections. While Plomer supporters attended Mr Simpson's Rooms to cast their votes, he claimed that Brereton sent his books around for absentee or ill supporters to record theirs.[54] Whether this is an accurate assessment or a smear tactic is challenging to determine. According to Plomer, he polled 267 votes on 1 April, whereupon both candidates claimed the majority of support and title of 'King'. The partisan poll lists of the voters' names were printed following the election, just as they were following parliamentary elections, highlighting the names and support of fashionable subscribers for public consumption.

Printed poll lists allowed the names and numbers of supporters to be scrutinised (Table 8.1) and enable demographic analysis. By 1 April, there were reportedly 606 subscribers who paid the requisite fee in order to vote. According to Plomer's statistics, 86 were neutral or absentee, abstaining from the fray. Of his 267 supporters, 186 were male, representing 69.6 per

Electing the Arbiter Elegantiarum *in Bath and Beyond*   149

Table 8.1 Plomer's poll list from *The Bath Contest*, 47–50; Brereton's poll list from *The Conciliade*, 8–11.

Category of Voter	Plomer Number of Votes	Plomer Percentage of Total Votes	Brereton Number of Votes	Brereton Percentage of Total Votes
Male Total	186	69.6	160	59.7
Titled	9	3.3	15	5.6
Clergymen	11	4.1	11	4.1
Military	0	0	16	5.9
Female Total	81	30.4	108	40.3
Titled	10	3.7	13	4.8
Married untitled	56	20.9	61	22.7
Unmarried untitled	15	5.6	34	12.7
TOTAL	267	100	268	100

cent of those who voted in favour of his candidacy: nine were titled, while 11 were clergymen. The remaining 81 voters (30.3 per cent) were female, with 10 titled ladies alongside 56 married and 15 unmarried women. Notable voters included Admiral Sir John Moore who had served during the Seven Years' War; Sir Edward Clive, a Justice of the Common Pleas; Lady Bingley, the wife of the Baron Bingley (former MP for York); Lord Mountmorres, an Irish peer and politician and associate of John Wilkes; and James Leigh Perrot, Jane Austen's maternal uncle.[55]

Brereton's poll list, gathered from the early vote on 28 March claimed to have 268 supporters voting for him. Of Brereton's 268 voters, 160 were men, forming 59.7 per cent of his total votes, with 15 titled men and 11 clergymen. Many of the men listed in Brereton's list were gentlemen, using the title 'esquire', a suffix not included in Plomer's list. Since Brereton's list was published after Plomer's in *The Conciliade*, it is possible that these details could have been added to highlight the distinguished supporters of Brereton's campaign. Due to Brereton's military background, it is unsurprising to see 16 military men on Brereton's list, in comparison with the lack of military titles in Plomer's faction. Brereton's list also presents a higher proportion of ladies supporting his candidacy, with women forming 40.3 per cent of his supporters, 10 per cent higher than Plomer's female supporters. Of these 108 women, 13 were titled ladies; 61 were married women and 34 were unmarried. Supporters of note include the 1st earl of Blesington, an Anglo-Irish peer; Lady Lauderdale, the wife of the 7th earl of Lauderdale; and David and Eva Maria Garrick, the celebrated actor and theatrical dancer from London.[56] Indeed, Garrick was heavily involved during the campaign, writing and publishing letters in the press, and mediating following the entrenchment of factions.[57] Brereton's poll list

150 Bath and Beyond

demonstrates an effort to highlight the politeness and rank of his faction, claiming superiority in quality and quantity over his opponent. Publicising the lists of voters and their voting inclinations following an election was standard practice in parliamentary elections and could be useful for future elections of Masters of Ceremonies as they revealed how the subscribers had been factionally divided. They were also of interest to subscribers and their networks in Bath and beyond, allowing them to see how friends and acquaintances voted during this controversial contest.

Making the polling lists public revealed how close the race was, with the two contenders separated by only one vote. This further entrenched the candidates and their supporters. Misleading advertisements with differing locations for the elections were placed in the newspapers, with some subscribers accusing Plomer of trying to derail the rights of the voters and split the vote.[58] As both candidates claimed that they had been rightfully elected, either on 28 March or on 1 April, a stalemate occurred, ratcheting up the vitriol in the press and creating a flashpoint in the community. According to physician and writer George Smith Gibbes: 'The men were anxious and fervent in the cause they took up; but the ladies, who . . . had their equal right of voting, were most furious and resentful'.[59] When Plomer tried to hold a ball on 10 April at Simpson's Rooms, he was 'refused the Rooms and Music for his intended ball'. This led to a massive riot the following day.[60] The meeting on 11 April descended into 'Scandalous Epithets, and Blows', as the ladies

> partook more of the parlieus of *Wapping* than the refined circles of Bath. It, at length, became so disgraceful, and such a scene of riot and confusion ensued at the rooms, that . . . the tumult was not appeased till . . . the town clerk had read the Riot-Act three times.[61]

A month after the riot, the caricature, 'Female Intrepidity, or the Battle of the Belles on ye Election of a King of Bath', appeared in the *Oxford Magazine* depicting men and women exchanging blows, trampling each other, and pulling out each other's hair (Figure 8.1). It could be argued that dignity and politeness emerged from this *melee* with equally bedraggled hair. The caricature's accompanying text reveals that 'some of the ladies lost their temper so greatly, as to descend to blows, and mere Billingsgate language, such as to call their antagonists b[itche]s and w[hores]s'.[62] The election turned to violence which, while by no means unusual during contested parliamentary elections, was shocking as genteel ladies joined the fray.

Georgian elections were cacophonous, colourful, and sometimes violent civic events, with men, women, and children, voters, and non-voters alike actively engaging in streets, public houses, assembly rooms, and homes. The slimmer the margins in a heated contest or the stronger a candidate's

Electing the Arbiter Elegantiarum in Bath and Beyond

Figure 8.1 Female Intrepidity, or the Battle of the Belles on ye Election of a King of Bath, 1769, etching, 11.9 × 17.5 cm, Lewis Walpole Library, 769.05.00.01 Impression 1. Courtesy of The Lewis Walpole Library, Yale University.

charisma, the more likely violence became. Caricatures like 'The Brentford Election' (Figure 8.2) from 1768 depict women as victims of electoral violence, with a mob of men attacking each other, and targeting elderly women and mothers with children with bludgeons. Indeed, this riotous election was alluded to in the press by 'a neutral subscriber' who was shocked by Bath's 'almost Brentford Election of Bruisers and Bludgeons'.[63] The outbreak of violence in Bath in 1769, a constituency known for its electoral civility, likely stemmed from the noisy Middlesex elections in 1768 and 1769 surrounding the repeated election and ejection of John Wilkes from parliament. Indeed, the electoral violence in Brentford (the county town for Middlesex where polling took place) caused significant disruption to elections and corporate life across England. That women were depicted as equal perpetrators of the violence in the caricature of Bath's Master of Ceremonies election highlights not only their equal right within the franchise to vote in this election but also the paradoxical loss of dignity and politeness attending the election of the very man to govern and police their politeness at future assemblies.

Nearly two weeks after the election of the two unyielding candidates, proposals were brought forward to resolve the conflict: these included electing a third party and involving a cross-factional committee. With the

Figure 8.2 The Brentford Election, 1768, etching, 11 × 18 cm, Lewis Walpole Library, 768.12.00.01 Impression 1. Courtesy of The Lewis Walpole Library, Yale University.

election in turmoil, the mayor and acting justices of Bath's corporation were called in to mediate.[64] On 13 April, six gentlemen each from Plomer's and Brereton's factions met to make the ultimate decision, with William Wade emerging victorious as the new 'reigning Monarch'.[65] His first subscription ball on 18 April resulted in the 'Restoration of Harmony and Tranquility', likely due to the fact that his campaign was unmarred by factional strife and modelled around gentlemanly conduct.[66] Wade also maintained local status and historical roots in Bath as his great-uncle had served as MP for the city from 1722 to 1747. As a result, Bath's subscribers established a fund-raising subscription to create a gold medallion for Wade, a badge used to distinguish Bath's Master of Ceremonies for 145 years.

Maintaining Power

Naturally, the successful election of a Master of Ceremonies, uncontested or not, did not portend a 'reign' without strife. Dispute mediation and resolution were intrinsic to the role. If not handled firmly and diplomatically, disputes could precipitate challenges to the Master of Ceremonies' authority; conversely, reluctance to enforce established rules could erode respect for the office. Dancing master G.M.S. Chivers articulated this: 'In all disputes the Persons so concerned should leave the Room with the Master of Ceremonies, and not return 'till both parties are reconciled'.[67] This

Electing the Arbiter Elegantiarum *in Bath and Beyond* 153

was not a practice limited to Bath. In her diary, novelist Frances Burney described an encounter with a Mr Richard, the Master of Ceremonies at a London ball in April 1772, in which he described his role:

> which obliges me to call all the minuets—lead out the ladies—fix on the gentlemen—O! I have such a fuss to settle disputes!—every thing is referred to me—'Sir, was this not my dance?' 'No, sir, I am sure it was my turn'—'Now pray sir, tell me, did not this gentleman do so—or so?' Gad so! it is such fun![68]

The Master of Ceremonies' decisions could neither be ignored nor overruled. Understanding that the elected 'King's' word was final in Britain's assembly rooms meant that those involved in a dispute were required to acquiesce to his determination or withdraw from the rooms. Although precedence in rank was strictly observed, whether walking, sitting, or dancing, this stipulation paradoxically elevated the Master of Ceremonies above the nobility and gentry populating the assembly rooms, and rendered all subscribers equal under his judgment.[69] Balls reflected and reinforced Georgian social hierarchy, whether in formal minuets or informal country dances. Caroline Powys, a member of the gentry, attended a private ball at Fawley Court in Buckinghamshire in 1777, where the guest list was largely composed of the nobility. She remarked: 'No minuets that night: would have been difficult without a master of the ceremonies among so many people of rank'.[70] Correctly arranging the dancers according to precedence at a ball required an intimate awareness of each dancer's social status within the community. The Master of Ceremonies' attention to this level of detail was essential to avoid giving offence. An authoritative figure to regulate the dancing could forestall members taking offence if they perceived the strict order of precedence to have been perverted. A sharp eye 'to read the room', observe, prevent, or defuse any disputes was vital.

The rules of the assembly rooms, printed and published in city directories across Great Britain, asserted the determinative power of the Master of Ceremonies in disputes. However, in response to obstinate subscriber behaviour in Edinburgh's New Town in 1787, the Master of Ceremonies' decision was underscored by support from the assembly room's directors.[71] Similarly, the determinations of a Lady Directress were viewed as sacrosanct; in 1740s Derby, for instance, those flouting the rules were 'turned out' of the rooms.[72] Masters of Ceremonies were censured for any irregularity in the order and management of the ballroom; their attentiveness to each person's actions was essential to ensure fairness.[73] Famously, 'Beau' Nash required the duchess of Queensberry to remove her decorative apron, which was forbidden by his assembly room rules, remarking that 'none but Abigails [lady's maids] appeared in white aprons [to which] the

154   *Bath and Beyond*

good-natured dutchess [*sic*] acquiesced in his censure'.[74] However, there were also instances in which the Master of Ceremonies received resistance to his dictates. In January 1780, Edmund Rack recounted such a situation in his journal:

> Capt Dawson, Master of the Ceremonies [in Bath], & the Bishop of Worcesters [*sic*] lady had lately a dispute on a dress ball night. The lady came in with a hat on, which is contrary to the establishd rules. Capt D politely remonstrated—the lady would not obey. The Capt insisted— she would not, but retird into the tea room. The Capt followd her, & told her that if she would not comply, disagreeable as the task would be, he must be obligd to take her hat off himself. She was still obstinate and ordering her chair left the rooms. The conduct of Capt D was highly applauded, but the Bishop has been silly enough to resent it, & some abusive letters have appeard [*sic*] in the London papers on the occasion.[75]

Captain Dawson's conflict resolution strategy was affirmed by the subscribers, confirming that he had acted appropriately on behalf of their interests and had been successful in holding subscribers to account, rather than allowing a select few to disobey the 'constitution' mutually agreed upon by the 'electorate'.

Despite assertions of power, subscribers could also question the Master of Ceremonies' directives. In 1770, John Marsh (musician, gentleman composer, and Master of Ceremonies) made the 'mistake' of admitting Mr Day, organist and music master, to Romsey's assembly. According to Marsh, Day was fashionably dressed, well mannered, and fond of dancing. However, as the son of a shoemaker, he was deemed improper company for the assemblies at Southampton and Romsey. Mrs Daman told John Marsh that she was

> surprized [*sic*] to hear that 'Day the shoemaker's son' . . . had been suffer'd to become a subscriber . . . [and] that I ought as Master of Ceremonies to return them their subscriptions & not admit them into the room, or in short to <u>turn them out</u> if they presum'd to come in (emphasis in original).[76]

Although serving as Master of Ceremonies was prestigious, any misstep could result in a public meeting to investigate his conduct and a vote either to retain or to remove him from office.[77] In Edinburgh, subscribers displeased with the conduct or management of the Master of Ceremonies could address their concerns to the Directors, who investigated the complaints.[78] At the assembly room in Leamington Spa in 1816, the power

Electing the Arbiter Elegantiarum in Bath and Beyond   155

structure was made explicit; 'the power of direction over the Public Assemblies . . . is in the Ladies and Gentlemen, Subscribers to the Balls, and them only'.[79] Stemming from the subscribers, authority was delegated to the Master of Ceremonies to act on the community's behalf, while still 'subject to the cognizance and control of the Subscribers'.[80] Lord Auckland recounted in 1798 that one subscriber was dissatisfied with Richard Tyson's behaviour while in office in Bath, having been 'rash enough of late to hold the language of a democrat, and to defend it with a great degree of effrontery'.[81] Another subscriber, upon being asked by Tyson to attend his benefit ball, provided a list of 50 subscribers' names and a draught for 50 guineas, instructing that this sum of money was to be donated to the Treasurer of the Bath Hospital instead of Tyson's benefit.[82] Tyson reportedly 'received three hundred pounds less than usual, and was in extreme danger of losing his office' as a result of espousing radical political sentiments.[83] The Master of the Ceremonies, as arbiter of polite behaviour, needed to avoid aggressive, political debate in polite company. Personal indiscretions also might result in removal from office: William Wade was ejected by the subscribers from Bath's Upper Rooms in 1777 for his adulterous affair with Elizabeth Eustatia Campbell, which resulted in her divorce.[84] Inappropriate or impolite behaviour also resulted in reprisals from the subscribers. The Master of Ceremonies was answerable to his 'constituents' despite being their 'King'.

Conclusion

The disputes during the 1769 Bath Contest set precedents for future Master of Ceremonies' elections, particularly that the electorate include both residents and visitors to Bath, and that the electoral procedure be agreed upon before the campaign. The aberrant descent into impoliteness and violence by both candidates and the electorate provided a powerful impetus for upholding politeness in future elections. It also demonstrated the importance of hearing and acknowledging subscribers' voices in decisions directly affecting them. The danger of a frustrated electorate, whose authority had been threatened, clarified the importance of candidates and their supporters respecting the electorate's rights.

Subscribers to Bath's assembly rooms showed an acute familiarity with electoral practices, procedures, and publications, with an adept ability to translate these well-known practices to suit social spaces. They reproduced established modes of political communication via the press and squib books to the election of society's 'King'. Practices and procedures were copied and inverted as well, ensuring that electoral procedures and assembly room rules stemmed 'bottom-up' from the subscribers, and not 'top-down' from election officials and candidates. Women's involvement in these elections cannot be understated. The very fact that it was accepted and expected

156   Bath and Beyond

that women would vote is important, especially given how closely it echoed parliamentary election customs, adding to a growing understanding of women's voting practices in other religious, civic, and economic areas of life in the eighteenth century.

Ultimately, the 1769 election revealed the importance of Bath and its 'King' in the imaginations of assembly room subscribers and the wider reading (and dancing) public. Indeed, by the end of the year, the country dance tune, 'The Bath Frollick, or, The Successfull Campaign [*sic*]', was published, commemorating this contest and Wade's victory in Thompson's *Twenty Four Country Dances for the Year* 1769.[85] The character of the *arbiter elegantiarum* remained central to his electoral success and highlighted the source of his power in Georgian society. Bath's assembly rooms remained scenes of strategic manoeuvring by the Master of Ceremonies and subscribers, delicately balancing politeness and impoliteness. Schemes to overthrow or overrule the arbiter of elegant amusements were not unusual occurrences, including Wade's ejection from the Upper Rooms in 1777 and the 1803 failed coup to oust James King from the Lower Rooms. These tensions highlighted the tenuous character of the power the Master of Ceremonies held over the subscribers.

Assembly rooms were critical spaces in Georgian Britain, gathering places for polite society for concerts, gaming, and dancing. Domains of entertainment and social interaction, they were rife with contradictions. They were spaces which encouraged broader social mixing across social strata, while rigorously enforcing the preservation of the hierarchical rights of precedence. Their elections provided subscribers the opportunity to *elect* their 'King' or 'Queen', the Master of Ceremonies or Lady Directress. The 'King', of indifferent birth, was paradoxically endowed with absolute authority over the appearance, movements, and behaviours of his social superiors. However, despite this title and authority, he was still answerable to his 'constituents'. Masters of Ceremonies and Lady Directresses ruled society with a firm hand, yet governed the subscribers with *their* permission.

Underpinning the assembly rooms was a social contract between its directors, subscribers, and manager. To be commercially successful, the rooms needed continually to attract and retain suitable subscribers among the nobility, gentry, and middling sort. Having gathered these together, they needed to ensure a well-regulated and socially harmonious environment. To this end, authority was devolved from the rooms' directors and subscribers onto the Master of Ceremonies, to safeguard the enterprise by establishing and enforcing accepted codes of conduct, regulating behaviour, and mediating disputes. In fulfilling this contract, Masters of Ceremonies became iconic figures in Georgian society, especially in fashionable leisure resorts like Bath. Their images were enshrined in paintings, engravings,

Electing the Arbiter Elegantiarum *in Bath and Beyond* 157

and city guides, and their names echoed in Britain's ballrooms through published country dance tunes like 'Beau Nash', 'Captain Wyke', and 'Mr King's Waltz, the Master of Ceremonies at Bath & Cheltenham'.[86] By their charm and charisma, these powerful figures ruled over the ballroom, regulated subscribers, and policed politeness to ensure the ultimate success of the rooms through their smooth operation.

Notes

1 Phyllis Hembry, *The English Spa, 1560–1815: A Social History* (London: Athlone Press, 1990); Bruce Osbourne and Cora Weaver, *Rediscovering 17th century springs and spas* (Malvern: Aldine Press, 1996).
2 Thomas Tegg, *Analysis of the London Ball-Room* (London, 1825), 60.
3 Steven Gores, *Psychosocial Spaces: Verbal and Visual Readings of British Culture, 1750–1820* (Detroit, 2000), 71.
4 John Eglin, *The Imaginary Autocrat: Beau Nash and the Invention of Bath* (Profile Books, 2005), 15.
5 Samuel Derrick, *A Collection of Original Poems* (1755).
6 TNA, PROB/11/761/79.
7 Hester Lynch Piozzi, *The Piozzi Letters: 1817–1821*, ed. O. M. Brack, 6 vols. (London, 1989–2002), vi, 312.
8 G. N. Wright, *The Historic Guide to Bath* (Bath, 1864), 304–5.
9 Frank O'Gorman, *Voters, Patrons and Parties: The Unreformed Electorate of Hanoverian England, 1734–1832* (Oxford: OxfordUniversity Press, 1989), 67.
10 John Courtney, *The Diary of a Yorkshire Gentleman: John Courtney of Beverley, 1759–1768*, ed. Susan Neave and David Neave (Otley, 2001), 63.
11 *Saint James's Chronicle*, December 14, 1805.
12 *Kentish Gazette*, October 23, 1804; *Bath Chronicle and Weekly Gazette*, November 13, 1817.
13 *Kentish Gazette*, October 23, 1804.
14 *Saint James's Chronicle*, December 14, 1805; *Hampshire Chronicle*, December 16, 1805; *Salisbury and Winchester Journal*, November 20, 1815; *Hereford Journal*, November 27, 1816; *Northampton Mercury*, November 30, 1816.
15 *Bath Contest*, 16.
16 *Bath Contest*, 36–37.
17 *The Essex County Election: Report of the speeches delivered at the hustings* was printed and sold by Meggy and Chalk, proprietors of the *Chelmsford Chronicle* and *Essex Herald*. So, too, was William Pine (printer of the *Bristol Gazette*), responsible for publishing *The Bristol contest; the proceedings at the contested election* in 1781.
18 *The Bath Contest: Being a Collection of All the Papers, Advertisements, &c. Published before and Since the Death of Mr Derrick, by the Candidates for the Office of Master of the Ceremonies, and Their Friends* (Bath, 1769).
19 *Bath Chronicle*, April 27, 1769.
20 *HP Commons 1754–90*, iii, 366.
21 Elaine Chalus, "Women, Electoral Privilege and Practice in the Eighteenth Century," in *Women in British Politics, 1760–1860*, ed. Kathryn Gleadle and Sarah Richardson (Basingstoke: Palgrave Macmillan, 2000).
22 *Bath Contest*, 8; *Salisbury and Winchester Journal*, August 19, 1811; *Salisbury and Winchester Journal*, November 30, 1829.

158 Bath and Beyond

23 Jonah Miller, "Suffrage and the Secret Ballot in Eighteenth-Century London Parishes," *Historical Journal* lxvii (2024): 50; Sarah Richardson, *The Political Worlds of Women: Gender and Politics in Nineteenth Century Britain* (New York: New York University Press, 2013), 89–93; Sarah Richardson, "Petticoat Politicians: Woman and the Politics of the Parish in England," *The Historian* (2013): 12–13.

24 Ben Gilding, " 'No Distinction Exists as to Religion, Profession, or Sex': Imperial Reform and the Electoral Culture of the East India Company's Court of Proprietors, 1760–84," *Parliamentary History* xliii (2024): 130–33; Peter Auber, *Analysis of the Constitution of the East India Company* (1826), 349.

25 *Bath Contest*, 8–50.

26 *Bath Contest*, 24, 36, 59.

27 *Bath Contest*, 17. Numerous notices in Bath's newspapers printed conflicting locations for the same election, including both Mr Gyde's and Mr Simpson's Rooms.

28 Huntington Lib., mss HM 54457, xv, 160.

29 *Bath Contest*, 14.

30 *Bath Contest*, 35, 41.

31 *Bath Contest*, 16.

32 Yorkshire Election, *A Collection of the Speeches, Addresses and Squibs, Produced by All the Parties During the Late Contested Election for the County of York* (Leeds, 1807), 16–17.

33 *Bath Contest*, 13–14.

34 *Bath Contest*, 13.

35 Steve Poole, *The Politics of Regicide in England, 1760–1850: Troublesome Subjects* (Manchester: Manchester University Press, 2000), 9.

36 David Walsh et al., "The Cider Tax, Popular Symbolism and Opposition in Mid-Hanoverian England," in *Markets, Market Culture and Popular Protest in Eighteenth-Century Britain and Ireland*, ed. Adrian Randall and Andrew Charlesworth (Liverpool: Liverpool University Press, 1996), 69.

37 *Bath Contest*, 7–9.

38 *Bath Contest*, 7–9.

39 *Morning Advertiser*, January 6, 1818.

40 *Bath Contest*, 11, 35.

41 *Bath Contest*, 35.

42 *Bath Contest*, 37.

43 Peter Paul Pallet, *Bath Characters, or, Sketches from Life*, 3rd ed. (1808), viii; Peter Paul Pallet, *Decus & Tutamen, Or, Our New Money as Now Coined in Full Weight and Fineness Proved to be for the Honour, Safety, and Advantage of England* (1696).

44 *Bath Contest*, 11, 38.

45 *Bath Contest*, 7, 27–28.

46 *Bath Contest*, 27.

47 *Bath Contest*, 33.

48 *Bath Contest*, 32.

49 *Bath Contest*, 8, 37.

50 *Bath Contest*, 19–20.

51 *Bath Contest*, 20.

52 James Sketchley, *Sketchley's Bristol Directory* (Bristol, 1775).

Electing the Arbiter Elegantiarum *in Bath and Beyond* 159

53 *Bath Contest*, 34.
54 *Bath Contest*, 47.
55 *Bath Contest*, 47–50.
56 *Conciliade*, 8–11.
57 George Smith Gibbes, *The Historical and Local New Bath Guide* (Bath, 1835), 145.
58 *Bath Contest*, 28.
59 Gibbes, *The Historical*, 145.
60 *Bath Contest*, 56–57.
61 *Bath Contest*, 65; Egan, *Walks Through Bath*, 115.
62 *The Oxford Magazine; or University Museum*, 13 vols. (1769), ii, 188.
63 *Bath Contest*, 43.
64 *Bath Contest*, 50–53.
65 *Conciliade*, 3–7; *Bath Contest*, 66.
66 *Bath Chronicle and Weekly Gazette*, April 20, 1769; *Conciliade*, 16, 24.
67 G. M. S. Chivers, *A Pocket Companion to the French and English Country Dances* (1818), 39.
68 Frances Burney, *The Early Diary of Frances Burney, 1768–1778*, ed. Annie Raine Ellis, 4 vols. (London, 1907), i, 168–69.
69 Abraham Rees, *The Cyclopædia; or, Universal Dictionary of Arts*, 39 vols. (1819), xxviii, 396.
70 Caroline Lybbe Powys, *Passages from the Diaries of Mrs Philip Lybbe Powys of Hardwick House, Oxon. 1756 to 1808*, ed. Emily J. Climenson (1899), 185–86.
71 *Caledonian Mercury*, March 26, 1787.
72 *Derbyshire Courier*, November 6, 1847.
73 *The Southampton Guide* (Southampton, 1795), 95–96.
74 Oliver Goldsmith, *The Life of Richard Nash, of Bath, Esq: Extracted Principally from His Original Papers* (1762), 36.
75 BCL, MS B920: Edmund Rack, A Disultory Journal of Events etc. at Bath, January 22, 1780.
76 Huntington Lib., mss HM 54457, iii, 8–10.
77 H. Sharpe, *New Guide: An Historical and Descriptive Account of Warwick and Leamington* (Warwick, 1816), 185.
78 *Caledonian Mercury*, March 26, 1787.
79 Sharpe, *New Guide*, 185.
80 Sharpe, *New Guide*, 185.
81 William Eden, *The Journal and Correspondence of William, Lord Auckland*, 2 vols. (1861), ii, 479.
82 Eden, *The Journal*, ii, 479.
83 Eden, *The Journal*, ii, 479.
84 *Trials for Adultery, or, the History of Divorces*, 7 vols. (Clark, NJ, 2006), i, 70.
85 Charles Thompson and Samuel Thompson, *Twenty Four Country Dances for the Year 1769* (1769), 50.
86 John Johnson, *A Choice Collection of 200 Favourite Country Dances*, 6 vols. (1750), v, 64; Martin Platts, *Martin Platts' Periodical Collection of Popular Dances, Waltzes &c. No. 12* (c.1816), 2; Augustus Voigt, *A Selection, Elegant & Fashionable Country Dances, Reels, Waltzes &c. for the Ensuing Season 1809* (1809), 10.

160   *Bath and Beyond*

Bibliography

Manuscript Sources

Bath Central Library

MS B920: Edmund Rack, A Disultory Journal of Events etc. at Bath.

Huntington Library

mssHM 54457, John Marsh Journals

Primary and Secondary Sources

Anonymous, *Trials for Adultery, or, the History of Divorces*. Clark, NJ: Lawbook Exchange Ltd., 2006.

The Bath Contest: Being a Collection of All the Papers, Advertisements, &c. Published Before and Since the Death of Mr Derrick, by the Candidates for the Office of Master of the Ceremonies, and Their Friends. Bath: Archer and Cruttwell, 1769.

Burney, Frances. *The Early Diary of Frances Burney, 1768–1778*. Edited by Annie Raine Ellis. London: G. Bell, 1907.

Chivers, G. M. S. *A Pocket Companion to the French and English Country Dances*. London, 1818.

The Conciliade; Being a Supplement to the Bath Contest. Bath: Archer and Cruttwell, 1769.

Courtney, John. *The Diary of a Yorkshire Gentleman: John Courtney of Beverley, 1759–1768*. Edited by Susan Neave and David Neave. Otley: Dalesman Publishing Company Ltd., 2001.

Dain, Angela. "Assemblies and Politeness, 1660–1840." PhD diss., University of East Anglia, 2000.

Decus & Tutamen, Or, Our New Money as Now Coined in Full Weight and Fineness Proved to Be for the Honour, Safety, and Advantage of England. London, 1696.

Derrick, Samuel. *A Collection of Original Poems*. London: A. Millar, 1755.

Eden, William. *The Journal and Correspondence of William, Lord Auckland*. London: R. Bentley, 1861.

Eglin, John. *The Imaginary Autocrat: Beau Nash and the Invention of Bath*. London: Profile Books, 2005.

Gibbes, George. *The Historical and Local New Bath Guide*. Bath: C. Duffield, 1835.

Goldsmith, Oliver. *The Life of Richard Nash, of Bath, Esq: Extracted Principally from His Original Papers*. London: J. Newbery, 1762.

Gores, Steven. *Psychosocial Spaces: Verbal and Visual Readings of British Culture, 1750–1820*. Detroit: Wayne State University Press, 2000.

Gray, Jonathan. *An Account of the Manner of Proceeding at the Contested Election for Yorkshire in 1807*. York: Thomas Wilson & Sons, 1818.

Hembry, Phyllis. *The English Spa, 1560–1815: A Social History*. London: Farleigh Dickinson University Press, 1990.

Johnson, John. *A Choice Collection of 200 Favourite Country Dances*. London, 1750.

Namier, Sir Lewis, and J. Brooke, eds. *The History of Parliament: The House of Commons, 1754–1790*. London: Secker and Warburg, 1964.

Electing the Arbiter Elegantiarum *in Bath and Beyond*   161

O'Gorman, Frank. *Voters, Patrons and Parties: The Unreformed Electorate of Hanoverian England, 1734–1832.* Oxford: Clarendon Press, 1989.

The Oxford Magazine; or University Museum. London, 1769.

Pallet, Peter. *Bath Characters, or, Sketches from Life.* London: G. Wilkie & J. Robinson, 1808.

Piozzi, Hester. *The Piozzi Letters: 1817–1821.* Edited by O. M. Brack. London: Associated University Presses, 1989.

Platts, Martin. *Martin Platts' Periodical Collection of Popular Dances, Waltzes &c. No. 12.* London: Martin Platts, c.1816.

Powys, Caroline. *Passages from the Diaries of Mrs Philip Lybbe Powys of Hardwick House, Oxon. 1756 to 1808.* Edited by Emily J. Climenson. London: Longmans, Green & Co., 1899.

Rees, Abraham. *The Cyclopædia; or, Universal Dictionary of Arts.* London: Longman, Hurst, Rees, Orme & Brown, 1819.

Sharpe, H. *New Guide: An Historical and Descriptive Account of Warwick and Leamington.* Warwick: H. Sharpe, 1816.

The Southampton Guide. Southampton: A. Cunningham, 1795.

Tegg, Thomas. *Analysis of the London Ball-Room.* London, 1825.

Voigt, Augustus. *A Selection, Elegant & Fashionable Country Dances, Reels, Waltzes &c. for the Ensuing Season 1809.* London, 1809.

Wright, G. N. *The Historic Guide to Bath.* Bath: R.E. Peach, 1864.

9 The Undertakers of Eighteenth-Century Bath

Dan O'Brien

Hey-day! I hear a noise! What can it be?
The undertakers. I told you how it wou'd be—The dismal crew have had scent of your death; here they are.[1]

In the 1786 play *Better Late Than Never*, a piece created for private performance by William Davies, the affluent Bath resident Mr Peter Recluse feigns his death after a rival declares him dead in the local newspaper. This is not an entirely original tactic in eighteenth-century theatre, but it does allow the elderly gentleman to discover the plans of the nefarious Mr Swindal who intends to discredit Recluse's son and marry his sister Phoebe, purely for economic gain. The majority of scenes focus on the comic attempts of Recluse to remain 'dead' in the eyes of his family, aided by his butler, Mr Handy.

Recluse's 'deceased' state draws an unfortunate but humorous consequence at the beginning of the second Act, when three undertakers arrive at the house to perform his funeral. The men named Coffin, Grimly, and Finis are introduced in the midst of a furious argument on the doorstep of Recluse's household, disputing who arrived first at the property and should win first hearing. As the servant, Handy, questions each undertaker we are introduced to a series of behaviours which are far from the sober, solemn reputation of the trade. Slanders, bribes, and threats are used by the desperate undertakers, but none succeeds, and Coffin, Finis, and Grimly are sent away. The candid nature of this conversation is made more humorous by the undertakers' refusal to accept that Recluse is not actually dead. The undertakers return to the Recluse household in the fourth Act where they try to force entry aggressively in another comedic sequence, equally contradictory to the sobriety and solemnity expected from the funeral trade.

We should not, of course, interpret these characters as an authentic representation of Bath's undertakers, but as a joke which could only succeed if its audience recognised a kernel of truth or a familiar suspicion.

DOI: 10.4324/9781003393856-9

The Undertakers of Eighteenth-Century Bath 163

Undertakers were an inevitable part of life in a prosperous, fashionable city such as Bath—a city populated with affluent families and social climbers who were perfectly suited to the self-aggrandising products of the trade. We may therefore use these overdrawn and exaggerated gentlemen as a window on the reality of undertaking in Bath because they prompt us to consider what the trade looked like there and how it operated. What sorts of people were undertakers in Bath and how did they compete for custom?

This chapter intends to examine the early undertaking trade in eighteenth-century Bath, responding to a lack of writing on the development of funerary business in the city. The chapter commences by considering the origins of Bath's undertaking businesses and how they operated. It limits its focus to those who specifically chose the title 'undertaker', and it is necessary to consider contemporary knowledge of this title because it was novel in the eighteenth century and open to interpretation. Secondly, the chapter considers how Bath's undertakers promoted themselves and encouraged potential customers to trust their innovative businesses. An analysis of undertakers' advertisements identifies the qualities which were perceived to define a good undertaker: both the intangible quality of experience and the very tangible spaces in which the undertakers traded. Thus, a close analysis of major Bath funerals demonstrates how these occasions were a 'shop window' for the services of entrepreneurial undertakers seeking to present themselves as credible and comprehensive.

Introducing the Literature

The long eighteenth century has been presented as important to the history of the undertaking trade because it is perceived to be a period of expansion and development, bridging the gap between the origins of the trade in the late seventeenth century and the commercial boom of the 'Victorian Way of Death'. The number of practising undertakers in eighteenth-century England is unclear, but the individuals discussed as examples of early undertaking indicate that the trade was overwhelmingly metropolitan. Julian Litten identifies the pioneers William Boyce and William Russell but is clear that neither had an 'absolute monopoly' over the funeral trade in the early eighteenth century.[2] Clare Gittings notes that not only did the trade originate in London, as illustrated by Boyce and Russell, but that its influence was most profoundly felt in the city.[3] Paul S. Fritz argues that, as a 'solely profit-driven enterprise', undertaking depended on a large and conducive customer base which was only present in an urban centre, such as London.[4] This is not to suggest that the provinces were devoid of undertakers or the influence of their trade until the late eighteenth century. Existing literature identifies a few provincial undertakers who acted solely in the trade, of which the earliest known example is Richard Chandles of Shrewsbury,

164   *Bath and Beyond*

who operated in 1718.[5] Fritz observes that the emergence of provincial undertakers following the form of their metropolitan counterparts was limited to the 'last quarter' of the eighteenth century, and this accounts for the scarcity of named tradesmen in the records.[6] Trevor Fawcett has provided a limited but valuable account of some of the key undertakers in his history of trades in eighteenth-century Bath. His research identifies a few prominent and successful undertakers such as John Plura and William Cross, illustrating the existence of undertaking in the city and justifying a wider study to address the breadth of the trade including those speculative individuals who might not have achieved the same success.[7] Fawcett's account invites an appraisal of how these 'undertaking' businesses operated and what made them so distinct as to warrant a separate classification in both the historical record and the eyes of their contemporaries.

While the metropolitan and provincial undertaking trade may have developed at different paces, the early undertakers came from similarly diverse backgrounds. Early undertaking was opportunistic and entrepreneurial tradesmen entered into a fast-developing market, which would be directed and developed by their ingenuity. This trade is therefore presented as an unregulated and disparate institution, which had no criteria of entry nor rules of operation; as Litten summarises 'anyone could set themselves up as an undertaker.'[8]

Knowledge of the Role of Undertaker

In response to the irregularity of the early trade, this chapter specifically studies the Bath tradespeople who identified themselves publicly as 'undertakers'. It is important to clarify this approach, because many urban and rural tradespeople in the provinces provided for, or organised, funerals but did not choose to adopt the title of undertaker. We can identify at least 61 people who used the title of 'undertaker' in just the last three decades of the eighteenth century.[9] These individuals' adoption of the title was significant because it demonstrated an awareness of the trade in the city.

It is plausible that some of the early Bath undertakers had become aware of the title as a consequence of their other businesses, because visits to the warehouses and shops of London were common in the fabric and furnishing trades from which many early undertakers originated. Although these visits were intended for purchasing stock, they provided tradesmen with an opportunity to interact with members of the metropolitan funeral trade and observe their operations. Bath's undertakers consequently alluded to knowledge of their metropolitan counterparts in advertisements which reported that the proprietor had 'returned from London' or promised 'the same terms as the warehouses in London' or that 'undertakers may be supplied equally cheap as in London.'[10] Furthermore, it is also apparent that

The Undertakers of Eighteenth-Century Bath   165

some undertakers had worked in metropolitan businesses such as these, prior to establishing themselves in Bath. William Bartlett of St. James's Street had worked for the London undertaker Francis Deschamps at Rathbone Place in the 1750s before establishing himself in Bath.[11] It is plausible that Bartlett's decision to diversify his upholstering business was influenced by his experience of the funeral trade in London. Bartlett's business differed from the majority of Bath undertakers because he chose the dual titles of 'undertaker' and 'coffin maker,' possibly reflecting a particular specialism he had learned whilst working for Deschamps. Bath had few individuals who styled themselves specifically as coffin makers, and it would have been a skill which made Bartlett useful to other local undertakers who did not make their own coffins. Another Bath undertaker, named Treacher, advertised his former duties as a 'Groom of the Chambers to the Assembly House in Soho Square' as evidence for his pedigree as an upholder, appraiser, and undertaker.[12] It is apparent here that Treacher's experience in a social environment in London may have been advantageous as it demonstrated an awareness of taste and an ability to manage important occasions.

The Identities of Bath's Undertakers

The undertakers of *Better Late Than Never* were dedicated to funerary work and their testimony indicates that they were always engaged in the organisation of funerals or the acquisition of new businesses. The nature of their work seems to define their already exaggerated characters through their comic names and the way in which they speak about death in jargon, which they describe as 'the way we call it in the business.'[13] These factors give the undertakers a distinctive presence which is demonstrated when the butler Handy recognises them instantly outside the Recluse household.

It is apparent that most Bath tradesmen, who identified themselves as undertakers, were also engaged in other trades in which they had previously established their reputation. The continuation of their previous livelihoods mitigated the financial risks of establishing an entirely new business, particularly when that might initially have a low number of consumers and require a large stock of funerary goods. Similar to their London counterparts, the undertakers of Bath were men whose adoption of the trade was a diversification of existing work and, much as in the capital, textile and furnishing trades, provided the majority of the early proponents.

Many of the undertakers identified within this chapter worked concurrently as textile traders. Within the textile trades, linen drapery was the most common supplementary occupation for Bath's undertakers. This is an unsurprising development because of the longstanding importance of linen attire in funerary rites, specifically the shroud or winding sheet worn by the corpse. The popularity of linen led to the *Burying in Woollen Acts* of the

166   Bath and Beyond

late seventeenth century. These acts were intended to curb the use of linen by instructing the use of wool for burial clothes and imposing a £5 fine for transgression. Although the act was not repealed until 1815, its influence was challenged throughout the period by wealthy individuals' willingness to pay the fine and increasingly poor enforcement by local officials.[14] The persisting trade in linen goods for funerary use would therefore have provided a means by which tradesmen were introduced to the commercial opportunities of funerals. It also created a situation in which the linen draper was recognised as an essential tradesman for the supply of funerals, a status which would prove useful to anyone who wanted the public to trust his authority and credibility as a funeral supplier. George Chapman's shop at Upper Cheap Street advertised his services as an undertaker and sold a broad range of different linens alongside textiles such as bombazine and Norwich crape, which were used in funerary and mourning contexts.[15]

Mercery was the second most common supplementary trade for the undertakers identified here. The products of a mercer were diverse, as demonstrated by the undertaker George Strawbridge who also traded as mercer and linen draper.[16] Strawbridge's dual occupations reflect the similarity of mercery and linen drapery; mercers were also involved in the fabric trade and frequently consolidated several different clothing trades.

It can be argued that businesses which consolidated different textile and clothing trades were more likely to diversify into undertaking. Each different trade added skills and stock which reduced an early undertaker's dependence on other tradesmen for the numerous items that were required in the contemporary funeral. The potential stock of an early undertaker featured many items of clothing, and the trades which produced these items were fertile ground for new undertakers. Gloves were still distributed as gifts and were part of the stock sold by undertaker John Gale at his Wade's Passage hattery, hosiery, and haberdashery shop that he inherited from his grandfather.[17] Gale's business included several specialisms that offered an easy path into undertaking because they involved the production and sale of funerary goods. Hatters such as Peter Grigg and Thomas Creaser who both took the title 'undertaker' may have stocked the caps sold and rented for funerals.[18] Hosiers' skills enabled them to produce funerary goods such as pillows and shrouds which used delicate materials. The Stall Street undertaker and hosier Mr Smith advertised making and selling 'men, women and children's shrouds: men and women's from 4s. 6d. to one Guinea.'[19] The products of haberdashers, including ribbons and buttons, were used in the decorative attire of the funeral attendants, and undertakers such as Mayo & Co, also of Wade's Passage, were capable of providing these.[20]

The second largest group in Bath undertaking were members of the furniture trade such as upholsters, upholders, cabinetmakers, and joiners.

The Undertakers of Eighteenth-Century Bath   167

This trend complements Matthew Craske's description of undertakers as 'upholders in the sphere of death,' whose middle management of diverse trades mirrored the organising and centralising behaviour of the upholsterers, or upholders.[21] It is obvious that the skills required to manufacture a cabinet could be applied to the production of coffins, as both items were boxes of a sort, but there is more to the funerary effectiveness of the furniture maker. The skills of organisation and acquisition required in furniture manufacturing were beneficial during funerary preparations where an undertaker might need to act as middleman between various businesses. For example, the completion of a coffin might involve upholstery for the interior as well as a lead inner-coffin to contain the body for vault burial. The exterior might also require metal handles, nails, and a name plate, and perhaps the use of a silk wrap for the coffin wood. With the possible exception of the upholstery, all of these items would be sourced from outside of the undertaker's business and this necessitated an awareness of artisanal networks and arguably the nurturing of such relationships. Many of the undertakers who were furniture makers were also practitioners of allied trades, such as George Tar, whose shop at Fountain Buildings in Bath specialised in cabinetmaking and upholstery. Tar's business also sold interior furnishings, such as wallpaper and hangings, which were likely intended for affluent customers.[22] Similar to Tar, other upholders seized the opportunity to adopt a title which highlighted a specific aspect of their work such as William Orchard of Margaret's Buildings, who described himself as a 'cabinet and chair-maker' in an advertisement that also promoted his undertaking business.[23]

Auctioneering was another popular form of diversification for upholders who sold goods from local estates and businesses at the city's taverns, in addition to their work as undertakers. The notion of undertakers burying people and selling their goods at auction may seem ghoulish, but auctioneering involved the commercialisation of upholders' knowledge regarding the value of household items. It is arguable that funerary work enabled upholders to interact with bereaved families, creating an entrepreneurial opportunity for the sale of personal effects and properties. It is unsurprising that some of Bath's most successful auctioneers, such as Samuel Nichols and John Plura, were well-established undertakers.[24] It is also worthwhile noting that auctioneers were particularly adept users of print media, as this was the way in which they announced their auctions and described the goods which they wanted to sell.[25] It is probable that this made them more willing users of the media as undertakers because they were already familiar with newspaper advertising and its benefits.

It is evident that some people recognised the roles of auctioneer and undertaker to be mutually compatible or intrinsically linked. In 1784, Charles Abbott abandoned his work in haberdashery, hosiery, and lace

168   *Bath and Beyond*

to become an auctioneer and undertaker.[26] Abbott did not come from a typical auctioneer background, although the furnishing of funerals was a minor part of his earlier business. It can be argued that by adopting these two new titles at the same time, he was possibly motivated by the belief that it was viable and profitable to combine the two trades. The eight undertakers working successfully in Bath as auctioneers may have been sufficient evidence to persuade Abbott to pursue the opportunity.[27]

Competition between Undertakers

In *Better Late Than Never*, the undertakers of Bath are imagined as a cut-throat group of entrepreneurs, driven by desperation to promote their wares. In the real world of eighteenth-century Bath, there were two forms of competitive behaviour with which undertakers could attempt to bolster and improve their status as professionals. The relocation and redesign of shops was a material form of competitive behaviour which demonstrated the status and quality of the business. The undertakers' public claims of experience and qualification were often incorporated into advertisements, but these were harder for consumers to confirm.

The success of Davies's fictional undertakers is testified by their accounts of lavish lifestyles and esteemed company. Finis is related to members of the city corporation and possesses the right of free entry to the theatre, which he attempts to use as a bribe. Grimly describes a life of fine dining and good wine stating that 'there is a not a man at Bath can produce such a sample.'[28] The undertakers' ebullient descriptions prompt the butler, Handy, to remark that 'I fancy the business of an undertaker must be very profitable.'[29] What then were the real-world symbols of success and profitability that encouraged customers of good and reliable content?

In *Better Late Than Never*, the verbal conflict between Bath's competing undertakers is punctuated with statements of authority and qualification in matters regarding death. Discrediting the authority of his competitors, Davies's Mr Coffin argues, 'I was regularly brought up to the business; the others, there, are intruders, mere bunglers in it.'[30] In an increasingly competitive marketplace, the length of tradesmen's time as an undertaker was a quality which could distinguish them from those who had recently established their businesses. Believing that he had secured the household's custom, Coffin further disputes the abilities of his rival Finis, arguing that 'He can very ill afford such a premium; he's but a novice in the branch.'[31] The 'branch' mentioned by Coffin was the undertaking trade, subtly suggesting that longevity in funerary work mattered more than additional experience in other trades. The aggressive disputes between fictional undertakers were an exaggerated version of the professional disagreements which existed between many tradesmen including undertakers. Such disputes prompted

The Undertakers of Eighteenth-Century Bath   169

one undertaker William Pitman from neighbouring Bradford-on-Avon to use *Bath Chronicle* to explain that 'various efforts have been artfully made use of to injure me, (particularly in the funeral way by my opponents in that line).'[32] It is significant that Pitman identified his denigrators as workers in the funeral trade because he was concurrently involved in auctioneering and upholding, neither of which caused him the same damage.

The Undertakers' Experience and Qualification

In *Better Late Than Never*, longevity was an important quality of a 'good' undertaking business, and this was also the case on the streets of eighteenth-century Bath. The advertisements of Bath's undertakers presented longevity as evidence that an undertaker was adequately skilled and commercially successful. In a period when many new undertakers were establishing themselves, the businesses which had existed for an extended period could boast greater experience and rely on developed relationships with customers and suppliers.

Advertisements for undertakers often provided a limited account of the funerary goods which they sold, and there is a tendency to focus on the products of the undertakers' other businesses. This reflects a contemporary custom of deferring responsibility for the funeral to the undertaker, a practice which is represented in the frequently used statement 'funerals fully furnished.'[33] Although they may not give consistent detail on what undertakers sold, they do provide a useful account of who was using the title 'undertaker' and where they were located within the city.

When an undertaker died or retired it was often necessary for their successor to publish an announcement identifying themselves. It was also important because convention dictated that the business would continue in the name of the successor, and it was therefore necessary that customers associated the new name with the old business. Bath's undertakers followed a wider trend for press announcements which offered an opportunity for businesses to advertise themselves, even if they did not wish to promote their stock.[34] It has been observed that these advertisements stated the continuity between family members who inherited businesses, building on reputation, and encouraging trust.[35]

Following the death of successful upholsterer and undertaker Arthur Trimnell, his widow Mary took charge of the business along with her sons Charles and Thomas, promising that the business, 'will be carried on as usual' in an advert which emphasised their relationship as 'widow and sons of Arthur Trimnell.'[36] The Trimnell name was already established in Bath and this kind of promotion suggested that his family understood the sort of service his customers expected. In some instances, the inheritor did not share the surname of the deceased and to ensure continuity it was

170 *Bath and Beyond*

necessary to state publicly the nature of the relationship. In 1784, John Gale announced the arrival of a new stock of items including funerary goods at his diverse business in Wade's Passage; in addition to undertaking, he was also a hosier, hatter, haberdasher, and glover.[37] His advertisement identified him as 'successor to his grandfather, Mr John Bowden,' high-lighting his relationship to the elderly haberdasher and undertaker, who had died during the previous month. Thus death could also be the oppor-tunity for an employee to inherit an established funerary business with its stock and customers. Following the death of the undertaker Joseph Gawen, his successor, Abraham Holmes, announced his adoption of the premises and stock of his 'late employer' with a brief advertisement that called upon Gawen's customers and friends.[38] Holmes could not depend on familial ties, but his time in Gawen's business supported the idea that he could offer a continuation of the service that customers expected.

Working experience in an existing funerary business was often regarded as an asset which underscored ties of family or friendship; it was also particularly significant if an undertaker had left a continuing business to establish their own. References to work in the city's funeral businesses con-firmed a contemporary belief that knowledge of the trade could only be gained through experience, rather than education. In the mid-eighteenth century, Robert Campbell noted the absence of any particular qualifica-tion for undertaking and unfavourably concluded that undertakers 'require more money than brains.'[39] He suggested that artisans became undertak-ers through their employment in the trade and consequent experience of its unique duties. Such vocational instruction had been the premise of an earlier satirical ballad, *Funeral Discipline*, which depicted the tutelage of an undertaker's assistant named Paul Meagre. Knowledge of the secretive practices of the trade was received by Meagre whilst he assisted the chief undertaker with the preparation of a funeral. Meagre was a senior member of the undertaker's retinue, and it was made apparent that his instruction was intended to lead to his eventual inheritance of the business.[40] Many Bath undertakers followed a similar career path to the fictional Meagre by rising from the position of assistant to inherit the business of their deceased or retired employer. In 1793, George Tar advertised his business with a prominently placed reference to his 25 years of employment as a foreman to the Bath undertaker William Cross.[41] Tar appealed to his former master's customers because Cross had left the undertaking business and no other members of his family intended to continue in the trade. The length of Tar's service was important because it assured customers that they could expect the same service they had become accustomed to with Cross. These claims were made in the context of competition with the undertakers William and John Evill, who had been trading for many years in Milsom Street.[42] The Evills courted Cross's customers with claims of a close relationship with

The Undertakers of Eighteenth-Century Bath   171

the retired undertaker, although this was a professional relationship and the Evills had not worked for Cross.[43]

The longevity of an undertaker's service for their predecessor was frequently testified by advertisements which announced their establishment. Such behaviour clearly emphasised the continuity between predecessor and successor, assuring customers that they would receive the same service which they were used to. For a newly established undertaker, such as Abraham Holmes or George Tar, claims of long service in the trade were evidence of experience which might distinguish them from other competitors. There were many non-undertakers who traded in funerary goods in eighteenth-century Bath, and it is plausible that established undertakers competed with these individuals by using their own professional experience in funerary work.

Undertakers' Shops

The premises of Bath's numerous undertakers may be examined as another platform for competitive behaviour. This is possible because design and location gave a shop a sense of status or significance. Indeed, it is arguable that the undertakers' premises were representative of 'high-status' shops which are understood to have specialised in the retail of specific goods or services, reflecting greater affluence in the consumer base.[44] Some of these are observed to have already been in existence over a considerable period of time, such as mercers and drapers, trades which were well represented in Bath's undertaking.[45] Increasing demand has also been implicated in the emergence of specialist retailers such as booksellers and, significantly, cabinetmakers who are identified as having 'evolved' from more generalised artisanal trades.[46]

Existing literature has argued that shops were integral to retailers' promotion of their goods because items could be viewed on the premises or observed in window displays. Walsh describes how both high- and low-status shops used space to display as many goods as possible, providing a detailed account of what was on offer.[47] Stobart and Hann present the shop interior as a space which demonstrated the scope of the business and the qualities of the shopkeeper.[48] Berry observes the importance of retail spaces in promotion and is advocated in studies which examine the shop as a venue for polite consumptive activity.[49]

Funeral work was mostly conducted in the household of the deceased and the body was not usually kept at the undertaker's premises in the way bodies are now stored in a modern funeral director's shop. Yet, shops were still important to the early trade as they were often where the undertaker's workshops were located and where funerary goods owned by the undertaker might be stored. It is possible that funerary items, particularly

172 *Bath and Beyond*

accessories, may have been viewed in these locations, as the retailers sold other goods which could be viewed and interacted with. The status of these shops was also important to the competitive activity of the undertaker as it was a very public testament to the success of a business. When advertisements focused on the space within shops, they affirmed that a business was both successful and sufficiently well-equipped to require space for more stock or employees. Both George Strawbridge and Lionel Lee advertised expansion in the space of their premises, the former describing the 'commodious premises' of his new shop in Green Street near St Michael's church, which was an improvement on his previous shop in the same street. Space, rather than location, was the prime quality of this new shop, and his advertisement celebrated 'a large and genteel assortment of linen-drapery and mercery goods,' which could be observed in the new location.[50] Funerary textiles such as Norwich and yard-wide crapes were included in his lengthy list of items to see; even though the shop might not be a funeral home, it was still a place to encounter the paraphernalia of mourning. Demonstrating the importance of space over location, Lionel Lee chose to expand his building in the Market Place in 1784 and 'rendered his shop more commodious.'[51] Use of the term 'warehouse' suggested that a tradesman had a large and comprehensive stock of items, a detail which was an attractive quality for a specialist retailer who claimed to be able to serve all aspects of their trade. In Bath, several undertakers operated or opened warehouses where their funerary goods could be viewed alongside items from their other additional trades. In Bath, the undertakers operating warehouses came primarily from textile trades, such as drapery, haberdashery, or silk mercery.[52] We know about these premises because the opening of a warehouse was an important occasion, which made a positive statement about the capability of an undertaker's overall business.

In Bath, Lawton and Marsh declared their partnership as undertakers after opening a warehouse alongside Lawton's woollen drapery shop in the Abbey Churchyard. The warehouse performed a key role in the partners' new business because it enabled them to merge the stocks of their existing silk mercery and woollen drapery businesses, which included items that were useful in the funeral trade. As a consequence, they promised to serve funerals as cheaply as in London because the warehouse possessed a 'great stock of SILKS and SATTINS for funerals.'[53] In practical terms, a warehouse reduced an early undertaker's dependency on other tradesmen for the supply of funerary goods and diminished the additional costs to which this might contribute. Rather than going to the market whenever they received a funerary request, undertakers like Lawton and Marsh could rely on the readily available stock of their own warehouse. An undertaker in Bath might, therefore, argue that they could charge even less than their London-based counterparts, even though the London businesses were able

The Undertakers of Eighteenth-Century Bath 173

to draw upon a wide stock of readily available items. References to the capital also reflected the broader national scope of the businesses which formed warehouses. The undertaking brothers, William and John Evill, hosted their business in a 'Sheffield, Birmingham and London warehouse,' a designation which emphasised both the scope of their business and the comprehensive nature of their stock.[54] The Evills's business was distinguished by retailing items from 'northern manufactories' and 'London tradesmen.' It is notable that during the long eighteenth century Bath did not boast any specifically styled 'funeral warehouses,' similar to the premises operated by B. Belcher, undertaker in Bristol during the first decades of the nineteenth century.[55]

The location of the shop was also an informal indicator of the status of an undertaker's business. The shop's siting in a fashionable location carried the benefits of more affluent customers and greater prestige for the business. The concentration of undertakers in Milsom Street and Queen's Square is arguably a reflection of the additional trades performed by undertakers in Bath. Four undertakers opened prominent businesses in Milsom Street, which was occupied by fashionable textile and luxury tradesmen.[56] The region around the Abbey was a similarly popular location, particularly Wade's Passage where three different undertakers traded from shops.[57] The business of Mayo & Co. is significant because it occupied two locations in the city: a shop in Wade's Passage and a warehouse in the Market Place.[58]

Funerals as a Shop Window—The Funeral of James Blathwayt

Funerals were arguably one of the best opportunities for the early undertakers of Bath to promote their abilities and competence to an audience of local residents. Funerals travelled through the city streets using thoroughfares that teemed with potential spectators, who might observe something that would catch their attention and prompt a desire for the same display. The funeral of James Blathwayt provides an interesting demonstration of the capabilities of Bath's undertakers. Blathwayt died at his lodgings in 1788, and it was necessary for his body to be transported from Bath to Dyrham in nearby Gloucestershire. He was a member of the Blathwayt family from Dyrham Park, the second son of William III Blathwayt, and the grandson of the politician and statesman also named William (d.1717).[59] His body was conveyed to Dyrham for burial with fellow family members at the church of St Peter, and in this respect the occasion was similar to other funerals of individuals of status whose bodies were either taken out of Bath or transported through the city to a family plot.

The responsibility for organising and executing the funeral was given to one of the most established undertaking businesses in Bath, that of the Trimnell brothers, undertakers and upholders at Westgate Buildings. At the

174   *Bath and Beyond*

time of Blathwayt's death, the brothers Charles and Thomas ran a business which had started with their father, Arthur.[60] The funeral performed by the brothers travelled through the city and into the countryside at a total cost of £83 13s. and included the departure from the city and the journey to Dyrham.[61]

The Trimnells placed Blathwayt's body in an expensive three-layered coffin that was both a demonstration of personal wealth and a practical solution for vault burial. In the innermost coffin the body of the dead man was surrounded with quilted satin, his head rested on a satin pillow and a sheet was drawn halfway over his body. If the body was to be viewed by relatives, the sheet exposed the upper body. Those who went to see Blathwayt's corpse would note that a white cap was placed on his head and his hands were dressed with white gloves. This coffin was then placed in a lead coffin that was primarily a practical item intended to contain any material from decomposition when it was placed in a vault. The lead coffin was not purely practical, however, because the Trimnells included an inscription on the lid identifying the dead man. The lead coffin would have required the involvement of a plumber to seal and manipulate the material. Both inner and lead coffins were placed inside an extravagant outer coffin that featured a host of silvered handles and ornamental silvered nails. This external coffin was also covered with superfine grey cloth, which was a fashionable custom at the time, particularly outside of Bath where coffins for intramural burial were covered in black and red fabric.[62] The coffin would be at the centre of the Trimnells's elaborate funeral procession comprising vehicles, attendants, and gathered mourners. The brothers sourced a hearse, possibly part of the notable 'Black Work' and charged for velvet decorations to adorn both the vehicle and the horses which pulled it.[63]

The majority of the attendants who accompanied the funeral were dressed in black coats or gowns, with a cap worn on their heads, thus guaranteeing a tidy and uniform appearance. They carried truncheons supplied at cost to the Blathwayt family, not as a means of ensuring security, but as a legacy of the heraldic origins of the elaborate funeral which fashionable undertakers performed. Mutes were an example of this, recalling the heraldic duty of the castle porter, standing guard at the door of the deceased household and participating in the funeral procession, carrying a tall wooden staff called a 'stave.'[64] The Trimnells provided four mutes who processed on horseback, a custom which can be seen in contemporary trade paraphernalia depicting funerary journeys from the city to the countryside.

Not all funerary attendants wore black due to the contemporary custom of marking the death of unmarried individuals with the colour white. For this reason, white accessories were provided for the attendants closest to the coffin during the funeral, most notably the underbearers who stood beneath the pall, taking the weight of the coffin. The Trimnell brothers

The Undertakers of Eighteenth-Century Bath 175

both attended the funeral and included their white lutestring hatbands in the Blathwayt's funeral bill alongside other items purchased as funerary gifts for the mourners. A limited party of close mourners, most likely the pall bearers, were given white hatbands and scarves as well as kid gloves.[65] The material composition of the gloves reflected these individuals' close relationship to the deceased, and a larger, less-exclusive group of mourners received white lambskin gloves.[66] The enthusiastic donation of gloves in funerary giving had declined throughout the eighteenth century, but its continuing importance provided a way for glovers such as the undertaker Joseph Gale to enter the funeral trade.

Not all goods were purchased for the funeral because the Trimnell brothers also engaged in the practice of rental, which was common in London and offered a more convenient way for funerary goods to be used by both customer and undertaker. The customer did not need to acquire items which would be of limited use to them, and the undertaker did not need to replenish their stock after each funeral. The brothers rented the velvet pall at 15s. for a day's use, which included the departure of the coffin from Bath and its transportation for burial at St Peter's Dyrham.[67] Feathers were another item which the Trimnells rented out in large quantities for use at numerous points in the funeral procession. Ostrich plumes were more difficult to acquire in the eighteenth century because ostriches were not farmed at this time and feathers had to be sourced from hunted birds. The exclusivity of these items made them a striking inclusion in the decoration of the respectable funeral, with the undertakers using them on the horses, hearses, as well as placing them on the coffin.

Conclusion

This chapter has examined the early undertaking businesses of eighteenth-century Bath to present an aspect of the city's history which has traditionally been overlooked. In this period, the business of undertaking was performed by a range of tradesmen who often worked in more than one trade and did not focus solely on funerals, unlike their counterparts in the fictional Bath of *Better Late Than Never*. The highly diversified nature of their undertaking businesses mitigated some of the risk of establishing themselves in a new line of work with a title which had only recently been introduced to the city.

This was a competitive environment with many of the city's undertakers located close to each other and many having worked in each other's businesses in the past. The fictional undertakers fought at the doors of the bereaved household looking for custom, but their counterparts in the real city were engaged in less combative forms of competition. In lieu of qualifications the undertakers sought to distinguish themselves from each other in terms of their longevity in business, asserting that experience equated to quality and reliability. Bath's early undertakers' claims of credibility

176 Bath and Beyond

were reinforced by the spaces from which they traded; new and expanded premises did not play an integral role in the funeral, but they were a tangible demonstration of a successful business. Ultimately the funeral was a stage for the undertakers, and a shop window for prospective customers, who may have either seen it passing through the city or heard gossip from those who saw it. Undertakers could position themselves at the centre of high-status funerals, claiming responsibility for the successful execution of the funeral as it passed through the city streets.

Notes

1 William Davies, "Better Late Than Never," in *Plays Written for a Private Theatre* (1786), 261–364.
2 Julian Litten, *The English Way of Death: The Common Funeral Since 1450* (London: Hale, 1991).
3 Clare Gittings, *Death, Burial and the Individual in Early Modern England* (London: Croom Helm, 1984), 95.
4 Paul S. Fritz, "The Undertaking Trade in England: Its Origins and Early Development, 1660–1830," *Eighteenth-Century Studies* xxviii (1994): 249.
5 Chandles is identified by Litten, "The Funeral Trade in Hanoverian England, 1714–1760," 51. Another provincial undertaker in the literature is John Miller of Ipswich (*c*.1788): Fritz, "The Undertaking Trade in England," 248.
6 Fritz, "The Undertaking Trade in England," 248.
7 Trevor Fawcett, *Bath Commercialis'd: Shops, Trade and Market at the 18th Century Spa* (Bath: Ruton, 2002).
8 Litten, "The Funeral Trade in Hanoverian England, 1714–1760," 54.
9 These individuals have been identified through examination of the following texts during the chapter's focus period: *Bath Chronicle and Weekly Advertiser; Bath Journal; Felix Farley's Bristol Journal*; and William Bailey, *Bailey's Western and Midland Directory; or, Merchant's and Tradesman's Useful Companion, for the Year, 1783* (1783); William Bailey, *Bailey's Western and Midland Directory; or, Merchant's and Tradesman's Useful Companion, for the Year, 1784* (1784); *The New Bath Directory, for the Year, 1792* (1792).
10 *Bath Chronicle*, November 11, 1784, *Bath Chronicle*, December 4, 1788; *Bath Chronicle,* November 27, 1788.
11 *Bath Chronicle*, October 27, 1768.
12 *Bath Chronicle*, May 14, 1767.
13 Davies, *Better Late Than Never*, 290.
14 Phillis Cunnington, *Costume for Births, Marriages & Death* (London: A. and C. Black, 1972), 163–65.
15 *Bath Chronicle and Weekly Gazette*, April 26, 1764.
16 *Bath Chronicle*, March 26, 1795.
17 *Felix Farley's Bristol Journal*, October 3, 1789.
18 *Bath Chronicle*, October 24, 1782; *Bath Chronicle*, November 4, 1762.
19 *Bath Chronicle*, November 4, 1762.
20 *Bath Chronicle*, December 1, 1785.
21 Matthew Craske, "Design and the Competitive Spirit in Early and Mid-Eighteenth-Century England," *Journal of Design History* xii (1999): 215.
22 *Bath Chronicle*, December 18, 1793.

The Undertakers of Eighteenth-Century Bath   177

23 *Bath Chronicle,* June 11, 1795.
24 *Bath Chronicle,* November 4, 1799; *Bath Chronicle,* August 21, 1794.
25 Cynthia Wall, "The English Auction: Narratives of Dismantlings," *Eighteenth Century Studies* xxxi (1997): 6–7; Ivon Asquith, "Advertising and the Press in the Late Eighteenth and Early Nineteenth Centuries: James Perry and the Morning Chronicle, 1790–1821," *The Historical Journal* xviii (1975): 717–18.
26 *Bath Chronicle,* April 24, 1794.
27 The eight 'auctioneer-undertakers' in Bath at this time were: John Plura, Isaac Cooke, William Birchill, William Cross, Thomas Bird, Thomas Colebridge, James Evatt, Samuel Nicholls, William Evill, and Mr Treacher.
28 *Better Late Than Never,* 1786, 283.
29 *Better Late Than Never,* 1786, 284.
30 *Better Late Than Never,* 1786, 280.
31 *Better Late Than Never,* 1786, 288.
32 *Bath Chronicle,* August 28, 1788.
33 Litten, "The Funeral Trade in Hanoverian England," 59.
34 John Stobart, "Selling (through) Politeness: Advertising Provincial Shops in Eighteenth-Century England," *Cultural and Social History* 5 (2008): 312–16; Dinah Reed, Reed, Dinah, "Did Eighteenth-Century Shopkeepers Use Newspapers to Promote Their Goods? A Comparison of Manchester and Norwich 1765–1805," *History of Retailing and Consumption* 9, no. 1 (2023): 19–37.
35 Hannah Barker, *The Business of Women: Female Enterprise and Urban Development in Northern England 1760–1830* (Oxford University Press, 2006), 110–17; Deborah Simonton, "Invisibility, Presence and Absence: Scottish Businesswomen in the Eighteenth and Nineteenth Centuries," *Scottish Historical Review* 2 (2023): 298–300; Deborah Simonton, "Widows and Wenches: Single Women in Eighteenth-Century Urban Economies," in *Female Agency in the Urban Economy: Gender in European Towns, 1640–1830,* ed. Deborah Simonton and Anne Montenach (London: Routledge, 2013), 101–9.
36 *Bath Chronicle,* July 5, 1781.
37 *Bath Chronicle,* December 16, 1784.
38 *Bath Chronicle,* September 11, 1800.
39 Roger Campbell, *The London Tradesman: Being a Compendious View of All the Trades, Professions, Arts, Both Liberal and Mechanic, Now Practised in the Cities of London and Westminster* (1747), 329–30.
40 *Funeral Discipline: Or, the Character of Strip-Corps the Dead-Monger. According to the Instructions of Paul Meagre, Once Mourner in Chief to the Funeral Undertaker* (1725), 4.
41 *Bath Chronicle,* December 18, 1793.
42 William and John Evill were undertakers at 18 Milsom Street; they had advertised as early as 1778: *Bath Chronicle,* June 11, 1778.
43 *Bath Chronicle,* December 26, 1793.
44 Angus McInnes, "The Emergence of a Leisure Town: Shrewsbury, 1660–1760," *Past and Present* cxx (1988): 61; Jon Stobart and Andrew Hann, "Retailing Revolution in the Eighteenth Century? Evidence from North-West England," *Business History* xlvi (2004): 171–94, 180; Jon Stobart, "Shopping Streets as Social Space: Leisure, Consumerism and Improvement in an Eighteenth-Century County Town," *Urban History* xxv (1998): 3–21.
45 Christina Fowler, "Changes in Provincial Retail Practice During the Eighteenth Century, with Particular Reference to Central Southern England," *Business History* xl (1998): 40; Paul Glennie, "Consumption, Consumerism and Urban Form: Historical Perspectives," *Urban Studies* xxxv (1998): 934.

178 *Bath and Beyond*

46 The term 'evolved' is used in Stobart and Hann, "Retailing Revolution in the Eighteenth Century?." 189.
47 Walsh, "Shop Design and the Display of Goods," 164–71.
48 Stobart and Hann, "Sites of Consumption: The Display of Goods in Provincial Shops in Eighteenth-Century England," *Cultural and Social History* ii (2005): 171–72.
49 Helen Berry, "Polite Consumption: Shopping in Eighteenth Century England," *Transactions of the Royal Historical Society* xii (2002): 383–86.
50 *Bath Chronicle*, March 16, 1769.
51 *Bath Chronicle*, December 2, 1784.
52 These undertakers include: Charles Abbot, haberdashery *Bath Chronicle*, December 14, 1786; Percival and Cunditt, linen-draper *Bath Chronicle*, May 3, 1787; Londsdale and Butress, silk *Bath Chronicle*, December 4, 1788.
53 *Bath Chronicle*, November 27, 1788.
54 *Bath Chronicle*, June 11, 1778.
55 *Bristol Mirror*, June 21, 1817.
56 Milsom Street undertakers: John Plura 1780; William Birchill 1781; Percival & Cunditt 1787; William Bally 1794.
57 Undertakers include: John Bowden and John Gale, 3 Wade's Passage: *Bath Chronicle*, September 28, 1787; Meredith, "Wade's Passage": *Bath Chronicle*, January 13, 1785; Mayo & Co., "Wade's Passage": *Bath Chronicle*, November 24, 1785.
58 *Bath Chronicle*, January 13, 1785.
59 *HP Commons 1690–1715*, iii.
60 *Bath Chronicle*, July 5, 1781; *Bath Chronicle*, December 30, 1784.
61 Gloucester RO, D1799/A382: Receipted Funeral Account for Funeral of James Blathwayt, 1789.
62 C. Boston, A. Boyle, J. Gill, and A. Witkin. *'In the Vaults Beneath'—Archaeological Recording at St. George, Bloomsbury*, Oxford Archaeology Monograph No. 8 (Oxford: The Oxford Archaeological Unit Ltd., 2009), 163–64.
63 The Black Work was a set of funerary vehicles which was owned by a Bath tavern keeper. It included a mourning coach, hearse, and chariot. It was sold by John Plura in his capacity as an auctioneer, *Bath Journal*, June 30, 1794; it was purchased by Mr Phillott, *Bath Journal*, July 28, 1794.
64 Litten, *The English Way of Death*.
65 Gloucester RO, D1799/A382.
66 This practice has been observed in a North American context in: Steven Bullock and Sheila McIntyre, "The Handsome Tokens of a Funeral: Glove-Giving and the Large Funeral in Eighteenth-Century New England," *The William and Mary Quarterly* lxix (2012): 305–46.
67 Gloucester RO, D1799/A382.

Bibliography

Primary

Gloucestershire Record Office
'D1799/A382 [Receipted Funeral Account for Funeral of James Blathwayt, 1789].
Bailey, W. *Bailey's Western and Midland Directory; or, Merchant's and Tradesman's Useful Companion, for the Year, 1783*. Birmingham, 1783.

The Undertakers of Eighteenth-Century Bath 179

Bailey, W. *Bailey's Western and Midland Directory; or, Merchant's and Tradesman's Useful Companion, for the Year, 1784.* Birmingham, 1784.
Bath Chronicle and Weekly Advertiser.
Bath Journal.
Bristol Mirror.
Calcutta Gazette.
Campbell, R. *The London Tradesman. Being a Compendious View of All the Trades, Professions, Arts, Both Liberal and Mechanic, Now Practised in the Cities of London and Westminster.* London, 1747.
Davies, W. *Better Late Than Never.* London, 1784.
de Mandeville, B. *The Fable of the Bees.* London, 1723.
Felix Farley's Bristol Journal.
Funeral Discipline: Or, the Character of Strip-Corps the Dead-Monger. According to the Instructions of Paul Meagre, Once Mourner in Chief to the Funeral Undertaker. London, 1725.
The New Bath Directory, for the Year. *Containing an Historical Account of the Ancient and Present State of that Elegant City; the Salutary Properties of Its Waters, Its Bathing, and Amusements, with the Lodging-Houses, Account of the Posts, and the Mail and Other Coaches, with a Description of the Seats, Villages, and Curiosities in the Neighbourhood,* 1792.
Oxford Journal.
Stamford Mercury.

Secondary

Asquith, I. "Advertising and the Press in the Late Eighteenth and Early Nineteenth Centuries: James Perry and the Morning Chronicle, 1790–1821." *The Historical Journal* 18 (1975): 703–24. https://doi.org/10.1017/S0018246X00008864.
Barker, H. *The Business of Women: Female Enterprise and Urban Development in Northern England 1760–1830.* Oxford: Oxford University Press, 2006.
Bath Abbey Memorials. "Richard Randolph." Accessed February 12, 2024. www.bathabbeymemorials.org.uk/person/randolph-richard.
Berry, H. "Polite Consumption: Shopping in Eighteenth Century England." *Transactions of the Royal Historical Society* 12 (2002): 375–94. www.jstor.org/stable/3679353.
Boston, C., A. Boyle, J. Gill, and A. Witkin. *'In the Vaults Beneath'—Archaeological Recording at St. George, Bloomsbury.* Oxford Archaeology Monograph No. 8. Oxford: The Oxford Archaeological Unit Ltd., 2009.
Bullock, S. C., and S. McIntyre. "The Handsome Tokens of a Funeral: Glove-Giving and the Large Funeral in Eighteenth-Century New England." *The William and Mary Quarterly* 69 (2012): 305–46. https://doi.org/10.5309/willmaryquar.69.2.0305.
Cox, N. *The Complete Tradesman: A Study of Retailing, 1550–1800.* Aldershot: Ashgate, 2000.
Craske, M. "Design and the Competitive Spirit in Early and Mid-Eighteenth-Century England." *Journal of Design History* 12 (1999): 187–216. www.jstor.org/stable/1316282.
Cruickshanks, E., S. Handley, and D. Hayton, eds. *The History of Parliament: The House of Commons 1690–1715.* Cambridge: Cambridge University Press, 2002.
Cunnington, P. *Costume for Births, Marriages & Death.* London: A. and C. Black, 1972.

180   Bath and Beyond

Davies, William. *Plays Written for a Private Theatre*. London, 1786.

Fawcett, T. *Bath Commercialis'd: Shops, Trade and Market at the 18th Century Spa*. Bath: Ruton, 2002.

Fowler, C. "Changes in Provincial Retail Practice During the Eighteenth Century, with Particular Reference to Central Southern England." *Business History* 40 (1998): 37–54. https://doi.org/10.1080/00076799800000337.

Fritz, P. S. "The Undertaking Trade in England: Its Origins and Early Development, 1660–1830." *Eighteenth-Century Studies* 28 (1994): 241–53. https://doi.org/10.2307/2739202.

Gittings, C. *Death, Burial and the Individual in Early Modern England*. London: Croom Helm, 1984.

Glennie, P. "Consumption, Consumerism and Urban Form: Historical Perspectives." *Urban Studies* 35 (1998): 927–51. https://doi.org/10.1080/0042098984628.

Hoppit, J. *Risk and Failure in English Business, 1700–1800*. Cambridge: Cambridge University Press, 1987.

Howarth, G. "Professionalizing the Funeral Industry in England, 1700–1960." In *The Changing Face of Death: Historical Accounts of Death and Disposal*, edited by Peter Jupp and Clare Gittings, 120–34. Basingstoke: Macmillan Publishing, 1997.

Kirkham, P. A. "Samuel Norman: A Study of an Eighteenth-Century Craftsman." *The Burlington Magazine* 111 (1969): 500–13. www.jstor.org/stable/876064.

Litten, J. *The English Way of Death: The Common Funeral Since 1450*. London: Hale, 1991.

Litten, J. "The Funeral Trade in Hanoverian England, 1714–1760." In *The Changing Face of Death: Historical Accounts of Death and Disposal*, edited by Peter Jupp and Clare Gittings, 48–62. Basingstoke: Macmillan Publishing, 1997.

McInnes, A. "The Emergence of a Leisure Town: Shrewsbury, 1660–1760." *Past and Present* 120 (1988): 53–87. www.jstor.org/stable/650922.

Nineteenth Century Collections Online. "A Collection of Playbills from Theatre Royal, Bath, 1812–14." Accessed October 10, 2013. http://tinyurl.galegroup.com/tinyurl/Acgq6.

Reed, D. "Did Eighteenth-Century Shopkeepers Use Newspapers to Promote Their Goods? A Comparison of Manchester and Norwich 1765–1805." *History of Retailing and Consumption* 1 (2023): 19–37. https://doi.org/10.1080/23735 18X.2023.2168847.

Simonton, D. "Invisibility, Presence and Absence: Scottish Businesswomen in the Eighteenth and Nineteenth Centuries." *Scottish Historical Review* 2 (2023): 290–314. https://doi.org/10.3366/shr.2023.0615.

Simonton, D. "Widows and Wenches: Single Women in Eighteenth-Century Urban Economies." In *Female Agency in the Urban Economy: Gender in European Towns, 1640–1830*, edited by Deborah Simonton and Anne Montenach, 92–115. London: Routledge, 2013.

Stobart, J. "Selling (Through) Politeness: Advertising Provincial Shops in Eighteenth-Century England." *Cultural and Social History* 5 (2008): 309–28. https://doi.org/10.2752/147800408X331416.

Stobart, J. "Shopping Streets as Social Space: Leisure, Consumerism and Improvement in an Eighteenth-Century County Town." *Urban History* 25 (1998): 3–21. www.jstor.org/stable/44612931.

Stobart, J., and A. Hann. "Retailing Revolution in the Eighteenth Century? Evidence from North-West England." *Business History* 46 (2004): 171–94.

Stobart, J., and A. Hann. "Sites of Consumption: The Display of Goods in Provincial Shops in Eighteenth-Century England." *Cultural and Social History* 2 (2005): 165–88. https://doi.org/10.1191/1478003805cs019oa.

Wall, C. "The English Auction: Narratives of Dismantlings." *Eighteenth Century Studies* 31 (1997): 1–25. www.jstor.org/stable/30053642.

Walsh, C. "Shop Design and the Display of Goods in Eighteenth-Century London." *Journal of Design History* 8 (1995): 157–76. www.jstor.org/stable/1316030.

10 British Female Hospitality and Fashionable Society in Eighteenth-Century Nice, 1769–92

Isabelle Eve Carlotti-Davier

British hospitality, especially through the agency of female elite travellers, played a significant role in the development of Nice as a fashionable health resort in the eighteenth century. Studies on the Grand Tour in Italy have paid little attention to this minor destination in comparison with major cities such as Rome, Florence, Naples, and Venice. It may be explained by the fact that in the eighteenth century, Nice was no more than a provincial town belonging to the kingdom of Savoy (unlike today, where Nice is part of France), even if it was a convenient stopping point for those travelling by sea to Genoa or Marseilles on board local *feluccas*. Society was small with few noble families, and Nice did not have many cultural sites of which to boast. During the century, the Royal Family of Savoy only visited the town once. In 1713, Sicily was granted to the duke of Savoy, Victor Amadeus II, according to the Treaty of Utrecht. The future king and his wife, Anne of Orleans, passed through Nice before embarking to be crowned in Palermo (by 1720 they had been given, in place of Sicily, the Kingdom of Sardinia by the Holy Roman Emperor after the Spanish attack on these two islands in 1718). Victor Amadeus II's successors, Charles Emmanuel III and Victor Amadeus III, commissioned works to develop the town and the roads between Nice and Piedmont, but they did not visit Nice during their respective reigns.[1] Nice was never envisioned as a health resort for the Sardinian Royal Family and the court; it rather served political and diplomatic purposes, especially as a strategic naval base (with the cooperation of the British) to secure intelligence on the moves of the French fleet in Toulon.[2]

However, at the end of the Seven Years' War in 1763, Nice became a fashionable health resort for the British aristocracy and gentry. Most historians consider that the popularity of the place was the consequence of the publication of Tobias Smollett's *Travels through France and Italy* in 1766, the author himself being reckoned as the 'discoverer' of Nice which is to a certain extent true because it made the town known to British doctors as a good place to recommend to invalids. However, it is more convincing to consider that the attraction of Nice and its suitability for

DOI: 10.4324/9781003393856-10

elite British women, especially for ladies of the court, owed much more to the two visits of King George III's brother, the duke of York, in 1764 and 1767. Two years after the duke's second visit, Lady Charlotte Finch (1725–1813), royal governess for the children of George III and Queen Charlotte, decided to spend several months in Nice hoping for the recovery of her ill son. She was joined by other members of the English Court, including Countess Spencer (1737–1814) and Lady Holland (1723–1774). This provided royal and aristocratic patronage, guaranteeing the destination as a fashionable town which was confirmed by the presence of another of George III's brothers, the duke of Gloucester (1743–1805), who was travelling in Italy with his wife and children during the winters of 1783 to 1786.[3] Ladies of rank formed the majority of British female visitors in Nice in the eighteenth century, but from 1770 onwards, women of means from the middling sort were also able to travel to Italy and were willing to partake in the same elite voyage. Poorer travellers could try to join a richer family to save expenses by acting as servants or companions in exchange for their passage. Some doctors' and clergymen's wives and children used to accompany aristocratic families, but nevertheless travellers of fashion remained at the pinnacle of local society.

British female hospitality took place according to different rules than those in other spa resorts in Britain. Unlike Bath, there was no official Master of Ceremonies acting as 'regulator of diversions', 'overseer of the marriage market', or 'moderator of disputes at play'.[4] The system of welcome relied primarily on hostesses of rank, as was the convention in Italy.[5] Hospitality was mainly domestic as there were no public assembly rooms where the elite could meet, apart from at the principal theatre in Nice (known by various names during the eighteenth and nineteenth century, and now known as the Opéra de Nice). And even in the latter case, it was usually considered as a prolongation of domestic hospitality, as the boxes were used as private spaces for guests. Elaine Chalus has shown how in the first half of the nineteenth century elite women, foreigners, and local nobility managed to create a cosmopolitan 'Season' in Nice based on domestic hospitality and elite sociability. Women of the nobility and gentry were good social facilitators thanks to their education and social skills, with the ability to create quickly a small, exclusive society on an annual basis.[6]

However, for the eighteenth century, research has mostly been investigated by local historians on the basis of male travel diaries, while female sources have been ignored. On the whole, the operation of the system of hospitality, as well as the identification of hostesses, is under-explored. As the eighteenth century initiated a long tradition of British elite travel to Nice until Queen Victoria's visits in the nineteenth century, it appears relevant to understand, through the concept of hospitality, how Nice operated as a fashionable health resort at the very beginning of its creation and

184   *Bath and Beyond*

how female British travellers from the aristocracy and the gentry played an instrumental part in it. The study of elite hospitality has often been limited to fashionable entertainment and amusements, and where the town of Nice has been considered as a spa resort, many aspects of British women's agency within local society have been overlooked, especially the notions of mutual support and solidarity, which are rooted in traditional definitions of aristocratic hospitality.

This chapter is based on published and unpublished archival material, comprising letters, journals, and diaries relating to British female travellers from the aristocracy and the upper gentry. It refers to elite women's experiences in the second half of the eighteenth century, from 1769 to 1792, as being the best documented period at hand. After the French invasion of Nice in 1792, the British fled to Genoa and only returned to Nice in the winter of 1802–1803 following the Peace of Amiens. These sources are, by definition, subjective, but this research aims to describe women's perceptions of hospitality and how they represented themselves as hostesses in Nice's local society. It examines how they adapted British hospitality within a small reconstituted upper society, including few native noble families who were not wealthy. It considers how fashionable society in Nice created a temporary court during the visit of royalty and how British court ladies served as ladies-in-waiting or unofficial ambassadresses in a provincial town. These different parts played by British hostesses led to rivalries of power and precedence, which were eventually settled in favour of ladies most capable of representing the community at large by their rank and their public morality. In the context of Nice as a health resort, assistance to the sick and the bereaved was essential to ladies of fashion as the expression of their traditional responsibility towards the weaker members of the group. This reflected a hierarchical solidarity because it was mainly aimed at their social peers, even if British elite women offered occasional charity to the poor on their own initiative or sometimes upon the invitation of elite native nobility acting on behalf of the local church. This conforms with the image of prestige and power of the urbanised landed classes in eighteenth-century Britain, but it demonstrates at the same time the survival of the traditional codes of honour and Christian conduct at a time when the concept of hospitality was put into question by moralists and philosophers.[7] As a result, this chapter evaluates how hospitality enabled ladies of fashion to translate in a foreign society their authoritative status as members of the ruling class and how the British community and local nobility entrusted them to act for the benefit of others.

Entering Nice's Elite Society

On their arrival in Nice, British ladies were welcomed with cards that were sent by the local nobility, some officials (mostly the consuls), and other

British Female Hospitality and Fashionable Society 185

foreign travellers. Accreditation was compulsory according to rules of social nicety in Nice. Within the British community, acceptable individuals were either part of their existing networks of acquaintances or recommended to them by common connections or relations. Even though most visitors came at the beginning of January, many began to settle from October to December. The early presence of British members in late autumn was important as it allowed time to begin to settle in and offer hospitality to the newcomers. As Elaine Chalus has rightly noted in her study of Brighton and Nice in the first half of the nineteenth century (and this also applies to the eighteenth), the 'Pre-Season' was essential to the quick reconstitution of society, by finding the best accommodation suitable for receiving guests and creating ties with the wintering elite in advance of the full season.[8]

In 1769, it was easy for Lady Spencer to recreate a pleasant social circle because many court ladies were already residing in Nice. Her friends, Lady Charlotte Finch and her children, as well as Lady Holland, were installed in their apartments and villa, ready to welcome her and her family.[9] In 1778, Lady Polwarth's (1751–1833) situation was quite different, when she travelled to Nice with her sick husband, and an acquaintance, Mrs Barker, who appears to have been of a lower social standing. Due to the American Revolution, few British ladies and families of rank were present in Nice when she arrived in the first days of January.[10] Lady Polwarth on her arrival received several cards from Lady Drogheda (1744–1784), and from an unknown Mrs Yorke, who presented herself as a distant relative of her husband. As the sending of cards amounted to a visit, Lady Polwarth had to decide if she would return Mrs Yorke's civilities. This decision was postponed until the connection was finally confirmed by both her mother-in-law, Lady Marchmont, and Mrs Barker. Even though Mrs Yorke's family was from the lower gentry, Lady Polwarth eventually included them in her circle of relations in Nice, mainly because high society was very small there: 'they seem good sort of people and will do well enough to fill up the great blank of acquaintances'.[11]

In 1783 when peace in America was concluded, British travellers flocked to Italy in great numbers. Elizabeth Foster (1758–1824) who came from October to May in 1783, mainly for health reasons, found that 'the English swarm[ed]' in the town and 'the English name [was] venerated everywhere'.[12] She was recommended to many British ladies because of her wide connections made through her high-ranking family, the frequent travels of her father in Italy since 1765, and her association with the house of Devonshire. Several years later in 1787, Laetitia Houblon (1742–1828), a gentlewoman of Huguenot descent, was welcomed in Nice by the hostess, Lady Rivers (c.1725–1795), after having been her guest in her villa at Lyons.[13] One year later, Eleanor Egerton (d.1846), daughter of Lord Grey of Wilton (later earl of Wilton), travelled to Nice with her parents for the sake of her mother's health. They were integrated immediately into Lady Gordon's

186   *Bath and Beyond*

(*d*.1796) society as she opened her house every evening.[14] In 1792, the place was still overcrowded with British travellers and invalids. Lady Spencer was thus prepared to be faced with constant society as she had many acquaintances abroad and was a close friend of Lady Rivers.[15] As a result, the company on offer depended on rank and connections, but also on the number of British residents and travellers present in Nice at the time of the stay. Once admitted among the first people of the town, British ladies were in a position to return and offer hospitality themselves.

British Hostesses and Fashionable Entertaining

As a rule, it was assumed that the principal British families were expected to receive and entertain guests. Hospitality was presented as a social duty supported by the family unit. In female sources, more attention is paid to hostesses, although this does not mean that British men were not hosts in their own right. During the winter of 1778, a Mr Lee received guests at least once a week at his home for balls and some music, and it was common that captains would invite elite members on board their ships.[16]

As mentioned, due to the patronage by the British royal family of the town of Nice and the regular presence of court ladies, British hospitality was based on exclusive social circles and fashionable entertainment. Even though Nice had limited native nobility, several families and ladies of Nice maintained a reputation for good education and rank. The society of the governor and his wife was the most praised by British ladies, and emissaries from the court of Turin or the spouse of the president of Nice's Senate were considered respectable enough.

British hospitality was not the only alternative to native hospitality. French *emigrés* to Nice were numerous in the last decades of the century, such as Prince Camille de Rohan (Knight of Malta and former Field Marshal of Louis XVI). In 1788, Eleanor Egerton regularly attended the lavish parties he gave to elite society in Nice.[17] Even if they were a significant contribution to amusements in elite society at that time, it should be noted that in earlier periods, some French ladies were present and offered a larger choice of good company to the British. From 1769–1770, Lady Spencer entertained a close relationship with Madame Trudaine, Anne Marie Rosalie Bouvard de Fourqueux (1714–1776), wife of Louis XV's *intendant* of finance. The two ladies saw each other very frequently, paying and receiving civilities in turn.[18]

Abroad, the difference between British gentry and aristocracy seems to have been strictly marked. The more elevated the title, the better the ladies were received and respected. A title from the peerage was *de facto* an efficient and legitimate claim to authority among foreign society and within the British expatriate community. However, means were decisive in the

British Female Hospitality and Fashionable Society 187

ability to receive with elegance. Women, such as Lady Elizabeth Foster (née Hervey) or her sister Lady Erne (1753–1842), who were cut from marital ties and with no financial resources could only be guests, regardless of their high birth. Conversely, Laetitia Houblon, despite no title, but a good family fortune (as the daughter of a wealthy MP and granddaughter of a baronet), once succeeded in inviting more than one hundred guests to her villa.[19] However, when she met Lady Spencer in Nice in 1792, she was nevertheless considered friendly but 'vulgar'.[20] Distinction, even of degree in some cases, was essential in a hierarchical society; although it is well known that in the eighteenth century the British gentry and aristocracy intermarried and were well connected.[21] Sometimes differences would be underplayed if an aristocratic lady took a liking for a woman from the lower gentry who showed exemplary personal qualities, as in the example of Lady Spencer who considered the Irish Mrs Balfour as her *protegée*, and tried to convince her correspondent, Mrs Caroline Howe, that she should meet her on her return to London.[22]

Several factors had to be taken into account to be eligible as a hostess and even more to qualify for the position of a leading hostess. First, age mattered: British hostesses in Nice were usually aged over 30. In 1769, Lady Spencer was 32 years old and Lady Charlotte Finch was 44. Lady Spencer in 1792 was a dowager of means aged 55. In 1778, Lady Drogheda was 34 and, during the long-lasting 'reign' of Lady Rivers from 1779 to 1792, she received guests while herself aged 54 to 67. Laetitia Houblon was present during the winter of 1787–1788, aged 45 and, in 1792, aged 50. Additionally, long residence in Nice was undoubtedly a decisive element. Coupled with fortune and education, it helped secure a dominant position in local society, as the example of Lady Rivers embodies perfectly (Figure 10.1). Among her contemporaries, she was known as the main British hostess from 1779 to 1792, and is still remembered in local history books and biographical dictionaries. Her integration into local society enabled her to form many connections with the native nobility and with Sardinian government officials. Even if she was separated from her husband, Lord Rivers, she had £2,100 per annum which was enough to entertain on a large scale.[23] As the daughter of a baronet and wife of a baron (married 1776), she was well connected within the British *beau monde* and could present herself as a legitimate hostess of rank. After seven seasons in Nice, she decided to have a villa built in the *Faubourg de la Croix de Marbre* area, renamed 'the English district', only about a mile and a half from the new quarters of the town (Figure 10.2). This was a special privilege granted to her by the local authorities, probably to reward her for the beneficial effects of her great hospitality on the development of the town as a fashionable cosmopolitan place.

British lady travellers usually stayed at hotels before finding a long-term rental for the duration of their stay. *L'hôtel d'Angleterre* run by a British

Figure 10.1 Richard Purcell, *Penelope Rivers (née Atkins), Lady Rivers when Mrs Pitt*, c.1746, mezzotint, 35.1 × 25.1 cm, National Portrait Gallery, NPG D40255. © National Portrait Gallery, London.

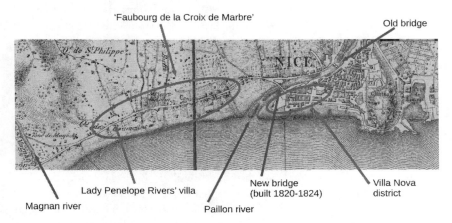

Figure 10.2 The different areas of residency of British female travellers in late eighteenth-century Nice. Joseph Rosalinde, *Carte topographique de la ville et de la campagne de Nice*, 1825, lithograph, Bibliothèque Nationale de France/GALLICA, GE F CARTE-5616. Courtesy of the Bibliothèque Nationale de France. Annotated by the author.

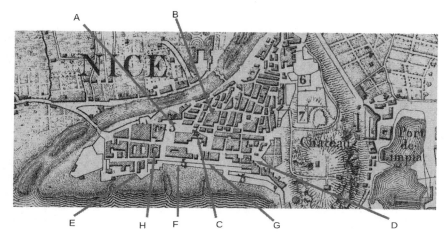

Figure 10.3 The main points of interest in late eighteenth-century Nice. Joseph Rosalinde Rancher, *Detail of the map of the town of Nice*, in *Guide des étrangers à Nice*, 1825, lithograph, Bibliothèque Nationale de France/GALLICA, GE F CARTE-5616. Courtesy of the Bibliothèque Nationale de France. Annotated by the author:

A: the 'Grande Place'
B: Cathedral and Bishop's Palace
C: Governor's house (Royal Palace)
D: the Senate of Nice
E: Theatre Royale (now the Opéra de Nice)
F: the 'Terrace'
G: the 'Cours' (Corso)
H: Héraud Palace ('Hôtel d'Angleterre' and the consul's house in 1792)

woman, Mrs Williams, in the Héraud Palace was highly recommended by British travellers. While the district of *Faubourg de la Croix de Marbre* was the preferred choice, other reasons, such as age, illness, or the remoteness of the area, led some British to settle in the quarters of *Villa Nova* on the right side of the Paillon, where the principal theatre was situated. They rented rooms in the palaces owned by noble native families, near the 'Grande Place' and the fashionable promenades of the elevated 'Terrace' (built over the ancient fortifications of the town) and of the 'Cours'. All offered beautiful views of the seaside and some had courtyards (Figure 10.3).

The wife of the British consul had an ambiguous position. The consul was not officially a diplomatic representative of the British government, even if he reported all sorts of first-hand sensitive information to the British envoy at Turin, as well as miscellaneous news on private individuals.

190   *Bath and Beyond*

Consuls were often considered by British fashionable ladies, such as Lady Polwarth, as no more than merchants. Nevertheless, she discovered when she arrived in 1778 that consuls were admitted into Nice's upper society.[24] In 1792, the British consul Nathaniel Green (1745–1799) enjoyed a good position in the local society because of his remarkable dedication to the British residents. His young wife was much liked in Nice and was reckoned to be educated with elegant manners. In the Héraud palace, Mrs Elizabeth Green was visited by all travellers of distinction, in particular the duchess of Ancaster (*d.*1793) and the duchess of Devonshire (1757–1806). At the birth of the consul's daughter, the duchess of Ancaster was chosen as godmother. Both ladies were to be found visiting the newborn almost daily— the duchess of Ancaster was much in physical pain and could not follow the gaieties of the place, whereas the duchess of Devonshire was exiled on the decision of her husband, the duke of Devonshire, and missed all her children. Her adulterous affair with Charles Grey had led to the birth of an illegitimate baby girl in Aix several weeks before. The newborn was immediately taken from her.[25] Mrs Elizabeth Green's hospitality and home were thus perceived as a comforting space for both of them.[26]

British hospitality was as much about entertaining travellers in a good or bad state of health, as it was an occasion for the ladies to demonstrate how well they were educated and assert their social standing within local high society. The framework of British female hospitality appears stable during the period 1769 to 1792 and answered to the rules and codes of conduct imported from Britain. It comprised visits, dinners, assemblies (often called after the Italian name *conversazioni*), and balls. Each event could be formal or informal, homosocial or heterosocial according to the number of guests, and if they were friends or distant acquaintances. Visits took place in the morning after breakfast until the main meal (dinner) and were resumed at the end of the afternoon. According to Lady Polwarth, newcomers owed the first visit to the members already residing in town.[27] During visits, British women could display their patriotism by offering tea to strangers.[28] The necessary accessories, including tea equipage, seem to have been brought from Britain. These consisted of luxurious materials, such as a tea-table (imported either from Asia or from a British manufacturer), a silver teapot, a boiler, a sugar pot, and porcelain or silver teacups.[29] Breakfast could also be prepared in an 'English' manner (although what this entailed is not described in Lady Rivers' letter), which stressed the desire of British hostesses to offer to their guests customs of home, even if they also adapted to local mores.[30]

Dinner, being the main meal of the day, was the most frequent invitation made and received by elite British women. In the second half of the eighteenth century, the fashionable British used to dine around three o'clock and most British hostesses in Nice adopted the same hours. However, politeness and the return of civilities towards the native nobility who dined at noon made some British hostesses change hours to conform to their customs. This shows a positive aspect in the relationships between foreign travellers and the native population, which has been overlooked by travel historiographies which regularly put forward negative perceptions of visitors, based on an alleged sense of British superiority and conventional prejudices. Excursions in the countryside and walks in the town also usually led to some modifications in the ladies' schedule. In comparison with Bath, where everybody was supposed to do the same activities and be at the same place at the same time, Nice offered a little more flexibility and freedom in daily activities.[31] These adaptations and self-organisation of time are visible in female-authored sources. In her 1769–1770 visit, Lady Spencer brought forward dinner to noon because she desired to invite the Governor and his wife, Monsieur and Madame de Nangis, even though she considered that noon was not convenient. She grumbled in her journal that it 'takes away all the morning' and it forced her to come back hastily from her promenades.[32] Some years later, Lady Polwarth found it more practical to have late dinners: 'Most of the English dine at three there but I thought it left so little time for dressing and walking, that I could not adopt the hour'.[33] Throughout the century, dinner gatherings were limited in number to the governor's family and the main noble local families, along with some British acquaintances and friends.

After dinner and before evening visits, British hostesses received company for cards or music. The card games were usually the ones played in local society or in other cities in Europe. As for music, as in England, it could be performed by the hostess, the guests, or professional musicians. In 1769–1770, Lady Spencer only referred to 'Company and cards' or 'Company and music'.[34] In 1788, Eleanor Egerton indicated that Felice Giardini, a Piemontese composer, was present during their assembly with a lady singer who was her pupil. They gave a concert to 'a good deal of company'.[35] On Lady Spencer's second visit in 1792, she declared that she received company every evening from seven to 10 o'clock for card parties.[36] In the same year, some balls were given at Lady Rivers's house or at Lady Landaff's (1752–1796). The latter was an Irish baroness who received magnificently: 'all the best company, sixteen couple of dancers, three rooms for cards, refreshments continually handed round but no supper'.[37] The absence of supper conformed with Italian hospitality rules. This again shows that some local elite practices were adopted by British hostesses.

It can therefore be argued that entertaining had different meanings in relation to different hostesses and implied a large variety of settings, taking into account wealth, accommodation, and a desire to maintain more selective circles in a more confidential atmosphere. In particular, the visit of royal members of European dynasties engendered a temporary need of

192   *Bath and Beyond*

hospitality by the leading hostesses in local society. British ladies played a significant role in this special context. The giver of hospitality thus enjoyed a privileged position in local society, because many people relied on their entertaining, and many social ties could be made to their benefit. However, this elevated status could give rise to contradictory emotions and feelings, which could lead either to rivalries and a spirit of revenge, or to benevolent and charitable conduct, as the next section will explore.

Rivalries, Friendship, and Mutual Assistance

The duke and duchess of Gloucester resided in Nice in the winter of 1786, mainly for medical reasons. A younger brother of George III, William, was not in good health and was a frequent visitor to spa towns and Brighton. In 1766, he had secretly married Maria Waldegrave (1736–1807), a widow and the illegitimate daughter of Sir Edward Walpole. After the birth of their daughter, Sophia, the marriage was disclosed to the king, who banned her from court. As a result, she remained the morganatic wife of the duke, without the rights and privileges attached to members of the British royal family. When the couple visited Turin in 1785, the Sardinian court made efforts to adapt its ceremonial procedure to be sure not to upset George III and at the same time, not to offend the duke.[38] On their way to Nice, they were attended by Lady Rivers, first in her villa at Lyons. She then accompanied them to Marseilles and on to Nice. According to Lady Rivers's daughter, Louisa Beckford (*c*.1754–1791), her mother was acting more or less as a lady-in-waiting: 'The G [Gloucesters] are at Lyons—and my mother obliged to attend them every where. . . . We are at this place [Marseilles] for four days with the Glocester [*sic*] who follow us incessantly to Nice'.[39] The apparent vindictive character and sharp tongue of the duchess caused disharmony in Nice's local society. The duchess complained that she was not received on equal terms as her husband.[40] This situation was aggravated, or caused, by the fact that the duke was, at the time, tired of his spouse and did not give her as much support as before. He was, in fact, travelling with his mistress, also a lady-in-waiting to the duchess, Almeria Carpenter (1752–1809). However, the duchess found powerful allies among some British hostesses, including Lady Maynard. Lady Maynard, previously known as Nancy Parsons (*c*.1735–1814), was a former courtesan and mistress to both the dukes of Grafton and Dorset. In 1776, she married Charles Maynard, 2nd Viscount Maynard, who was 20 years her junior. This advantageous alliance gave her both fortune and (technically) social status. Viscountess Maynard could have become a major social facilitator for the British, like Lady Rivers, because she was a long-term resident in Nice, from 1780 to 1792. However, she was shunned by the British, not only for her past, but also and mostly because she repeatedly

British Female Hospitality and Fashionable Society 193

created scandals by seducing young men in public. In practice, she was only partially excluded from local society, because she was careful to receive local nobility and other foreign travellers, who in turn included her in their circles. By virtue of reciprocal hospitality, Lady Maynard managed to be part of major events.[41] Still, her position remained controversial with the British elite, which in some ways made her a good candidate to embrace the duchess's complaints against the duke, as she was already considered a scandalous outsider.

The strategy was to humiliate the duke by not respecting his royal position in public, which was in reality, exactly what the duchess was experiencing daily by the non-recognition of her title. Lady Rivers was left unimpressed:

> She [Lady Maynard] has a ball and supper every Wednesday which makes the Nizzards so partial to her that I have no doubts but the D [uke] stay'd, she would have influenced some of them to behave ill for the marquis of Fèrrer [Ferrero de Gubernatis] gave her [the duchess] a ball the other night, to which the Duke was not reckon'd [sic] tho' they live in the same house and the Villegarde who is her intimate friend and worthy the honour will not speak to the Duke; in short, there is such a cabaling [sic] with *these witches* that all comfort and serenity is destroy'd [sic], and the place made quite disagreeable (emphasis in original).[42]

Action was taken not only in the domestic sphere but also at the principal theatre. In order to weaken the duke's respectability in public, Lady Maynard had an accomplice in the young duke of Bedford (1765–1802), who was making his Grand Tour in 1785–1786. Lady Rivers nicknamed him Lady Maynard's 'cub'.[43] A scheme was designed and carried out in which the duke of Bedford was to refuse to bow before the duke and to act offensively towards him in front of all the British and the assembled local nobility. This included putting his elbow so close to his Highness's face that Lady Rivers thought that he would 'heat [sic] the teeth down his throat'.[44]

Precedence could also cause rivalries between titled ladies, especially in the context of an improvised court society. The problem arose during the visit of Ferdinand, archduke of Milan, and his wife, Beatrix of Austria, which took place just after the duke and duchess of Gloucester's departure from Nice. Among the titled hostesses residing in Nice every winter for several years, Lady Maynard, as the wife of a viscount, in spite of her low birth, had precedence of rank and was eligible to be the first to host the couple. However, Lady Rivers was given the preference. The fact that she was only the daughter of an English baronet was countered by her education, her close association with the duke of Gloucester, and her dominant

194 *Bath and Beyond*

status in Nice local society.[45] She invited the couple for a 'breakfast *a l'angloise*' at her house, which served as a meeting point to go to a villa in the countryside where the archduke and his wife were to entertain guests. She had the honour of keeping her privileged position as the leading British lady in Nice during the whole day.[46] Lady Rivers indicates that 'Lady Maynard and her men were ask'd [*sic*]', which means that she was behind her in the order of precedence. In another party at a villa in Villefranche, a town near Nice, the archduke confirmed her position, as he made her walk out of the room even before her wife, the duchess, and paid her much attention.[47] Despite the fact that Lady Rivers declared to Lady Erne that she 'does not love Royalty in general', she contrived to serve royal visitors as best as she could and seemed happy to receive some gratification and social recognition in return for the hospitality she offered in Nice.[48]

Lady Rivers' close associations with royalty also gave her the ability to act as a very efficient social facilitator to the benefit of her native friends. In introducing one of the main local hostesses, Baroness Rosalie Tonduti de Falicon (*b*.1730), to the duke and duchess of Gloucester, she indirectly gave her support to this assembly in preference to others in town, with the exception of the governor's house. This remained the most prestigious assembly among elite foreigners, even if some British ladies complained that people of 'any fashion' were received, which did not comply with their expectations of social exclusivity. When the duke honoured the baroness by his visit, all the British travellers who were admitted to Nice high society flocked to see him in person. Lady Rivers thus used her leadership to intercede on behalf of the baroness's family and it appears that the duke agreed to offer them his help:

> The poor Tondut [Tonduti] family are in great affliction for their brother who is involved in the disgrace of his Colonel . . . after 36 years service to be disgraced and become a beggar is a melancholic thing and they are all much to be pity'ed [*sic*]. Our dear Duke has behaved like an angel to them.[49]

As a result, hospitality could prove reciprocal and also beneficial to the whole community, especially for members in distress. These aspects have been often downplayed in the study of travel in Italian cities in the eighteenth century. The notion of friendship and female alliances are, however, very useful categories of analysis to better understand gendered sociabilities and the role of women within communities such as the British abroad.[50] In the eighteenth century, the concept of hospitality was linked to the codes of politeness and civility in elite society, but also encompassed charity and mutual support, as inherited from Christian tradition and aristocratic values.

British Female Hospitality and Fashionable Society   195

Hostesses considered it their duty not to overlook elderly people in society either. In 1770, Lady Spencer's mother, Margaret Georgiana Poyntz (*d*.1771), was staying in Nice with her grandchildren. She praised the hospitality from British ladies, especially that received from Lady Charlotte Finch who came to visit her very often, as it made her feel included in society.[51] Isolated elite women accompanying a relative in a bad state of health were in general not totally deprived of company, even if they could not throw large parties themselves. Visits and visiting offered an outlet for those unable to host on a large scale. In 1778, morning visits allowed Lady Polwarth to enjoy the support of friends because her husband could attend to no more than one guest at a time. Playing backgammon with Countess della Valle and Mrs Barker compensated a little for her loneliness and her lack of amusement. Mrs Barker endeavoured to put her sewing skills to good use to help Lady Polwarth finish a formal dress for the christening of the Swiss consul's son, for whom she had been chosen godmother. She was also thoughtful, bringing good books and letters—such as Madame de Sévigné's letters—to read aloud. The British ladies in general enjoyed reading her epistles in Nice and in the South of France because her descriptions of local scenery were a stimulating subject of discussion. Furthermore, her evocation of separation from her daughter echoed their own sense of distance from home and family. For Lady Polwarth, returning Lady Drogheda's visits at the end of the afternoon, around six o'clock, was a legitimate excuse to leave her house and enjoy a larger society.[52] Lady Drogheda was herself quite isolated because of her husband's nervous complaints.[53] It was also an opportunity for Lady Polwarth to return Countess della Valle's hospitality and friendship by rendering her the service of inviting her into her coach to go to Lady Drogheda's.[54] The countess did not own a carriage herself, like most of the local noble families, and it was difficult to ride back on her horse by moonlight from the *Faubourg de la Croix de Marbre*.[55]

During the last decades of the century, Lady Rivers appeared as not only the main British hostess in Nice, but also a 'maternal' benefactress to young, separated wives, those in marital difficulties, and even unmarried elder ladies. This is exemplified in her support of Lady Elizabeth Foster and her sister Lady Erne, as well as their parents Lord and Lady Bristol. In 1783, when Lady Elizabeth Foster was in a difficult position, having fled her abusive husband, she was left alone to maintain her establishment and status in society.[56] Lady Rivers offered her support. Additionally, her parents, Lord and Lady Bristol, the former having decided to live apart from his wife, relied separately on Lady Rivers' protection in Nice.[57] In 1788, Lady Elizabeth Foster's sister, Lady Erne, whose marriage was also disastrous in spite of her family's high expectations, was invited to stay at Lady Rivers's houses in Nice and Lyons. Lady Erne's husband allowed her a very limited income, which compelled her to rely on her father's support

196   *Bath and Beyond*

and friendly hospitality, such as from Lady Rivers.[58] In reality, this meant a restrained lifestyle (even abroad), dependent on others' travel schemes. Unmarried women, even of a certain age such as Laetitia Houblon, who was past the age of 40, were relieved to know that she and her young cousin could have confidence in Lady Rivers' assistance if needed: 'Lady Rivers hearing I was ill, came and sat an hour, which revived us a little'.[59]

Hospitality was understood in a wide sense which included domestic hospitality, mutual mental support, and some material and medical assistance. British ladies of fashion, such as Lady Spencer, had the means to travel with a family doctor who could give advice or tend to serious cases. It was considered important that the British did not rely on native practitioners. When Lady Charlotte Finch was in Nice in 1770, the duchess of Beaufort (1719–1799) was accompanying her very ill daughter, Lady Mary Somerset (1756–1831) (later duchess of Rutland), but thanks to the help of Lady Spencer's physician, the crisis was averted. The incident was reported through the correspondence of Lady Mary Coke, who was exchanging letters with Lady Charlotte from Aix:

> Lady Charlotte Finch writes me word that Ly [*sic*] Mary Somerset . . . has been dying of a fever; she seems to be very lucky that Ly [*sic*] Spencer was not gone, who you know has always a physician with her and a very good one and seems to be serviceable on this occasion, for Ly [*sic*] Charlotte says there is no assistance at Nice.[60]

In 1778, Lady Polwarth related the presence of many valetudinarians in Nice. Her husband's doctor was required for several difficult cases. It was reassuring for the British community as a whole to rely on wealthy families and their physicians. Although for the physicians themselves, it was rarely a good opportunity for publicity, because, in Lady Polwarth's opinion, they were often called when all hopes of recovery were lost.[61] On the grounds of friendship, medical assistance was extended to the local nobility, as in the example of Lady Drogheda, who offered the services of her personal physician to Countess della Valle to have her child inoculated.[62] In 1792, Lady Spencer was approached by other British families in distress, consenting again to 'lend' her physician and for herself to give counselling to husbands and fathers. This orchestrating of physical and emotion care could be said to place Lady Spencer in the role of 'mistress of the ceremonies of medicine', a term coined by the physician Thomas Beddoe in reference to authoritative dowagers doing such works at the turn of the century in British spa resorts.[63] The role and term can thus also be seen to be relevant to those British hostesses in Nice. It also shows that besides female solidarity and alliances, ladies of fashion played a significant role of assistance to the whole British community, regardless of gender.

That same year Lady Spencer was solicited by Thomas Graham, later Lord Lynedoch, on account of his wife, Mary (1757–1792), daughter of the 9th Lord Cathcart, whose death was imminent. Lady Spencer made daily calls to Mary Graham's house, as did her daughters, Lady Duncannon (1761–1821) and the duchess of Devonshire, who were her close friends. Mary Graham's last wish was to go back to England to meet her sister again and to be buried in Scotland, but it was no longer possible for her to travel long distances by road, and instead a sea voyage home was imagined, or a shorter crossing to Naples. Thomas Graham sought Lady Spencer's advice. The presence and actions of British ladies of fashion in Nice were instrumental in helping Mary Graham 'prepare' for her death, especially by receiving and accepting her instructions for the sake of her relatives after her death. She entrusted Charlotte Nugent to announce her death to her sister, Lady Stormont, in England, according to a specific and anticipated order to try to lessen her grief. She requested the duchess of Devonshire 'to continue to see as much of Charlotte Cathcart [Mary's young unmarried sister] as she can, and to love her, and tell her exactly anything that occurs to her' and to thank Lady Spencer for all the kindness to her.[64] It seems that Lady Spencer and her daughter were put in the position of reliable and good protectresses, because of their dominant position in society in Britain and abroad, as well as for their charitable characters. The reputation of Lady Spencer as a fervent evangelical devotee does not mean that she was an isolated case. Notably this characteristic of charitability in British hostesses in Nice was not wholly spurred by religious duty, as it was common for female travellers to take care of their counterparts regardless of their religious beliefs. Even differences in religion were not a deterrent to mutual support. In 1792, Laetitia Houblon, with other Protestant ladies, visited the Catholic Mary Eyre (d.1804), (daughter of Thomas Belasyse, Earl Fauconberg) daily, who had just lost her husband in Nice. To ensure she would not be alone during the removal of the corpse, Laetitia Houblon invited her to her house.[65]

Conclusion

This chapter has examined through eighteenth-century female diaries and letters the role played by British hostesses in Nice elite society. It has been shown that they contributed in a significant way to transform the reputation of Nice as a provincial town into a fashionable spa resort. Exclusive domestic hospitality was a strong incentive for members of the British *beau monde* to come to Nice, because they were sure that they would find a distinguished company (albeit a small one) and common social codes abroad. The presence of ladies of fashion was a guarantee against estrangement and too much novelty in adapting to a foreign context. Lady travellers of

198 *Bath and Beyond*

rank were thus introduced 'smoothly' into Nice's local elite society. Acting as 'Mistresses of the Ceremonies', they reinforced ties of transnational and national friendship and gave relief to elite members in distress. They gave a sense of belonging to the 'exiled' British who could feel as much part of a community and a national entity as of a cosmopolitan high society.

Notes

1 Conseil Général des Alpes-Maritimes, *Le comté de Nice et la maison royale de Savoie* (Milan: Silvana Editoriale, 2010), 129–65.
2 Christopher Storrs, "The British Diplomatic Presence in Turin: Diplomatic Culture and British Elite Identity, 1688–1789/98," in *Turin and the British in the Age of the Grand Tour*, ed. Paola Bianchi and Karin Wolfe (Cambridge: Cambridge University Press, 2017), chap. 4.
3 Phyllis Hembry has demonstrated the same system of royal patronage in English spa resorts. Phyllis Hembry, *The English Spa, 1560–1815: A Social History* (London: Athlone Press, 1990).
4 John Eglin, *The Imaginary Autocrat: Beau Nash and the Invention of Bath* (London: Profile Books, 2005).
5 Maria Luisa Betri and Elena Brambilla, eds., *Salotti e ruolo femminile in Italia tra fine Seicento a primo Novecento* (Venice: Marsilio, 2004).
6 Elaine Chalus, "Cette fusion annuelle: Cosmopolitanism and Identity in Nice, *c.*1815–1860," *The Urban History Journal* xli (2014): 606–26; Elaine Chalus, "Spaces of Sociability in Fashionable Society: Brighton and Nice, *c.*1825–35," in *Gendering Spaces in European Towns, 1500–1914*, ed. Elaine Chalus and Marjo Kaartinen (New York: Routledge, 2019), 75–86.
7 Felicity Heal has shown that the representation of aristocratic hospitality ideals evolved in early modern England as the landed elite began to neglect their social duties towards the neighborhood community in favour of an ostentatious quest of power and prestige in highly competitive urban settings. Felicity Heal, "The Idea of Hospitality in Early Modern England," *Past and Present* cii (1894): 66–93; Felicity Heal, *Hospitality in Early Modern England* (Oxford: Oxford University Press, 2013). The decline of traditional hospitality was also debunked by the French philosophers of the Encyclopedia, claiming that the rise of commercial institutions for accommodation and entertainment converted elite true hospitality into self-interest. "Hospitality," in *L'Encyclopédie ou Dictionnaire raisonné des sciences, des arts et des métiers* (Paris, 1766), viii, 314–16.
8 Chalus, "Spaces of Sociability," 79–83.
9 BL, Add MS 75611: Lady Spencer to Caroline Howe, December 6–7, 1769.
10 On the contrary, Lady Polwarth was of high birth. She was the daughter of Philip Yorke, 2nd earl of Hardwicke, and Jemima, Marchioness Grey.
11 BLARS, L 30/9/60/124: Lady Polwarth to Marchioness Grey, January 23, 1778.
12 East Sussex Archives, AMS 5440/113: Lady Foster to Lady Sheffield, October 1783.
13 Alice Frances Houblon, *The Houblon Family, Its Story and Times*, 2 vols. (London: Archibald Constable, 1907), ii, 188.
14 The Hon. Miss Egerton, *Diary of the Honorable Miss Egerton Afterwards Marchioness of Westminster During 1787 and 1788 Given an Account of a Tour in France and the North of Italy* (1855), 97. Mary Allsopp, daughter of Thomas Allsopp of Loughborough, was the wife of Sir William Gordon (1726–1798).

British Female Hospitality and Fashionable Society 199

15 BL, Add MS 75640: Lady Spencer to Caroline Howe, February 13, 1792.
16 BLARS, L 30/13/12/47: Lady Polwarth to Jemima Robinson, February 24, 1778.
17 Egerton, *Diary of the Honorable Miss Egerton*, 98, 101.
18 Chatsworth, CS5 2014–1–252: Lady Spencer's Journal, January 1770.
19 Houblon, *The Houblon Family*, ii, 218.
20 BL, Add MS 75640: Lady Spencer to Caroline Howe, April 24, 1792. Laetitia Houblon was nevertheless a member of London fashionable society and was admitted at St James' Court.
21 John Cannon, *Aristocratic Century: The Peerage of Eighteenth Century England* (New York: Cambridge University Press, 1984); Hannah Grieg, *The Beau Monde: Fashionable Society in Georgian London* (Oxford: Oxford University Press, 2013); Katherine Glover, *Elite Women and Polite Society in Eighteenth-Century Scotland* (Woodbridge: Boydell & Brewer, 2011), 16–17.
22 BL, Add MS 75640: Lady Spencer to Caroline Howe, March 2–3, 1792.
23 BL, Add MS 75640: Lady Spencer to Caroline Howe, April 1, 1792.
24 BLARS, L 30/9/60/126: Lady Polwarth to Marchioness Grey, May 11, 1778.
25 Amanda Foreman, *Georgiana, Duchess of Devonshire* (HarperCollins, 1998).
26 Houblon, *The Houblon Family*, 244.
27 BLARS, L 30/13/12/46: Lady Polwarth to Jemima Robinson, January 30, 1778.
28 Egerton, *Diary of the Honorable Miss Egerton*, 106.
29 Ellis Markman, "The Tea-Table, Women and Gossip in Early Modern England," in *British Sociability in the Long Eighteenth-Century. Challenging the Anglo-French Connection*, ed. Valérie Capdeville and Alain Kerhervé (Woodbridge: Boydell Press, 2019), chap. 4; Brian Dolan, *Ladies of the Grand Tour* (New York: HarperCollins, 2001), 130.
30 SCA, Wh M 544–3: Lady Rivers to Lady Erne, March 3, 1786.
31 Peter Borsay qualified Bath's society as a 'corporate style of life'. Peter Borsay, "Urban Life and Culture," in *A Companion to Eighteenth Century Britain*, ed. H. T. Dickinson (Malden: Blackwell Pub., 2002), chap. 15.
32 Chatsworth, CS5 2014–1–252: Lady Spencer's Journal, December 2, 1769, January 29, 1770. Jean-Baptiste Noyel de Bellegarde (1701–78) and her wife, Anna Genna di Cocconato (1726–1811).
33 BLARS, L 30/13/12/47: Lady Polwarth to Jemima Robinson, February 24, 1778.
34 Chatsworth, CS5 2014–1–252: Lady Spencer's Journal, February 11 and 13, 1770.
35 Egerton, *Diary of the Honorable Miss Egerton*, 101.
36 BL, Add MS 75640: Lady Spencer to Caroline Howe, March 5, 1792.
37 Houblon, *The Houblon Family*, ii, 195.
38 TNA, FO 67–5: John Trevor to the marquess of Carmarthen, November 8, 1786. The duke and duchess of Gloucester were travelling incognito which implied an already simplified protocol.
39 J. W. Oliver, *The Life of William Beckford* (Oxford: Oxford University Press, 1937), 145, 149.
40 SCA, Wh M 544/1: Lady Rivers to Lady Erne, January 1786.
41 SCA, Wh M 544/1–3: Letter from Lady Rivers to Lady Erne, January and March 1786; Egerton, *Diary of the Honorable Miss Egerton*, 99.
42 SCA, Wh M 544/2: Lady Rivers to Lady Erne, January 11, 1786.
43 SCA, Wh M 544/2: Lady Rivers to Lady Erne, January 11, 1786.
44 SCA, Wh M 544/2: Lady Rivers to Lady Erne, January 11, 1786.
45 Even if Lady Rivers was old and deaf; she was obliged to use a cornet to communicate with her guests.

200 Bath and Beyond

46 SCA, Wh M 544/3: Lady Rivers to Lady Erne, March 3, 1786.
47 SCA, Wh M 544/3: Lady Rivers to Lady Erne, March 3, 1786.
48 Lord Herbert gives a detailed account of Lady Rivers's hospitality towards the duke and his family. *The Pembroke Papers: Letters and Diaries of Henry, Tenth Earl of Pembroke and His Circle*, ed. Lord Herbert (Jonathan Cape, 1950), 244–46.
49 SCA, Wh M 544/1: Lady Rivers to Lady Erne, January 1786.
50 Amanda Herbert made a brilliant contribution on this subject in the field of British spa resorts. See Amanda Herbert, *Female Alliances: Gender, Identity and Friendship in Early Modern Britain* (New Haven: Yale University Press, 2014), chap. 4.
51 BL, Add MS 75572: Lady Poyntz's Journal, February 21 and March 2, 1770.
52 Leeds Archive Service, WYL150: Lady Polwarth's Journal, June 8, 1778.
53 BLARS, L 30/9/60/128: Lady Polwarth to Marchioness Grey, March 3, 1778.
54 Vittoria della Valle (*d*.1831) was the goddaughter of one of the governors of Nice, the Count of Nangis. From 1769 to 1792, the British ladies held her in high esteem as she spoke English well which was extremely rare among the local nobility.
55 BLARS, L 30/9/60/125–126: Lady Polwarth to Marchioness Grey, March 3, 1778.
56 On the consequences of desertion, see Lawrence Stone, *Broken Lives: Separation and Divorce in England (1660–1857)* (Oxford: Oxford University Press, 1993), 18.
57 Vere Foster, *The Two Duchesses: Family Correspondence (1777–1859)* (1898), 94, 97.
58 W. S. Childe Pemberton, *The Earl Bishop: The Life of Frederick Hervey, the Bishop of Derry and Earl of Bristol* (New York: E. P. Dutton, 1924), ii, 365.
59 Houblon, *The Houblon Family*, ii, 200.
60 Lady Mary Coke, *The Letters and Journals of Lady Mary Coke* (Bath, 1889–96), iii, 211.
61 BLARS, L 30/9/60/126: Lady Polwarth to Marchioness Grey, February 10, 1778.
62 BLARS, L 30/9/60/125: Lady Polwarth to Marchioness Grey, February 6, 1778.
63 Thomas Beddoes, *Manual of Health or the Invalid Conducted Safely Through the Seasons* (1806), 332.
64 E. Maxtone Graham, *The Beautiful Mrs Graham and the Cathcart circle* (Boston: Houghton Mifflin Co., 1928), 282.
65 Houblon, *The Houblon Family*, ii, 245.

Bibliography

Beddoes, Thomas. *Manual of Health or the Invalid Conducted Safely Through the Seasons*. London: J. Johnson, 1806.
Betri, Maria Luisa, and Elena Brambilla. *Salotti e ruolo femminile in Italia tra fine Seicento a primo Novecento*. Venice: Marsilio, 2004.
Borsay, Peter. "Urban Life and Culture." In *A Companion to Eighteenth Century Britain*, edited by H. T. Dickinson, chap. 15. Malden: Blackwell Pub., 2002.
Cannon, John. *Aristocratic Century: The Peerage of Eighteenth Century England*. New York: Cambridge University Press, 1984.
Chalus, Elaine. "Cette Fusion Annuelle: Cosmopolitanism and Identity in Nice, c.1815–1860." *The Urban History Journal* 41, no. 4 (Autumn 2014): 606–26. https://doi.org/10.1017/s0963926813000710.

British Female Hospitality and Fashionable Society 201

Chalus, Elaine. "Spaces of Sociability in Fashionable Society: Brighton and Nice, *c*.1825–35." In *Gendering Spaces in European Towns, 1500–1914*, edited by Elaine Chalus and Marjo Kaartinen, 75–94. New York: Routledge, 2019.

Childe-Pemberton, W. S. *The Earl Bishop: The Life of Frederick Hervey, the Bishop of Derry and Earl of Bristol*. New York: E. P. Dutton, 1924.

Coke, Mary (Lady). *The Letters and Journals of Lady Mary Coke*. Bath: Kingsmead Reprints, 1970.

Conseil Général des Alpes-Maritimes. *Le comté de Nice et la maison royale de Savoie*. Milan: Silvana Editoriale, 2010.

Dolan, Brian. *Ladies of the Grand Tour*. New York: HarperCollins, 2001.

Foreman, Amanda. *Georgiana, Duchess of Devonshire*. New York: HarperCollins, 1998.

Foster, Vere. *The Two Duchesses: Family Correspondence (1777–1859)*. Blackie & Son, 1898.

Egerton Grosvenor, Eleanor, Marchioness of Westminster. *Diary of Hon. Miss Egerton, afterwards Marchioness of Westminster, During 1787 and 1788 Given an Account of a Tour in France and the North of Italy*. London: H. Massey, 1855.

Eglin, John. *The Imaginary Autocrat: Beau Nash and the Invention of Bath*. Profile Books, 2005.

Glover, Katherine. *Elite Women and Polite Society in Eighteenth-Century Scotland*. Woodbridge: Boydell Press, 2011.

Grieg, Hannah. *The Beau Monde: Fashionable Society in Georgian London*. Oxford: Oxford University Press, 2013.

Heal, Felicity. *Hospitality in Early Modern England*. Oxford: Oxford University Press, 1990.

Heal, Felicity. "The Idea of Hospitality in Early Modern England." *Past and Present* 102, no. 1 (Winter 1984): 66–93. https://doi.org/10.1093/Past/102.1.66.

Hembry, Phyllis. *The English Spa, 1560–1815: A Social History*. London: The Althone Press, 1990.

Herbert, Amanda. *Female Alliances: Gender, Identity and Friendship in Early Modern Brittain*. New Haven: Yale University Press, 2014.

Herbert, Henry, Earl of Pembroke, ed. *The Pembroke Papers: Letters and Diaries of Henry, Tenth Earl of Pembroke and His Circle*. London: Jonathan Cape, 1950.

Houblon, Alice Frances, ed. *The Houblon Family, Its Story and Times*. London: Archibald Constable, 1907.

Jaucourt, le Chevalier de. "Hospitality." In *L'Encyclopédie ou Dictionnaire raisonné des sciences, des arts et des métiers*. Paris: Briasson David, Le Breton, Durand, 1766.

Markman, Ellis. "The Tea-Table, Women and Gossip in Early Modern England." In *British Sociability in the Long Eighteenth-Century. Challenging the Anglo-French Connection*, edited by Valérie Capdeville and Alain Kerhervé, chap. 4. Woodbridge: Boydell Press, 2019. https://doi.org/10.1017/9781787444904.007.

Maxtone-Graham, E. *The Beautiful Mrs Graham and the Cathcart Circle*. Boston: Houghton Mifflin Co., 1928.

Oliver, J. W. *The Life of William Beckford*. Oxford: Oxford University Press, 1937.

Stone, Lawrence. *Broken Lives: Separation and Divorce in England (1660–1857)*. Oxford: Oxford University Press, 1993.

Storrs, Christopher. "The British Diplomatic Presence in Turin: Diplomatic Culture and British Elite Identity, 1688–1789/98." In *Turin and the British in the Age of the Grand Tour*, edited by Paola Bianchi and Karin Wolfe, chap. 4. Cambridge: Cambridge University Press, 2017.

11 The 'Bath Revolution'?
Musical *Distractions* in French Spas, *Cercles*, and *Salons*

Phil Bonjour

At the beginning of the nineteenth century, *cercles* were instituted almost everywhere in France as establishments designed to accommodate communities of people, generally consisting of several rooms and *salons*, offering various leisure, cultural, or social activities including conversation, music, and dancing. These *cercles* and *salons* aimed at gathering the maximum numbers of *étrangers* [or 'foreigners'] together and offering *distractions* (or 'entertainments') alongside thermal cures.[1] These four terms, maintained in French throughout this chapter, were embedded in the administrative and literary vocabulary of French spa towns.[2] Along with gambling, music was at the very heart of activities in *cercles* and *salons*. In German historiography, this music is the subject of a separate and established field of study and a separate name, *Kurmusik*, because music played a central role in the economic, social, and political history of spa towns, which were themselves central to the development of the places where they were located, particularly in the nineteenth century.[3] On the other side of the Rhine, French historians refer to the nineteenth century and the first three decades of the twentieth century as *l'âge d'or du thermalisme* ['the golden age of thermalism', 'heyday of balneotherapy', or 'age of watering-places'].[4] While taking care not to endorse this meliorative chrononym, a quick historical rereading of the *âge d'or* focuses on the circulation of thermal and (proto)tourist practices as cultural transfers throughout Europe.[5] In French historiography, these spa practices, and their European market, during the *âge d'or* were a transposition of an ancient model: that of 'Beau' Nash's Bath.[6]

In the 1980s, French historian Marc Boyer extended the understanding of early twentieth-century French scholar Alfred Barbeau's notion of the 'Bath Revolution', an established notion in the French historiography.[7] French historians consider the development of assembly rooms as central to the 'Bath Revolution'.[8] The French historiography of tourism explores how Bath's assembly rooms served as a model to organise the sociability of *étrangers* by developing the infrastructure of reception (hotels, restaurants,

DOI: 10.4324/9781003393856-11

The 'Bath Revolution'? 203

and refreshments) and *distractions* (gambling, balls, concerts, and other entertainments). More specifically, many of the community practices invented in Bath were imported to France, such as the publication of lists of *étrangers* newly arrived in the spa town, the meticulous organisation of balls, and the spatial organisation of leisure activities within the spa town by the Master of Ceremonies. Studying *Kurmusik* means adopting an analytical approach to the *âge d'or du thermalisme*, which has traditionally reduced this *âge d'or* to being merely a source of *distractions* for *étrangers*. Therefore, studying the musical practices of *cercles* and *salons* constitutes a bottom-up analysis that allows us to question the veracity of the 'Bath Revolution'.

Boyer argued that there was a 'sense of tourism history' given by the quest for distinction of 'dominant socio-cultural groups' whose practices then spread to the rest of society.[9] According to him, the first 'invention of distinction' of this order took place in Bath in the eighteenth century, devoting a section of his history of southeastern French spa towns to the 'Bath Revolution'[10]:

> Why this exception for Bath? . . . There was nothing exceptional about its Roman past. . . There was nothing exceptional about the quality of the water or the fact that Bath is located in a deep valley in a crystalline massif! The meaning of this invention must be sought in socio-cultural history. It is part of a set of inventions by which the United Kingdom fundamentally distinguished itself from the rest of the world during the 18th century: we know about the Industrial, Agricultural, Demographic and Maritime Revolutions, which are the best-known aspects of the British *take-off* [in English in the text], but we do not know about the Tourist Revolution: when the British aristocracy distinguished itself from the continental nobility and from the new English bourgeoisie of merchants and manufacturers by the journey of distinction (emphasis in original).[11]

According to Boyer, hierarchical distinction was a common goal of *étrangers*, seeking to make a place for themselves in the community. At the same time, spa town leaders competed for the most prestigious clientele to distinguish themselves from other European spa towns, organising the life of the *étrangers* in such a way that they could create and maintain their own distinctions. Such an undertaking required that every sector of the spa town's activities, including music, be directed towards distinction. The 'Bath Revolution', according to Boyer, is characterised by the sociable practices of 'fashionable' people who sacrificed practicalities to follow fashion[12]; and by 'puff', a creative expression in which the commercial end itself constitutes the means, both fuelling and mirroring the tourists'

204 Bath and Beyond

appetite for music.[13] Boyer's argument for this British socio-cultural invention was inherited from Alfred Barbeau. Barbeau argued:

> Between the French water cities of the time and the English ones, there are only inevitable similarities. In both of them, it is necessary that the patient follows a similar regime; that they look for ways to relax, which will necessarily be conversation, walk, music, dance, game. . . . How could it be otherwise? These are features common to the thermal spas of all times and all countries, and which have nothing characteristic. But, on the contrary, what distinguishes Bath or Tunbridge [Wells] at the time we are dealing with . . . we find it nowhere in France, I mean the society glitter, the ordered train of pleasures, the extent and the variety of the clientele, the universal appeal . . . . The emergence of the English water cities and their subsequent development are original and spontaneous phenomena . . . which owe nothing . . . to continental influence.[14]

This analysis suggests that all French thermal towns were the same, in their modesty and boredom, in comparison with the Bath model. Barbeau linked the socio-economic and musical practices of spa towns through '*l'éclat mondain*' [the society glitter] '*le train réglé des plaisirs*' [the ordered train of pleasures], and '*l'universel attrait*' [the universal appeal].[15] This chapter therefore provides a musical extension of the scholarship of Boyer and Barbeau within the 'Bath Revolution'. Its aim is not to show that this 'Bath Revolution' was a musical revolution, or even a revolution *through* music; rather, it aims to characterise music (in the German sense of *Kurmusik*) as revealing a paradigm shift and rupture in the history of tourism. French *Kurmusik* stands as a testament to the evolution of social practices developed around Thermalism in the wake of principles established in eighteenth-century Bath.[16]

This chapter is motivated by recent renewed interest in European spa towns, demonstrated by the 'Great Spa Towns of Europe' UNESCO World Heritage nomination in 2021, and by French heritage promotion initiatives.[17] These developments have highlighted the importance of musical practices in the heyday of France's spa towns, in particular in Évian-les-Bains, Vichy, and Aix-les-Bains (also called Aix-en-Savoie).[18] The case studies of the last two have been selected because they were the two dominant French spa towns of the nineteenth and early twentieth centuries. Aix is particularly interesting because of its location in a region of decisive importance in relations between France and Italy during the Risorgimento (the unification of Italy in the 1850s), in which Savoie was instrumental.[19] Close to Aix geographically, Évian was selected as a smaller counterpart (and direct competitor) to Aix. The thermal seasons for these three towns took place in the summer, hosting multiple venues for the *étrangers* to meet and enjoy music. This chapter compares the musical organisation of the *cercles* and *salons* in Vichy, Aix, and Évian to establish the links between their organisation and the 'Bath Revolution' described by both French contemporaries and historians. It delves into the influence of the 'Bath Revolution' on French spa musical seasons and provides insights into the economic, political, and social stakes of musical practices that are still often disregarded in France because of their perceived triviality.

Analysing early musical spa practices is challenging due to a lack of source material. Most of the first French *cercles* were created in the 1820s, such as the Cercle d'Aix-les-Bains in 1824.[20] However, prior to 1824, there are very few surviving administrative documents. Musical programmes were not published in newspapers until the 1850s. The patchy corpus of sources confirms the chronological limits suggested by the historiography: the introduction of *distractions* in French spa towns occurred well after Bath's golden age. The gaps in the corpus are not simply due to issues of preservation and survivability, but also due to the status of early musical practices accorded by the press, spa leaders, and fashionable clientele.

'*L'éclat Mondain*' [The Society Glitter]

French spa towns were microcosms of a strictly structured aristocratic society. The traditional style of music in spa towns at the end of the eighteenth century and at the beginning of the nineteenth century can be considered as *musique d'ameublement* [ornamental 'furniture music'], a style favoured by aristocratic clientele in their homes and the early French *cercles* that provided an aural backdrop for other entertainments. One of the few identifiable musicians from these French spas is Isaac Strauss (unrelated to Johann Strauss). He was conductor of the orchestra of the salons of the Cercle d'Aix from 1824 to 1843, and then at Vichy from 1844 to 1857.[21] That orchestra principally played for balls and concerts, but also provided background music for social activities like talking, taking the waters, and playing cards. When Strauss left Aix, he was replaced by Simon Lévy, a member of Strauss's orchestra. They were friends and colleagues with similar roots: Jewish musicians from Alsace who, like many French provincial musicians, had travelled through France pursuing successful careers.[22] Their musical performances in the Cercle d'Aix can likely be reconstructed from the musical scores published by Lévy and Strauss (Figure 11.1).[23] The instrumentation was often composed of a string quartet or quintet, accompanied by a piano, or more rarely, a flute. The melody was systematically entrusted to the first violin accompanied by the rest of the ensemble, sometimes with simple question-and-answer motifs. The musical structure of these dances was rigid, with rare inventions of rhythmic figures. There is

206 Bath and Beyond

Figure 11.1 Simon Levy, *Valses favorites du cercle d'Aix les bains. Nouveau recueil suivi d'un galop pour le piano avec accompagnement de violon, flûte ou flageolet ad libitum composé et dédié à son ami Strauss, artiste du Théâtre des Italiens et directeur des Concerts d'Aix par Simon Lévy*, undated, In-fol. oblong, Bibliothèque Nnationale de France, VM12 G-8320 [*Favourite waltzes from the Aix les bains circle. New collection followed by a galop for piano with accompaniment by violin, flute, or flageolet ad libitum composed and dedicated to his friend Strauss, artist at the Théâtre des Italiens and director of the Concerts d'Aix by Simon Lévy*]. Courtesy of the Bibliothèque Nationale de France.

nothing to differentiate their style from other waltzes published by Lévy, such as *Les Soirées de Lyon*.[24]

In both the private homes and the music rooms of the *cercles*, women of high social status demonstrated their musical skills, an integral part of their upbringing, in front of other members of the community. Napoleon I's niece, Maria-Letizia Bonaparte (Marie de Solms), was exiled from France to Aix (at that time part of the kingdom of Sardinia) during the 1840s and 1850s. While there, she organised salons at her residence, with musical performances playing an important role. She also opened the Théâtre du Chalet, a public theatre where female *étrangers* to the spa town performed, sang, and played alongside renowned artists.[25] The programme from 30

The 'Bath Revolution'? 207

Figure 11.2 Martin Cadenat d'après Sorrieu, *Souvenir d'Aix-les-bains. Sale* [sic] *de danse du casino* [Casino Ballroom], in *Journal d'Aix-les-Bains*, 1853, lithograph, Bibliothèque Nationale de France, JO-7116. Courtesy of the Bibliothèque Nationale de France.

208 Bath and Beyond

July 1859 reveals that the cellist Joseph van der Heyden shared the stage with *étrangers* and Marie de Solms herself, playing pieces from their local repertoire as well as compositions by the hostess.[26] These salons encouraged amateur musical performances, supporting local sociability while also bringing together famous European artists with female tourists. The repertoire consisted mainly of sonatas for solo instrument or accompanied by a piano, as well as the *mélodie française* [French art song, similar to the German *Lied*], such as Louis Niedermeyer's *Le Lac* based on a poem by Alphonse Marie Louis de Lamartine.[27] From the 1870s and 1880s onwards, musical salons gradually disappeared from French spa towns, as the managers concentrated their efforts on the construction of new performance and concert spaces: casino theatres and bandstands.

Only a small group of artists and intellectuals continued to host music salons. This is notably the case of poetess Anna de Noailles and her family. Anna de Noailles was the daughter of Rachel de Brancovan (née Mousouros), herself a pianist and the daughter of the Turkish ambassador in London from 1861. Rachel Mousouros married Grégoire Bibesco-Bassaraba de Brancovan [son of Romanian Prince Georges Bibesco] on 28 May 1874 in London. The couple settled in a villa on the shores of Lake Geneva in Amphion, near Évian, where they spent their summers. Their guests included members of the European aristocracy and a number of renowned artists and well-known personalities, such as Marcel Proust and his family.[28] The press reported that private concerts were performed at the Bassaraba villa. Indeed, Polish musician and politician Ignacy Jan Paderewski, for example, stayed in Bassaraba's villa before dedicating his *Polish Fantasy on Original Themes* (1893) to Rachel de Brancovan.[29] In *Le Livre de ma vie*, Anna de Noailles described a few memories of society at Amphion:

> Mon père, lui, avait pour les réunions fastueuses autour de sa table, ainsi que pour l'accueil qu'il faisait à ses hôtes d'Amphion, une inclination qui tenait du digne amour du décor, d'une sorte d'éloquence dans l'organisation, à quoi se mêlait le besoin de voir croître autour de soi le bonheur dispensé par sa puissance.[30]
>
> [My father, for his part, had an inclination for sumptuous gatherings around his table, as well as for the welcome he gave to his guests from Amphion, which stemmed from a dignified love of décor, a kind of eloquence in organisation, with which was mixed the need to see the happiness dispensed by his power grow around him.]

Balls in grand salons and amateur concerts provided opportunities for *étrangers* to show themselves to advantage through aesthetic and social performances, helping to establish their social power within an international community. Many of Proust's characters in *À la recherche du temps perdu* were inspired directly by his stays with the de Noailles family, as well as by time spent at Évian and other French resorts.[31]

Urban development significantly reshaped the socio-cultural practices of these spa towns. For the first few decades, the Cercle d'Aix housed a theatre where plays were performed regularly. From the 1850s onwards, changes became palpable with two vital developments: first, the Cercle moved to a new, larger building; and secondly, Marie de Solms founded the Théâtre du Chalet, bringing these two establishments into direct competition with each other. Le Chalet had no orchestra, but it offered a musical programme in keeping with the private and less formal practices mentioned earlier: concerts by amateurs or soloists. At the same time, the Grand Hôtel des Bains d'Évian continued to offer these two types of musical performance until the 1870s. In 1859, the Cachat water company, owner of the Hôtel des Bains, built a new, more prestigious, state-of-the-art establishment, becoming the Grand Hôtel des Bains.[32] My previous research has demonstrated how this urban development reshaped the spa's musical practices. The relocation of the Cachat establishment permitted the maintenance of an aristocratic inner circle with its own elite music practices, while the managers of the spa in the city centre wanted to expand outwards to the lake, organising new kinds of music activities.[33] The remaining *salons* were pushed outwards to the city's edge.

'Le Train Réglé Des Plaisirs' [The Ordered Train of Pleasures]

From the 1870s onwards, other establishments began to challenge the monopolies of the Cercle in Aix and the Cachat company in Évian. In 1873, the Évian town council decided to open its own spa and casino to generate more revenue for the town.[34] In Aix, the Chalet de Marie de Solms theatre was demolished in 1880, although it had stopped giving regular performances in the 1860s.[35] A competitor, the Casino de la Villa des Fleurs, appeared in 1879.[36] Each of these new establishments had its own orchestra. Évian also reckoned with the neighbouring competition of the orchestra from the casino in nearby Amphion-les-Bains for a few seasons in the mid-1870s.[37] While competition between Aix and Évian stimulated the development of spa music over the following decade, competition within the two communes did so even more.

To maintain a competitive advantage over local and international spa towns, several columnists in the thermal magazines (published in every spa town) asked for the spa towns to change, prompting *Kurmusik* to evolve, shifting away from an intimate atmosphere that favoured amateur music-making and small balls, to the expansion and modernisation of leisure spaces and times, including musical ones. One of these columnists was Joseph Dessaix from Évian, a supporter of an independent Savoie and

210 *Bath and Beyond*

defender of its territory. Dessaix regretted the closing of the Cachat society's 'small glassed-in *salon* of the thermal establishment'[38] that had been located in the main street of the city: 'when it was open, the greatest animation reigned in the town until midnight'[39];

> the orchestra threw its joyful fanfares into the air. Today . . . all the excitement is concentrated on the terrace and in the *salon* of the new hotel [built away from the city centre] and the city looks like a tomb. Why shouldn't there be two *salons*?[40]

Dessaix also wrote of the *salon* built in the new Grand Hôtel des Bains by the Cachat society:

> The refusal of the salon makes us want to build an independent casino even more strongly. Why should we not have a *kursaal* in the style of the German cities, where all the pleasures that can be provided for bathers are combined. . . . The day when such an establishment is inaugurated will mark the era of prosperity that we foresee for Évian. Then this pretty city will be able to rank among the most popular seaside resorts in Europe.[41]

Dessaix referred to the cramped conditions of the Cachat society's Grand Hôtel des Bains, which did not have the necessary infrastructure to organise several *distractions* at the same time, forcing the organisers to decide between activities, sometimes to the detriment of the music:

> All the spa towns are distinguished, during the thermal season, by the splendour of the festivals and distractions which they offer to the *étrangers*. In France and in Germany, no opportunity is missed to attract and retain foreigners and to offer them, in the spa town to which they are obliged to go to seek health, all the desirable amenities. Dances, concerts, shows, races, day and night parties, everything is done to vary the pleasures and to welcome with eagerness the *baigneurs* [bathers] who arrive from all over Europe. We do not want to compare our little town with Vichy or Hamburg, but we have said many times that, except for the unrivalled nature and the enchanting sites, it is difficult to find elsewhere fewer pleasures than in Évian. One only has to be willing and able to put one's hand to it. . . . If we do not have yet to offer to the *baigneurs* the pleasures which they find in the big spa towns of France and Germany, we can at least encourage them to take advantage of the beautiful days to know our surroundings.[42]

With the consistent increase in number and affluence of *étrangers*, spa town leaders sought to capitalise on these *distractions*. In addition to maintaining

The 'Bath Revolution'? 211

and increasing musical offerings, the leaders felt compelled to innovate to compete with their rivals. The minutes of the Aix syndic indicated:

> While the establishments of Vichy, Plombières, Louèche, Uriage, etc. are becoming more beautiful and receiving improvements which are multiplying as if by magic; while those of Baden, Wisbaden and the Pyrenees are competing with them to offer the foreigner all the possible pleasures, we remain stationary to the extent that we do not even offer him all those which nature seems to have lavished on us as if by design . . . .I should even say that we have remained more than stationary, because we have not maintained what existed.[43]

In Aix, but also in Évian, newspaper columnists and local elected officials were ambitious and demanding of the entrepreneurs of the *distractions* sector, a development which spurred the age of the Casino-Théâtres and spa town Operas later in the century.

With the multiplication of music venues and the diversification of programming, music was no longer background sound but a main entertainment in its own right. The programmes of the Cercle d'Aix advertised both the famous Parisian comic singer Levassor and the young Italian violinist Ferni twins in 1854.[44] In Vichy, Strauss set up a special bandstand for his orchestra in a new private park near the windows of the *cercle*. With the advertisement of renowned musicians and more impressive performance venues, audiences for these musical *distractions* increased. As in Bath, mornings in the refreshment room, and evening concerts, performances, and balls in the grand salon punctuated each day, creating a rhythmic cycle of activity in French spa towns. With more regular cycles of activity within these spa towns, visibility among spa visitors increased, illustrated by publicly displayed lists of *étrangers*,[45] and the inspection of applicants for membership by previous members of the *cercles*:

> Only persons who, by virtue of their dress, education and conduct, are what we call people of good company, will be admitted to the Salon du Cercle. A committee, of which foreigners will be successively invited to be a member, will examine the persons presented and, by secret ballot, decide on admission or refusal.[46]

This is very similar to published lists of arrivals in Bath and recording of visitors' names in the Pump Rooms. There were also subscription practices similar to British assembly rooms, in which existing subscribers were required to vouch for new members, with time for subscribers to list any objections. Further regulation of the *étrangers* manifested in the public display of *salon* rules in Aix and Vichy and the creation of the position of the Ball Commissioner in Aix responsible for organising balls (though

212   *Bath and Beyond*

fulfilling a less dominant role than, for example, Bath's Master of Ceremonies, as explored in Rachael Johnson and Hillary Burlock's chapters).[47] French *salon* leaders were also increasingly under surveillance by the prefect and the police commissioner because of the regulation of gambling by the French administrative authorities and the security problems posed by the influx of *étrangers* from all over Europe.[48]

Music was also used to regulate spa visitors through a very significant concentration of daily and seasonal musical programming over the course of the nineteenth century. In the new building occupied by the Cercle d'Aix from 1850 onwards (renamed the Grand Cercle d'Aix), the orchestra enjoyed greater visibility than in the past as their concert' programmes were publicised in spa newspapers. It also corresponded to an intensification of the *Cercle*'s activities and an increase in its membership. A concert and ballroom were built that also served as a 'mobile theatre'.[49] Balls gradually lost their monopoly in the pages devoted by the press to spa music, as the interest of *étrangers* gradually shifted from the ballroom to the concert hall.[50] This was also the case for the orchestra at the Grand Hôtel des Bains d'Évian, Casino municipal d'Évian, and the Villa des Fleurs, generating greater competition between these venues. By the end of the 1860s, the Cercle d'Aix orchestra played daily in the evenings until 11pm, extending to 1am two days a week for balls.[51] The number of daily concerts and performers also continued to grow throughout the 1870s and 1880s. During the 1880 season, a year after the opening of the new Casino de la Villa des Fleurs, the orchestra had between 40 and 50 musicians, performing twice a day.[52] The Cercle d'Aix orchestra had at least 25 musicians, according to the lease, and was also required to play twice a day.[53] In Évian, the orchestra at the Grand Hôtel des Bains was made up of around 15 musicians, performing once a day.[54] The Casino Municipal orchestra had the same number of musicians, but played twice a day.[55] The repertoire of those orchestras thus expanded to include a wide range of musical genres in order to satisfy the tastes of as many *étrangers* as possible. Concert programming favoured light music in the early afternoon, generally outdoors under the bandstands, culminating in full operas or ambitious symphonic works in the evening.

During this period, spa orchestras expanded massively, but also divided into smaller ensembles to perform more frequently. In addition to evening concerts, some musicians performed hourly, providing aural regulation to the daily life of bathers.[56] Every hour of the day was animated by a 'phalanx' of the orchestra (Table 11.1).[57] As identified by Marie-Claire Mussat, the spa orchestra ensured the omnipresence of music in the life of the spa town. Music served as a framework for spa rituals.[58] In parks, one or two concerts were given each afternoon, and in Évian, musicians were also heard in the morning performing near the spring. New initiatives were

The 'Bath Revolution'? 213

Table 11.1 Musical *distractions* during the 1902 water season in Aix.[59]

Schedule	Distraction	Conductor
Grand cercle		
1pm	Musical *matinée* performed by 'the small orchestra'	E. Provinciali or Restiau
4pm	"Five o'clock concert" performed by 'the septet' *and/or* Children's ball	E. Provinciali
8pm	Opera or *opéra-comique* or Classical and modern music concerts	Léon Jehin Léon Jehin
Villa des Fleurs		
1pm	Concert in the 'Salle d'Ombrage'	Gérin
3pm	Concert in the park by the 'Grand Orchestre'	A. Brunetti
4pm	Music Hall (performances interspersed by the orchestra)	
8pm	Symphonic concert *or* opera	N. Gervasio

implemented by both the Grand Cercle and Villa des Fleurs. In 1899, for example, a music hall was inaugurated at the Villa des Fleurs.[60] This truly became a 'liner of pleasures' according to French historian Jérôme Penez, with its 'grand hall' for concerts, park and bandstand, theatre, and music hall.[61] The construction of new musical venues in the 1890s and 1900s resulted in a programme of densely packed musical days to entertain the *étrangers* with variety.

'L'universel Attrait' [the Universal Appeal]

Évian columnist Joseph Dessaix reiterated time and again that thermal cures had no social or economic benefit without music. Dessaix believed that the urban planning of spa towns ought to have been entirely designed to facilitate the pleasure of *étrangers*. He was a visionary in the early 1860s, as French municipalities and private establishments expanded spaces for leisure, gambling, and scenic and musical performances. Dessaix wrote in *La Nymphe des Eaux*:

> The organisation of balls and concerts will come later; for such *distractions*, men are needed who take care of them in a special way, and it will always be difficult in Évian, because the baths are private properties and the city does not have to worry about what happens there. On the other hand, the *maîtres d'hôtels* have other things to do and the owner-landlords don't care much about them. Foreigners have shown

214 *Bath and Beyond*

little taste for such pleasures up to now, musical evenings are mostly deserted, and the artists do not pay for them. It is due to something, it seems to be in the air.[62]

Dessaix recognised that the musical success of a spa town required the recruitment of staff with specific professional skills. Isaac Strauss was one of those rare ones. He first worked in Aix in the context of furniture music as a violinist leading a small ensemble (usually four to seven musicians) that played at balls and concerts in the first decades of the century. Strauss was then central to the competition between these spa towns, as he moved from Aix to Vichy in summer 1843 where the French Minister of Agriculture, responsible for the thermal baths owned by the French state, personally made him a financially advantageous proposal.[63] Theatrical and musical performances in France, until the 1864 liberalisation decree, was a privilege that had to be requested from central government, and the *Kurmusik* of Vichy was no exception.[64]

In the opinion of contemporary observers and historians, Isaac Strauss played a decisive role in Vichy's remarkable success. His reputation in the spa towns was such that he was noticed during the winter season in Paris, where he became the conductor of the Opera balls.[65] He is sometimes considered as Napoleon III's 'official musician' because of his proximity to power.[66] In 1854, Strauss became leaseholder of Vichy Casino private garden and director of the new municipal theatre, consolidating a musical monopoly in Vichy. He was also under obligation to the city, mentioned in an administrative document 'Specifications of requirements between the city of Vichy and Isaac Strauss':

art. 3: The Director will have to pay the poor tax. This tax is fixed, for the present year, at the sum of 10 francs for each performance.

art. 4: The number of performances will not be less than 3 per week during two and a half months of the water season, on Sunday, Tuesday and Thursday of each month, starting from June 15th until August 31st of each year.[67]

Musicians could therefore use the spa phenomenon for their own personal success. Strauss's career was emblematic of what musicians could achieve in the competitive music market spurred by France's golden age of spa towns. He retired as a musician in 1872 to become one of the first French collectors of Jewish art.[68] Musical practices were organised in order to have a 'puff' effect in the distinction of spa leaders and musicians.

Considering the increasing number of concerts and musicians, the spa orchestras' conductors developed new managerial and technical strategies. In musical terms, this translated into a very large number of scores

The *'Bath Revolution'?* 215

to manage. The Municipal Archives of Aix-les-Bains houses a collection of more than 10,000 edited scores, from the former musical library of Aix's casino.[69] The size of the collection indicates a great deal of flexibility required on the part of the musicians. Mastery of musical arrangement was necessary for musical directors as well, a field in which Henri Kling, a Swiss French horn player and conductor of several *Kurorchester*, including Évian, distinguished himself. Kling was also a great teacher and arranger, author of treatises for young musicians and several arrangements published by major music publishers.[70] His well-known books include *Populäre Instrumentationslehre mit genauer Beichreibung der Eigenthümlichkeiten jeden Instruments bearbeitet und durch viele Notenbeispiele [Popular instrumentation theory with precise description of the peculiarities of each instrument, edited and illustrated with many musical examples]*, published in German in 1882, and *Théorie élémentaire et pratique de l'art du chef d'orchestre, du directeur de musique d'harmonie, de fanfare et de société chorale [Elementary theory and practice of the art of the conductor, the director of wind bands, brass bands and choral societies]*, published in French in 1901. In his treatises on instrumentation and conducting, Henri Kling drew on his experience in the *Kurorchester* to outline the principles of orchestration, focusing more on the swiftness of arranging and simplicity of conducting gestures than the sophistication or scholarly depth of these disciplines:

> Of course I have considered all the genres used in music, and indicated the best way to use each instrument in this or that way.[71]
>
> The field of the conductor is very vast; it embraces all types of music, from the simple song to the most complicated pieces, as well as all styles and all schools. Putting together a programme for a concert is a difficult thing to do. First of all, it must not be too long; secondly, it must be made as attractive and varied as possible; the conductor must not have a favourite school, but must endeavour to popularise all well-made, well-conceived, well-written music, both modern and ancient, for well-composed works are always beautiful, whatever school they belong to.[72]

Kling repeatedly emphasised the musical diversity with which the conductor had to contend, including both the aesthetic choices in the arrangements and selection of repertoire.[73] The author provided insight into the challenges of conducting, including pitiful rehearsal time and anticipating gross performance errors made by second-rate musicians. Kling's concerns can be seen as a confirmation of the historical analysis of *Kurmusik* by German historians, who have argued that the aesthetics of casino music cannot be understood without a comprehensive examination of the socio-economic

216   *Bath and Beyond*

factors surrounding musical production, and the conductor's ways of working and conceptualisation of his profession.[74]

Diplomacy and Cosmopolitanism

As spa towns became cosmopolitan hubs of activity for foreign visitors, they also served as spaces for diplomatic encounters. When Napoleon III came to Vichy for a cure in 1861, he stayed at Isaac Strauss's house.[75] Queen Victoria also visited Aix during the water seasons of 1885, 1887, and 1890, resulting in the significant presence of English tourists in Aix.[76] The *cercles* and musicians of Aix were at the heart of diplomatic relations between France and the Kingdom of Sardinia, whose sovereign was a descendant of the House of Savoy. Cavour, the Sardinian politician at the heart of Italian unification, shaped Aix's trajectory as a spa town by sending one of his most trusted men, the entrepreneur Victor Bias, to manage the *distractions* of the *Cercle*.[77] Bias replaced Levy and Strauss with Italian orchestras whose soloists came directly from the Royal Chapel of Turin (capital of Savoy), including the conductor and cellist Leonardo Moja, whose scores annotated in Italian have been preserved.[78] The assumed cosmopolitanism of spa leaders increased tourism in Aix, Vichy, and Évian, despite the events of the 1870–1871 Franco-Prussian War. Spa musicians were seen as servants to the cause of great leaders and their political and economic ambitions, further shaping the spa towns' musical practices and performances.

The diplomatic status of French spa towns obtained in the nineteenth century was bolstered by the exceptional musical variety of spa town orchestras' repertoire, sometimes referred to as *potpourri*, and by the diversity of musicians and audiences. The repertoire of the orchestra of the Grand Hôtel des Bains d'Évian conducted by Henri Kling consisted mainly of Beethoven, Mozart, or Weber overtures, and *virtuoso* pieces for soloists.[79] Representative examples include fantasias for flute on operas by Gounod or Donizetti, written by Jules Hermann (one of the most renowned virtuoso flautists of his time), or transcriptions of Verdi operas for violin by Henri Vieuxtemps. It was not uncommon for compositions by local conductors to be featured, but unfortunately, no trace of them has been discovered in Évian. To make music accessible to as many visitors as possible, the spa town offered open-air concerts. Parades took place in the streets, and an orchestra performed in the harbour square in the afternoon.[80] The repertoire was that of *orphéons* (French choral societies) and military music, with *bravura* pieces requiring great technical skill and agility for piston or trumpet by Jean-Baptiste Arban, including *La neige qui brille*. Men's choruses were in fashion, including those by Laurent de Rillé, one of the most prolific choral composers at the time. From 1890 onwards, the orchestra at the Grand Hôtel des Bains gave concerts specifically defined as 'classical

The 'Bath Revolution'? 217

and modern music concerts', although I have not been able to find the programmes.[81] Prior to this, evening and afternoon concert programmes commonly featured romantic overtures (mainly by Mendelssohn); excerpts from Mozart's operas, overtures, and fantasias; and orchestral transcriptions of memorable works by Schubert (*Marche militaire* no. 1), Chopin (*Nocturnes*), and Boccherini (the famous 'Menuet' from the *String Quintet op. 11*, no. 5). Romance and song were also an important part of *Kurmusik*, and there is even evidence of a performance by the singer Thérésa (born Désirée Emma Valladon), one of France's first singing stars, who 'took up residence' in Évian in 1865.[82] Lastly, salon dances formed a solid basis of the repertoire, whether in the Viennese (Carl Millöcker and the Strauss family's polkas, gallops, and mazurkas), Italian, or French style with its quadrilles. The repertoire was international, and the historical range was very broad, from Boccherini's eighteenth-century repertoire to contemporary compositions.

There was a confusion of genres, so much so that *Kurmusik* can be defined by the sequence in which these were performed: a classical overture, followed by a composition by the conductor, excerpts from operas and *bravura* pieces for soloists, various pieces, and ending with a piece performed by the whole orchestra. On 22 June 1889, *Le Journal d'Évian* reported:

> The Casino has just resumed its concerts. Every evening the gardens and the quays are alive with people coming to relax. The musicians have the good sense to be eclectic; they range from Haydn to Léo Delibes, from Beethoven to Massenet. Classical music is mixed with light music. You have to please everyone . . . and his father![83]

With this sentence, the columnist summarised one of the main aspects of *Kurmusik*: its expensive eclecticism. The genre, style, and function of the music were intertwined, creating a diverse programme featuring operatic arias, classical overtures, extracts from symphonies, military marches, dance music, and popular songs (*chansons*). Visitors to the spa were not dismayed by this tangle of genres, as they demonstrated a cosmopolitan sensibility and aesthetic that dominated sociability. A disparate variety of artistic sensibilities created harmony, an approach, outlined by French historian Marie-Claire Mussat, 'to bring people together, to create the illusion of a community for the duration of the music'.[84]

What is the Bath Revolution?

Certainly, there are important differences between the golden age of the Bath Assembly Rooms and the *cercles* and *salons* of Vichy, Aix, and

218 Bath and Beyond

Évian. These French spa towns came to prominence 50 years later, during which time European musical practices evolved independently of what was happening in the spa towns. They also created their own spa seasons and calendars of activity between May and November, differentiated from Bath's season between October and May. But there were also similarities between Bath and its French and Savoyard emulators, in the organisation of the *distractions* and the musicians' methods, as well as the significant English clientele in Aix, and the influence of 'Beau' Nash's management of balls. Music maintained and supported the pillars of sociability in watering places. It created an atmosphere that welcomed fashionables, facilitating the individualistic performances of *étrangers* by showcasing their musical talents. The organisation, programming, and venues for music reflected the public's taste both for simplicity and for a constant renewal and innovation. The musical industry of French spa towns created an ecosystem of 'puff', in which the commercial ends constitute the means, both feeding and reflecting the spa visitors' voracious desire for music.

The 'Bath Revolution' was not an invention of new musical practices (programming, composing, or performing) or performance forms (salons, balls, outdoor music, bandstands, and private or public concerts), as these existed in large cities and prior to the spa's golden age. Rather, the 'Bath Revolution' was a new way of articulating sociocultural dynamics in a cramped urban space. Early spa *cercles* featured smaller ensembles with opportunities for *étrangers* to distinguish themselves through amateur musical performances. Yet, over the course of the nineteenth century, music venues and ensembles expanded in size and number, flooding the tourist market of spa towns with cosmopolitan music. Spa towns operated on business and management models that were flexible enough to offer an endless renewal of *distractions*, sometimes favouring quantity over quality. These musical performances showcased the distinction of the wealthiest international visitors in the sophisticated and aestheticised form of social 'self-segregation' known as *entre-soi*.

Notes

1 Paul Gerbod, "Loisirs et santé: les cures thermales en France (1850–1900)," in *Oisiveté et loisirs dans les sociétés occidentales au XIXe siècle,* ed. Adeline Daumard (Abbeville: Imprimerie F. Paillart, Centre de recherche d'histoire sociale de l'Université de Picardie, 1983).

2 During the rest of the nineteenth century, the terms *cercles* and *salons* gave way to *casinos*. And in the twentieth century, *touristes* replaced *étrangers* and *loisirs* (tr. leisure) and *divertissements* replaced *distractions*.

3 See, for example, the recent study day organised by the University of Tubingen: "Tagung: Im Bad wöll wir recht fröhlich sein. Bade- und Kurmusik in der

Frühen Neuzeit," 2022; Peter Stahcel and Cornelia Szabó-Knotik, Oesterreichisches Musiklexikon Online [Online], "Kur und Sommerfrische," accessed January 2024, www.musiklexikon.ac.at/ml/musik_K/Kur_und_Sommerfrische. xml; Mathias Spohr, "Geschichte der Kurmusik: Marktplatz der Musiker und Musikstile," *Das Orchestrer* i (2010): 14–15; Reto Parolari, "Die Vergessenen: Kuorchester in Deutschland," *Das Orchestrer* i (2010): 10.

4 Marie-Ève Férérol, "Lust, Tranquillity and Sensuality in French Spa Towns in the Heyday of Balneotherapy (the Belle Époque and the Roaring Twenties)," *Via* xi–xii (2017); Dominique Jarassé, *Les thermes romantiques: Bains et villégiatures en France de 1800 à 1850* (Clermont-Ferrand: Institut d'études du Massif Central, 1992); Marie-Ève Férérol, *2000 ans de thermalisme. Économie, patrimoine, rites et pratiques*, ed. Dominique Jarassé (Clermont-Ferrand: Institut d'études du Massif central, 1996); Françoise Breuillaud-Sottas, *Évian mondain; L'âge d'or du thermalisme* (Milan: le Vieil Annecy, 2018).

5 Béatrice Joyeux-Prunel, "Les transferts culturels. Un discours de la méthode," *Hypothèses* vi (2003): 149–62; Michel Espagne, "La notion de transfert culturel," *Revue Sciences/Lettres* i (2013) [online].

6 Rémy Knafou, ed., *Tourismes 2—Moments de lieux* (Paris: Belin, 2005).

7 For example, a reference French online geographical glossary presents Bath as 'the matrix from which other tourist locations were developed. English society was the pioneer of this innovation, which then spread by following the British community around the world along trade and colonisation routes' (Géoconfluences: Ressources de géographie pour les ensignants [Online], "Écoumène touristique," accessed January 2024, https://geoconfluences.ens-lyon.fr/glossaire/ecoumene-touristique; Marc Boyer, *Histoire générale du tourisme* (Paris: L'Harmattan, 2008), 66; Philippe Clairay and Johan Vincent, "Hommage à Marc Boyer (1926–2018)," *Mondes du Tourisme* xv (2019) [Online]; Bernard Toulier, "Les réseaux de la villégiature en France," *In Situ* iv (2004) [Online]; Christine Matthey, *Construire l'Europe en voyageant. Enjeux du tourisme culturel pour le développement d'une identité européenne* (Geneva: Institut Européen de l'Université de Genève, 2008), 135; Saskia Cousin, Bertrand Réau, "Genèses," in *Sociologie du tourisme* (Paris: La Découverte, 2016), 5–18.

8 Rémy Knafou, "Bath et les *Assembly Rooms*," *Les lieux du voyage* (Paris: La Découverte, 2012), 135–37.

9 Marc Boyer, "Comment étudier le tourisme?," *Ethnologie française* xxxii (2002): 393–404.

10 Marc Boyer, "La révolution de Bath," in *Le thermalisme dans le grand Sud-Est de la France* (Grenoble: Presses Universitaires de Grenoble, 2005), 37–41.

11 'Pourquoi cette exception de Bath? . . . Son ancienneté romaine n'avait rien d'exceptionnel . . . Rien d'extraordinaire dans les qualités des eaux, ni dans le fait que Bath se trouve dans une vallée encaissée d'un massif cristallin ! Il faut chercher le sens de cette invention dans l'histoire socioculturelle. Elle fait partie de cet ensemble d'inventions britanniques du XVIIIe siècle par lesquelles le Royaume-Uni se distingue fondamentalement du reste du monde: on connaît les Révolutions industrielle, agricole, démographique, maritime . . . qui sont les aspects les plus connus du take off britannique, on méconnaît la Révolution touristique . . . l'aristocratie britannique se distingue des noblesses continentales et de la nouvelle bourgeoisie anglaise de négociants et manufacturiers par le voyage de distinction'. Boyer, "La révolution de Bath," 37–38.

12 Boyer, *Le thermalisme dans le grand Sud-Est*, 160–62.

13 Boyer, *Le thermalisme dans le grand Sud-Est*, 60–61.

220 *Bath and Beyond*

14 'Entre les villes d'eaux françaises du temps et les anglaises, il n'y a que les ressemblances inévitables qui sortent de la nature des choses. Dans les unes et les autres, il faut bien que le malade suive un régime analogue; qu'ils cherchent des moyens de se désennuyer, qui seront nécessairement la conversation, la promenade, la musique, la danse le jeu . . . Comment se pourrait-il autrement? Ce sont là traits communs aux stations thermales de tout temps et de tout pays, et qui n'ont rien de caractéristique. Ce qui distingue Bath au contraire ou Tunbridge à l'époque qui nous occupe . . . on ne le trouve nulle part en France, je veux dire l'éclat mondain, le train réglé des plaisirs, l'étendue et la variété de la clientèle, l'universel attrait . . . L'éclosion des villes d'eau anglaises, et leur développement ultérieur sont des phénomènes . . . originaux et spontanés, et qui ne doivent rien, au moins de façon immédiate, à l'influence continentale'. Alfred Barbeau, *Une ville d'eaux anglaise au XVIIIe siècle, la société élégante et littéraire à Bath sous la reine Anne et sous les Georges* (Paris: A. Picard et fils, 1904), 13–14.
15 Barbeau, *Une ville d'eaux anglaise*, 13–14.
16 Annick Cossic, "Fashionable Diseases in Georgian Bath: Fiction and the Emergence of a British Model of Spa Sociability," *Journal for Eighteenth-Century Studies* xl (2017): 537–53; Annick Cossic, "The Digital Encyclopedia of British Sociability in the Long Eighteenth Century," *Bath (and the Reinvention of Spa Sociability)*, accessed January 2024, www.digitens.org/en/notices/bath-and-reinvention-spa-sociability.html; Annick Cossic and Karl Wood, "The Digital Encyclopedia of British Sociability in the Long Eighteenth Century," *Spa Sociability in Bath and Pyrmont*, accessed January 2024, www.digitens.org/en/notices/spa-sociability-bath-and-pyrmont.html.
17 Great Spa Towns of Europe Association, *Annual Review 2021–2022* (Baden-bei-Wien, 2023). Some local organisations are now working hard on the heritage status of their cities, such as: the Société d'art et d'histoire d'Aix-les-Bains which is publishing *Arts et mémoires*, a local history review with several articles about musical practices; the Villa du Châtelet in Évian-les-Bains, Lake Geneva cultural centre which organises exhibitions, conferences, concerts, balls, and various events about Évian's heritage; and the Vichy Opera Museum where the archives of the spa opera are conserved and promoted through exhibitions.
18 *Faites vos jeux! La vie musicale dans les casinos français (19e–21e siècles)*, conference organised by Martin Guerpin and Étienne Jardin (Paris, 2021), with publication in Actes Sud/Palazzetto Bru Zane forthcoming in Spring 2024.
19 Nathalie Arpin, "Au-delà de la mondanité: pouvoirs et réseaux à Aix-les-Bains (1848–1914)," (PhD, Savoie University, Forthcoming).
20 Comte de Loche, "Histoire d'Aix-les-bains," *Mémoires de l'Académie des sciences, belles-lettres et arts de Savoie* iv (1900), 317.
21 Laure Schnapper, *Musique et musiciens de bal. Isaac Strauss au service de Napoléon III* (Paris: Hermann, 2023).
22 Schnapper, *Musique et musiciens de bal.*
23 *Marie. Souvenir d'Aix-les-bains, polka-mazurka pour piano* (Paris, 1853); *Valses favorites du Cercle d'Aix les Bains* (Paris, undated); *Les Soirées d'Aix les bains* (Paris, 1840); *Mazurkas du Cercle royal d'Aix* (Paris, 1845).
24 Simon Lévy and J. Strauss, *Soirées de Lyon* (Strasbourg, undated).
25 Zoltan-Étienne Harsany, *Marie de Solms, femme de lettres* (Chambéry, 1983).
26 Théâtre du Chalet programme, July 30, 1859, *Les Matinées d'Aix-les-Bains* (Chambéry, 1859).
27 Théophile Bonjour, "La valorisation musicale des grands lacs périalpins: L'ennui ou la fête," *Collection EDYTEM* xxi (2021): 167–84.

The 'Bath Revolution'? 221

28 At the end of September 1880, a festival was held in honour of Hussein Kamal Pacha, son of the Egyptian king Ismaïl Pacha. In 1882, the villa welcomed the famous American singer Marie Vanzandt, as part of a meeting with Baroness Julie von Rothschild, the Princess of Brancovan and Prince Edmond de Polignac. *Le Gaulois*, September 30, 1880; *Le Ménestrel*, September 3, 1882; Jean-Michel Henny, *Marcel Proust à Évian* (Auvernier: Chaman, 2015).

29 Musée Paderewski, BRANCOVAN-1889–03–13: Princess Rachel Bibesco Bassaraba to Ignacy Jan Paderewski, March 13, 1889.

30 Anna de Noaille, *Le Livre de ma vie* (Paris: Hachette, 1932), chap. 7. With the exception of the writings of the poet Anna de Noailles, published here in French and translated to English by the author, all quotations from publications in French or German, old or recent, are translated directly into English by the author.

31 Henny, *Marcel Proust à Évian*.

32 François Breuilaud-Sottas, *Évian, aux sources d'une réussite* (Annecy: Le Vieil Annecy, 2008).

33 Théophile Bonjour, *Musique et thermalisme: l'exemple d'Évian-les-Bains (1860–1892)* (Paris: EHESS/CNSMDP, 2016), 6.

34 Françoise Breuillaud-Sottas, *La prodigieuse ascension des eaux d'Évian (1790–1914)* (Lille: Chambéry, 2003), 153.

35 *Journal d'Aix-les-Bains*, September 5, 1880; *Journal d'Aix-les-Bains*, September 14, 1879.

36 Aix-les-Bains Municipal Archives, 1O169, n°21: *Autorisation de bâtir accordée à M. Mottet pour construire dans la Villa des Fleurs un bâtiment devant servir de salle de réunion, de bals, de concerts et théâtres*, March 31, 1879.

37 Bonjour, *Musique et thermalisme*, 33.

38 Joseph Dessaix, *La Nymphe des eaux* (Évian, 1863), no. 5.

39 Dessaix, *La Nymphe des eaux*, no. 5.

40 Dessaix, *La Nymphe des eaux*, no. 5.

41 Joseph Dessaix, *La Nymphe des eaux* (Évian, 1864), no. 4.

42 Joseph Dessaix, *La Nymphe des eaux* (Évian, 1860), no. 3.

43 Aix-les-Bains Municipal Archives, 2F11: "Délibération concernant moyen d'aviser à la construction d'un nouveau cercle," January 22, 1847.

44 *Le Journal d'Aix-les-Bains*, May 21, 1854.

45 Savoie Departmental Archives, 1FS2820: Liste des étrangers.

46 Savoie Departmental Archives, 1 FS 2821: Séance du Décembre 27, 1826, December 27, 1826.

47 Savoie Departmental Archives, M 776: Règlement des salons, undated; 37F1: Lettre du Commissaire pour les bals, June 18, 1873.

48 Savoie Departmental Archives, M 775: Fonds de la préfecture, Police administrative, Jeux: cercles et casinos, Aix.

49 Marie-Reine Jazé-Charvolin, Joël Lagrange, and Johann Thibaudier, "Casino Grand-Cercle," in *Inventaire général du patrimoine culturel* (Aix-les-Bains: Ville d'Aix-les-Bains, 2005).

50 For example, several issues of the *Courrier d'Aix-les-Bains* in July 1864.

51 *Nouveau guide pratique médical et pittoresque aux eaux d'Aix en Savoie* (Chambéry, 1864), 48–49.

52 M. Lévy et al., *Eaux minérales de la Savoie* (Paris, 1880), 25; *L'Europe-artiste*, July 11, 1880.

53 Aix-les-Bains Municipal Archives, 2F11: Propositions de Fermage du Casino, October 12, 1876.

54 He did not begin his 'day concerts' until 1882. *Saison d'Évian*, July 1, 1882.
55 *Évian. L'été,* July 1880, supplement to issue no. 1.
56 At the Casino municipal d'Évian, the number of musicians rose from 14 in 1878 to 27 in 1889. *Évian. L'été*, June 27, 1878; *Saison d'Évian*, June 15, 1889.
57 Military term constantly used by the press (*Évian. L'été*, June 28, 1877; *Saison d'Évian*, July 17, 1884; *'L'Europe-artiste,* July 27, 1884).
58 Marie-Claire Mussat, "Les kiosques à musique dans les villes d'eau," in *2000 ans de thermalisme. Économie, patrimoine, rites et pratiques*, ed. Dominique Jarrassé (Clermont-Ferrand: Institut d'études du Massif central, 1996), 234.
59 Aix-les-Bains Municipal Archives, 19Z3 bis: Daily programmes for the artistic season (incomplete season).
60 *L'Avenir d'Aix-les-Bains*, May 7, 1899.
61 Jérôme Penez, *Histoire du thermalisme en France au XIXe siècle* (Paris: Economica, 2005), 198.
62 Dessaix, *La Nymphe des eaux*, no. 3.
63 Laure Schnapper, "Isaac Strauss et Vichy," *Bulletin de la Société d'histoire et d'archéologie de Vichy et des environs* (2019): 43–60.
64 Vichy Municipal Archives, 2R/348/1253: Correspondence with the central authority.
65 Schnapper, *Musique et musiciens de bals*.
66 Jean-Claude Yon, "Les fastes du Second Empire," *Isaac Strauss, musicien et collectionneur sous le Second Empire* (Paris: EPHE, 2018).
67 Vichy Municipal Archives, 3N/210/19: Cahier des charges, June 14, 1854.
68 Dominique Jarassé, *La collection Isaac Strauss* (Le Kremlin-Bicêtre: Editions Esthétiques du Divers, 2018).
69 Aix-les-Bains Municipal Archives, 20Fi.
70 W. A. Mozart, *Concert für Clarinette mit Begleitung des Orchesters. Arrangement für Clarinette mit Begleitung des Pianoforte von H. Kling* (Leipzig, 1883). This arrangement, while being published by Breitkopf & Härtel, shows Kling's reputation as an arranger, although it does not demonstrate great creativity beyond academic writing.
71 Kling, *Populäre Instrumentationslehre mit genauer Beichreibung der Eigenthümlichkeiten jeden Instruments bearbeitet und durch viele Notenbeispiele* (Hanover, 1882).
72 Henri Kling, *Théorie élémentaire et pratique de l'art du chef d'orchestre, du directeur de musique d'harmonie, de fanfare et de société chorale* (Lausanne, 1901).
73 Kling, *Théorie élémentaire*.
74 Kling, *Théorie élémentaire*; Kling, *Populäre Instrumentationslehre*.
75 Schnapper, "Strauss à Vichy."
76 Claire Delorme-Pégaz, *La reine Victoria et la Savoie* (Chambéry: La Fontaine De Siloe, 2022).
77 Nathalie Arpin, "Jean Louis Victor Bias (1814–1901). Itinéraire d'un 'casinocrate' célèbre inconnu d'Aix-les-Bains," *Arts & Mémoire* xxxix (2022): 39–48.
78 Savoie Departmental Archives, 37F3: Fonds Guilland (accounting and administrative documents).
79 All the information about the musical repertoire comes from an analysis of the concert programmes of the spa orchestras, choirs, and brass bands published in the *Évian. L'été* from 1873 to 1877.
80 *Évian. L'été,* July 3, 1874.
81 *Saison d'Évian*, September 13, 1890.

82 Jacqueline Blanche, *Thérésa, première idole de la chanson française (1837–1913)* (La Fresnay-sur-Chedouet, 1981); Nouvelles diverses', *Le Ménestrel*, August 13, 1865.
83 *Le Journal d'Évian*, June 22, 1889.
84 Mussat, "Les kiosques à musique," 236.

Bibliography

Barbeau, Alfred. *Une Ville d'eaux anglaise au XVIIIe siècle: La société élégante et littéraire à Bath sous la reine Anne et sous les Georges. Thèse présentée à la Faculté des lettres de l'Université de Paris.* Paris: A. Picard et fils, 1904.

Boyer, Marc. *Le thermalisme dans le grand sud-est de la France.* Grenoble: Presses Universitaires de Grenoble, 2005.

Breuillaud-Sottas, Françoise. *Évian, aux sources d'une réussite: 1790–1914.* Annecy: le Vieil Annecy, 2008.

Breuillaud-Sottas, Françoise. *La prodigieuse ascension des eaux d'Évian (1790–1914).* Lille: ANRT, 2003.

Cossic, Annick. "Bath (and the Reinvention of Spa Sociability)." In *The Digital Encyclopedia of British Sociability in the Long Eighteenth Century.* www.digitens. org/en/notices/bath-and-reinvention-spa-sociability.html.

Cossic, Annick. "Fashionable Diseases in Georgian Bath: Fiction and the Emergence of a British Model of Spa Sociability." *Journal for Eighteenth-Century Studies* 40, no. 4 (2017): https://doi.org/10.1111/1754-0208.12506.

Gerbod, Paul. "Loisirs et santé: les cures thermales en France (1850–1900)." In *Oisiveté et loisirs dans les sociétés occidentales au XIXe siècle*, edited by Adeline Daumard, 195–203. Abbeville: Imprimerie F. Paillart, Centre de recherche d'histoire sociale de l'Université de Picardie, 1983.

Jarrassé, Dominique. *Les thermes romantiques: Bains et villégiatures en France de 1800 à 1850.* Clermont-Ferrand: Institut d'études du Massif Central, 1992.

Jarrassé, Dominique, ed. *2000 ans de thermalisme: Économie, patrimoine, rites et pratiques.* Clermont-Ferrand: Institut d'études du Massif central, 1996.

Knafou, Rémy, ed. *Tourismes 2—Moments de lieux.* Paris: Belin, 2005.

Mussat, Marie-Claire. "Les kiosques à musique dans les villes d'eau." In *2000 ans de thermalisme: Économie, patrimoine, rites et pratiques*, edited by Dominique Jarrassé. Clermont-Ferrand: Institut d'études du Massif central, 1996.

Parolari, Reto. "Die Vergessenen: Kuorchester in Deutschland." *Das Orchester* (January 2010): 10–13.

Schnapper, Laure. *Musique et musiciens de bal: Isaac Strauss au service de Napoléon III.* Paris: Hermann, 2023.

Spohr, Mathias. "Geschichte der Kurmusik: Marktplatz der Musiker und Musikstile." *Das Orchester* (January 2010): 14–15.

Stahcel, Peter, and Cornelia Szabó-Knotik. "Kur und Sommerfrische." In *Oesterreichisches Musiklexikon Online*, 2022. https://doi.org/10.1553/0x000269eb.

12 Bath, Abroad

How British American Colonists Imagined and Encountered the Famed Spa City

Vaughn Scribner

A visit to Bath confounded Matthew Bramble, a protagonist in Tobias Smollett's *Humphry Clinker* (1771). Ever the traditionalist, Bramble found his once-beloved spa city 'so altered, that I can scarce believe it is the same place that I frequented about thirty years ago'.[1] But the city's alterations extended well beyond brick and mortar. Having remarked upon Bath's physical transformations, Bramble ridiculed the 'upstarts of fortune' who now attended Bath. In Bramble's estimation, these 'planters, negro-drivers, and hucksters from our American plantations . . . hurry to Bath, because here without any farther qualification they can mingle with the princes and nobles of the land'.[2]

Though vocalised by a fictional character, Bramble's remarks revealed core developments in the physical, personal, and perceived nature of Georgian Bath. As 'the queen of spas', a 'fashionable residential centre' built around status and health, eighteenth-century Bath became a key space in Britons' imperial imaginations: 'a city dependent upon image-making', in Peter Borsay's contention. He continued to explain, 'perhaps more than any other town in eighteenth-century Britain, [Bath's] success and its very identity depended not upon what it was, but what it was imagined to be'.[3]

And, as alluded to by Bramble's notation of visitors from 'our American plantations', Britons abroad were critical in upholding Bath's imaginative power. By mid-century, wealthy British American colonists—Britons born, or who had permanently settled, in the 13 American colonies—embarked on a campaign of connection with Great Britain. Many British Americans, in fact, considered Great Britain their true 'home', and accordingly hoped to experience elements of the homeland and recreate spaces like Bath in their colonial locales.[4] New Jersey's governor, William Franklin, revealed as much in April 1763, exclaiming:

> We have often wished that we could put Great Britain under sail, bring it over to this country and anchor it near us, we could then enjoy the

DOI: 10.4324/9781003393856-12

pleasure which that delightful spot affords, as well as you whose happy destiny it was . . . [to have] been born there.[5]

While well-heeled British American colonists wanted to 'mingle with the princes and nobles of the land' in person, they were also intent on bringing British urbanity and health 'over to this country'.

Yet, after 1775, many residents of the Thirteen Colonies came to view themselves as American rather than British—rebellious visionaries who hoped to correct the supposed ills of the crumbling British monarchical system through a radical form of revolutionary republicanism. But political rupture hardly equalled total estrangement. British American colonists had, after all, spent the past 150 years as ardent members of the British Empire, and thus had a hard time shedding many British ideological and cultural tenets.[6] As was especially revealed by their attempts at recreating British spa culture in America, citizens of the United States emulated as much as, if not more than, they defied British monarchical culture.[7]

This chapter builds upon the keen insights of Bramble (via Smollett), Borsay, and Franklin to demonstrate the extent of Georgian Bath's 'image-making' campaign. British American colonists, and American citizens thereafter, imagined Bath as the ultimate 'resort and fashionable residential centre', perhaps only second to London in terms of gentility, consumerism, health, and sociability.[8] British Americans accordingly relied upon a broad range of literature—newspapers, books, pamphlets, letters, and hearsay—to formulate their own visions of the spa city and, in turn, the British imperial imagination.[9] But not everyone had to imagine Bath from abroad, as hundreds of white, wealthy British Americans visited Bath during the eighteenth century.[10] For men who had spent their lives frequenting colonial imitations of Bath, attending this ultimate arena of British leisure made them feel more British than perhaps ever before and, importantly, only fuelled their desires of recreating Bath abroad.

Yet, British American colonists' figurative representations of, and literal encounters with, Bath remain understudied. Such an oversight is surprising, as Bath is one of the most popular sites of analysis among scholars of eighteenth-century Britain. From sociability to health to urban planning, historians continue to chart the vast depths of Bath's chalybeate waters.[11] So, too, have British American colonists' efforts at metropolitan emulation harboured massive scholarly attention over the past 75 years.[12] The concurrent rise of 'New British' and 'Atlantic World' history has further crumpled geographic and temporal boundaries to reveal how colonists navigated a 'vast Early America'.[13] Finally, various historians have studied how colonists' expeditions to Great Britain during the seventeenth and especially eighteenth centuries fostered in them a deep sense of Britishness.[14]

226 *Bath and Beyond*

This chapter combines these disparate historiographical threads to demonstrate how British American colonists and, eventually, residents of the United States imagined, encountered, and attempted to re-create the famed spa city. Bath held considerable sway over these diverse Americans' visions of leisure, health, and gentility, whether lolling in a Pennsylvanian spa or rubbing elbows with the nobility in Bath's famed assembly rooms. In many ways, it still does.

Imagining Bath

In 1724, the English clergyman and historian Hugh Jones remarked, 'The *Habits*, *Life*, *Customs*, *Computations*, &c. of the *Virginians* are much the same as about *London*, which they esteem their *Home*' (emphasis in original).[15] Jones's observations were not without merit. Various historians have argued that, especially by the mid-eighteenth century, British American colonists 'were becoming *more* British than was in fact British'.[16] These Britons abroad took their identities as British imperialists seriously, and it showed. Mid-century British American colonists enjoyed a higher standard of living per capita than any such population in human history.[17] This 'golden age' of colonial America, as colonist Thomas Jones called it, translated into massive commercial, urban, and agricultural success. By the outbreak of the American Revolution (1775–1783), British American colonists were some of the wealthiest, thriving, and (ironically) loyal of all British subjects.[18]

But there was plenty of tarnish to this golden age. White colonists violently enforced their supposed superiority, enslaving tens of thousands of kidnapped Africans to farm their valuable crops, destroying indigenous peoples, stealing their land, and waging war on competing empires.[19] Because of their distance from the British metropole, moreover, many colonists worried they could never enjoy many of those advantages—large cities, aristocratic interaction, and true civility—bestowed upon their British brethren. This is where Bath came in. Unlike London, whose size and diversity outstripped colonists' most fantastical imaginations, Bath steadily ascended in the colonial mindset as a paragon of London's virtues in a more attainable form. Its population more closely resembled that of America's largest cities, as did its rural location, which fostered an ideal balance of leisure, gentility, commerce, and health. Bath, in short, represented a dream of British urbanism which might be recreated in America. British American newspaper editors especially fuelled this fantasy. The terms 'news from Bath' and 'we hear from Bath' became rather commonplace by the middle of the century, with newspapers covering royal visitors, gentlemen's gossip, new buildings, and imperial power. Through this press-fuelled frenzy, imagination, image-making, and collective memory

Bath, Abroad 227

drove Bath's transatlantic fame, which was exactly how its proprietors, and visitors, wanted it.

British American news stories about the celebrated spa town often concentrated upon royal and aristocratic company. Bath's proprietors, after all, 'went to great lengths to celebrate and publicise a royal sojourn, so that the memory of the occasion would linger long after the principal actors had departed'.[20] These accounts, moreover, provided colonial readers with a link to an 'imagined community' of royalty and aristocracy which they rarely, if ever, physically encountered on American shores.[21] In an especially telling instance, the 6 January 1735 issue of Boston's *Weekly Rehearsal* covered the extended sojourn of George II's second daughter, Princess Amelia, to Bath in September 1734. 'They write from Bath', the article opened, 'that the Princess Amelia continues drinking the Waters twice a Day, plays at the publick Rooms almost every Night, was present at a Ball last Week, and is very cheerful'. As colonists read this juicy piece, they could imagine themselves flitting through the spa city. And the author was sure to mention that, besides the princess and her coterie, Bath also hosted 'a great deal of Company, and were in Expectation of a very great Season'. But just referencing genteel company was not enough, hence the inclusion of those celebrities 'present at Bath the following Persons of Distinction', including the duke of Grafton, Lord Palmerston, Lady Torrington, and Sir Robert Rich.[22]

The article discussed earlier joined dozens of newspaper pieces detailing royalty and nobility in Georgian Bath. On 14 June 1736, for instance, the *New York Weekly Journal* republished an 'Extract of a Letter from Bath, dated March 2' which recounted in painstaking detail how 'those Noble Personages' congregated in Bath to celebrate Queen Caroline's birthday.[23] Here was the ultimate British celebration, defined by monarchical allegiance, charity, aristocracy, and balls. Bath stood front-and-centre. 'The morning was ushered in with the usual Demonstration of Joy', the author noted, 'but the Noon brought on more uncommon, but more valuable Entertainments'. Lord Palmerston held a gratis dinner for Bath hospital's infirm patients, and Mr Pointz, 'who delights in relieving Necessities, and communicating Happiness', provided clothing and provisions to 20 poverty-stricken women. 'Many of the Nobility and Gentry were present at these truly Love Feasts', watching as onlookers happily recorded their largess. By evening, the celebrations turned from charity to revelry, as 'Every body of any Fashion was admitted to the most crowded Ball that ever was in this Place at this time of the year, and equal to that of the fullest Seasons'. The countess of Pembroke presided over the affair, where around 3,000 feasted on the finest food, 'in a much higher Taste than we had ever seen in this part of the World', and enjoyed great fulfilment 'in paying the Highest Respect to the best of Queens'.[24]

228   *Bath and Beyond*

Gentility and order created an orgy of opulence in this ultimate party. Yet, it was a celebration that colonists could not have, because there were no royals or aristocrats in the Thirteen Colonies. Nor was there a Bath. But that did not halt their visions of genteel leisure. On the contrary, various articles on Bath's royal and aristocratic connotations continued to dot American newspapers over the next decades.[25] Newspapers—those key purveyors of 'the MANNA of the day . . . the true and genuine food of the mind'—gorged colonists with a buffet of Bath's royal revelries.[26] Because colonial American coverage of Bath was either re-printed or adapted from British broadsheets, furthermore, British societal barbs often coloured these stories. Gossip, scandal, and shocking accounts, after all, were imperative for British celebrity image-making.[27] What better place to trace such exploits than Britain's playground for the rich and famous?

Quarrels and drunkenness among Bath's 'polite' company especially incited public interest. The 1 June 1752 edition of the *Boston Post Boy* reported a duel 'between two Gentlemen . . . at the Lebeck's Head [tavern]' which came to a gory end when one of the men stabbed the other through his neck and shoulder. 'It seems strange', the author jeered, 'that our English Gentry should be more prone to fight in Time of Peace, than in Time of War'.[28] In another example of gentlemanly squabbles, readers of the *New York Gazette* learned in October 1751 of a recent argument during which 'a Young Adventurer, who had more Money than Wit, being guilty of some rude Gallantry to a Lady, was called to Account for it, by a Gentleman, who gave him some Nose-Correction'. Nursing a broken nose and a bruised ego, the libertine escaped Bath rather 'than risk spoiling his Fortune' through shame and dishonour.[29]

With disputes over taxation and control of the American colonies erupting in the late 1760s, Bath's already-exciting environs became even more politically driven. Genteel supporters of the radical British politician John Wilkes frequented the city alongside equally elite detractors to the American cause. Social mixing was often a veritable tinderbox. In April 1769, readers of the *Providence Gazette* learned of a fracas earlier that year after 'an officer [at Bath] took an opportunity . . . in the hearing of a lady pretty nearly related to Mr Wilkes, to speak of that gentleman in a disrespectful and virulent manner'. When the anti-American officer spat 'damn [Wilkes], I wish I had his head', the bold woman quipped,

I wish, Sir, you had half his head . . . Because you would not then, Sir, have rendered yourself so ridiculous as to calumniate an absent man, who . . . is greatly above being guilty of so mean, unmannerly an act.[30]

From duels to drunkenness and debates, Bath's company provided plenty of celebrity, scandal, and intrigue.

Though newspapers held sway over the most colonial readers, other Bath-related publications—especially books and pamphlets—arrived in America during the second half of the eighteenth century touting similar promises. Yet cost, combined with relatively low literacy rates, meant that only wealthy, educated colonists purchased books, at least in vast numbers. These tactics were largely intentional, as the volumes' content, prose, and themes boasted an intentionally elitist, biting, and satirical tone which was usually aimed at more 'polished' readers throughout the empire.[31] Thus, while newspapers generally played to colonists' fantasies of royal and aristocratic company, scandal, and gossip, books often considered Bath society through a combination of tongue-in-cheek satire and *belles lettres*, which might help colonists become more genteel.

In *The New Bath Guide* (1766), Englishman Christopher Anstey employed imaginary 'memoirs' to rub elbows with Bath's genteel company, while still maintaining a safe distance from which to cast slings and arrows.[32] In one instance, 'Mr B–n–r–d' arrived in Bath to the tolling of bells (a common occurrence to celebrate a gentleman's entrance to the city). 'Some think it strange they should make such a riot; In a place where sick folk would be glad to be quiet', Mr B–n–r–d quipped. Yet, as Anstey concluded with rather ironic prose, 'you know there is nothing diverts or employs; The minds of *great* people like making a noise'.[33] Profligacy and paradox melded into an intoxicating brew at Bath, where elite company celebrated their own extravagance at the same time that they mocked the very society in which they thrived. Anstey's *New Bath Guide* became a bestseller, necessitating 10 new editions within a decade of its publication.[34] The book also appeared in bookstores across the northeastern American seaboard, including John Mein's 'London Book-Store, North-Side King-Street, Boston', Garrat Noel's New York City bookstore 'next Door to the Merchant's Coffee-House', and a printer's shop in Philadelphia's Market Street. One Boston bookseller described the *New Bath Guide* as 'exhibiting a humorous detail of the Ceremonies, Taste, Spirit, Diversions, and polite Conversations, together with some tender Scenes, and unfortunate Incidents, which lately happened at that seat of Dissipation and Pleasure'.[35]

Yet, the *New Bath Guide* was only one among many Bath-bred books that appeared on America's shores during the eighteenth century.[36] In 1767, the Irish writer Samuel Derrick published his *Letters* to celebrate the supremacy of Bath's sociable opportunities. Perhaps no one was more qualified than Derrick to extol Bath's virtues, as he had recently been elected Master of Ceremonies at Bath (following in the lineage of Richard 'Beau' Nash), thus making Derrick the *de facto* director of Bath's famous rules of decorum, fashion, and order.[37] At its core, Derrick's *Letters* was little more than a self- and Bath-promoting publicity scheme, deeming Bath

230   *Bath and Beyond*

'one of the most elegant, pleasant, and convenient spots in Europe'. The spa city's 'plays, music, cards, balls, and so many different amusements', Derrick continued, made Bath '*the* Region of Pleasure'. And if a visitor grew tired of such sociable amusements, they could retreat to the more exclusive Pump Room for therapeutic water and quiet conversation. 'There is no place in the world', Derrick insisted, 'where a person may introduce himself, on such easy terms, to the first people of Europe, as in the rooms at Bath'. And just outside lay a world of possibilities: Derrick declared Bath's streets, squares, and buildings 'the grandest I ever saw', and the Circus 'beyond description magnificent'.[38] Unsurprisingly, booksellers from Boston to Charleston and Williamsburg soon advertised Derrick's *Letters* among their diverse inventories.[39] Bath was a wonder unto itself, a fantastical place which colonists consumed with greedy pleasure.

Encountering Bath

On 28 September 1774, the 30-year-old British American lawyer and radical American patriot Josiah Quincy Jr left Salem, Massachusetts for England. As a supporter of the rebellious American cause, Quincy voyaged to England for purposes of shrewd politicking. Unfortunately, his efforts stalled from the beginning, and by mid-December Quincy decided that Britain's leaders were 'not fit to represent the inhabitants of North America'.[40] But political setbacks did not stop Quincy from enjoying his English sojourn. Having exhausted his resources in London, Quincy headed to Bath. Quincy realised that Bath was a resort for British politicians and leading thinkers, namely because of its relative accessibility to Westminster and variety of genteel spaces, places, and company. This included the English historian Catharine Macaulay, who ardently supported the American cause. Quincy had a few 'improving conversations' with Macaulay and tried to bend the ear of other possible allies during his resplendent tour of the spa city.[41] He also, of course, soaked in the city's various opportunities for leisure and gentility.

When Quincy arrived in Bath on the evening of 30 December 1774, he attended 'a grand ball at the Lower Rooms', where he watched about 300 spa-goers dancing. For the next five days, Quincy's time at Bath played out like a common English holiday. After chatting with Macaulay on 31 December, Quincy rushed to 'see the Circus and the Crescent and other places of public resort and notice at Bath'. Guided by fellow Bostonian, John Temple, Quincy spent the rest of his day rambling 'about two hours round at a distance from the town, where on the hills encircling this splendid city I had a most enchanting prospect'. The next day (1 January 1775), Quincy sipped water with polished company at the Pump Room, attended service at Bath's Abbey Church, and 'went to several Coffee-houses of public resort, where [he] had an opportunity of seeing much of the manners of people at Bath'.[42]

But Quincy's brushes with grand buildings, and powerful political figures, were not over. His third day in the spa city brought even more enchanting surprises, as he visited a 'very splendid and full' ball at the Upper Assembly Rooms. Of all Quincy's Bath ramblings thus far, the new, fashionable assembly rooms especially impressed the judgmental colonist: 'the rooms are most magnificently elegant, and the paintings which cover the windows, taken from the draft of the figures found at the ruins of Herculaneum have fine effect'. Quincy found himself drawn to the majesty of the Herculaneum paintings and, as the young man reflected upon the past of Greece and the future of the British Empire, he engaged in a pithy exchange with Colonel Isaac Barré, MP for Wycombe. This was not Quincy's first interaction with Barré, as he 'had about half an hour's conversation' with the Anglo-Irish politician concerning 'American affairs' while lounging in the Pump Room the previous day. But, as Quincy and Barré reflected upon the ruins of Herculaneum, Barré warned the young American of many British citizens' ignorance—even condescension—towards the American colonies. And, though Barre assured Quincy that 'America was always a favorite [sic] with me', Quincy ultimately dismissed Barré's words as hollow, recording 'Col. Barré was among those who voted for the Boston port Bills'.[43] Here was a keen example of how, though British and American citizens still largely agreed upon notions of civility, political actions could prove almost-wholly destructive to compromise. Despite the genteel setting and company of this conversation, Quincy deemed Barré as untrustworthy because of his support for the Boston Port Act of 1774, part of the larger series of measures colonists called the 'Coercive Acts', which closed Boston's port to outside trade, a change in stance for Barre, who was a follower of Pitt and Shelburne. Though Parliament hoped this act might isolate Boston and stifle further rebellion, it actually accomplished the exact opposite, as it turned even more colonists against Parliament and, increasingly, the British monarchy.[44]

From political pugilism to raucous balls to grand architecture, Quincy's Bath experiences lived up and, politically, perhaps, down to his expectations. And Quincy was hardly alone, for during the eighteenth century, hundreds of British American colonists visited the famous spa city. In doing so, they expanded their understanding of Bath from an imagined to tangible space. Quincy had surely read about Bath before he arrived. His actions reveal as much, as Quincy knew who to reach out to, or at least identify (Macaulay, Temple, and Barré, among others), where to go (the Pump Room, Upper Assembly Rooms, and Circus), and the most fashionable diversions (countryside perspectives and Herculaneum paintings). For colonists like Quincy, a visit to Bath became tantamount with British

232   *Bath and Beyond*

sociability, consumption, and gentility, even if political differences coloured his experiences in new ways.

A full survey of every colonist who visited Bath during the eighteenth century is beyond the scope of this chapter. Nevertheless, most colonists who visited Bath did so with a carefully curated set of expectations, most of which were shaped by their previous (imaginary) interactions with the renowned spa. Somehow, Bath managed to equal almost every colonist's vaulted projections. And, through this process, colonists felt closer to the mother country than perhaps ever before, even if they visited Bath during a time of imperial and monarchical disillusion.

Various historians have demonstrated how eighteenth-century British Americans felt drawn to Britain, and how 'knowing London, experiencing it personally' became a 'crowning achievement' for the elite in the Thirteen Colonies.[45] To this end, scholars estimate that at least 1,000 wealthy British American colonists lived in London after 1750. As Julie Flavell contended, before the Continental Congress gathered at Philadelphia in 1774, 'the elites who were to become its members were more likely to meet each other in London than in any American city'.[46] But, for many colonists, the scope, complexity, and capriciousness of London proved at once attractive and repulsive. At times, this 'little world' of London felt *too* big, *too* mercantilist, and *too* foreign, even to the most 'British' of Americans.[47] Colonists needed something more intimate, a microcosm of London society which was at once challenging, yet still accessible. Bath fit the bill.

As Bath's public buildings, private lodgings, shops, gardens, and thoroughfares multiplied in the mid-to-late eighteenth century, more visitors flocked to this 'melting pot of society' than ever before.[48] Reflecting the spa city's 'urban renaissance', colonists who journeyed to Bath in the three decades before the American Revolution concentrated on the city's genteel accoutrements as much as its healing waters. In 1750, Peter Manigault, the 19-year-old son of wealthy Lowcountry planters, summarised an 'ordinary' day at Bath. 'About seven in the morning', he began, 'Folks get up, & go to the Wells to drink the Mineral Waters'. From there, however, interest in the waters slowed to a trickle. At 10am spa-goers congregated at the Coffee House for breakfast, from whence they either went for a ride, 'or what is more common, go to the public Room, and play at Cards till three O'Clock in the afternoon'. Bath society spent the rest of their day 'imployed in Dining, & equip[ing] . . . themselves for the Assembly, where they [dance] or play at Cards, till about 12 at night'. In Manigault's experience, these diversions were 'the Trade every Day' at Bath.[49]

Bath's proprietors intended this well-rehearsed schedule to bring comfort to the most visitors possible.[50] Upon experiencing 'all the pleasures of Bath' in May 1753, South Carolinian Eliza Lucas Pinckney professed, 'was I to live at a distance from London I don't know any place so agreeable

Bath, Abroad 233

as Bath'.[51] Benjamin Franklin, then living in London, also made multiple sojourns to Bath with his son, William, between 1760 and 1768, but provided little description of his journeys beyond needing the 'exercise I have yearly been accustomed to'.[52] The same went for Connecticut colonist Eliphalet Dyer, who, while visiting London as an agent for the Susquehanna Land Company in 1763–1764, only recorded 'have been at Bristol and Bath'.[53] Even though Franklin and Dyer did not provide specific accounts of their journeys to Bath, these busy men's decisions to visit the spa city during otherwise critical political appointments highlight the whirlpool-like pull of Bath.[54]

Though medical therapy remained a key draw, genteel diversions especially attracted colonists to Bath in the 1770s. Philadelphian Francis Hopkinson gushed in 1767, 'was I to choose a Residence in England I think I should not hesitate a Moment in giving the Preference to Bath beyond any other place'.[55] Arthur Lee from Virginia and William White from Philadelphia concurred. Having lived for years in London during the early 1770s, Lee exclaimed, 'at Bath I had a very extensive acquaintance; and there is not in the world a more agreeable place to one so circumstanced'.[56] White similarly professed that, though he 'made several journeys to different parts of [England]', Bath proved 'the most interesting of my excursions'.[57] Even though Thomas Parke, a Philadelphian who studied in London from 1771 to 1773, did not want to live in Bath permanently, he had to admit, 'it certainly exceeds any place I have seen yet, for high Life & Grandeur'.[58]

Bath had something for almost everyone. For colonists, that 'something' revolved around the spa city's unsurpassed ability to blend high society, consumption, and architecture. The New Jerseyan Stephen Kemble's tour of Bath especially revealed these prospects. Upon approaching the city on 27 August 1773, Kemble remarked 'Ancient Bath . . . was only famous for the Baths hot and cold, but is now admired for the Elegance of its New Buildings, which exceed anything in England'. Kemble spent the rest of the day touring the 'broad' streets lined with 'magnificent' houses. He concluded by remarking, 'the Ball Room, Tea Room, Card Room, &c. are of the first order and far surpass anything of the Kind in England'.[59]

Kemble was hardly unique in his effusions. Travelling from South Carolina, Henry Laurens Sr visited Bath numerous times from 1771 to 1772. Laurens revelled in 'viewing and contemplating the amazing Improvements in [Bath] and the adjacent Country'. He especially appreciated the 'Sereneness and Silence' offered during the evening and morning hours, which allowed him and his sons to soak in the city 'free from the Hurry and Bustle which I suppose never cease to disturb and divert the attention, while the Throng of Company is in motion'.[60] Of course, such company had become a part of the very fabric of Bath by the 1770s; stone, spa, and sinew melded into one. When Josiah Quincy Jr visited the spa city in 1774, the 'amazing

234   *Bath and Beyond*

Improvements' which Laurens noted were in many ways complete. The Circus (1754–1767), Upper Assembly Rooms (1768–1771), and Royal Crescent (1767–1774) were complete, thus providing an architectural grandeur which could finally match Bath's famous sociability, shops, and spas.[61]

Recreating Bath

British American colonists' insatiable thirst for monarchical connection, urban development, genteel association, and material culture coalesced in their imagination(s) of Bath. The spa city became a model of British leisure, as it encompassed a wide variety of purpose-built, ever-evolving venues— 'pump rooms, assembly rooms, theatres, chapels, walks, gardens, squares, and circuses'—which guaranteed visitors a unique experience.[62] Because of Bath's more conservative size, location, and (more) concentrated amenities, the 'queen of spas' represented to colonists an approachable model for emulation that London simply exceeded.

Visiting Bath especially fuelled colonists' desire to recreate certain facets of British society.[63] Benjamin Franklin—who spent a considerable portion of his adulthood living in England and made multiple trips to Bath—was obsessed with crafting his home city of Philadelphia in the image of London or, more specifically, his *idealised version* of the British metropolis. Franklin accordingly established various public, 'enlightened' urban institutions in Philadelphia after the London model, including the Junto Club (1726), Library Company of Philadelphia (1731), Union Fire Company (1736), American Philosophical Society (1743), Pennsylvania Hospital (1750), and the College of Philadelphia (1755).[64] Franklin's efforts proved successful because of colonists' intense desire for British-style urban spaces and institutions. Yet, even with Franklin's relative success, Philadelphia never got close to equalling London in size, social diversity, or metropolitan maturity. Franklin, and so many other colonists like him, steadily came to realise that they needed to change the bar for British-style leisure, sociability, gentility, and health in America. And, through a potent combination of figurative and literal encounters, Bath became that bar.

Colonial Americans enjoyed unprecedented access to a slew of genteel leisure spaces in the late eighteenth century, ranging from exclusive coffeehouses to mineral spring spas, to public pleasure gardens, to playhouses, to verdant promenades, and accompanying assembly rooms. Yet, unlike Bath, which combined all of these sociable venues into one space, colonists still had to make do with more scattered, tenuous options. The finest public pleasure gardens blossomed in New York City, while the best mineral spring spas gurgled up around Philadelphia and Boston.[65] Every major city boasted genteel coffeehouses, but their select, often-subscription-based, clientele could be icy to strangers, let alone those they did not consider their

Bath, Abroad   235

social equals.[66] Playhouses, meanwhile, ebbed and flowed with the shifting tides of empire, as George Whitefield campaigned against these burgeoning venues at the same time that the first British acting troupes arrived in the colonies.[67]

Such a boom in leisure spaces bred fierce detractors. In 1761, a group of Philadelphia ministers penned a public address to the governor of the city, in which they observed, 'with the greatest concern . . . among our Fellow Citizens, an immoderate and growing Fondness for Pleasure, Luxury, Gaming, Dissipation, and their concomitant Vices'.[68] The recent public subscription lottery intended 'for erecting public Gardens, with Baths or Bagnios, among us' was the last straw for these religious leaders. Where the citizens of Philadelphia were once lauded for their 'Sobriety, their Frugality, their Industry, their serious Turn of Mind', such spaces of unchecked sociability would surely derail the once-pious populace. Why should the city not construct hot and cold baths at the hospital instead? 'And as to a publick place of Walking', they continued, 'the State House Green or Garden, by a Law of the Province, is already set apart for that Use'. Ultimately, these Philadelphia church-men professed that 'Gaming Tables, a House of Entertainment, Places of Drinking, and the like' would necessarily accompany this Bath-inspired public spa venue and, in turn, upset their decades-long efforts at pious civility.[69]

Though similar opposition continued to emanate from colonial pulpits, parlours, and public venues, the British American leisure sector continued along with aplomb.[70] A brief survey of Pennsylvania's emerging mineral spring spa facilities between 1760 and 1775 especially reveals how the spectre of Bath impelled this process. Carl Bridenbaugh contended that, in the late eighteenth century, 'the spas of the Philadelphia area took on a sophistication which provided the nearest American approach to Bath'.[71] Initially, proprietors hoped to attract Philadelphians to the nearby Yellow Springs Spa and Bristol Spa, which ignited a craze within the Quaker city for 'taking mineral waters'.[72]

In 1765, John White thumbed his nose at religious leaders by opening a mineral spa facility within Philadelphia's neighbourhood of 'New Bath'. It was no coincidence that this neighbourhood took Bath as its namesake, as White capitalised upon locals' hopes at converting its springs into 'public Gardens, with Baths or Bagnios'.[73] And, while Bristol Spa's rural location necessitated the construction of 'Long Rooms', Philadelphia's urban location—rife with assembly halls in city taverns, coffee houses, and other public spaces—meant that White did not have to worry about building his own version of Bath's famed Upper Assembly Rooms.[74] Yet, White mimicked Bath in other ways. In the style of the famous spa city, White promised 'to accommodate Ladies and Gentlemen with Breakfasting, on the best of Tea, Coffee or Chocolate'. White also guaranteed visitors 'whose Health

236   *Bath and Beyond*

may require their going into the Bath' access to 'Brushes and proper Towels'. White headed off religious opposition, asserting he hoped 'to prove himself capable of conducting every Thing, so as to answer the many public Advantages, and salutary Purposes' that a spa might provide Philadelphia's eager citizens.[75]

White's 'Rose of Bath' spa proved a runaway success, and predictably soon had competition. In 1766, William Johnson opened a similar venue across the street, complete with cheesecake, 'commodious rooms', a water fountain, and 'engine'-powered bathing room. Once again, Johnson did not open out-right assembly rooms, such as those in Bath, England, but he did provide every other luxury which spa-goers might demand. And apparently it worked. 'Those who've seen the famous Baths in England', Johnson asserted, 'say these are quite equal to them'.[76] As the rural Yellow Spring and Bristol spas boomed and urban proprietors opened similar venues, the search for new mineral springs in and around Philadelphia continued unabated until the outbreak of the American Revolution. Through it all, owners hoped to 'equal . . . the famous Baths in England', of which Bath reigned supreme.

Although Pennsylvania's spas 'took on a sophistication which provided the nearest American approach to Bath', Americans never equalled the spa city.[77] And they never really could. Beyond physical constraints such as size, amenities, architecture, and access, colonial American spa complexes lacked perhaps the most important asset of Bath: its long-held, carefully crafted reputation.[78] Ultimately, Bath was far more than its Upper Assembly Rooms, genteel promenades, or bustling balls. It was the promise of grandeur, the imagination of something better—an escape from the real world that no other place in the British Empire could ever truly match. But that did not stop colonists from trying.

Beyond Bath?

The American Revolution (1775–1783) tore mid-century British American notions of deference and sociability to shreds. America's once-blossoming leisure sector withered under the flames of war. General George Washington commandeered Yellow Springs Spa as his medical headquarters; the British military transformed New York City's once-thriving pleasure garden, Ranelagh, into a military hospital; urban city taverns and coffee houses descended into overcrowded haunts for beleaguered soldiers and refugee citizens.[79] Ordinary colonists, meanwhile, thumbed their noses at mid-century ideals of hierarchy and order, commandeering taverns for their own rebellious means and even burning the New York Vauxhall Garden to the ground.[80] Such transformations made Bath feel farther away than perhaps ever before. Watching their power wither by the day, some loyal colonists escaped to Bath, as this 'parallel society sealed from the outside world' was perfectly primed for colonials' wartime diversions.[81] Not only did Bath harbour a diverse set of visitors with an equally diverse set of political views, but it also offered visitors a variety of venues through which to reflect upon their tenuous position(s) within the empire.

American rebels, meanwhile, reconfigured notions of British leisure, health, and gentility to fit emerging visions of American liberty, republicanism, and natural bounty. And, whether or not they realised it, British customs remained critical in such endeavours.[82] With gardens overgrown, taverns overtaken, spas converted, orchards felled, and promenades pulverised, Americans faced a considerable task. Not only must they rebuild their leisure spaces, but they should do so in a way that distinguished their new spaces from their Old-World counterparts. They achieved these goals, if only partially, as most American spaces continued as veritable copies of their British counterparts, with perhaps more allusions to environmental superiority added to their local recipe of leisure and sociability.

Post-revolutionary Americans touted their land as unsurpassed in natural bounty. One 1783 American newspaper article invited beleaguered Britons to 'the fertile plains of Independent America' as an escape from their supposed destitution. Where Great Britain was 'a land which holds out to them nakedness, want and penury', the author promised prospective Britons that America 'flow[ed] with milk and honey'.[83] Such natural plenty, Americans reassured themselves, would surely guarantee future success in terms of governance, economy, agriculture, and, of course, leisure.

But, it was not a binary undertaking. Americans' accomplishments in reconstructing (and constructing) new urban leisure spaces were commendable. The Yellow Springs and Bristol Spas became more popular than ever before in the early Federal Era, and ignited an unsurpassed frenzy for 'resort' spas throughout America's eastern seaboard.[84] Business owners opened taverns and fine hotels around these sites, in addition to promenades, restaurants, orchards, assembly rooms, tea houses, and stage-coach stops.[85] Yet, as ever, they did so upon the Bath model. Americans could tout their sites' 'uniqueness', but ultimately, they tarried in springs, sipped coffee, and danced in venues which hoped to match the queen of spas. Americans' mentalities alluded to as much. One contributor to the *Columbian Herald* in 1786 remarked that newly discovered springs were 'not inferior in their effects to . . . Bath in England', and hoped that 'it will be the Bath of South-Carolina and the adjoining states'.[86] So too did another hopeful American assert that, though New York's New Lebanon mineral springs were still in their infancy, 'the hot springs of Bath in England' also 'owe their present flourishing situations to small beginnings'.[87] News stories beginning with 'we hear from Bath' continued to dot American newspapers, and elite Americans still travelled to Bath for extended vacations.[88]

238 *Bath and Beyond*

'Becoming American' was as much about 'unbecoming British' as anything else, yet Bath maintained its strangle-hold over even the most ardent Americans' mindsets. This should come as no surprise, since being British was all most 'Americans' knew, and Bath was the most iconic space of gentility, leisure, and health in the British empire.[89] Even a brutal revolution could not destroy the queen of spas' multi-decade 'image-making' campaign, as Americans continued to imagine, encounter, and recreate Bath.[90] Georgian Bath's success rested in its ability to satisfy visitors' imagined and physical encounters with the spa city. Publishers capitalised upon interest to provide colonials with a wide array of Bath-concentrated prose, which helped them not only connect with Bath society, but also better understand the spa city's physicality. Yet, for certain colonists, reading about Bath was simply not enough. In travelling to Bath, some British American elites managed to turn fantasy into reality, and their experience did not disappoint. Feeling more inspired to emulate their homeland than perhaps ever before, those same colonists returned to America and attempted to recreate Bath, abroad, through a carefully planned network of spas, pleasure gardens, taverns, coffeehouses, orchards, playhouses, and promenades.

This transatlantic promotion campaign worked. Bath retains its status as the ultimate Western spa centre, with tens of thousands of Americans visiting the splendid city's Roman baths and honey-coloured buildings every year. And, upon returning to home, they visit local imitations of the famous spa city. But, they cannot equal Bath. They never really could!

Notes

1 Tobias Smollett, *Humphry Clinker* (New York: The Century Co., 1906), 32, 35; Alfred Barbeau, *Life and Letters at Bath in the Eighteenth Century* (London: William Heinemann, 1904), 196–98.
2 Smollett, *Humphry Clinker*, 196–98.
3 Peter Borsay, *The Image of Georgian Bath, 1700–2000* (Oxford: Oxford University Press, 2000), 9, 19, 241. This article is indebted to Peter Borsay's various works. If Bath was the 'queen of spas', Dr. Borsay was surely the king (historian) of Bath.
4 This chapter uses the same definition of British American 'colonist' which historian William L. Sachse employed in 1956: 'The criteria which will be employed in this work are either native birth or a determination to settle, to plant, to become a permanent co-member of the colonial community, with the hope of growing and flourishing with it'. William L. Sachse, *The Colonial American in Britain* (Madison: University of Wisconsin Press, 1956), 5; Stephen Conway, "From Fellow Nationals to Foreigners: British Perceptions of the Americans, circa 1739–1789," *William and Mary Quarterly* lix (2002): 74.
5 Charles Henry Hart, ed., "Letters from William Franklin to William Strahan," *Pennsylvania Magazine of History and Biography* xxxv (1911): 427.
6 Many of these British Americans would have been from England, Scotland, Ireland, and Wales. In their correspondence, they often used 'British' and 'English' interchangeably in their discussions of their travels to the British Isles.

7 Elisa Tamarkin, *Anglophilia: Deference, Devotion, and Antebellum America* (Chicago: University of Chicago Press, 2008).

8 Borsay, *Image of Georgian Bath*, 19.

9 Peter Borsay, *The English Urban Renaissance: Culture and Society in the Provincial Town, 1660–1770* (Oxford: Clarendon Press, 1989), 277.

10 Julie Flavell, *When London Was Capital of America* (New Haven: Yale University Press, 2010), 249–50.

11 Borsay, *Image of Georgian Bath*; Borsay, *English Urban Renaissance*; Roy Porter, ed., *The Medical History of Waters and Spas* (London: Wellcome Institute for the History of Medicine, 1990); Phyllis Hembry, *The English Spa, 1560–1815: A Social History* (London: Athlone Press, 1990); Barbeau, *Life and Letters at Bath*; R. S. Neale, *Bath, 1680–1850: A Social History or a Valley of Pleasure, Yet a Sink of Iniquity* (London: Routledge, 1981); Amanda E. Herbert, "Gender and the Spa: Space, Sociability and Self at British Health Spas, 1640–1714," *Journal of Social History* xliii (2009): 361–83. Trevor Fawcett wrote a litany of books on the history of Bath, which may be accessed at the History of Bath Research Group [Online], "Collection of Fawcett Papers and Books," accessed February 25, 2022, https://historyofbath.org/fawcettpapers/fawcettpapers.

12 Carl Bridenbaugh, *Cities in the Wilderness: The First Century of Urban Life in America, 1625–1742* (Oxford: Oxford University Press, 1938); Carl Bridenbaugh, *Cities in Revolt: Urban Life in America, 1743–1776* (New York: Alfred A. Knopf, 1955); Richard Bushman, *The Refinement of America: Persons, Houses, Cities* (New York: Alfred K. Knopf, 1992); Tristram Hunt, *Cities of Empire: The British Colonies and the Creation of the Urban World* (New York: Metropolitan Books, 2014), 19–63; Sharon V. Salinger, *Taverns and Drinking in Early America* (Baltimore: The Johns Hopkins University Press, 2002); Benjamin Carp, *Rebels Rising: Cities and the American Revolution* (Oxford: Oxford University Press, 2007); Vaughn Scribner, "Cultivating 'Cities in the Wilderness': New York City's Commercial Pleasure Gardens and the British American Pursuit of Rural Urbanism," *Urban History* xlv (2018): 275–305; Eric Hinderaker, "The 'Four Indian Kings' and the Imaginative Construction of the First British Empire," *William and Mary Quarterly* liii (1996): 487–526; Flavell, *When London Was Capital of America*; Kariann Akemi Yokota, *Unbecoming British: How Revolutionary America Became a Postcolonial Nation* (Oxford: Oxford University Press, 2011); Brendan McConville, *The King's Three Faces: The Rise and Fall of Royal America, 1688–1776* (Chapel Hill: University of North Carolina Press, 2006).

13 J. G. A. Pocock, "British History: A Plea for a New Subject," *Journal of Modern History* xlvii (1975): 601–21; Richard Bourke, "Pocock and the Presuppositions of the New British History," *The Historical Journal* liii (2010): 747–70; Bernard Bailyn, *Atlantic History: Concept and Contours* (Cambridge, MA: Harvard University Press, 2005); Peter A. Coclanis, "Atlantic World or Atlantic/World?", *William and Mary Quarterly* lxiii (2006): 725–44; Karin Wulf, Aeon [Online], "Vast Early America," accessed February 25, 2022. https://aeon.co/essays/why-the-history-of-the-vast-early-america-matters-today.

14 Sachse, *The Colonial American in Britain*; Flavell, *When London Was Capital of America*; Daniel Kilbride, *Being American in Europe, 1750–1860* (Baltimore: Johns Hopkins University Press, 2013); Julie M. Flavell and Gordon Hay, "Using Capture-Recapture Methods to Reconstruct the American Population in London," *Journal of Interdisciplinary History* xxxii (2001): 37–53; Richard Godbeer, *World of Trouble: A Philadelphia Quaker Family's Journey*

240   *Bath and Beyond*

Through the American Revolution (New Haven: Yale University Press, 2019), 26–27.

15 Hugh Jones, *Present State of Virginia* (New York: Joseph Sabin, 1865), 43.

16 Benjamin H. Irvin, "Smashing Idols," *Commonplace: The Journal of Early American Life* viii (2008); McConville, *The King's Three Faces*, 119–36.

17 Alice Hanson Jones, "Wealth Estimates for the American Middle Colonies, 1774," *Economic Development and Cultural Change* xviii (1970): 130.

18 Thomas Jones, *History of New York During the Revolutionary War*, ed. Edward Floyd De Lancey, 2 vols. (New York: New York Historical Society, 1879), i, 12.

19 Woody Holton, *Liberty Is Sweet: The Hidden History of the American Revolution* (New York: Simon & Schuster, 2021); Kathleen DuVal, *Independence Lost: Lives on the Edge of the American Revolution* (New York: Random House, 2015).

20 Borsay, *English Urban Renaissance*, 241.

21 Benedict Anderson, *Imagined Communities* (London: Verso, 2006).

22 *Weekly Rehearsal*, January 6, 1735.

23 *New York Weekly Journal*, June 14, 1736.

24 *New York Weekly Journal*, June 14, 1736.

25 *Boston Evening Post*, August 22, 1737; *Virginia Gazette*, July 13, 1739; *Pennsylvania Journal*, March 3, 1768.

26 Richard Owens, "Essays First Published in *The World*, 1753–1756," in *The Works of Richard Cambridge, Esq: Including Several Pieces Never Before Published*, ed. George Owen (Cambridge, 1803), lxx, May 2, 1754.

27 Brian Cowan, Oxford Handbooks [Online], *News, Biography, and Eighteenth-Century Celebrity*, available from www.oxfordhandbooks.com/view/10.1093/oxfordhb/9780199935338.001.0001/oxfordhb-9780199935338-e-132?print=pdf (accessed 1 Mar. 2022).

28 *Boston Post Boy*, 1 June 1752.

29 *New York Gazette*, 28 Oct. 1751.

30 *Providence Gazette*, 1 Apr. 1769.

31 David Shields, *Civil Tongues and Polite Letters in British America* (Chapel Hill, 1997), 11.

32 Christopher Anstey, *The New Bath Guide: Or, Memoirs of the B—r—d Family, in a Series of Poetical Epistles* (5th edn, 1767), 34; Shaun Regan, 'Bathing in Verse: Christopher Anstey's *The New Bath Guide* and Georgian Resort Satire', in *Spa Culture and Literature in England, 1500–1800*, ed. Sophie Chiari and Samuel Cuisinier-Delorme (New York, 2021), 136, 138.

33 Anstey, *The New Bath Guide*, 34.

34 Regan, 'Bathing in Verse', 135.

35 *Boston Gazette*, 15 June 1767; *New York Gazette and Weekly Mercury*, 16 July 1770; *Pennsylvania Ledger*, 4 Apr. 1778; *Boston Evening Post*, 31 Aug. 1767.

36 Borsay, *Image of Georgian Bath*, 20–59.

37 Samuel Derrick, *Letters Written from Liverpool, Chester, Corke, the Lake of Killarney, Dublin, Tunbridge-Wells, Bath* (2 vols, 1767), ii; R.D.E. Eagles, ODNB [Online], Samuel Derrick (1724–1769), available from www.oxforddnb.com/view/10.1093/ref:odnb/9780198614128.001.0001/odnb-9780198614128-e-7536 (accessed 2 Mar. 2022).

38 Derrick, *Letters*, 83, 86–8.

39 *Boston Gazette*, 6 July 1767; *South Carolina Gazette*, 31 Jan. 1770; *Virginia Gazette*, 1 Aug. 1771.

40 Josiah Quincy Jr., 'Journal of Josiah Quincy, Jun., during His Voyage and Residence in England from September 28th, 1774, to March 3d, 1775', *Proceedings of the Massachusetts Historical Society*, l (1916), 434; *Memoirs of Josiah Quincy, Junior, of Massachusetts: 1744–1775*, ed. Eliza Susan Quincy (2nd edn, Boston, 1874), 230; Bob Ruppert, Journal of the American Revolution [Online], *Josiah Quincy Jr.*, available from https://allthingsliberty.com/2019/06/josiah-quincy-jr/ (accessed 3 Mar. 2022).
41 Quincy, 'Journal', 451.
42 Quincy, 'Journal', 451–3.
43 Quincy, 'Journal', 451–3.
44 Benjamin L. Carp, *Defiance of the Patriots: The Boston Tea Party and the Making of America* (New Haven, 2010), 204–217.
45 Flavell, *When London was Capital of America*, 10.
46 Flavell and Hay, 'Using Capture-Recapture Methods', 38–42, 48; Flavell, *When London was Capital of America*, 249.
47 Sachse, *The Colonial American in Britain*, 23.
48 Borsay, *English Urban Renaissance*, 271.
49 Peter Manigault, 'Peter Manigault's Letters (Continued)', ed. Elizabeth Heyward Jervey and Mabel L. Webber, *South Carolina Historical and Genealogical Magazine*, xxxii (1931), 275.
50 Borsay, *English Urban Renaissance*, 270.
51 Eliza Lucas Pinckney, *The Letterbook of Eliza Lucas Pinckney, 1739–1762*, ed. Elise Pinckney (Chapel Hill, 1972), 80, 121.
52 *The Papers of Benjamin Franklin*, ed. Leonard W. Labaree (37 vols, New Haven, 1970), xiv, 224–6; Skemp, *William Franklin*, 35; Labaree, et. al., *Autobiography*, 308.
53 'A Selection from the Correspondence and Miscellaneous Papers of Jared Ingersoll', ed. Franklin B. Dexter, *Papers of the New Haven Colony Historical Society*, ix (1918), 289.
54 Of course, other colonial spa-goers had more intimate goals. In 1763, Charles Carroll of Maryland utilised Bath's famous marriage circuit, penning an (unsuccessful) letter to a young woman's father in the hope that he might welcome matrimony. Charles Carroll, *Unpublished Letters of Charles Carroll of Carrollton and His Father, Charles Carroll of Doughoregan*, ed. Thomas Meagher Field (New York, 1902), 81–4.
55 *Papers of Benjamin Franklin*, xiv, 171–3.
56 Richard Henry Lee, *Life of Arthur Lee, LL.D.* (2 vols, Boston, 1829), ii, 392.
57 William Stevens Perry, 'Ancestry and Early Life of William White', *Historical Magazine of the Protestant Episcopal Church*, vi (1937), 29.
58 Whitefield J. Bell Jr., 'Thomas Parke's Student Life in England and Scotland, 1771–1773', *Pennsylvania Magazine of History and Biography*, lxxv (1951), 239–40.
59 'The Kemble Papers, Volume 1', in *Collections of the New-York Historical Society for the Year 1883* (New York, 1884), 17.
60 Henry Laurens, *The Papers of Henry Laurens*, ed. George C. Rogers, David R. Chesnutt, Peggy J. Clark (16 vols, Columbia, 1980), viii, 17. Laurens returned to Bath in January and February of 1772, and then again in May 1772. See Laurens, *Papers*, viii, 156–9, 180–3, 350.
61 Borsay, *English Urban Renaissance*, 100–1, 151–3, 236, 273, 336–7; Borsay, *Image of Georgian Bath*, 13.
62 Borsay, *English Urban Renaissance*, 273.

242 *Bath and Beyond*

63 Kilbride, *Being American*, 14.
64 Peter Clark, *British Clubs and Societies, 1580–1800: The Origins of an Associational World* (Oxford, 2000); Flavell, *When London was Capital of America*, 194–5.
65 Scribner, 'Cultivating Cities in the Wilderness', 275–305; Scribner, 'The Happy Effects of these Waters', 440.
66 Vaughn Scribner, *Inn Civility: Urban Taverns and Early American Civil Society* (New York, 2019), 21–41.
67 Vaughn Scribner, 'Transatlantic Actors: The Intertwining Stages of George Whitefield and Lewis Hallam, Sr., 1739–1756', *Journal of Social History*, l (2016), 1–27.
68 *Pennsylvania Gazette*, 20 Aug. 1761.
69 *Pennsylvania Gazette*, 20 Aug. 1761.
70 *Boston News-Letter*, 10 July 1750.
71 Bridenbaugh, 'Baths and Watering Places', 164.
72 Bridenbaugh, 'Baths and Watering Places', 171.
73 *Pennsylvania Gazette*, 22 Aug. 1765.
74 *Pennsylvania Gazette*, 11 June 1772; Peter Thompson, *Rum Punch and Revolution: Taverngoing & Public Life in Eighteenth-Century Philadelphia* (Philadelphia, 1999); Daniel P. Johnson, *Making the Early Modern Metropolis: Culture and Power in Pre-Revolutionary Philadelphia* (Charlottesville, 2022).
75 *Pennsylvania Gazette*, 11 June 1772.
76 *Pennsylvania Gazette*, 15 May 1766, 13 June 1766; Bridenbaugh, 'Baths and Watering Places', 172.
77 Bridenbaugh, 'Baths and Watering Places', 164.
78 Borsay, *Image of Georgian Bath*, 9.
79 Janet Mace Valenza, *Taking the Waters in Texas: Springs, Spas, and Fountains of Youth* (Austin, 2000), 19; Scribner, 'Cultivating Cities in the Wilderness', 30; Scribner, *Inn Civility*, 137–70; Carp, *Rebels Rising*, 62–98.
80 Scribner, *Inn Civility*, 109–76; Scribner, 'Cultivating Cities in the Wilderness', 29.
81 Borsay, *English Urban Renaissance*, 277; Kate Davies, *Catharine Macaulay and Mercy Otis Warren: The Revolutionary Atlantic and the Politics of Gender* (Oxford, 2005), 2, 132; Quincy Jr., 'Journal', 452; *The Diary and Letters of His Excellency Thomas Hutchinson, Esq.*, ed. Peter Orlando Hutchinson (2 vols, Boston, 1884–86), i, 345–54; South Caroliniana Library, University of South Carolina, Manigault Family Papers: Gabriel Manigault to Ann Manigault, 21 Dec. 1777; Samuel Curwen, *The Journal and Letters of Samuel Curwen*, ed. George Atkinson Ward (Boston, 1864), 145, 170, 229; Elkanah Watson, *Men and Times of the Revolution; or, Memoirs of Elkanah Watson, Including Journals of Travels in Europe and America, from 1777 to 1842*, ed. Winslow C. Watson (New York, 1856), 172–3; New York State Library [Online], *Biographical Notes: Elkanah Watson Papers, 1773–1784*, accessed January 24, 2023, www.nysl.nysed.gov/msscfa/sc13294.htm.
82 Eric Nelson, *The Royalist Revolution: Monarchy and the American Founding* (Cambridge: Cambridge University Press, 2014).
83 *New Jersey Gazette*, May 14, 1783.
84 Theodore Corbett, *The Making of American Resorts: Saratoga Springs, Ballston Spa, Lake George* (New Brunswick: Rutgers University Press, 2011); Conevery Bolton Valenčius, *The Health of the Country: How American Settlers Understood Themselves and Their Land* (New York: Basic Books, 2002).

Bath, Abroad 243

85 A. K. Sandoval-Strausz, *Hotel: An American History* (New Haven: Yale University Press, 2007).
86 *Columbian Herald*, May 4, 1786.
87 *Columbian Herald*, June 19, 1786.
88 *New York Journal, & Patriotic Register*, December 7, 1791; *Independent Ledger*, October 10, 1785. Kilbride, *Being American in Europe*, 45–80.
89 Yokota, *Unbecoming British*; Jon Butler, *Becoming America: The Revolution Before 1776* (Cambridge: Cambridge University Press, 2000).
90 Borsay, *Image of Georgian Bath*, 9.

Bibliography

Manuscript Sources

South Caroliniana Library

Columbia Manigault Family Papers, Manuscripts Division.

Printed Primary and Secondary Sources

Anderson, Benedict. *Imagined Communities*. London: Verso, 2006.
Anstey, Christopher. *The New Bath Guide: Or, Memoirs of the B-r-d Family, in a Series of Poetical Epistles*, 5th ed. London: J. Dodsley, 1767.
Bailyn, Bernard. *Atlantic History: Concept and Contours*. Cambridge, MA: Harvard University Press, 2005.
Barbeau, Alfred. *Life and Letters at Bath in the Eighteenth Century*. London: William Heinemann, 1904.
Bell Jr., Whitefield J. "Thomas Parke's Student Life in England and Scotland, 1771–1773." *Pennsylvania Magazine of History and Biography* 75, no. 3 (July 1951): 237–59.
"Biographical Notes: Elkanah Watson Papers, 1773–1784." New York State Library. Accessed January 24, 2023. www.nysl.nysed.gov/msscfa/sc13294.htm.
Borsay, Peter. *The English Urban Renaissance: Culture and Society in the Provincial Town, 1660–1770*. Oxford: Oxford University Press, 1989.
Borsay, Peter. *The Image of Georgian Bath, 1700–2000*. Oxford: Oxford University Press, 2000.
Bourke, Richard. "Pocock and the Presuppositions of the New British History." *The Historical Journal* 53, no. 3 (September 2010): 747–70.
Bridenbaugh, Carl. "Baths and Watering Places of Colonial America." *William and Mary Quarterly* 3, no. 2 (April 1946): 151–81.
Bridenbaugh, Carl. *Cities in Revolt: Urban Life in America, 1743–1776*. New York: Alfred A. Knopf, 1955.
Bridenbaugh, Carl. *Cities in the Wilderness: The First Century of Urban Life in America, 1625–1742*. Oxford: Oxford University Press, 1938.
Bushman, Richard L. *The Refinement of America: Persons, Houses, Cities*. New York: Alfred K. Knopf, 1992.
Butler, Jon. *Becoming America: The Revolution Before 1776*. Cambridge: Cambridge University Press, 2000.
Carp, Benjamin L. *Defiance of the Patriots: The Boston Tea Party and the Making of America*. New Haven: Yale University Press, 2010.

244 Bath and Beyond

Carp, Benjamin L. *Rebels Rising: Cities and the American Revolution.* Oxford: Oxford University Press, 2007.

Carroll, Charles. *Unpublished Letters of Charles Carroll of Carrollton and His Father, Charles Carroll of Doughoregan.* Edited by Thomas Meagher Field. New York: United States Catholic Historical Society, 1902.

Clark, Peter. *British Clubs and Societies, 1580–1800: The Origins of an Associational World.* Oxford: Oxford University Press, 2000.

Coclanis, Peter A. "Atlantic World or Atlantic/World?" *William and Mary Quarterly* 63, no. 4 (October 2006): 725–44.

Conway, Stephen. "From Fellow Nationals to Foreigners: British Perceptions of the Americans, circa 1739–1789." *William and Mary Quarterly* 59, no. 1 (January 2002): 65–100.

Corbett, Theodore. *The Making of American Resorts: Saratoga Springs, Ballston Spa, Lake George.* New Brunswick: Rutgers University Press, 2011.

Cowan, Brian. "News, Biography, and Eighteenth-Century Celebrity (September 2016)." Oxford Handbooks Online. Accessed March 1, 2022. www.oxfordhandbooks.com/view/10.1093/oxfordhb/9780199935338.001.0001/oxfordhb-9780199935338-e-132?print=pdf.

Curwen, Samuel. *The Journal and Letters of Samuel Curwen.* Edited by George Atkinson Ward. Boston: Little, Brown and Company, 1864.

Davies, Kate. *Catharine Macaulay and Mercy Otis Warren: The Revolutionary Atlantic and the Politics of Gender.* Oxford: Oxford University Press, 2005.

Derrick, Samuel. *Letters Written from Liverpool, Chester, Corke, the Lake of Killarney, Dublin, Tunbridge-Wells, Bath.* Vol. 2. London: L. Davis and C. Reymers, 1767.

Dexter, Franklin B., ed. "A Selection from the Correspondence and Miscellaneous Papers of Jared Ingersoll." *Papers of the New Haven Colony Historical Society* 9 (1918): 201–472.

DuVal, Kathleen. *Independence Lost: Lives on the Edge of the American Revolution.* New York: Random House, 2015.

Eagles, R. D. E. "Samuel Derrick (1724–1769)." In *Oxford Dictionary of National Biography*, September 23, 2004. Accessed March 2, 2022. www.oxforddnb.com/view/10.1093/ref:odnb/9780198614128.001.0001/odnb-9780198614128-e-7536.

Fawcett, Trevor. "Collection of Fawcett Papers and Books." *History of Bath Research Group.* Accessed February 25, 2022. https://historyofbath.org/fawcettpapers/fawcettpapers.

Flavell, Julie M. *When London Was Capital of America.* New Haven: Yale University Press, 2010.

Flavell, Julie M., and Gordon Hay. "Using Capture-Recapture Methods to Reconstruct the American Population in London." *Journal of Interdisciplinary History* 32, no. 1 (Summer 2001): 37–53.

Franklin, Benjamin. *The Papers of Benjamin Franklin. Vol. 14, January 1 Through December 31, 1767.* Edited by Leonard W. Labaree. New Haven: Yale University Press, 1970.

Franklin, William. "Letters from William Franklin to William Strahan." Edited by Charles Henry Hart. *Pennsylvania Magazine of History and Biography* 35, no. 4 (1911): 415–62.

Godbeer, Richard. *World of Trouble: A Philadelphia Quaker Family's Journey Through the American Revolution.* New Haven: Yale University Press, 2019.

Hembry, Phyllis. *The English Spa, 1560–1815: A Social History.* London: Athlone Press, 1990.

Herbert, Amanda E. "Gender and the Spa: Space, Sociability and Self at British Health Spas, 1640–1714." *Journal of Social History* 43, no. 2 (Winter 2009): 361–83.

Hinderaker, Eric. "The 'Four Indian Kings' and the Imaginative Construction of the First British Empire." *William and Mary Quarterly* 53, no. 3 (July 1996): 487–526.

Holton, Woody. *Liberty Is Sweet: The Hidden History of the American Revolution*. New York: Simon & Schuster, 2021.

Hunt, Tristram. *Cities of Empire: The British Colonies and the Creation of the Urban World*. New York: Metropolitan Books, 2014.

Hutchinson, Thomas. *The Diary and Letters of His Excellency Thomas Hutchinson, Esq*. Edited by Peter Orlando Hutchinson. Boston: Houghton Mifflin Publishers, 1884–1886.

Irvin, Benjamin H. "Smashing Idols." *Commonplace: The Journal of Early American Life* 8, no. 4 (July 2008). Accessed February 26, 2022. http://commonplace. online/article/smashing-idols/.

Johnson, Daniel P. *Making the Early Modern Metropolis: Culture and Power in Pre-Revolutionary Philadelphia*. Charlottesville: University of Virginia Press, 2022.

Jones, Alice Hanson. "Wealth Estimates for the American Middle Colonies, 1774." *Economic Development and Cultural Change* 18, no. 4, Part 2 (July 1970): 98–127.

Jones, Hugh. *Present State of Virginia*. New York: Joseph Sabin, 1865.

Jones, Thomas. *History of New York During the Revolutionary War*. Edited by Edward Floyd De Lancey. New York: New York Historical Society, 1879.

"The Kemble Papers. Vol. 1." In *Collections of the New-York Historical Society for the Year 1883*. New York: New York Historical Society, 1884.

Kilbride, Daniel. *Being American in Europe, 1750–1860*. Baltimore: Johns Hopkins University Press, 2013.

Labaree, Leonard W., Ralph L. Ketcham, Helen C. Boatfield, and Helene H. Fineman, eds. *The Autobiography of Benjamin Franklin*. New Haven: Yale University Press, 2003.

Laurens, Henry. *The Papers of Henry Laurens. Vol. 8: October 10, 1771–April 19, 1773*. Edited by George C. Rogers, David R. Chesnutt, and Peggy J. Clark. Columbia, SC: University of South Carolina Press, 1980.

Lee, Richard Henry. *Life of Arthur Lee, LL.D*. Boston: Well and Lilly, 1829.

Manigault, Peter. "Peter Manigault's Letters (Continued)." Edited by Elizabeth Heyward Jervey and Mabel L. Webber. *South Carolina Historical and Genealogical Magazine* 32, no. 4 (October 1931): 270–80.

McConville, Brendan. *The King's Three Faces: The Rise and Fall of Royal America, 1688–1776*. Chapel Hill: University of North Carolina Press, 2006.

Neale, R. S. *Bath, 1680–1850: A Social History or a Valley of Pleasure, Yet a Sink of Iniquity*. London: Routledge, 1981.

Nelson, Eric. *The Royalist Revolution: Monarchy and the American Founding*. Cambridge: Cambridge University Press, 2014.

Owens, Richard. "Essays First Published in *the World*, 1753–1756." In *The Works of Richard Cambridge, Esq: Including Several Pieces Never Before Published*, edited by George Owen. Cambridge and London: L. Hansard, 1803.

Perry, William Stevens. "Ancestry and Early Life of William White." *Historical Magazine of the Protestant Episcopal Church* 6 (1937): 4–35.

Pinckney, Eliza Lucas. *The Letterbook of Eliza Lucas Pinckney, 1739–1762*. Edited by Elise Pinckney. Chapel Hill: University of North Carolina Press, 1972.

Pocock, J. G. A. "British History: A Plea for a New Subject." *Journal of Modern History* 47, no. 4 (December 1975): 601–21.

246 *Bath and Beyond*

Porter, Roy, ed. *The Medical History of Waters and Spas*. London: Wellcome Institute for the History of Medicine, 1990.

Quincy, Eliza Susan, ed. *Memoirs of Josiah Quincy, Junior, of Massachusetts: 1744–1775*. Boston: Little, Brown, 1874.

Quincy Jr., Josiah. "Journal of Josiah Quincy, Jun., During His Voyage and Residence in England from September 28, 1774, to March 3, 1775." *Proceedings of the Massachusetts Historical Society* 50 (October 1916): 433–71.

Regan, Shaun. "Bathing in Verse: Christopher Anstey's *The New Bath Guide* and Georgian Resort Satire." In *Spa Culture and Literature in England, 1500–1800*, edited by Sophie Chiari and Samuel Cuisinier-Delorme, 135–58. New York: Palgrave Macmillan, 2021.

Ruppert, Bob. "Josiah Quincy Jr." *Journal of the American Revolution* (June 4, 2019). Accessed March 3, 2022. https://allthingsliberty.com/2019/06/josiah-quincy-jr/.

Sachse, William L. *The Colonial American in Britain*. Madison: University of Wisconsin Press, 1956.

Salinger, Sharon V. *Taverns and Drinking in Early America*. Baltimore: The Johns Hopkins University Press, 2002.

Sandoval-Strausz, A. K. *Hotel: An American History*. New Haven: Yale University Press, 2007.

Scribner, Vaughn. "Cultivating 'Cities in the Wilderness': New York City's Commercial Pleasure Gardens and the British American Pursuit of Rural Urbanism." *Urban History* 45, no. 2 (May 2018): 275–305.

Scribner, Vaughn. " 'The Happy Effects of These Waters': Colonial American Mineral Spas and the British Civilizing Mission." *Early American Studies: An Interdisciplinary Journal* 14, no. 3 (Summer 2016): 409–49.

Scribner, Vaughn. *Inn Civility: Urban Taverns and Early American Civil Society*. New York: New York University Press, 2019.

Scribner, Vaughn. "Transatlantic Actors: The Intertwining Stages of George Whitefield and Lewis Hallam, Sr., 1739–1756." *Journal of Social History* 50, no. 1 (Fall 2016): 1–27.

Shields, David. *Civil Tongues and Polite Letters in British America*. Chapel Hill: University of North Carolina Press, 1997.

Skemp, Sheila L. *William Franklin: Son of a Patriot, Servant of a King*. Oxford: Oxford University Press, 1990.

Smollett, Tobias. *Humphry Clinker*. New York: The Century Co., 1906.

Tamarkin, Elisa. *Anglophilia: Deference, Devotion, and Antebellum America*. Chicago: University of Chicago Press, 2008.

Thompson, Peter. *Rum Punch and Revolution: Taverngoing & Public Life in Eighteenth-Century Philadelphia*. Philadelphia: University of Pennsylvania Press, 1999.

Valenčius, Conevery Bolton. *The Health of the Country: How American Settlers Understood Themselves and Their Land*. New York: Basic Books, 2002.

Valenza, Janet Mace. *Taking the Waters in Texas: Springs, Spas, and Fountains of Youth*. Austin: University of Texas Press, 2000.

Watson, Elkanah. *Men and Times of the Revolution; or, Memoirs of Elkanah Watson, Including Journals of Travels in Europe and America, from 1777 to 1842*. Edited by Winslow C. Watson. New York: Dana and Company, 1856.

Wulf, Karin. "Vast Early America." *Aeon* (July 15, 2021). Accessed February 25, 2021. https://aeon.co/essays/why-the-history-of-the-vast-early-america-matters-today.

Yokota, Kariann Akemi. *Unbecoming British: How Revolutionary America Became a Postcolonial Nation*. Oxford: Oxford University Press, 2011.

13 Bath Assembly Rooms
Then, Now, and Next

Tatjana LeBoff

Georgian Bath, although not unique, is an interesting example of how a city flexed and reformed around its identity of tourism, health, and entertainments, mediated by its shifting population of tourists, visitors, and residents. Bath had many guises as hospital, home, pulpit, rostrum, playground, workplace, and a convenient political home for several high-ranking Members of Parliament. For its visitors and residents, Georgian Bath offered a myriad of opportunities, with the city carving out a niche for itself as a place for recuperation—based on its thermal spa waters—and revelry—catering to the growing tourist market which demanded to be entertained. For those of a political inclination, they were able to make sure of the narrow corporation to enable easy elections and use the social circuit as a stage for soft politics. Wealthy tourists brought in not only social variety, but also money and employment, supplementing the regular economic and social cycles of the city, which were supported by the resident population. Additionally, the professional, artistic, merchant, and labouring classes could see the advantages the tourist economy of Bath could offer. As this book has demonstrated, Georgian Bath became a stage on which social rituals, political networks, economic trades, urban developments, and familial relationships played out, either in person or at a distance through correspondence, the press, and print culture.

Bath and Beyond is not intended to be a complete study of Georgian Bath's spa and assembly cultures and its influences abroad, but instead a starting point to enhance our understanding of the complexities of this small, yet ambitious city, and others that sought to emulate it. This book endeavours to provide a platform for new research into often under-explored areas, including that of the role of women within politics and society; colonial histories and the interplay between the commercial commerce of enslavement and that of the entertainment sphere; and the histories of corporeal experience, such as Dan O'Brien's consideration of death and burial in Georgian Bath. Utilising previously under-used primary sources, such as collections of correspondence, newspapers, and accounts,

DOI: 10.4324/9781003393856-13

248 *Bath and Beyond*

individual chapters have sought to expand the collective knowledge about Georgian Bath and the Bath Assembly Rooms. Questions such as where did the money come from? what was the lived experience of the Bath ballroom? and what are the legacies of the city? come into focus through different prisms. By probing these lesser-examined areas of city life, from the business of undertaking to understanding Bath's ability to inform spa culture in foreign climes, the volume hopes to advance our knowledge of the intricacies of a city and the people who inhabited, shaped, and reshaped it. While some topics are often spoken about with reference to Georgian Bath, such as that of music, husband-hunting, and the personalities of the Masters of Ceremonies, the chapters addressing these themes have offered alternative insights through cross-pollination of ideas and sources, as exemplified by Rachel Bynoth's emotionally considered unpicking of the marriage mart through the epistemological relation between mother and daughter; and Rachael Johnson's chapter on the symbiotic relationship between spa towns and the Masters of Ceremonies. These chapters have sought to turn a critical lens on these areas, incorporating cross-disciplinary approaches, to reframe Georgian Bath and the Bath Assembly Rooms.

Understandably, this book does not offer complete answers to these questions. In the time between the 2021 conference and writing this section, further original research has been undertaken, and continues to take place. One such example is the research the National Trust curatorial team at the Bath Assembly Rooms is undertaking as part of the developing visitor experience at the Bath Assembly Rooms. This work is broad, exploring multivarious aspects of Georgian society, and is being conducted in consultation with other curators and academics. While this research is not yet publicly available, some elements are being shared through academic channels, such as at the British Society for Eighteenth-Century Studies annual conference, and through a series on public tours of, and events at, the Bath Assembly Rooms themselves.

Although this book speaks to the influence the Bath Assembly Rooms and the spa city had on establishments and social culture in eighteenth- and early nineteenth-century Europe and North America, it only briefly touches on the broader and more complex topics of globalism and colonialism. Rupert Goulding and Timothy Moore's chapter begins to bring out the Assembly Rooms' original subscribers' connections to enslavement, but more research is needed—and more is currently underway by National Trust curators. Along with exploring the Rooms' original and subsequent investors and managing committee, research is also being carried out using historic marriage, death, and baptismal records, wills, newspapers, and first-hand accounts in order to gain a better understanding of the realities of the global and colonial connections of the Rooms and the Georgian city, both at home and abroad. Research is also continuing to be carried out into the global population of Georgian Bath, with current research focusing on Black, Indian, and South Asian communities, informed by those global connections of the Rooms' subscribers and the city's visitors and residents. Preliminary findings have uncovered over a hundred named Black individuals who were predominantly involved with domestic service in Bath, some of whom may have been employed at the Assembly Rooms as well, although research is still seeking evidence of this. We do know that the Bath Assembly Rooms were accepting of these communities, hosting not only performers and artists, such as the celebrated Black virtuoso violinist George Bridgetower, who performed in the Bath Assembly Rooms in December 1789 as detailed in the *Bath Journal* and *Bath Chronicle and Weekly Gazette*,[1] but also attendees from these global populations, such as Nathaniel Wells (1779–1852), son of a white, Welsh St Kitts plantation owner, and Juggy—later Jordine Wells—a Black enslaved worker educated in England, who moved to Bath in the early 1800s.[2]

The perception of Bath and impression of the city from global minority figures is something that could also be investigated further. Previous studies, such as Peter Borsay's seminal book *The Image of Georgian Bath, 1700–2000*, offer important insights, but lacks global and minority perspectives. It would be fruitful for future research to consider more fully not only the influence Georgian Bath had across the globe, but also, conversely, the influence of non-English culture on Bath. This is hinted at through a mainly Eurocentric lens in many of the chapters: from the influence of Italian musicians on the city's concerts, to Roman antique and Classical architecture on the built city. Furthermore, it would be wonderful to consider the changing image of Georgian Bath post-2000, something that the National Trust is considering in relation to the current and future role of the Assembly Rooms and what assembly now means in the twenty-first century.

The aims of the National Trust are to reaffirm that the Rooms are part of the living city of Bath, for both its residents and tourists, sharing it as a place for connection and celebration, much as it was when it opened in 1771. While the Rooms in the eighteenth century may have been considered open to a wider range of people—allowing artisans and tradesmen to attend, mixing with the gentry and aristocracy—they were, in reality, highly exclusive and socially hierarchical, as chapters by Hillary Burlock and Jemima Hubberstey have demonstrated. The National Trust are now seeking for the Rooms to be openly inclusive—offering a welcoming space with relevant and relatable dynamic programming (ticketed and free), from small-scale pop-up events to large take-overs of the space for concerts and balls, reminiscent of those entertainments which first enticed people to Bath and the Rooms. The curators are also actively taking an inclusive approach to research. Not only are they exploring under-researched areas

250 *Bath and Beyond*

and considering the historic lived experiences of people from global majority communities, but they are also considering how age, gender, disability, health, class, wealth, and marital status all played a role in affecting peoples' experience of the balls, concerts, and social activities which took place in the Assembly Rooms. By taking this comprehensive approach—that everyone's history is our history and a variety of experiences are valid—the Bath Assembly Rooms looks to not only make the physical building and the programme on offer more inclusive and accessible but also the way in which these and the visitor experience is developed, curated, programmed, and shared by inviting in others throughout the process. By working in consultation, collaboration, and co-creation with academics, students, specialists, curators, conservators, architects, and local community members, the National Trust aims to refashion the building and reframe the meaning of assembly for the society we live in now, adapting to shifting needs while still celebrating the architecture, purpose, and historic lives of this building, which is ultimately and fundamentally centred around the people of Bath and beyond.

Notes

1 See the *Bath Journal*, December 7, 1789 and the *Bath Chronicle and Weekly Gazette*, December 3, 1789, December 10, 1789 and December 17, 1789.
2 See Anne Rainsbury, "Nathaniel Wells: The Making of a Bla ck Country Gentleman," in *Britain's Black Past*, ed. Gretchen H. Gerzina (Liverpool University Press, 2020).

Appendices

Appendix 1: Transcribed List of Subscriber Names, as They Appear on the Articles of Agreement

Timothy Moore and Rupert Goulding

1. Rob Sutton
2. Will Davenport
3. Christopher Talbot
4. Ch.s Mein
5. Richard Salter
6. Henry Powys
7. James Leigh Perrott
8. Jon. Morton Pleydell
9. Benj. Adamson
10. Edw. Greenly
11. And.w Sproule
12. Dan. Danvers
13. William Colborne
14. Jn. Wood
15. Benj. Colborne
16. Sir Peter Denis Bar.t
17. Mrs Jane Denis
18. Mrs Towers
19. Sam.l Roffey
20. Will. Bennett
21. G. Brune
22. W. Harrington
23. David Nagle
24. John Charnock
25. P. Dehany
26. S. Gordon

252   *Appendices*

27. Phil. Francis
28. Frank Bennett
29. Charles Owen
30. Arthur Cookson
31. Marg.t Rambouillet
32. Will. St. Quintin
33. Fr. D. Birkhead
34. Thos. Haviland
35. M. Smith
36. Alice Horsman
37. Jane Horsman
38. John Brent
39. Wm. Robinson
40. Thos. Bowdler
41. Thos. Coward
42. Jn. Pigott
43. Wm. Provis
44. Miss Coward
45. Wm. Smith
46. Katherine Wright
47. Joseph Salvador
48. Dr Paterson
49. Walter Wiltshire
50. Dyonisia Thresher
51. Marg. Gordon
52. Sarah Snee
53. John Monck
54. Edward Drax
55. Wm. Street
56. Will Greenwood
57. Sam Stephens
58. J. Wadman
59. Jasp. Morris
60. Rich Horsford
61. William Adams
62. Willm. Primatt
63. George Wrought

Appendix 2: Rauzzini Bath Subscription Concert Repertoire, 1780–1786

The information given in the following sections has been gathered from advertisements published in the *Bath Chronicle and Weekly Gazette*. The presentation is in a similar format to Paul F. Rice, who comprehensively

Appendices 253

recorded details of the subscription concerts that took place from November 1786 to January 1810. My aim here is to complete the record for those concerts under Rauzzini's sole direction, focusing specifically on the winter subscription concerts only. There were also benefit concerts, and other concerts that took place at the Upper Assembly Rooms under Rauzzini's direction, but these are not included here since they are not the main topic of discussion in this chapter.

Brianna E. Robertson-Kirkland

1780–1781 Concerts

Ten concerts were presented between 1 November 1780 and 27 January 1781. Subscription costs (not advertised, but likely the same as the previous season): [2 pounds, 2 shillings (gentlemen); 1 pound, 1 shilling (ladies); non-subscribers admittance 7 shillings, 6 pence (gentlemen); 5 shillings (ladies)]. Concerts began at 6.30pm.

Principal Vocal Performers: Signor [Giusto Fernando] Tenducci, Miss Pollon, and Rauzzini.

Principal Instrumental Performers: [Giuseppe] Puppo (first violin), [George] De Camp (flute), Johann Christian Fischer (principal oboe)—'(at the request of the company)'. Later, Mr. Legard [possibly Le Gard] (pedal harp) joined the concerts.

Dates the subscription concerts took place: 1 November 1780; 8 November 1780; 15 November 1780; 22 November 1780; 29 November 1780; 13 December 1780; 27 December 1780; 13 January 1781; 20 January 1781; 27 January 1781.

1781–1782 Concerts

Ten concerts were presented between 24 October 1781 and 2 January 1782. Subscription costs: 2 guineas (gentlemen); 1 guinea (ladies); non-subscribers admittance 7 shillings, sixpence (gentlemen); 5 shillings (ladies). Concerts began at 7pm for the first three concerts. Thereafter concerts began at 6.30pm.

Principal Vocal Performers: Signor [Giusto Fernando] Tenducci, Maria Storer, and Rauzzini. [Francesca] Corri performed 'for the first four nights'.

Principal Instrumental Performers: Johann Peter Salomon (first violin), [John] Mahon (Clarinet), Johann Christian Fischer (principal oboe)— '(at the request of the company)', [Jane Mary] Guest (piano forte).

Dates the subscription concerts took place: 24 October 1781; 31 October 1781; 7 November 1781; 14 November 1781; 21 November 1781; 28 November 1781; 5 December 1781; 12 December 1781; 26 December 1781; 2 January 1782.

Plus two additional subscription concerts: 16 January 1782; 23 January 1782.

254   *Appendices*

1782–1783 Concerts

Eight concerts were presented between 30 October 1782 and 1 January 1783. Subscription costs: 1 guinea (gentlemen); 1 guinea (ladies); non-subscribers admittance: 5 shillings. Concerts began at 7pm.

Principal Vocal Performers: Signor [Giusto Fernando] Tenducci, Maria Storer, [Ann] Cantelo (appearing 11 December 1782), and Rauzzini.

Principal Instrumental Performers: Mr. Scheener [possibly Schöner] (first violin), [Johan Alexander] Herschell (Violoncello), Johann Christian Fischer (oboe), [Jane Mary] Guest (piano forte).

Dates the subscription concerts took place:

30 October 1782: *Orfeo* by Gluck; *Amintas* [pasticcio English opera]; several cantatas by eminent composers.

6 November 1782: *Orfeo* by Gluck; *Amintas*; several cantatas by eminent composers.

13 November 1782: *Orfeo* by Gluck with full choruses.

20 November 1782: *Serenata of Aurora* by Johann Christian Bach.

27 November 1782: *Orpheus* 'at the particular desire of the Subscribers'.

4 December 1782: *Rinaldo and Armida* by Johann Christian Bach.

11 December 1782: A Miscellaneous Concert.

1 January 1783: [Repertoire not advertised].

1783 Concerts

Eight concerts were presented between 5 November 1783 and 24 December 1783. Subscription costs: 1 guinea (gentlemen); 1 guinea (ladies); non-subscribers admittance: 5 shillings. Concerts began at 7pm.

Principal Vocal Performers: [Ann] Cantelo and Rauzzini.

Principal Instrumental Performers: [Diedonné Pascal] Pieltain (first violin), [George] De [C]amp (flute), Johann Christian Fischer (oboe), [Jane Mary] Guest (piano forte), J. Pieltain (french horn) [joined for the final four concerts].

Dates the subscription took place:

5 November 1783:

Act I. New Overture, Haydn; Song, Miss Cantelo, Sarti; Concerto Flute, Mr. De [C]amp; Duetto Miss Cantelo and Mr. Rauzzini; Concerto Violin, Mr Pieltain.

Act II. Overture, la Buona Gigliola, by particular desire; Concerto Piano Forte, Miss Guest; Song, Miss Cantelo, Kozeluck [Koželuch], (accompanied on the Violin by Mr. Pieltain, and on the Piano Forte by Miss Guest) Concerto Oboe, Fischer; Song, (Queen Mary's Lamentation) Miss Cantelo; Full Piece.

Thereafter the repertoire is not advertised.

Appendices 255

12 November 1783; 19 November 1783; 26 November 1783; 3 December 1783; 10 December 1783; 17 December 1783; 24 December 1783.

1784–1785 Concerts

Eight concerts were presented between 10 November 1784 and 5 January 1785. Act I consists of Ancient Music, and Act II consists of Modern Music. Subscription costs: 1 guinea; non-subscribers admittance: 5 shillings. Concerts began at 6.30pm.

Principal Vocal Performers: [Ann] Cantelo, [Marie] Chanu, and Rauzzini.

Principal Instrumental Performers: [Diedonné Pascal] Pieltain (first violin), [Johan Alexander] Herschell (violoncello), [Tebaldo] Monzani (German flute), Johann Christian Fischer (oboe), [Jane Mary] Guest (piano forte). J. Pieltain (french horn) [joined for the final four concerts].

Dates the Subscription Concerts Took Place: 10 November 1784; 17 November 1784; 24 November 1784; 1 December 1784; 8 December 1784; 15 December 1784: Guest's [benefit] concert; 22 December 1784; 29 December 1784; 5 January 1785.

26 January 1784: [additional subscription concert] Rauzzini introduces [Antonio] Lolli, principal violin to the Empress of Russia to perform 'for one night only'.

1785–1786 Concerts

Eight concerts were presented between 9 November 1785 and 25 January 1786. Act I consists of Ancient Music, and Act II consists of Modern Music. Subscription costs: 1 guinea; non-subscribers admittance: 5 shillings. Concerts began at 6.30pm.

Principal Vocal Performers: [Ann] Cantelo, and Rauzzini.

Principal Instrumental Performers: [Diedonné Pascal] Pieltain (first violin), [Johan Alexander] Herschell (violoncello), [Tebaldo] Monzani (flute), Johann Christian Fischer (oboe), [Jane Mary] Guest (piano forte and organ).

Dates the Subscription Concerts Took Place: 9 November 1785; 16 November 1785; 23 November 1785; 30 November 1785: Act I selected from Handel's Music; 14 December 1785; 28 December 1785; 11 January 1786; 25 January 1786.

Index

Note: Page numbers in *italic* indicate a figure, and page numbers in **bold** indicate a table on the corresponding page.

Abel, Carl Friedrich 98
Acts of Parliament: Boston Port Act (1774) 231; Stamp Act (1765) 145; Sugar Act (1765) 145
Adam, Benjamin 30
Adam, James 41, 42, 54n11
Adam, Robert 39–42, 44–6, 48–53: designs for Ball and Concert Room *40, 46–8, 50, 52*
Adams, William 23, 25, 252
Addison, Joseph 66
Aix-les-Bains (Aix-en-Savoie) 204–5, *207*, 215, 220n17; Cercle d'Aix 205, 209, 211, 212; Chalet de Marie de Solms Theatre (Théâtre du Chalet) 209
Allen, Ralph 6, 118
Amelia, Princess 227
America (North) xiv, 3, 7, 106, 178n66, 185, 225–6, 228–9, 234, 238, 248
American Revolution 9, 185, 226, 232, 236
Amphion-les-Bains 208, 209
Ancaster, duchess of *see* Bertie
Anne of Orleans 182
Anson, Elizabeth, Lady 9, 57, 60, 62, 63, 66–7, 70, 74n27, 74n32
Anson, George, Lord 63, 69, 71
Anstey, Christopher 229
Ash, John 3
Ashe, Andrew 97
Atwood, Thomas Warr 39, 53n1
Auckland, Lord *see* Eden

Auld Robin Gray 110
Austen, Jane 9, 18, 29, 57, 78, 81–2, 88, 118, 149; *Northanger Abbey* 78, 84, 91; *Persuasion* 88; *Pride and Prejudice* 81–2

Bach-Abel concert series 98, 101, 103, 107–8
Bach, Johann Christian 98, 104–5, 112; *Rinaldo and Amida* 105, 254; *Serenata of Aurora* 105, 254
Badcock, Mr 85
Balconi, Signora 105
Baldwin, Thomas 39, 52
Barker, Mrs 185, 195
Barré, Colonel Isaac 7, 231
Bath, city of; Abbey 25, 27, 54n21, 173; Agricultural Society 23; Black Bear Inn 15; Bladud's Buildings 23, 30, 32n10; Brock Street 16, 32n10, 33n31; Circus 16, 18, 23, 26, 28, 33n31, 39, 43, 51, 142, 230, 231, 234; Corporation 41, 119, 121, 144, 152, 168, 247; Cross Bath 68; Fire Insurance Corporation 18; Funerals in 173, 176, 163, 165, 166, 168, 172, 173, 175; Gay Street 32n10, 142; General Hospital 23, 24; Great Pulteney Street (Parade Gardens) 29, 41, 52, 79; Guildhall 24, 39, 144; Gyde's Rooms 4, 8, 16–7, 144, 158n27; Lebeck's Head Tavern 228; Lower Assembly Rooms (formerly Simpson's) 96, 99,

144–5, 148, 150, 158n27; Margaret Buildings 5; Market Place 172, 173; Milson Street 79; New Sydney Place 52; 'New Town', plans for 52; North Parade 96; Northumberland Buildings 39; Octagon Chapel 24, 89, 142; Orchard Street 28; Paragon 24, 29, 32n10, 39; Pierrepont Street 28; Pulteney Bridge 41, 42, 51–2, 54n17; Pump Room 68, 70, 79, 86, 89, 117, 130, 211, 230, 231; Queen Square 7, 15–6, 18, 27, 39, 43, 54n15, 142; Royal Crescent 5, 18, 30, 39, 143, 234; St James Square 39; St James's Street 143; St Michael's Extra Muros 23, 172; Simpson's Rooms *see* Lower Assembly Rooms: Sydney Gardens 81; Sydney Place 52; The Parade 144; Trim Street 24, 25; Upper Assembly Rooms xiii, 1–2, 3, 4–5, 7–8, 9, 16–7, 19, 20–1, 23–31, 42, 80–1, 86–7, 96–100, 102, 105, 109, 111–2, 117, 130–1, 134, 231, 234, 253 (Balls 80, 249; Building Committee 23; Concerts and music in 44, 96–105, 107, 108–9, 111–2, 250, 252–5; Furnishing Committee 23, 25; Law Committee 22; Subscribers to 15–32, 251–2 (Connections to enslaved people 17, 22, 28, 29, 30)); Wade's Passage 166, 170, 173, 178n57; Westgate Buildings 18, 27, 173
The Bath Contest (1769) 116, 117, 126–7, 139, 141, 143, 145–6, 148, 149, 155
Bath, earl of *see* Pulteney
'Bath Revolution' 202–5, 217–8
Bathwick 41–3, 51, 52, 53n5, 55n35
Baumgarten, Charles Frederick 109
Beaufort, duchess of *see* Somerset
Beau monde, the 10, 60, 66, 70, 71–2, 127, 128, 187, 197
Beckford, Louisa 192
Beckford's Tower xiv
Beddoe, Thomas 196
Bedford, duke of *see* Russell
Beethoven, Ludwig van 108, 216, 217
Belasyse, Thomas, Earl Fauconberg 197

Bennet, Elizabeth 82
Bennet, Mrs 81
Bennett, Francis 18, 22
Bennett, Walter 22, 23, 25, 33n29
Bertie, Mary, duchess of Ancaster 190
Bessborough, countess of *see* Ponsonby
Bibesco, Prince Georges 208
Billington, Elizabeth 96
Bingley, Lady *see* Fox-Lane
Birch, Thomas 59
Bleaney Rofrer, Mr 84
Blesington, earl of *see* Stewart
Blue Ribbon *see* Cordon Bleu
Bombelles, Marc Marie, marquis de 4
Bonaparte, Maria-Letitizia (Marie de Solms) 206
Bonaparte, Napoleon (Napoleon I) 206
Borsay, Peter xvii, 2, 3, 78, 98, 116, 118, 199n31, 224, 225, 249
Boston, Massachusetts 229–30, 231; John Mein's London Book Store 229; *Weekly Rehearsal* 227
Boston Spa, Yorkshire 139
Bouvard de Fourqueux, Anne Marie Rosalie 186
Boyle, Richard, 3rd earl of Burlington 45, 50
Braham, John 96
Bramble, Matthew 1, 224–5
Brancovan, Grégoire Bibesco-Bassaraba de 208
Brancovan, Rachel de 208
Brent, John 252
Brereton, Major William *see* Masters of Ceremonies
Bridgetower, George xiv, 96, 249
Brighton, Sussex 10, 116, 125, 126–9, 130, 134, 142, 185, 192
Brown, Lancelot 'Capability' 20, 64
Brunetti, A. 213
Burke, Edmund 26
Burlington, earl of *see* Boyle
Burney, Frances 153; *Evelina* 57
Burns, Robert 108
Burr, Thomas Benge 119, 123
Buxton, Derbyshire 139
Byng, Charlotte, Viscountess Torrington 227

258 Index

Cachat Water Company 209–10
Cahusac, Thomas 5
Cahusac, William 5
Cambridge, University of 25, 59
Campbell, Elizabeth Eustatia 129, 155
Campbell, John Hooke 129
Canning, Elizabeth (Bess) 79, 81–8, 90, 91
Canning, George 85
Canning, Mehitabel (Hitty) 81–5, 87–8
Canning, Stratford 81
Cantelo, Ann 105–7, 109, 110–11, 254, 255
Caribbean: Barbados 22, 26, 28, 29, 30 (St George, Bridgetown 30); Jamaica 29, 30; St Kitts 249
Caroline, Queen 227
Carpenter, Almeria 192
Cathcart, Charles Schaw, 9th Lord Cathcart 197
Cathcart, Charlotte 197
Causey, Bell 121–2, 123, 134, 135n24
Cavendish Bentinck, Margaret, duchess of Portland 57, 67
Cavendish Bentinck, William, 3rd duke of Portland 25
Cavendish, Georgiana, duchess of Devonshire 5, 81, 185, 190, 197
Chambers, Ephraim 3
Chandles, Richard, of Shrewsbury 163
Chanu, Marie 109, 255
Charles Emmanuel III, King of Sardinia 182
Charnock, John (Jonathan) 22, 26, 29–30, 32n13, 251
Cheltenham, Gloucestershire 10, 129, 139, 157
Chesterfield, earl of see Dormer Stanhope
Chivers, G.M.S. 152
Cholmeley, Jane 29
Cholmeley, Robert 29
Cider Tax (1763) 145
Clementi, Muzio 109
Clive, Robert, Lord Clive (Clive of India) 21, 30, 32n15, 33n21, 33n31
Clive, Sir Edward 149
Coffin, Mr 168
Coke, Lady Mary 196

Collett, Jacques see Master of Ceremonies
The Conciliade 148, 149
Conyngham, Ellen Conyngham, Countess 7
Cookson, Revd Arthur 23, 25, 26, 252
Cookson, William (Alderman) 25
Cookson, William (brother of Arthur) 25
Cordon Bleu 10
Corri, Domenico 110
Corri, Francesca 102, 113n28, 253
Courtney, John 141
Coventry, Barbara, countess of 7
Coventry, George William, 6th earl of 7
Coventry, Henry 59; Philemon to Hydaspes 59
Coward, Miss 35n59, 252
Coward, Thomas 252
Creighton, Mary Caroline, Viscountess (Countess) Erne 187, 194, 195
Cross, Mr, collection of wild animals 28
Cross, William 164
Cumberland, Lieutenant-Colonel 142
Curtis, Mrs 86

D'arcy, Captain 141
Dalacourt, Mr 141
Dalacourt, Mrs 141
Daman, Mrs 154
Dancing xiii, 1, 2, 3, 4–5, 79, 82–3, 84, 86–7, 125, 144, 153, 154, 156, 202, 230; Cotillion Balls 89; Country Dances 2, 4, 5, 153, 156–7; Gallops 217; Mazurkas 217; Minuets 2, 4, 5, 85, 86–7, 153; Polkas 217; Ridottos 1–2, 16
Danvers, Daniel 23, 24, 25, 26, 251; Cam, Clutterbuck, Whitehead, Danvers & Phillott Partners (Bath Bank) 25
Davies, William 162, 168; Better Late than Never 10, 162, 165, 168–9, 175
Dawson, Captain William see Masters of Ceremonies
Decamp (De Camp), George (flautist) 107, 254
· De Grey, countess see Hume Campbell
Dehany, David 30

Index   259

Dehany, Margaret *31*
Dehany, Philip 30, *31*, 32n12, 35n66, 35n68, 251
Delaney, Mary 67
Denis, Jane 27, 35n59, 251
Denis, Sir Peter, bt. 20, 32n12, 251
Derrick, Samuel *see* Master of Ceremonies
Desgodetz, A.B. 49
Dessaix, Joseph 209–10, 213–4
Devonshire, duchess of *see* Cavendish
Dillon, Henry, 11th Viscount Dillon 7
Diocletian, Emperor 49; Palace of, Split, Croatia *49*
Donnellan, John 129
Dormer Stanhope, Philip, 4th earl of Chesterfield 87
Dougharty, John 59
Douglas, Catherine, duchess of Queensberry 66, 153
Drake, Mr (from Oxford) 90
Drax, Edward 23, 25, 26, 29, 32n12, 35n66, 35n68, 35n70, 252
Drogheda, Lady *see* Moore
Duncannon, Lady *see* Ponsonby
Dyer, Eliphalet 233

East India Company 18, 28, 144
Eden, William, Baron Auckland 155
Edinburgh 41–2, 101, 102, 153, 154; Assembly Rooms 55n30
Edward, duke of York 183
Edwards, Thomas 59
Egerton, Eleanor 185, 186, 191
Egerton, Thomas, Lord Grey of Wilton (later earl of Wilton) 185
Elliot, Anne 9, 88
Elliot, Sir Walter 9
Epsom, Surrey 2, 139
Erne, Lady *see* Creighton
Erskine, Thomas Alexander, 6th earl of Kellie 7
'Even and Odd' (EO) 123
Évian-les-Bains 204–5, 208–9, 210, 211, 212–3, 215–8
Exeter, Devon 51, 55n30
Eyre, Mary 197

Fauconberg, Earl *see* Belasyse
Finch, Lady Charlotte 183, 185, 187, 195–6

Finis, Mr 162, 168
Fischer, Johann Christian 253–5
Fitzroy, Augustus, 3rd duke of 192
Fleming, Anna 5, 86
Fleming, Catherine 5
Foster, Lady Elizabeth (later duchess of Devonshire) 187, 195
Foster, Mr 85
Foster, Rebeccah 85
Fox, Caroline, Baroness Holland 183, 185
Fox, Charles James 81
Fox-Lane, George, Baron Bingley 149
Fox-Lane, Harriet, Lady Bingley 149
Fraine, Captain Joseph 27
France 182, 195, 202–6, 210, 214, 216, 217; Revolutionary Wars (1793–1802) 85, 88
Frances (Francis), Sir Philip 21, 32n13, 35n66, 252
Franco-Prussian War 216
Frank, Black servant of Leigh-Perrot family 29, 36n74
Franklin, Benjamin 233, 234
Franklin, William, governor of New Jersey 224
Fry, Mr 142

Gainsborough, Thomas 9, 23
Garrick, David 149
Garrick, Eva Maria 149
Garvey, Edmund 23
Genoa 182, 184
George I 6
George II 227
George III 4, 10, 145, 183, 192
Germain, Lord George *see* Sackville
Gervasio, N. 213
Giardini, Felice 191
Gibbes, George Smith 150
Giordani, Tommaso 108
Gloucester, duchess of *see* Maria
Gloucester, duke of *see* William Henry
Gluck, Christoph Willibald 105, 254
Goldsmith, Oliver 118, 120, 122, 123
Gordon Riots (1780) 26
Gordon, Magaret 252
Gordon, Mary, Lady 185, 198n14
Gordon, S. 251
Gordon, Sir William 198n14
Grafton, duke of *see* Fitzroy

260 *Index*

Graham, Mary 197
Graham, Thomas (later Lord
Lynedoch) 197
Grantham, Lord *see* Robinson
Green, Elizabeth 190
Green, Nathaniel 190
Greenwood, Captain William 23,
26, 252
Greenwood, Rev. William 23
Grey, Charles (later Earl Grey) 190
Grey, Marchioness *see* Yorke
Grimly, Mr 10, 162, 168
Guadagni, Gaetano 105
Guest, Jane Mary 101–2, 104, 105,
107, 109, 111, 253–5

Handel, George Frideric 108, 109–10,
111, 112, 255; *Messiah* 111
Handy, Mr 162, 165, 168
Hardenhuish, Wiltshire 22
Hardwicke, earl of *see* Yorke
Harrington, Dr Henry 22–3, 26
Harrington, William 251
Harris, Jack 124; *Harris's List of
Covent Garden Ladies* 124
Harrogate, Yorkshire 139
Haviland, Thomas 32n13, 252
Haydn, Joseph 107–8, 109, 111, 112,
217, 254
Hayward, Robert 25
Heathcote, Margaret 59
Henley, Robert, earl of Northington 6
Hennessy, Richard 26
Herbert, Henry, earl of Powis
20, 33n21
Herbert, Mary, countess of
Pembroke 227
Hermann, Jules 216
Herschell, Johan Alexander 255
Hewetson, Captain 141–2
Hoare, Henry ('The Magnificent') 23
Hoare, Mary 23
Hoare, Sir Richard 23
Hoare, William 9, 23, 24, 117
Hogarth, William 69
Horsman, Alice 27, 252
Horsman, Ann 27
Horsman, Jane 27, 252
Horsman, Margaret 27
Houblon, Laetitia 185, 187, 196, 197,
199n20

Howard, Henrietta, countess of
Suffolk 71
Howe, Caroline 187
Hudson, Thomas 20
Hume Campbell, Amabel, Lady
Polwarth (later countess de Grey)
185, 190, 191, 195, 196, 198n10
Hume Campbell, Elizabeth, countess of
Marchmont 185
Hunter, Anne 108

Incledon, Charles 111

Jehin, Léon 213
Johnson, William 236
Jones, Charles *see* Masters of
Ceremonies
Jones, Rev. Hugh 226
Jones, Thomas 226

Kellie, Lord *see* Erskine
Kelly, Michael 106
Kemble, Stephen 233
King of Bath *see* Nash
Kingston, William 25, 26
Kling, Henri 215, 216
Koželuch (Kozeluck), Leopold 107,
108, 254
Kurmusik 202, 203, 204, 209, 215, 217

Lady Directresses 139, 141, 142,
153, 156
L'âge d'or du thermalisme 202
Lamartine, Alphonse Marie Louis
de 208
La Motte, Franz 96–7, 98, 99–100,
101, 112
Landaff, Lady *see* Mathew
Lauderdale, earl of *see* Maitland
Lauderdale, Lady *see* Maitland
Laurens, Henry, senior 233–4
Lawry, John 59
Le Fanu, Alicia 88, 89
Le Fanu, Harry 89
Le Mercier, Mademoiselle 86
Lee, Arthur 233
Lee, Mr 186
Legard (Le Gard), Mr 253
Leigh, Elizabeth (Bess) 82
Leigh, Mr (uncle of Bess Canning) 84,
85, 86

Index 261

Leigh, Mrs (aunt of Bess Canning) 82, 83
Leigh-Perrot, James 29, 32n8, 32n15, 35n66, 36n68, 36n74
Leo, Leonard 103
Lévy, Simon ix, 205, 206; *Les Soirées de Lyon* 206
Lichfield 63; races at 74n32
Ligonier, Sir John (later Earl Ligonier) 6
Linley, Thomas (the Elder) 96, 98, 99, 113n5
Linley, Thomas (the Younger) 99
Lolli, Antonio 255
London 4, 5, 7, 23, 30, 42, 43, 58, 60, 66, 82, 98, 99, 101, 103–4, 105, 107–8, 110, 124, 128, 143, 149, 153, 163, 164–5, 172–3, 187, 208, 225, 226, 229, 230, 232–4; Adelphi 42; Almack's 128; Billingsgate 81; Drury Lane 100; Hanover Square Rooms 99; King's Theatre 97, 99, 100, 101, 108; St James's Palace 4, 87; Season 89, 128; Wanstead 82
Lyncombe Spa 25

Macaulay, Catharine 230, 231
Madden, Lucretia 100
Madden, Mary 100
Mahon, John 109, 253
Maitland, James, 7th earl of Lauderdale 149
Maitland, Mary, countess of Lauderdale 149
Manigault, Peter 232
Mara, Gertrud 96
Marchmont, Lady *see* Hume Campbell
Maria, duchess of Gloucester (formerly dowager Countess Waldegrave) 192, 193, 194, 199n38
Marseilles 182, 192
Marsh, John 154
Martini, Giambattista 111
Masters of Ceremonies 80, 99, 116, 132, 134, 139, 140, 141, 144, 147, 150, 153, 156, 248; Amsinck, Mr 142; Blake, J. 127, 128; Brereton, Major William 126, 129, 130–1, 140, 143–4, 145, 146, 147–9, 149, 152; Collett, Jacques 116; Dawson, Captain William 130–2,

134, 154; Derrick, Samuel 116, 124–6, 128, 140, 142–4, 229–30; Heaviside, James 140; Jervois, Lieutenant-Colonel William 140; Jones, Charles 126, 127, 128, 142; King, James 156; Le Bas, Charles 141; Moreau, Simon 129; Nash, Richard ('Beau') xiii, 5, 8, 65, 79–80, 102, 116–24, 129, 133–5, 136n35, 140, 153, 157, 202, 218, 229; Plomer, R. 126, 143–9, 149, 150, 152; Richard, Mr 153; Tyson, Richard 116–7, 130, 132–4, 155; Wade, Captain William 2, 23, 99, 116, 126–30, 134, 140, 142–3, 145, 152, 155, 156, 166; Walker, James 130; Webster, Captain 117, 135n2 (Elections 7, 8, 126–30, 131, 133–4, 140–8, 150–2, 155–6, 247)
Mathew, Catherine, Baroness (later countess of) Landaff 191
Maynard, Charles, Viscount Maynard 192
Maynard, Nancy (née Parson), Viscountess Maynard 192–3
Mcchuse, Rebeccah *see* Foster
McPherson, William 28
Mein, Charles 28, 35n66
Mein, Patrick 28
Meyler, William 109
Michelangelo 45
Milan, Beatrix of Austria, archduchess of 194
Milan, Ferdinand, archduke of 194
Milborne, Dorset 22
Millöcker, Carl 217
Milton, Lord *see* Fitzwilliam
Moja, Leonardo 216
Monck, John 252
Montagu, Elizabeth 57, 67, 123
Monzani, Tebaldo 109, 255
Moore, Admiral Sir John 149
Moore, Anne, countess of Drogheda 185, 187, 195, 196
Moor Park 65
Morland, Catherine 84, 90
Morres, Hervey Redmond, 2nd Viscount Mountmorres 149
Mountmorres, Viscount *see* Morres

262   *Index*

Mozart, Wolfgang Amadeus 108, 216–7
Murray, Louisa, Viscountess Stormont (later countess of Mansfield) 197

Nagle, David 25–6, 251
Nagle, Honora (Nano) 26
Nangis, Madame de 191
Nangis, Monsieur de 191
Napoleon III 214, 216
Nash, Richard ('Beau') *see* Master of Ceremonies
National Trust xiii-xv, 248, 249, 250
Nelson, John Wood 30
New Bath Guide 17, 80, 229
Newmarket 81
Newspapers: *Bath Chronicle and Weekly Gazette* 54n15, 54n16, 80, 86, 106, 107, 113n5, 126, 129, 130, 143, 145, 146, 169, 249, 252; *Bath Journal* 103, 249; *Boston Post Boy* 228; *New York Weekly Journal* 227; *Providence Gazette* 228
New York 234, 236; Garrat Noel's bookstore 229; New Lebanon mineral springs 237
Nice 7, 9, 182–7, *188, 189*, 190–8; Faubourg Croix de Marbre, known as 'the English district' 187, 189, 195; L'hôtel d'Angleterre 187, *189;* Villa Nova 189
Niedermeyer, Louis 208
Noailles, Anna de 208, 221n30
North, Brownlow, bishop of Worcester 154
Nugent, Charlotte 197

Orchard, William 167
Orford, earl of *see* Walpole

Paderewski, Ignacy Jan 208
Palladio, Andrea 45
Palmerston, Lord *see* Temple
Paris 62, 69, 71, 214
Parke, Thomas 233
Pellet, Dr 119
Pembroke, countess of *see* Herbert
Penrose, Revd John 9
Perceval, Letitia 82
Petty, William, 2nd earl of Shelburne (marquess of Lansdowne) 231

Philadelphia 232–6; American Philosophical Society 234; Bristol Spa 235–6; College of Philadelphia 234; Continental Congress 232; Junto Club 234; Library Company of Philadelphia 234; 'New Bath' 235; Pennsylvania Hospital 234; Union Fire Company 234; Yellow Springs Spa 235, 236, 237
Philips, Edward 3
Piccinni, Niccolò 108
Pieltain, Diedonné-Pascal (violinist) 107, 109, 111, 254, 255
Pieltain, J. (French horn-player) 255
Pinch, John 52
Pinckney, Eliza Lucas 232
Pitt, George, Baron Rivers 187
Pitt, Penelope, Baroness Rivers 185–7, *188*, 190, 191, 192, 193–4, 195–6
Pitt, William (the Elder), earl of Chatham 6, 70, 144
Pleydell, Edmund Morton, 22
Pleydell, Jonathan Morton 22, 26, 251
Plura, John 164
Polwarth, Lady *see* Hume Campbell
Ponsonby, Henrietta, countess of Bessborough (formerly Lady Duncannon) 5, 81
Poole, Maria 111
Porter, Sarah 122
Portland, duchess of *see* Cavendish Bentinck
Portland, duke of *see* Cavendish Bentinck
Powerscourt, Lord *see* Wingfield
Powis, earl of *see* Herbert
Powys, Caroline Lybbe 153
Prat, Anne, du 25
Prior Park 6
Proust, Marcel 208
Provinciali, E. 213
Provis, William 252
Prudom, Maria 100
Pulteney, Frances 41–2
Pulteney, General Harry 41
Pulteney, William, earl of Bath 41
Pulteney, William Johnstone 41–3, 51

Queen Charlotte 183
Queensberry, duchess of *see* Douglas

Index   263

Queen Victoria 183, 216
Quincy, Josiah, junior 230, 231, 233

Rack, Edmund 154
Rambouillet, Colonel Charles, de 25
Rambouillet, Margaret 35n59, 252
Rauzzini, Venanzio 96–112; *The Village Maid* 110
Recluse, Peter 162
Recluse, Phoebe 162
Rich, Sir Robert 227
Rillé, Laurent de 216
Rivers, Lady *see* Pitt
Rivers, Lord *see* Pitt
Robinson, Frederick (Fritz) 10
Robinson, Sir William 21, 25
Robinson, Thomas, 2nd Baron Grantham 10
Rochestown, Dublin 22
Roffey, Samuel 18, 251
Rohan, Prince Camille de 186
Rome 39, 40, 44, 48, 51, 53; Baths of Caracalla 49; Baths of Diocletian 8, 49, 50; Pantheon 48; St Peter's Basilica, Vatican City 45
Romsey, Hampshire 154
Rossi, Lucy, de 5
Royal Leamington Spa, Warwickshire 139, 154
Russell, Dr Richard 126
Russell, Francis, 5th duke of Bedford 193
Russell, John, 4th duke of Bedford 6

Sackville (Germain), Lord George (later Viscount Sackville) 6–7
Salem, Massachusetts 230
Salter, Margaret 30
Salter, Richard 23, 26, 30, 35n66, 35n68, 251
Salvador, Joseph 32n13, 35n66, 252
Sarti, Giuseppe 107–8, 254
Savile, Gertrude 8
Savile, Sir George, 8th bt. 8
Scampston Hall, Yorkshire 20
Scarborough, Yorkshire 2, 10, 126, 139, 142
Scofton Hall, Nottinghamshire 25
Sea-bathing 33n31, 68, 127
Seven Years' War 23, 145, 149, 182
Seymour, Charles, 6th duke of Somerset 80

Shakespeare, William 4
Shelburne, earl of *see* Petty
Sheridan, Elizabeth (Betsy) 79, 81, 88, 91
Sheridan, Richard Brinsley 1
Shrewsbury Castle 42, 54n13
Shugborough Hall 63
Sibbald, Susan 86–7
Sir John Soane's Museum 40
Sketchley's Bristol Directory (1775) 148
Smith, Margaret 26, 30, 35n59
Smith, William 252
Smollett, Tobias 182, 225; *Humphry Clinker* 224; *Travels through France and Italy* (1766) 182
Snee, Sarah 26, 35n59
Somerset, 6th duke of *see* Seymour
Somerset, Elizabeth, duchess of Beaufort 196
Somerset, Lady Mary (later duchess of Rutland) 196
Southampton, Hampshire 68, 110, 130, 131, 132, 134
Spencer, Margaret Georgiana (née Poyntz), Countess Spencer 185, 186–7, 191, 195, 196–7
Sprange, J. 121, 122
Sproule, Andrew 22, 26, 33n31, 251
Spry, William, governor of Barbados 29
Stamitz, Carl Philipp 109
Stewart, William, earl of Blesington 149
Storace, Anna Selina 96, 106
Storer, Maria 102, 253, 254
Stormont, Lady *see* Murray
Stourhead, Wiltshire 23
St Peter's, Dyrham 175
St Peter's, Leeds (Leeds Minster) 25
Strauss, Isaac 205, 211, 214, 216, 217
Street, William 18, 23, 24, 32n13; Horlock, Mortimer, Atwood, Anderdon, Goldney & Street Partners (Bath & Somerset Bank) 24
Suffolk, countess of *see* Howard
Sutton, Robert 25
Swindal, Mr 162

Talbot, Catherine 59, 65, 66, 72
Talbot, Christopher 17, 251

264 *Index*

Teignmouth, Devon 22
Temple, Henry, Viscount
  Palmerston 227
Temple, John 230
Tenducci, Giusto Fernando 101, 102–3,
  104, 105, 106, 112, 253, 254
Terringham, Mr 84
Thomson, George 108
Thomson, James 69, 70; *Castle of
  Indolence* 69
Thrale, Hester 119
Thresher, Dyonisia 35n59, 252
Tilney, Henry 78
Tippin, Mr 85–6
Tivoli, Italy 49
Tonbridge, Kent 119
Tonduti de Falicon, Rosalie,
  Baroness 194
Torrington, Lady *see* Byng
Towers, Elizabeth 22, 26–7, 28,
  35n59
Towers, Revd Samuel 28
Treaty of Utrecht (1713) 182
Trudaine, Madame 186
Tunbridge Wells 8, 61, 63, 89, 116–7,
  119–28, 130, 132, 133–4, 141,
  204, 220n14; Chapel of King
  Charles the Martyr 119
Tunbridge Wells Guide (1780) 121, 132
Tunbrigalia (1722) 121
Turin, Savoy 186, 189, 192, 216
Tyson, Richard *see* Masters of
  Ceremonies

UNESCO 204

Valladon, Désirée Emma (known as
  Thérésa) 217
Valle, Countess della 195
Vestris, Gaetan ('God of Dance') 5
Vichy 204–5, 210–11, 214, 216, 217
Victor Amadeus II, duke of Savoy and
  King of Sardinia 182
Victor Amadeus III, King of
  Sardinia 182
Vieuxtemps, Henri 216
Virginia 9, 233

Wade, Captain William *see* Masters of
  Ceremonies
Wade, Field Marshal George 6, 140
Waldegrave, Maria, dowager Countess
  see Maria, duchess of Gloucester

Walpole, Horace (4th earl of
  Orford) 67
Walpole, Sir Edward 192
Watson, James *21*
Webster, Sally, Mr Bowman's maid 141
Wells, Jordine (formerly Juggy) 249
Wells, Nathaniel 249
Westminster 6; Palace of 8; School 25
Weymouth, Dorset 10; Stacie's Hotel
  and Assembly Room 33n31
Whatcombe, Dorset 22
Whitefield, George 235
White, John 235–6; Rose of Bath
  Spa 236
White, William 233
Wilberforce, William 30
Wilkes, John 5, 7, 149, 151, 228
Wilkes, Mary (Polly) 5
Willes, Edward 7
William Henry, duke of Gloucester
  183, 193
Williams, John 22
Wilton, earl of *see* Egerton
Wiltshire, Walter 18–19, 252
Wingfield, Richard, 6th Viscount
  Powerscourt 6
Wood, Elizabeth 24
Wood, John (the Elder) 40, 52, 55n34
Wood, John (the Younger) 24, 25, 28,
  40, 42–3, 45, 51, 52, 53, 54n15,
  55n31, 63, 96, 118
Workman, Thomas 29
Wray, Daniel 59, 65, 66
Wrest Park, Bedfordshire 59, 61, 63,
  69–70, 72; *Triumvirate*, the 59;
  Wrestiana 59, 60
Wrey, Sir Bourchier, 6th bt. 21
Wright, Joseph, of Derby 33n31, 34n51
Wright, Katherine 27, 35n59, 252

Yates, Mrs 141
York 45, 50, 149; Burlington's
  Assembly Rooms 55n29
Yorke, Elizabeth *see* Anson
Yorke, Jemima (*née* Campbell),
  Marchioness Grey 58, 59, 60, 62,
  69, 71–2
Yorke, Margaret *see* Heathcote
Yorke, Mrs 185
Yorke, Philip, 2nd earl of Hardwicke
  58, 59, 60, 62, 69, 71–2
Yorke, Philip, earl of Hardwicke (Lord
  Chancellor) 58

Printed in the United States
by Baker & Taylor Publisher Services